THE COMPLETE GUI

To Duncan,

Best wishes!

Earl Wm-Fee

Disclaimer Notice

This book is intended as a guide and a reference volume to assist your fitness and exercise program. It is not claimed as a substitute for professional fitness advice or medical advice. While an honest, best effort was made to advise and to list precautions, some potential problems may not be mentioned. Problems can arise if an individual is unfit, proceeds too intensely or rapidly, or has some bodily weakness. The advice may not be suitable for every individual. Caution is advised in all new exercises or programs and in the taking of new supplements, therefore check with your doctor before you begin. The opinions, advice, accuracy and completeness of the information herein are not guaranteed or warranted to produce any specific results or to avoid all problems.

EARL W. FEE

THE COMPLETE GUIDE TO RUNNING

HOW TO BE A CHAMPION FROM 9 TO 90

MEYER
& MEYER
SPORT

British Library Cataloguing in Publication Data
A catalogue record for this book is available from the British Library

Earl W. Fee:
The Complete Guide to Running
How to Be a Champion from 9 to 90
Oxford: Meyer & Meyer Sport (UK) Ltd, 2005
ISBN 1-84126-162-9

Aachen, Adelaide, Auckland, Budapest, Graz, Johannesburg,
New York, Olten (CH), Oxford, Singapore, Toronto
Member of the World
Sports Publishers' Association
www.w-s-p-a.org
Printed and bound by: TZ Verlag, Germany
E-mail: verlag@m-m-sports.com
www.m-m-sports.com

CONTENTS

ACKNOWLEDGMENTS

I express a debt of gratitude to Meyer & Meyer Sport, who agreed that this 2nd Edition would be of benefit to the running community, and to the staff (especially Thomas Stengel) for their efficient dedication.

The great spirit and camaraderie of the Saugeen Track Club, the achievements of these young athletes, and the dedication of the coaches has been an inspiration to me. The assistance and training with the North York Track Club in Toronto for over 14 years, and their encouragement in getting me started after a 33-year layoff is gratefully acknowledged. In particular, the coaching, often one-on-one from David Welch (President of NYTC), prepared me to break many world masters' track records; many of the middle distance/anaerobic workouts in this book were his creation. Also, my enduring friends at the Credit Valley Marathon Club and Gladstroke T&F Club have been an example of inspiration.

The assistance of the following resulted in a higher quality book and are also gratefully acknowledged:

- The generous editorial services of Duncan Mounsey
- The many photographers who supplied inspirational action photos (see the photos for credits)
- The large number of research papers on fitness and nutrition from physical education teacher Ken Glance, which added considerably to my knowledge;
- The many individuals (experts) and publishers (especially Human Kinetics) whose material for the book increased it's authenticity (see the credits and references). Special recognition and gratitude is acknowledged to the following for their valuable material: Dr. D. Costill, Dr. I. Lynch, and Dr. W. Scott, Charlie Francis, Payton Jordan, Ed Whitlock, Geordie and Earl Farell.

I express gratitude to Physiotherapy One (in particular, Vince Agostino), chiropractor Dr. Robert Taylor, chiropractor Dr. Astrid Trimm, chiropractor Dr. Michael Hardie, sports physician Dr. Anthony Galea, physician Dr. Edric Sum, the Mississauga YMCA and staff, and my many training partners (see Chapter 5, Principle 6); they all assisted me greatly to attain and sustain world record form; without the world records, no book would have been attempted. Finally, my thanks go out to my family and friends for their patience and understanding while I neglected them during this huge, but tremendously rewarding, project.

Earl W. Fee

FOREWORD

Earl Fee revealed his training secrets in the very successful self published book "How To Be a Champion from 9 to 90." In this Second Edition appropriately titled "The Complete Guide To Running", the previous edition has been updated, many action photos included, and the following new material added: new chapters on plyometrics, dynamic warm-up and inspirational quotations, the latest information on stretching, additional information on weight training, new magic supplements, best treatments for injury, effect of age on stride length and frequency, new training workouts, and more.

Earl Fee reveals his training secrets in *The Complete Guide to Running.* Earl Fee as a world-class master runner for over 18 years (including nine world masters track and field championships), has gathered extensive knowledge on physiology, and all aspects of fitness and running; this was largely based on a careful observation of effects in his own body. This knowledge has contributed to the achievement of many world masters records from the 300-meter hurdles to mile races. His quality training enabled him to develop particularly into one of the world's top 800-meter runners. Earl's experience also in the demanding nuclear power "Candu" industry as design engineer supervisor/technical writer/consultant in writing many exacting reports has no doubt contributed to his concise, correct and complete writing style.

All health enthusiasts, coaches, athletic trainers, parents of young athletes, and especially runners from beginner to elite will benefit from this in-depth book. The special emphasis on nutrition, mental training and inspiration (in addition to the physical training) will be of interest to athletes of all ages.

The latest techniques and fitness aspects are discussed in 22 chapters, and include: 26 training principles (many new), anaerobic threshold training, VO_2max (aerobic capacity) training, vVO_2max (velocity at VO_2max) training, central nervous system neural training, running in the water, stretching techniques, self-massage, weight training, "magic" supplements including creatine, injury prevention, and special training considerations for extreme young and old athletes. The 19 anti-aging tips (which I also heartily advocate) could assist you to "age slower than your rivals", and live decades longer with a higher quality of life.

All aspects of running training for sprinting, middle and long distance, and marathon are covered in detail except clothing and altitude training. I know of no other body of work on this subject that is so inclusive and practical. It is absolutely outstanding.

Payton Jordan, Head Track Coach Stanford University 1957-1979
1968 U.S. Olympic Track Coach

INTRODUCTION

"If you're going to be a champion, you must be willing to pay a greater price than your opponent" (Bud Wilkinson). You must pay the price with sacrifice. Success is not just training hard—it's a way of life. Do your sacrifices exceed your over-indulgences? This book will show you the way of the champion. And the inspirational chapters are designed to instill some enthusiasm for the dedication and determination required to be a champion.

This is a book for all fitness enthusiasts from a young age to 90, those with a dream, those who want to improve, those who want to learn the why and not just the how of running, and those who dare to excel. The basic principles of training are applicable to all ages. With proper training, the body, mind, and spirit are each fully used and in harmony. This book aims for this perfection to assist you in the serious play of athletic excellence, and to attain your fullest success in your sport, especially in running.

Proof of the effectiveness of the workouts and training schedules described herein (apart from my world records) is shown below by my age-graded percentage mainly for my 800-meter races over the past nine years. (Note, 100% age grade is equivalent to the open class world record.)

For example:

- 100.5% at Buffalo World Masters WAVA, 1995 (age 66)
- 99.49% at South Africa World Masters WAVA, 1997 (age 68). Second highest of all male races (1st: Robertson, NZL, 102.7% in the steeplechase at age 56)
- 102.04% at Boston US Masters Indoor, 1998 (age 69)
- 100.62% at Boston US Masters Indoor, 1999 (age 70)
- 99.71% at Gateshead World Masters WAVA, 1999 (age 70). Second highest of all male races (1st: Bradford, AUS, 99.93% in steeplechase at age 60. Mueller, GER, had 99.1% in 300-meter hurdles at age 60)
- 100% at Puerto Rico World WAVA, 2003 (age 74), average of 3 races

What are the principles of training and tips in few words? Work the five energy systems. Build a strong base before the speedwork phase. Train to increase the VO_2max (aerobic capacity) and increase the lactate threshold. Speed should not be neglected any time of the year. Have a plan and adapt gradually to your faraway goal. Practise periodization. Ensure proper nutrition and rest.

Use legal 'magic' supplements. To avoid injury, stress recovery in training, and practice cross-training, e.g., running in the water (my favorite). Run with good form and relaxation; be quick but don't hurry. Do not neglect stretching, strength training, and working the central nervous system neural pathways; older athletes particularly will benefit from these anti-aging exercises. Develop and practice the mental techniques. Race often, when ready. Taper. All the above are of no avail without desire, determination, and dedication. And, most important, look at each workout as a body, mind, and spirit experience. All the above are discussed, including the methods (secrets if you like) that I used to break over 40 world records in the 300-meter and 400-meter hurdles, 400-meters, 800-meters, 1500-meters, and mile in masters' track competitions."

The information herein is applicable to general fitness and many sports since 10 chapters are applicable in general and 12 chapters are specific to running. All the important fitness aspects are covered to make you faster, stronger, healthier and more knowledgeable; this book is meant to enhance mental preparation and physiological improvement and to inspire. Therefore, the total chapters provide a complete training system, but the individual chapters were written to be independent (stand-alone). A lot of the information has been obtained by careful observation of the effects of various training on my own body—observations recorded in detailed logs on running training for the past 18 years—what worked and what didn't. The supporting views and experience of others are included and referenced; many experts in their field have been quoted.

This is a book useful to the experienced runner but also to the serious beginner. The training workouts for 400-meter and middle distance runners in Chapters 6 and 8 respectively are applicable to all runners of all caliber and most ages of runners since they are based on race pace times.

We all need inspiration and motivation. We should have our favorite inspirational sayings to keep us going forward toward our goals. In Chapter 22, and throughout the book, you will find yours from the many examples listed (some by myself). These will complete your body, mind, spirit training.

CHAPTER 1

A mechanic must understand the workings of a car to make it run smoothly and efficiently. Similarly, a coach and athlete must understand the physiological aspects of the human body to condition it to run smoothly and efficiently.

PHYSIOLOGICAL PRINCIPLES

Changes to Your Body from Consistent Intense Exercise

When you train consistently for a few years, particularly if exercise is intense, you will find some beneficial changes in your body, such as:

1 Loss of body weight. The good news is you can increase your 5K and 10K running speed by one percent by lowering your weight by one percent.

2 Loss of body fat. Along with losing some weight, your body fat will decrease. Most sedentary females have about 27% body fat and sedentary men have about 20%. For runners, high body fat represents excess baggage. After about 12 years of consistent aerobic and anaerobic intense training, and a healthy low-fat, low-sugar diet, my body fat went down to 5%.

3 Resting heart rate decrease. With intense regular exercise, one or more of the following is likely to occur: the heart enlarges, heart ventricals become stronger, or coronary arteries enlarge. This results in more stroke volume or blood pushed on every stroke. So your resting heart rate will decrease. The normal resting heart rate is about

72 beats per minute for men and slightly higher for women. Generally, a low resting heart rate is indicative of a very fit individual. My resting heart rate has dropped to 41 beats per minute after 18 years of training.

4 Maximum heart rate, MHR, declines at a slower rate with age. Every decade, the sedentary person's MHR decreases by about 10 beats per minute. But with intense training, your MHR can stay nearly constant for decades. My MHR has stayed nearly the same for 17 years—near 190 beats per minute, due to consistent intense training. With a higher MHR, more blood is pumped, resulting in more oxygen utilization.

5 Mitochchondria and capillaries increase in muscle cells. Thus, more oxygen is utilized by the body resulting in more energy.

6 Slow twitch and fast twitch muscle fiber enlarges. A distance runner experiences slow twitch fiber enlargement, and a sprinter experiences fast twitch fiber enlargement.

Most of the above changes take years to reach a plateau of improvement. This is perhaps the major reason for a delay of about seven years for an athlete to normally reach a peak in performance. See further details below on these and other important physiological aspects.

To run faster and/or longer, an understanding and application of the physiological reactions of training are essential to athletes and coaches. "The athlete should understand the physiological reaction they are trying to achieve and should know when they have had enough and why they feel that way" (Lydiard[6]). By applying physiological data in a meaningful way, training and racing effectiveness are improved. Some of the more important physiological aspects are discussed below: the energy systems, muscle fiber, the respiratory system, anaerobic threshold, VO_2max, the heart, blood volume, mitochondrial enzymes, and lactic acid.

ENERGY SYSTEMS

There are three primary sources of energy available to the muscle for training and races. Tables 1.1, 1.2 and 1.3 on the next pages show the relative proportion of these energy systems depending on the length of the exercise. The three systems are the **creatine phosphate** or **power** system, the non-oxidative or **anaerobic lactate** system, and the oxidative or **aerobic** system. It is essential that the athlete train to exercise all three systems since all are used in running. Training must concentrate on those energy systems mainly used in the athlete's particular event(s).

The various chemical reactions in these systems are shown below. ATP, adenosine triphosphate (a high energy molecule) is the main source of energy for muscle contraction in the three energy systems. (One mole of ATP represents about 46 kilojoules, or 11 kilocalories[2].) ADP, adenosine *di*phosphate, is another important energy molecule in the reaction.

Power or Creatine Phosphate System

Power is defined as strength (force) times speed (velocity).

This power system is immediate acting for events such as shot put, weightlifting or sprinting where maximum muscle strength, with a burst of maximum energy, is required. It is important in a 100-meter or 200-meter dash, and also in the final sprint at the end of a middle- or long-distance race. The other two systems are too slow to supply this sudden energy. Creatine combines with an enzyme in the body to produce **creatine phosphate** (CP). The energy comes from breakdown of creatine phosphate producing more creatine and ATP. In the process, highly acidic hydrogen ions, H^+, are removed. The initial start to the reaction is from minimum ATP already in the cell. This energy source is useful only for exercises up to about 30 seconds. The equation below shows the importance of creatine in short, intense events. See Chapter 15 on creatine supplement.

$ATP + H_2O$–––––$ADP + H_3PO_4$
Creatine + enzyme–––CP
$CP + ADP + H^+$–––creatine + ATP
The cycle repeats itself over and over.

Note: Running fast repeats under about 20 seconds results in little acidic buildup, hence less fatigue. From above, it is seen this is due to creatine in the body that assists in removing the H^+ ions.

Anaerobic Lactate System

This speed system is of major importance for events such as the 400-meter and 800-meter. In this energy system, the demand for oxygen exceeds the rate at which oxygen is delivered. In the absence of oxygen, ATP is derived from the breakdown of glucose (in blood) and glycogen (stored in muscle and the liver). The anaerobic enzymes for this reaction are present in fast twitch muscle fibers. In view of the high speed, the aerobic system cannot produce energy fast enough to keep the muscles supplied; an oxygen debt is incurred and energy is supplied by the anaerobic system. The chemical process is called **anaerobic glycolysis**:

Glucose———-2ATP + 2 lactic acid

Glucose has the chemical formula $C_6H_{12}O_6$.
The lactic acid produced dissociates into negative lactate ions and positive H^+ ions (commonly called protons). The "H+ ions eventually inhibit the enzyme reactions for fuel metabolism" (Martin and Coe[2]). The accumulation of H^+ and lactate ions reduces blood pH into the acid range and impairs muscle contractions.

Up to about one minute of speed exertion the anaerobic system produces increasingly more energy; thereafter, the anaerobic system supplies less and less energy as the aerobic supplies increasingly more. The time period of one to two minutes represents a transition period from mainly anaerobic glycolysis to mainly aerobic glycolysis. About 120 seconds of intense effort uses 55% anaerobic and 45% aerobic energy (see Table 1.3 on page 20).

Aerobic System

For endurance events lasting more than about two minutes, the aerobic system supplies the majority of the energy with a constant supply of oxygen from the cardiovascular system. For events longer than a 5K, the energy from the anaerobic source is less than about 7%, eventually reducing to less than 1% for the marathon. ATP for endurance events is generated from several sources, including sugars, carbohydrates, fatty-acids ($C_{16}H_{32}O_2$), and to a much lesser extent, from amino acid proteins[3] (the latter chemical reaction is not given below). The aerobic enzymes required for these reactions are present in slow twitch muscles. The chemical reaction is called **aerobic glycolysis.**

Glucose + $6O_2$————36ATP + $6CO_2$ + $6H_2O$
Fatty acid + $23O_2$————130ATP + $16CO_2$ + $16H_2O$

The body obtains more energy from fats than carbohydrates after about 30 minutes of running. After about one hour of running at marathon pace the fat burning/glycogen burning ratio has increased to about 3/1 for the athlete. At two or three hours of exercise, nearly all of the energy is from fatty-acid metabolism. Thus it is important for the long distance runner to train long enough to activate the fatty-acid chemical reaction.

Note: By comparing the energy release from anaerobic glycolysis to aerobic glycolysis, the anaerobic metabolism of glucose requires 18 times more glucose to produce the same amount of ATP. The aerobic metabolism is more efficient. Also note the large amount of ATP from fatty acids.

% Of Each Energy Source Used In Running Races

It is important that the coach and athlete know the percentage of each of the three energy systems or sources used in the athlete's specialty event. The training can then be directed to cover all three systems but with more concentration on the major energy system(s). The breakdown of energy source versus events from the 100 meters to marathon for men's 1987 world records is shown in the Table below from Peronnet and Thibault[7]. The anaerobic energy system consists of creatine phosphate energy and anaerobic lactate energy. The creatine phosphate energy is mainly significant up to about 20 seconds (contributing an average of about 65% of total energy between zero and 20 seconds) but dropping off rapidly after this to near zero at about two minutes. Hence it is important to train for the three energy systems: creatine phosphate, anaerobic lactic, and aerobic.

Table 1.1 • Energy Contribution Vs Race Distance

Event	1987 World Record	% Energy Contribution	
Meters		Aerobic	Anaerobic
100	9.83	8	92
200	19.75	14	86
400	43.29	30	70
800	1:41.73	57	43
1500	3:29.46	76	24
3000	7:29.45	88	12
5000	12:58.39	93	7
10 000	27:08.23	97	3
Marathon	2:06:50	99	1

The above shows reasonable agreement with other references, e.g., Sparkes and Bjorklund[4].

Note: It would appear from the breakdown that little effort need be put on the speed and anaerobic training for the 10 000-meter and marathon. This would be incorrect. To achieve your maximum potential and fast times, they still need a lot of attention and cannot be neglected.

Similarly, Tables 1.2 and 1.3 (from Bangsbo, et al.[13]) show the "approximate relative contributions of anaerobic (phosphate + anaerobic lactate energy) and aerobic energy sources" during sequential and cumulative periods of exhausting exercise lasting 180 seconds.

Table 1.2 • Sequential Energy Distribution

Period Sequential	Anaerobic %	Aerobic %
0–30s	80	20
30–60s	60	40
60–90s	42	58
90–120s	36	64
120–80s	30	70

Table 1.3 • Cumulative Energy Distribution

Period Cumulative	Anaerobic %	Aerobic %
0–60s	70	30
0–90s	61	39
0–120s	55	45
0–180s	45	55

The above tables clearly show the great importance of aerobic training for runs longer than one minute.

MUSCLE FIBER

During the fall, while training for cross country and building a base, I transform my body from a sprinter/middle distance runner into a long distance runner (this is a slight exaggeration). Some of the fast twitch fibers (FT Type IIb) take on aerobic qualities and there is *possibly* enlargement of the slow twitch (endurance) fibers. See discussion below. The improvements in endurance are quite evident after about six to eight weeks of cross-country/base type of training.

Some of the main characteristics of fast and slow muscle fibers are:

Fundamental Differences. The fast twitch fibers (Type II) are light in color and have a relatively fast contraction time and a predominance of *anaerobic glycolytic* (breakdown of glycogen and glucose) enzymes which can utilize glycogen *without oxygen*. These fibers provide rapid movements in a short period of time. There are two types, FT Type IIa (white) and FT Type IIb (grey). FT Type IIa also contain *aerobic oxidative-glycolytic* enzymes referring to capability for *oxidative* metabolism, as well as glycolytic. FT Type IIb have low aerobic enzymes.

Type IIa fibers are often referred to as FOG fibers (fast oxidative glycolytic) and Type IIb fibers are called FG fibers (fast glycolytic).

Fast twitch fibers, when compared to slow twitch, have greater strength, faster contraction, poorer endurance, fatigue quicker, and have fewer mitochondria and capillaries[2].

The slow ("oxidative") twitch fibers (Type I, ST or SO) are dark in color with a slower contraction and a predominance of aerobic enzymes, which utilize oxygen for metabolism.

Sequential Operation. The slow twitch fibers are used throughout light to maximum levels of exercise, while the fast twitch fibers are utilized over the range of moderate to maximum effort. As effort is increased, the FT Type IIa fibers are then activated followed by FT Type IIb fibers during maximal effort or speed. The number of fibers used has increased with the effort until all three types are used at 100% effort. Costill[1] states: "Great mental concentration is required to maintain a given pace near the finish of a race. Much of the mental effort is probably used to activate the FT Type IIb fibers that are not easily recruited."

Sprinters versus Distance Runners. As the names indicate, the athletes with a predominance of fast twitch fibers have superior speed and those athletes mostly with slow twitch fibers have superior endurance. A muscle biopsy from Alberto Salazar's calf (gastrocnemius) revealed it was 93% slow twitch, 7%FT Type IIa, and no FT Type IIb fibers[1]. Fourteen elite distance runners showed an average of 82% of the cross sectional area (gastrocnemius) was composed of ST muscle[2]. Elite sprinters' muscles are composed predominately of FT Type IIa fibers. However, an average individual has roughly 50% ST, 25% FT Type IIa, and 25% FT Type IIb in the gastrocnemius leg muscles1.

One can guess the composition fairly well based on performance over a range of races. Also, if you can jump 16 inches or higher from standing and have little endurance, you have predominately fast twitch muscles. If you have little speed and lots of endurance you have mainly slow twitch muscles.

Genetically Fixed or Trained. The ratio of fast and slow twitch fibers is genetically determined according to Mangi et al[3]. Costill[1] also reports that studies have indicated: "The fraction of slow twitch and fast twitch fibers appears fixed and unaffected by training." This suggests this quality is inherited. Some are born with the potential to be sprinters, middle distance, or marathoners, depending on the parents.

Genetically Fixed but One Exception. The consensus is that fibers are genetically fixed with one exception: FT Type IIb fibers can take on the characteristics of FT Type IIa fibers with continued endurance distance running. This provides a greater oxidative capacity for the working muscles. "This alteration is strictly an effect of distance training and not a permanent change in the fiber itself" (Sparks and Bjorklund[4]). "The opposite, FT IIa to FT IIb fibers, can occur with strength training" (Martin and Coe[2]).

Hypertrophy or Selective Enlargement of Fibers. "Experts have proposed that the training for endurance may result in selective enlargement (of existing cells) of slow twitch fiber and strength training *may* result in fast twitch fiber enlargement" (Costill[1]). New evidence may not support this (Costill).

The muscle micrograph of Mary Decker supports the theory that slow twitch fibers enlarge with endurance training[4]. Sparks and Bjorklund[4] report: "She is primarily 65% fast twitch and 35% slow twitch but at the micrograph time of all endurance training, based on the actual *area* distribution the fast twitch to slow twitch ratio was about 50:50."

Continual Speed to Retain Fast Fiber Response. Martin and Coe[2] emphasize the importance of periodic inclusion of fast training throughout the year. "Without any training at higher intensities for a long period the FT fibers will have minimal training stimulus to improve their performance or to ensure maintenance of their performance." This suggests that *the FT neural pathways have become "rusty."* Hence it is important to retain some speed during the base building period. Charlie Francis, past coach of Ben Johnson, also believed in and taught retaining speed year round. See also Principle 24-"Neural Training" in Chapter 5.

THE RESPIRATORY CYCLE BETWEEN OXYGEN SUPPLY AND CO_2 DISCHARGE

The cycle starts with air (which is 20% oxygen) inhaled into the lungs through the mouth and nose. From the millions of minute alveoli in the lungs, oxygen diffuses into the hemoglobin of the blood. The blood is pumped by the heart to the capillaries where oxygen is transferred from the hemoglobin across the capillary membrane to the myoglobin in the muscle tissue.

The muscle cells receive the oxygen and tiny molecule food nutrients for producing energy. **Digestive** enzymes aid in producing these tiny molecule nutrients, such as glucose from carbohydrates, glycerol and fatty acids from fats, and amino acids from protein. These food nutrients pass through the small intestine into the lymph and blood.

The mitochondria, those tiny powerhouses of the cell, use **oxidative** enzymes in the presence of oxygen to breakdown these food nutrients into energy in the form of ATP. The muscles use the ATP as fuel and the waste, CO_2, is returned to the blood in the veins via the capillaries. Water and cellular waste go to the large intestine. At the lungs, the CO_2 diffuses from the blood through the minute alveoli into the discharged air. At VO_2max, the volume of CO_2 production (exhaled) has exceeded the volume of O_2 consumption (inhaled) and the athlete experiences high levels of acid in the blood.

RESPIRATORY SYSTEM

The maximum volume of air that can be expelled in a single breath (vital capacity) increases with years of distance running training. I recall being able to show a significant increase only one year after I started my running comeback after a 33-year layoff. A large group of cross-country runners measured 5.7 liters compared to 4.8 liters for a group of untrained similar age men[1].

The maximum *breathing capacity* for an untrained runner varies from as low as 120 liters (L) per minute and typically about 180L/min for a highly trained distance runner. Breathing capacity = breathing frequency (usually about 50 times per minute maximum during running) x volume of a breath. To accomplish this, I have noticed some good runners have a shallow rapid breathing compared to deeper slower breathing (myself).

The average person breathes at rest five to six liters of air per minute; this takes about one percent of the body's total energy need. An untrained runner could sustain about 100 L/min for a few minutes only, but a distance runner sustains about 100-120 L/min. for long periods which represents about 9% of total energy. Costill[1] further states, "Respiratory ventilation is probably not a limiting factor except at high altitude." It has been my understanding (from past reading) that breathing is not a major limiting factor. Therefore, it would appear no point in practicing running with holding the breath or other such tricks. (Zatopek used to hold his breath while running to get the feeling of oxygen debt.) However, proper breathing from the belly is important and also running with chest high rather than slouched. More efficient breathing would bring in more oxygen per minute and theoretically should result in improved performance.

For proper breathing[18], as the opera singers do, practice belly breathing. As you inhale, your belly should rise. As you exhale, the belly moves in. This is most easily practiced when sitting with your hands on your belly but can also be practiced when walking. When running slowly, I have sometimes concentrated on this, but it is impossible to think about when running fast. Also, by keeping the chest out, shoulders back, and hips forward when running, your lungs will open more to aid breathing. Breathe through the nose and mouth.

Before a race, it is helpful to take some deep breaths. A sigh or two will help to move the blood from your belly to your muscles and brain.[18]

Morehouse and Gross[18] also state, "Breathing is best left to nature. The less you think about and try to control your breathing, the more economical it will be. Natural breathing costs less than trying to breathe with a *contrived rhythm*." I agree; do not tamper with the *rhythm* of breathing, but practice belly breathing.

Oxygen Debt

The oxygen debt for a trained athlete for events from 200 meter to marathon is about 17 liters. An untrained individual can rarely tolerate more than 10 liters oxygen debt.
Total O_2 requirement = O_2 intake + O_2 debt.

Based on oxygen intake and oxygen debt, the aerobic and anaerobic energy percentages can be estimated:

Aerobic energy = O_2 intake/ O_2 total requirement
Anaerobic energy = O_2 debt/ O_2 total requirement

ANAEROBIC THRESHOLD AND VO_2 MAX

See also Chapter 7 for advantages, description, and training for anaerobic threshold and VO_2max thresholds. These thresholds increase with higher levels of training as described in Chapter 7.

Anaerobic Threshold

The running pace where lactate acid begins to increase at a much greater rate than previously is commonly called the **anaerobic threshold (AT) or lactate threshold (LT).** "At this working level: the elevated removal of CO_2 can no longer maintain blood acidity (pH) within reasonable limits; the blood lactate production greatly increases, the rapidly rising H^+ ion concentration and corresponding falling blood pH provides an additional powerful ventilatory stimulus" (Martin and Coe[2]). Therefore, at the same running pace to produce the AT and LT, the **ventilatory threshold (VT)** also occurs, wherein the breathing starts to become heavier and somewhat labored, resulting in an increased rate of oxygen intake. This threshold can often be observed by the athlete because of the noticeably increased breathing rate. A marathon runner must run a few percent just below this threshold to avoid the lactate buildup. Therefore, the AT is the best predictor of marathon performance.

For runners, the anaerobic threshold is roughly as follows: novice = 0.65 to 0.75 MHR, experienced = 0.80 to 0.85 MHR, elite = 0.85 to 0.90 MHR. With training, the AT occurs at a higher percentage of maximum heart rate, MHR, and VO_2max.

Below the AT, the aerobic metabolism provides essentially all the required energy, e.g., less than one percent anaerobic. In between the AT and VO_2max, there is an aerobic-anaerobic transition. As the running pace increases above the AT, there is an increased percentage of anaerobic metabolism and a corresponding decrease in percentage of aerobic metabolism (as seen in Table 1.1).

VO_2max

A one percent reduction in body weight will improve the VO_2max by one percent! And a one percent increase in VO_2max will improve your 5K or 10K race time by about one percent.

Description: Maximum aerobic power or VO_2max represents the maximum amount of oxygen that can be removed from circulating blood and used by the working tissues during a specified period. The units are milliliters of oxygen/kg of body weight/minute. "Once 100% VO_2max is achieved, anaerobic glycolysis provides the additional energy for continued work" (Martin and Coe[2]). An elite athlete, after having reached this maximum oxygen intake, cannot operate at VO_2max for more than a few minutes (5 to 8 minutes). However, some elite athletes can run a marathon at near 90% VO_2max.

Typical values of VO_2max ml/kg/min are:

- 70 to 85 for elite (world class) runners
- 50 to 60 for competitive club runners
- 35 to 50 for average healthy individuals

Prediction of VO_2max by Chart: Based on race times, a runner can predict his or her VO_2max from charts showing race times vs. VO_2max.

Table 2.4 from Noakes[8] is one source where VO_2max can be predicted from race times for 1500 meters up to a marathon and even for a 56K race. This chart is based on data in *Oxygen Power* from a 1979 book by Jack Daniels and J.R. Gilbert. A similar Table, 3.1, is found in *The Running Formula* by Jack Daniels. My VO_2max is about 52 to 56 based on the race time chart Table 2.4 in Noakes[8]. Since this table is based on race times, it takes care of the lower VO_2max for older runners.

Prediction of VO_2max by Formula: VO_2max can be predicted within + or – 4% by my simple formula below. This was obtained by an examination of the above tables.

VO_2max = 1000/5K race time in minutes

This formula gives the same VO_2max as the above tables at a 5K race time of about 20 minutes (e.g., VO_2max = 50). It overpredicts for slower runners (by +4% at 24 minute 5K), and underpredicts for elite runners (by -5% at 15 minute 5K).

Predictor of Performance. VO_2max is commonly mentioned as the best predictor of performance in the 3K, 5K and 10K. "The true predictors of the potential of runners are the peak running velocities or work loads they achieve during maximal test, not the actual VO_2max values" (Noakes[8], 1989 and 1990). Also in modern VO_2max studies, only half of all tested showed true plateau in oxygen consumption during maximal exercise. [Noakes suggests] "that factors related to muscle, not cardio-vascular system prevented half from reaching VO_2max.[8] This is quite conceivable: for example, in view of my limited experience on the bike, my running muscles prevent me from reaching a heart rate as high as 120 beats/minute. So untrained muscles could limit an individual in achieving VO_2max.

Effect of Training. "Because VO_2max can only be improved by about 15% with intensive training, it is clear that the average individual will never achieve the high values of the elite athletes" (Noakes[8]). However, Martin and Coe[2] state "Untrained people over a broad range of ages, on a serious fitness program can raise their sedentary lifestyle VO_2max as much as 40%." [It appears the Noakes figure is more applicable to experienced runners where percentage gains are more difficult (a case of diminishing returns). Also those with predominant slow twitch fibers should show greater improvement. Both references would agree genetic endowment is a major factor in the percentage achievable; one cannot make a thoroughbred race horse out of a donkey.]

Effect of Reduced Training. Hickson and co-workers[9] showed that training induced increases in VO_2max and heart size can be maintained when training is reduced from six to two days per week provided the intensity of exercise is high (85 to 100%).

The effects of detraining for four weeks was studied by Madsen, et al.,[17] in nine well-trained endurance athletes. Detraining consisted of one short high intensity bout per week compared to the normal 6-10 hours per week on a cycle ergometer. The test consisted of time to exhaustion at 75% VO_2max. There was no effect on VO_2max, but endurance capacity decreased by 21%. Glycogen stores in resting muscle were 20% lower after detraining. Also, there was significant reduction in the utilization of free fatty acids.

Coyle[14] reports after 21 days of detraining in highly trained athletes VO_2max reduced by about 7% due to a reduction in maximum stroke volume of the heart. Further decline at a slower rate was due to decline in oxygen extraction rate until the increases produced by training are all lost in three months.

Effect of Four Weeks of Inactivity. In 1992, after a prostate operation, I had four weeks of inactivity except for walking. Then I had six weeks of cross-training, followed by six weeks of running training. After this total of four months, I raced in Jalapa, Mexico, in the 400-, 800- and 1500-meter races on separate days, but was still more than 2 or 3% slower than before the operation. This was at age 62, a younger athlete should be able to recover quicker.

%VO_2max Used vs. Length of Race. The percent VO_2max increases as the length of the race becomes shorter hence faster. For the marathon to 3000 meters, it would vary from about 80% to 100% VO_2max.

THE HEART

Maximum Heart Rate

Maximum heart rate, MHR, and maximum VO_2max can be determined by monitoring an athlete while running to exhaustion on a treadmill or riding an exercise bike while breathing into a device that measures gas volume. Fortunately, there are easier ways to determine the MHR.

Note: Heart rate in beats/minute = b.p.m. in the discussion below.

The usual MHR formula for men, i.e., (220-age) b.p.m., or (226-age) for women is more appropriate for an untrained person, like the average sedentary person, or novice runner. One finds this formula in many books and it is even used at the local health clubs, e.g., YMCA, to determine the working exercise range, based on age, usually 60% to 85% of MHR. It would not be accurate for a runner with many years of experience because trained runners can show little reduction in heart rate over several decades. Also, some individuals have MHR significantly below normal; for example, Hal Higdon[10] reports that his MHR at age 60 was 153 b.p.m. and has been within a few beats of that for 20 years. Studies of very fit athletes have shown no change nor insignificant decrease in MHR for at least two decades. Also, I believe my MHR has remained close to about 195 b.p.m. from 60 to 70 years of age due to consistent intensive training.

My own experience with a heart rate monitor indicates my MHR is of the order of 195 b.p.m. but the formula above would predict only 150 b.p.m. at age 70.

Determine MHR

The following methods are suggested to determine the MHR.

Method 1

This method makes use of the expected ratio of anaerobic (or ventilatory) threshold to MHR. As mentioned above, an observant runner can detect fairly accurately his or her ventilatory threshold, VT, due to the noticeably increased breathing at this pace. Then, using a heart rate monitor, the heart rate HR@VT at this pace is determined, and the MHR is determined using this information as follows.

Runner	VT/MHR*	MHR
Novice	0.70	HR@VT/0.70
Experienced	0.83	HR@VT/0.83
Elite	0.88	HR@VT/0.88

*The 2nd column lists representative averages accurate to about + or- 4% to 5% so the formula is about + or – 6% or 7% accurate considering also the error in HR@VT. (For example, an experienced runner with VT of 163 b.p.m. has a MHR = 163/.83 = about 195 b.p.m.)

The above formula accounts for those individuals who have a much lower MHR than normal (i.e., larger than normal blood volume pushed on each heartbeat), such as Hal Higdon, and/or for athletes who have trained intensely for decades.

Method 2

The MHR can be determined by running to near exhaustion as explained below:

1. When in good shape, do fast intervals after a good warm-up. Run about 4 x 200 meters or 3 x 300 meters at 95% effort with 5 or 6 minutes rest between. Immediately after the last interval, measure the heart rate.

2. A 1500-meter or one mile race would produce close to MHR just before the end of the race or immediately after. The heart rate monitor is recommended for the above as it is impossible to measure by watch when heart rate is this fast and when one is exhausted and bent over with hands on the knees.

3. After a good warm-up, run 4 or 5 x 200 meters at 600-meter race pace. Rest between reps equals time for the run. Take the pulse immediately after the last interval. Without a heart monitor, have someone take the pulse for you.

Taking the Pulse

Without a heart rate monitor, place the fingers of the left hand on the artery at the top inside of the right wrist. When pulse coincides with one of the seconds call this zero. Thereafter, count all beats for 15 seconds. Multiply by four to get beats per minute. The error can only be less than one half beat in 10 seconds.

Benefits of Pulse Measurements

1. **Indicates sickness or lack of recovery next day.** Take pulse every morning before getting out of bed. If the pulse is about five beats per minute above normal you are possibly catching a cold or flu, or the training the day before was too hard. In either case, take it easy that day. If the resting pulse remains higher than about five b.p.m. or more above normal for five days or more the athlete is overtrained. It could take several weeks to get over this over-training; see page 416 of Noakes[8].

2. **Indicates severity of workout.** After a workout take the pulse about 15 minutes after the cool down. If the pulse is still too high, e.g., about 25 b.p.m. or higher above the resting value, this indicates the workout was too hard; in this case take it easy or easier the next day. The important thing is to take the pulse at a consistent time after the workout, for a variable time will only confuse the matter. With experience one can relate the effect on the body by the high or low recovery heartbeat. I have often found that my heartbeat seems to want to settle at 60 b.p.m. for a fairly long time after a workout, and I have suspected that the wrist watch is having some effect on my recovery pulse. After a hard workout, I have found my pulse is sometimes still up to about 15 b.p.m. above the resting value 90 minutes after the workout.

3. **Train in the recommended range.** The main advantage of pulse keeping is to train in the recommended range or to keep just within the anaerobic threshold; from experience, the athlete will know what value will keep him or her just below the AT. With training, the athlete notices at the same heart rate, the pace eventually becomes faster due to adaptation, increase in VO_2max, and/or improved running economy.

4. **Indicates when the next "rep" can start.** The rapidity with which the heart recovers during interval training is useful to determine the correctness of the pace, the length of the run, and the interval rest time. Ideally, the heart rate should decrease to 120 b.p.m. within 90 seconds; otherwise, the pace is too fast or the length of the run is too long or both. However, I had found that when in good shape in doing sets of 200-meter repeats at age 65 at 800-meter race pace (about 34 seconds) I could

start the next repetition at about 135 b.p.m. after about 45 seconds. Usually there were three or four "reps" in a set.

5. **Indicates improvement in fitness.** The heart rate can be used to determine the degree of fitness by measuring heart rate immediately after a set of intervals. For example, this method was used by Lasse Viren. The faster speeds for 200-meter repeats and the lower heart rate compared to previous months indicated much improved fitness.[8] See also "Heart Rate Monitoring" at the end of Chapter 7.

Resting Heart Rate

Exercise puts a moderate to intense stress on the heart causing it to be stronger, larger, and more muscular. The resting heart rate in a trained athlete usually reduces with training over several years. An experienced athlete has nearly one half the beats per minute of the average person, e.g., for an experienced male about 40 b.p.m. or less compared to the average of about 72 b.p.m. The athlete's heart works less, rests more and consequently takes longer to wear out. There are exceptions to the lowered resting heart rate, e.g., Jim Ryun (world record miler) had a resting heart rate of 72 b.p.m. Mine is 43 to 44 b.p.m. before getting out of bed. During hard training in the summer; at age 65, when training was less intense in the fall, it sometimes dropped to 40 to 41. After a long run, it often goes several beats below normal the next morning. Following a couple of easy days, it would often be down by about two beats per minute. With a bad cold or the flu, it goes up four or five b.p.m. for a day or two.

ENLARGED HEART, CORONARY VESSELS, AND INCREASED STROKE VOLUME

Enlarged Heart

An enlarged heart due to distance training is common in trained athletes, particularly rowers, swimmers, cyclists and runners. This results in the ability to pump more blood at much higher than normal volumetric rates, hence with greater oxygen delivery. Costill[1] reported the following for world class runners:

- Prefontaine, holder of many USA running records had a heart 30% to 40% larger than the average man of his age and size.
- The marathoner Hal Higdon has a heart about 50% bigger than that of a similar, but untrained man.

Heart size increases in proportion to the volume of miles trained, e.g., marathoners have much larger hearts than sprinters.[11] Costill[1] states, "Heart volume does not always increase following training but the ventricals may be stronger and able to empty more fully." [Also], "Left ventricular volume shows little increase due to training in older runners (above 40 or 50)." [I only know that there were changes in my heart several years after resuming running at age 56 (after a 33-year lay-off) as my resting heart rate dropped from about 54 to about 43 b.p.m.]

Enlarged Coronary Vessels

The advantage of enlarged coronary vessels may also be common in distance runners although less well documented. Costill[1] reports: "Clarence DeMar [Canadian] winner of the Boston marathon seven times, had a heart size somewhat larger than normal but had very large coronary vessels, two to three times normal size."

Stroke Volume

The trained athlete has larger cardiac output than an untrained or novice athlete due to increased heart stroke volume.

The stroke volume increases both at rest and during exercise due to an increase in size of the ventricular heart chambers, left and right, and an increase in mass of heart muscle with heart wall thickness unchanged (Martin and Coe[2]). The increased stroke volume along with the slower resting heart rate of the trained athlete results in the maintenance of the required cardiac output at rest.

Oxygen delivery to the body is a function of the following three factors:

Oxygen delivery = heart rate x stroke volume x oxygen extraction from the blood.

The above equation shows that for a trained athlete at a given heart rate during exercise: oxygen delivery may be increased due to a larger stroke volume and increased oxygen extraction from the blood. The latter results mainly from increased skeletal muscle capillary density from years of aerobic training.

HEART IRREGULARITIES

Well-trained runners have a high incidence of abnormal heart rhythms that are normal and do not indicate heart disease.[11] These irregularities in the heart beat are not serious but there is a danger of misinterpretation of their electro-cardiogram (EKG)[12]. (Note there are variations in time between heartbeats that occur during inhaling and exhaling, which are not discussed here as they are normal.) A well-trained runner can often detect some *abnormal* irregularities when taking the pulse, particularly after a hard workout. Palpitations and irregular pulse are sometimes seen as a sign of exhaustion; runners might taper off training when they occur[12]. This is not to imply that all heart irregularities in an athlete are not serious; some will require checking by a physician. The following are some of the studies and observations made on this subject:

- Twenty-five percent of all runners over 40 years of age have irregular EKGs[5].

- Dr. George Sheehan, world famous heart specialist and runner/author, reported[12] on an Italian study by Vererando and Raulli at the Rome Olympics. Nearly all of the 89 world class marathoners tested had abnormal EKGs; however, it was concluded the changes were not related to decreased heart function or disease.

- Dr. Sheehan[12] also discussed cardiac arrhythmias–continued runs of extremely rapid beats. The majority of arrhythmias occur in healthy hearts and have no effect on general health. Such benign irregularities are common among ordinary runners, as well as world class runners. I have experienced this erratic fast heart beat (also called atrial tachycardia) myself on several occasions; this sometimes occurs after a stressful situation of hard exertion like shoveling heavy snow, or even in a restful mode, but not during racing when I am well warmed up and rested from easier days beforehand. Usually this would occur after taking caffeine and/or when the body was tired from too many hard workouts close together. In the fall, when training is less intense, I rarely get this problem even with increased caffeine consumption. This indicates that it is mainly brought on by over-training and tiredness. Usually I can rid myself of this in 5 to 40 minutes by lying down and breathing deeply in complete relaxation and concentration. Excessive rapid heartbeat is sometimes stopped by lying down with feet above the head and propped against a wall. For prolonged rapid pulse lasting several hours or more, it is recommended to visit the hospital to bring the pulse down. Don't wait three days as I did once. See also the section on caffeine in Chapter 15 if you have this problem.

Once this condition occurred while doing fast 200-meter intervals with the heart monitor too tightly on the chest. My heart reached higher than 200 b.p.m. After about 15 minutes, my heart calmed down and I was able to run even faster than before. This, and a similar experience, made me think there is a benefit to a warm-up during which the heart beat gets up to near maximum. On another occasion, after atrial fibrilation or tachycardia occurred (due partly to warm-up too intense), I foolishly completed two 500-meter accelerations before my heart had calmed down to normal. In the last 50 meters of each, I never had so much lactate or felt so exhausted.

THE BLOOD

Increased Blood Volume and Red Blood Cells

When you train regularly over a long period of time, your body's blood volume increases. "Physical activity significantly increases the volume of plasma, the watery part of the blood" (Costill[1]). This results in a greater flow of oxygen to a greater number of cells over the body.

Costill[1] states: "The amount of oxygen carried by the blood is determined partly by the number of red cells and hemoglobin in the blood; therefore VO_2max is closely related to the athletes red cell volume. Experts generally agree that years of training will increase the number of red blood cells without changing the amount of hemoglobin in each cell."

Intense exercise training usually increases blood volume by approximately 500mL, i.e., 8% to 10%. This adaptation is gained after a few bouts of exercise and is quickly reversed when training ceases. However, blood volume can be restored within days after training is re-initiated (Coyle[14]).

pH Of Blood

In hard intense running, such as the 400-meter race, the pH of the blood (and muscles) drops from the alkaline range, i.e., slightly above the neutral pH value of 7.0, into the acid region. "This increased acidity due to lactate and H^+ ions limits the muscle's ability to produce energy and muscles have difficulty to contract" (Costill[1]). This acts as a safety valve preventing the pH from going excessively low. Anaerobic interval training consists of working intensely during a "rep" to get the pH to go down. Rest, let it come up during the rest interval, and start the next "rep" still with some residual acidity.

Recovery of one or two days may be required to allow the pH to return to normal. If pH is low when training in following days, the whole system is upset and the athlete will not be able to perform optimally. If a workout is too intense with too much volume, recovery from training is poor, appetite is affected and there is loss of sleep and staleness.

MITOCHONDRIAL ENZYME ACTIVITY

The mitochondria are those tiny powerhouses within the muscle cell that turn nutrients into ATP in the presence of oxygen. Oxidative enzymes within the mitochondria speed the reaction resulting in efficient performance. Measurements of these oxidative enzymes are used to indicate the capacity of the muscles to do work; they are a measure of endurance performance ability. Also, researchers have used the decrease in mitochondria enzymes content when training stops as a measure of rate of loss of fitness (Coyle[14]).

The investigations of Coyle[14] reveal the following:

- **Mitochondria enzyme activity the limiting factor.** It is likely that mitochondria enzyme activity is the limiting factor in determining the time to return to the pre-trained state.

- **Cessation of training.** Moderate training of only two to four months duration increases mitochondria enzyme activity by 20 to 40%, but this is lost in one to two months after training stops.

- **Detraining.** After 10 days of detraining mitochondria enzyme activity has reduced 50%. It takes over 40 days of re-training to regain the trained state.

PHYSIOLOGICAL DIFFERENCES BETWEEN MEN AND WOMEN

Women have slower speeds (generally about 11%) in world record performances than men from Noakes[8] Figure 16.1, for example:

- 100 meters (- 9.4%)
- 5K and 10K (-15%)
- Marathon (-11%)

The reasons for the above are due mainly to the following; compared to men, women have:

- About 12% smaller heart size
- Lower hemoglobin concentration in blood (hence less oxygen carrying capacity)
- More body fat
- Smaller bones and less muscle
- At least 25% less body strength
- Lower oxygen uptake

YOUR FRIEND, LACTIC ACID

This chapter would not be complete without clarifying some misconceptions about lactic acid. It has the reputation of being the "bad guy" responsible for fatigue and sore muscles. During intense-prolonged exercise it does cause some pain or discomfort but it is removed quickly, usually cleared from muscles within an hour or less after the activity. The soreness that remains is due to inflammation and tiny microtears in the muscles. Actually, lactic acid is more friend than foe since it is a key substance in providing energy during submaximal exercise.

Increased breakdown of muscle glycogen **(glycogenolysis)** or breakdown of blood glucose **(glycolysis)** lead to increased lactic acid in the blood.

The following summarizes some of the important points from the excellent research article by Dr. George A. Brooks[15]:

- "Seventy-five percent of the lactic acid produced during steady-state submaximal exercise is rapidly used as a source of aerobic energy production." Also, "Conversion of glucose in the liver and kidneys account for approximately 25% of lactic acid disposal during exercise."

- With adaptation due to high intensity and prolonged submaximal training: cardiovascular, mitochondrial and capillary capacity are increased resulting in decreased lactic acid production and formation.

- Also lactic acid may be supplied from inactive muscles to the liver and kidneys where it is converted to glucose; this glucose is released to general circulation and is used by active muscles.

REFERENCES

1. Costill, D., *Inside Running, Basics of Sports Physiology*, Benchmark Press, Carmel, IN, 1986.
2. Martin, D., and Coe, P., *Better Training for Distance Runners,* Leisure Press, Champaign, Illinois, 1997.
3. Mangi, R., Jokl, P., and Dayton, O. W., *Sports Fitness and Training,* Pantheon Books, New York, NY, 1987.
4. Sparks, K., Bjorklund, G., *Long Distance Runner's Guide to Training and Racing,* Prentice Hall, Englewood Cliffs, NJ, 1984.
5. Mirkin, G., and Hoffman, M., *The Sports Medicine Book,* Little Brown and Co., Boston, Toronto, 1978.
6. Lydiard, A., and Gilmour, G., *Running With Lydiard,* Hodder and Stoughton, Aukland, London, Sydney, Toronto, 1983.
7. Peronnet, F., and Thibault, G., "Mathematical analysis of running performance and world running records", *Journal of Applied Physiology, 67,* 453-465, 1989.
8. Noakes, T., *Lore of Running,* Leisure Press/Human Kinetics, Inc., Champaign, IL, 1991.
9. Hickson, R. C., et al, Reduced training intensities and loss of aerobic power, endurance and cardiac growth, *Appl. Physiol.,* 58: 492-499, 1985.
10. Higdon, H., *Run Fast, How to Train for a 5K or 10K Race,* Rodale Press, Emmaus, PA, 1992.
11. Pantano, J., and Oriel, R.J., "Prevalence and nature of cardiac arrhythmias in apparently normal well-trained runners", *American Heart Journal 104*, 762-768.
12. Sheehan, G., *Medical Advice for Runners,* World Publications, Mountain View, CA, 1978.
13. Bangsbo, J., et al, Anaerobic energy production and O2 deficit–debt relationship during exhaustive exercise in humans, *J. Physiol.* (London) 422:539-559, 1990.
14. Coyle, E. T., Detraining and retention of training-induced adaptations, *Gatorade Sports Science Institute, Conditioning and Training,* Volume 2, Number 23, March 1990.
15. Brooks, G. A., "Blood lactic acid: sports 'bad boy' turns good," *Gatorade Sports Science Institute,* Volume 1, Number 2, April 1988.
16. Watts, D. C. V., and Wilson Harry, *Middle and Long Distance Marathon and Steeplechase,* British Amateur Athletic Board, London.
17. Madsen, K., et al, "Effect of detraining on endurance capacity and metabolic changes during prolonged exhaustive exercise", *J. Appl. Physiol. 75* (4): 1444-1451, 1993.
18. Morehouse, L., and Gross, L., *Maximum Performance,* Simon and Shuster, New York, NY, 1977.
19. Cooper, K. H., *Aerobics,* M. Evans and Company, Inc., New York, NY, 1968

Bundeswehr
asics
Krombacher
55
asics

CHAPTER 2

Think of your mind as a well-trained harnessed thoroughbred, going into battle in control, disciplined and fearsome.

MENTAL TRAINING

INTRODUCTION

With body, mind, and spirit in harmony, there will be sublime athletic moments, and a life more complete and ideal. These would not be possible with an agitated mind and/or emotions in turmoil. Techniques to achieve these psychophysical experiences in training, competition and in the game of life are described in this chapter.

Long ago, the great Paavo Nurmi said: "Mind is everything—muscles pieces of rubber. All that I am, I am because of my mind." This indicates the importance of mental training. Unfortunately, the average athlete spends no time on mental training. Think what improvements and great strides forward you, can make when the powerful mental techniques are added to your arsenal of tricks.

Norman Vincent Peale[24] refers to Duke Kahanamoku of Hawaii, one of the greatest swimmers of all time; he knew that to be a great victor you have to give everything with all your body, mind, and spirit. He proved this by winning the 100-meter freestyle in the Olympics in 1912 and 1920 but lost to Johnny Weissmuller by inches in 1924. "It is practice, practice, practice," he said. "That is absolutely necessary. But also it is to use all your resources of body, mind and spirit—not part of them, not a fraction of them, but all of them."

In its application sports psychology still lags behind the physical aspect at least for the average athlete. Over 40 years ago, the great Australian world record holder many times over, Herb Elliot, incorporated mental techniques, including Zen philosophy and yoga; these were introduced by his legendary coach, Percy Cerutty. The Russians pioneered sports psychology and applied it with great success in training for the Olympics. Although most serious runners are spending 10 to 20 hours a week on training their bodies, very few are spending as much as 15 minutes a week on mental training. However, most elite athletes know the benefits; 85% of 633 Olympic hopefuls practiced some form of mental practice[25].

Quite often, competitors have little difference in strength, technique, or training; the winning difference comes in psychology. "The winners are able to get 'up,' to achieve the state of psychic balance that allows them to perform consistently at their best" (John Jerome[16]). Mental training techniques not only combat negative reactions, but also are able to release hidden reserves of energy and endurance[22]. ***Mental training should be practiced at least a few minutes every day; make use of your many spare moments.***

HARMONY OF BODY, MIND, AND SPIRIT

On my nearly daily trips to my local YMCA, I see the motto, "Body, Mind, and Spirit." Most members however are working exclusively on the body with little or no practice on mental techniques although spirit may not be lacking. I suspect that most have no idea about body, mind, spirit experiences or the desirable benefits in achieving this harmony. Dr. Jerry Lynch and Dr. Warren Scott in *Running Within*[1] state, "Perhaps you haven't experienced such psychobiological phenomena; maybe you have, but failed to make the connection or have forgotten about it."

As for myself, I had only part of the puzzle until reading the above book. I knew of the mental techniques and practiced them. I knew that to get the most from my workouts I had to enjoy them and this would lead to more rapid progress; this I learned from the great Derek Turnbull, probably the male master athlete of the last century. Also, I had experienced some psychophysical highs (not the endorphin high) while training and racing. I still recall an experience some 50 years ago when I surpassed myself in a race and felt I could run faster than ever without effort. But for many years, I had not put it all together. The discussion below involving Zen Buddhism and the way of the warrior athlete will assist you to achieve this perfection, i.e., harmony of body, mind, and spirit.

What is Spirit?

We know that the mind is the rider and the horse is the body. The spirit, the "heart mind," is an emotion encompassing many admirable abilities and convictions such as courage, determination, enthusiasm, joy, confidence, and peacefulness. The result is an emotion of the highest order. It is the core of the moving experience.

Zen Buddhism and Satori

"One of Zen Buddhism's basic beliefs is that there is a Buddha (the perfect ideal) in all of us who wants to be awakened."[19]

Body, mind, spirit harmony is the state of Satori. It is not describable in words according to Zen Buddhism since it is a spiritual experience to be felt and lived. It is also an experience to be felt in the body[19]. One finds many contradictions and negations in trying to understand it with the logical mind. However, the following is sufficient for this chapter:

Satori[19] is attained through dynamic meditation, which involves forgetting mind and body, making no special effort, moving from thought to no thought, i.e., when thoughts arise, they are quickly discarded. When immersed in Satori, you will experience a peaceful state of nothingness—a no-mind-ness, but still a state of alertness and not sleepiness. After considerable practice, the meditation results in inner vision, detachment, stability of the mind, calm, ecstasy, control, freedom, power, energy and mystery. "During meditation the mind is free of internal distraction and has pure attention to the present moment; the emotions are free of tension, and the body is fully relaxed and vitalized" (Millman[5]). The main objective of Satori for the devout Zen Buddhists is enlightenment; for example: empathy with all others, non-judgmental, the end of ignorance, the end of craving (stop desire), etc.[19].

Similarly, the warrior runner during peak experiences while running can feel the same benefits as achieved during Zen meditation such as peace, freedom, ecstasy, calm and energy. This transcendental mental state occurs when a runner feels the harmony of body, mind, and spirit—everything is in order. This experience is described by Lynch and Scott[1] as "going beyond our psychobiological limits and as much broader in scope than the release of endorphins" (which combat pain and stress). These magical times do not happen frequently. Normally they require a calm mind, quiet emotions, and a fit, energized body and good surroundings. They can occur on a slow run surrounded by the beauty of nature or even in a race surrounded by thousands of spectators. You will be lost in the seemingly effortless running-floating, gliding like a deer. You will say to yourself, "This is what it is all about."

My poem was inspired by words in *Running Within* by Lynch and Scott.

Running In Satori

Enjoy the body flow;
Gliding—floating—
Effort free.
Enjoy the now;
Enjoy the inner you.
This time is yours alone
To revel in—
As you breathe in—
The beauty
All around.

Let your senses sing;
Let your feelings ring;
Feel the hymn within;
Feel the peace within.
Body, mind, and spirit
All in harmony;
That's what it's all about.
Let your body shout
It's silent vitality;
Let the mind run free;

In Satori:
Forgetting self,
Going beyond,
Becoming more.
Feel the dynamic
Meditation
And rejoice in the play,
The mystical
Dance of life,
Where the journey
Exceeds the inn.

The discussion below will assist the athlete to experience Satori or harmony of body, mind, and spirit and will describe the ways of the warrior athlete.

The Warrior Athlete

In times of internal conflict, an athlete can choose the right path by referring to the ways of the warrior athlete. The way of the warrior athlete is the body-mind-spirit way where these three centers are all in control and in balance.

Some description of the warrior athlete from Lynch and Scott[1] follows: The warrior of the past, such as the Japanese Samurai, exhibited great inner strength and spirit. They realized the true battle was the internal war waged against their inner fears rather than against external events. "The warrior possesses a multidimensional (body-mind-spirit) approach to competition." Competition is a race against themselves. Also with inner success achieved, there is less stress, anxiety, and pressure to win, and with less anxiety and pressure, it is easier for the steady warrior to achieve victory. The warrior runner settles and calms the mind by daily practice of meditation, relaxation, visualization and affirmations.

In competition, the warrior athlete concentrates on performing rather than antagonistic competing. For example, Al Oerter, four-time Olympic champion, often competing while injured says it all, "I don't compete with the other discus throwers. I compete with my own history." Similarly, the incomparable Katarina Witt says, "When I go out on the ice, I just think about my skating. I forget it is a competition." The message is: Don't worry and fret about your competitors, just try to be better than yourself.

See the list of ideal qualities in the section below, which come from a knowledge and practice of all the mental techniques. Also, *In the Zone*, by Murphy and White describes hundreds of magical peak experiences of athletes while possessing all of the important characteristics of the Ideal Performance State.

For meditation, goal setting, solving problems, decision making or clearing the mind and emotions the warrior athlete uses slow body movements in peaceful surroundings. Slow walking, swimming, running in the water (see Chapter 11) or jogging I have found to be effective for these purposes. But walking or hiking in the embrace of nature is best; it follows that the warrior athlete is a lover of nature as are the Zen Buddhists who regard nature as a living friend. Similarly, the quiet, poise, balance, grace, rhythm and concentration involved in yoga and tai chi make them highly effective for meditation, clearing the mind and emotions, and integration of body, mind, and spirit.

The Correct Attitude for Harmony of Body, Mind and Spirit

- Lynch and Scott[1] recommend the following: "When you focus on the beauty and essence of the run (the journey, the preparation) you will cease to experience the anxiety and pressures associated with outcomes and results. 'Wanting' to win is healthy, but detach your ego from winning. Don't obsess about 'needing' to win or outcomes or results; this depletes your energy, creates anxiety and slows you down; simply run to show others your greatness and fitness. Concentrate on 'effortless effort' to simply run your best for that day rather than a must-do-well outlook. Focussing on the mental aspects (relaxation, visualization and affirmations) before and during workouts is essential in mastering the body, mind and spirit journey."

- "Have an objective to have fun and enjoyment in the workouts. When you begin to enjoy the 'dance,' you widen and expand your focus and create a bridge to link your body, mind and spirit" (Lynch and Scott[1]). Also, motivation and interest will not last if there is too much stress and not enough enjoyment in your sport. But it's focused fun; the focus has to be maintained also to provide valuable experience for competition. See also the section below on "Benefits of Laughter."

- Striving for perfection is too result-oriented, leading to focus on faster times, longer distances and harder and harder workouts. This can be destructive. In 1999 by trying too hard, the 400-meter outdoor world record for age group 70-74 eluded me all summer although I had tied it indoors on tighter turns at the USA Masters Indoor meet in Boston in March. Basically, I was somewhat over trained and always went out too fast. Trying harder is counter-productive. If I had forgotten about the record (competing against the clock) and concentrated on the joy of running, success may have been more likely. Also the two workouts per day normally, and intense intervals three times per week had worn my 70-year-old body down with too many winning workouts. Less often results in more. "Practice aikido, the less resistance, force and effort you create, the more efficient you become" (Lynch and Scott[1]).

How to Achieve a Psychophysical Workout

The following five steps during warm up will assist to achieve a mind-body-spirit workout:

1. Review the objectives of the training session.
2. Reflect on your overall goals.
3. Remind yourself how this workout will help to achieve your overall goals.
4. Remind yourself that if there is discomfort or fatigue, it is the only way to succeed.
5. With imagery, picture and feel yourself enjoying the session and completing it successfully, energetically and with enthusiasm.

These steps should result in a training session that is focused, enthusiastic, and satisfying.

Rewards of the Warrior Athlete or Body-Mind-Spirit Harmony

- Lynch and Scott explain[1]: "On the journey of mastery, preparation or practice is the reward." With this realization, the workouts become an enjoyable physical, emotional and spiritual experience. "The true prize is the practice, the in–the–moment warrior inner experience." Once inner success is achieved, there is less anxiety and pressure in competitive situations resulting in improved performance.

- When athletics are practiced with harmony of body, mind, and spirit, the valuable lessons and habits are carried over to daily pursuits.

- In your pursuit and achievement of harmony of body, mind, and spirit, you should come to a greater appreciation of your existence and realization that every day is a gift. In "the mystical journey," "the ultimate game of life," you will encounter the "beauty of being alive" (Lynch and Scott[1]).

- Finally, the warrior athlete or ideal athlete with self-realization and inner strength achieved, moves gracefully through life with the poise and carriage of a modest champion.

THE IDEAL STATE OF THE MIND

The "ideal state of mind" prior to and during competition is a Zen mindset that has all the characteristics and benefits of Zen Buddhism meditation. Dr. James Loehr[23, 31] lists twelve aspects of the ideal internal climate for performing optimally:

- Physically relaxed
- Low anxiety
- Optimistic
- Effortless
- Alert
- Self–confident
- Mentally calm
- Energized
- Enjoyment
- Automatic
- Mentally focused
- In control

Dr. Loehr determined the above "Ideal Performance State" after interviewing hundreds of peak performers in a variety of sports[31]. See also Charles Garfield[22] for a similar list of ideal characteristics for an athlete. Many athletes refer to it as playing "in the zone." Ideally, to perform at one's best, the athlete must have the above positive feelings. Before practice or competition, practice the mental techniques to achieve this ideal frame of mind.

From my own observation in setting over 40 world records in track events, breaking a world record generally does not feel like super effort at the time; in a superb performance, the athlete has the above characteristics and all is on autopilot. All this is possible from the thousands of hours of physical and mental preparation at near-the-race situation during workouts.

An example of a relaxed phenomenal athlete is Ralph Romain, holder of world records in the 400 meters for age category 55-59 and 60-65, e.g., an amazing 53.90 seconds in the latter category. He even has time to wave at the crowd during the race. Before the 800-meter final in the World Veterans Championships in Buffalo in 1995, he asked why I was warming up about one and a half hours before the race. I said it was to get rid of some nerves. He said, "When I'm in the starting blocks, I could go to sleep," and I believe him.

When in this ideal state during a performance, John Jerome calls it the Sweet Spot Theory of Performance[16]. For example, when a batter hits the perfect home run everything comes together to produce the perfect trajectory. In the ideal performance, such as the unbelievable long jump of Bob Beamon at the 1968 Mexico Olympics, shattering the world record by about 2 feet, there was "a combination of hundreds of variables including near perfect mental preparation and state of mind" (Jerome[16]). On the contrary, trying too hard in competition counteracts relaxation, and reduces speed, power and accuracy.

THE BENEFITS OF LAUGHTER

It is no secret that laughter, happiness and a sense of humor has many psychological advantages, such as a good mental outlook, a positive attitude, a relaxed and stress-free mind.

Have fun during the workouts and you will be more relaxed; the hard ones will seem much easier and this will translate into faster races and avoidance of staleness. We called ourselves the "Invalids" (my 1998/99 running partners at North York T &F Club). We all had nicknames; there was "Big Mouth," "Pervert," "Crazy Legs or Bonkers," and "Old Fogy" (guess who?).

Laughter has other important advantages:

- Strengthen the immune system
- Aid in treating illness and injury
- Relieve pain and physical tension
- Longevity

Focus on the positive aspects of life rather than the negative to achieve happiness. Look on the bright side to achieve a sense of humor.

RELAXATION TECHNIQUES

"By fully relaxing the muscles, one can in turn relax the mind; Edmund Jacobson demonstrated this over fifty years ago" (Garfield[22]).

There are several reasons for clearing the mind and relaxing completely (Terry Orlick[13]):

- To fall into restful sleep the night before an important competition
- To prepare for a top performance
- To speed recovery between events or after a meet
- To prepare the mind and body for imagery, or assertive self statements
- To prepare for any stressful situation as before an exam, or interview, or giving a speech
- To adjust to a stressful situation requiring calm communication

After completing one of the methods below, you should be calm, energized, relaxed, centred and ready to begin visualization. In a relaxed state of mind, your mental system is most receptive to the mental images focused upon or to the self-assertive statements.

Methods of Relaxation. There are many different methods to relax the body and mind. In the case of relaxation before a competition, it will be necessary to increase the tension after the deep relaxation to achieve the optimum tension for competition, for one should not be too relaxed for peak performance. See Method 2. Some typical or popular methods are described below:

Method 1. The relaxation technique by Terry Orlick[13] described briefly below is fairly typical:

1. Get yourself into a comfortable position sitting or lying down. Breathe easily and slowly. Think relaxation into all body parts in the following order: toes, feet, lower legs, upper legs, behind, lower back, upper back, fingers, forearms, upper arms, shoulders, neck, jaw, and head. Let each part totally relax then move to the next part. Think warmth into your fingers. "Scan your body for possible areas of tightness and relax these areas. Imagine your body encircled with soothing warmth and relaxation."
2. Now concentrate on diaphragmatic breathing, i.e., where the stomach rises on inhale and falls on exhale. Relax on each breath particularly the exhale as you "sink deeper and deeper into warm, calm, complete relaxation."
3. Now go to your special place of peace and tranquility.

Method 2. Some references, such as[3,23,29], describe the "tense, hold, and release" technique (Edmund Jacobson system) moving through all body parts from the upper body to the toes or in the reverse direction, one body part at a time. This is called "Progressive Muscle Relaxation." Lie flat on your back, arms at the side. Let the limbs relax and flop. Hold tension for 10 seconds or so in each part. Then let the tension go for about 10 seconds. On each breath, inhale new energy and vitality; exhale tiredness and tension[3]. Alternatively tense all parts together on a count of 10; then count backward from 10 relaxing all parts; now bring your tension up a level that you feel right for competition.

However, according to Terry Orlick[13], "Tensing the muscles before they are relaxed is a commonly recommended procedure developed initially by psychologists for non-athletes; it is generally not popular with athletes who are more in tune with their muscles."

Method 3. Kay Porter and Judy Foster[3] describe the short form of relaxation once you have mastered relaxing quickly: Take a quiet moment, close eyes, and center on your breathing. Breathe in deeply and hold it for a moment—exhale, letting your mind and body relax and become empty and peaceful. Notice if there are any areas of tightness. "If so, send it some energy and peace and let it go." When you are fully relaxed and centered you are ready to begin your visualization.

Method 4. Autogenic Training. This method of training concentrates on your muscles, functions related to the heart and breathing, and on your mental state. Autogenic means "self-create" or having control over oneself by concentration. The method relies on the words "heavy" and "warm" that are connected with feelings of relaxation. One variation of the method developed by Johannes Schultz is briefly as follows:

1. While in a quiet place and sitting or lying comfortably, close your eyes and start with deep diaphragmatic breathing.
2. Concentrate on each arm for over a minute. Repeat to yourself, "My arm feels heavy, becoming heavy, becoming heavier and heavier, becoming very heavy."
3. Concentrate on each leg with similar repeated statements, feeling this leg become increasingly heavier and relaxed.
4. Concentrate on each arm for over a minute. Repeat to yourself, "My arm feels warm, becoming warm, becoming warmer and warmer, becoming very warm."
5. Concentrate on each leg with similar repeated statements feeling the leg becoming increasingly warmer and relaxed.
6. Garfield[22] explains:
   Repeat the following four to six times "My chest feels calm and pleasant. Finally repeat, "I feel supremely calm and relaxed."
   Proceed exactly as above repeating the following statements[22]:
   "My heartbeat is calm and steady."
   "My stomach feels soft and warm."
   "My forehead feels cool."
7. Begin the self-assertive statements and/or visualization.

For a more complete session include the shoulders, head and feet. In that case do both arms together and both legs together to keep the session within 10 minutes. Millman[5] described a method similar to the above but without the warmth steps. When relaxed, "On inhalation feel yourself floating up and on exhalation, float back down."

Method 5. The book *Creative Visualization*[29] by Shakti Gawain has sold over 2 million copies starting from a self published book of 2,000 copies. One relaxation method from this book, described briefly, results in energization, exhilaration and deep relaxation following the steps below:
1) Lie down, arms at side, eyes closed, relax, breathe gently, deeply and slowly.
2) Imagine a glowing sphere of golden light emanating from your *head* as you breathe the slowly in and out five times, concentrating on this light. Similarly repeat this process for the *throat, chest* and *navel area, pelvic area* and *feet*. Think of the light as energy radiating and expanding through your body.
3) Now imagine all six spheres of light glowing all at once and radiating energy.
4) Imagine energy flowing down one side of your body from head to feet as you exhale deeply, and energy flowing upward on the other side as you inhale deeply. Complete three such circuits around the body.
5) Similarly visualize energy flowing down the front of your body and returning along the back. Breathe as above and complete three circuits.

6) Finally, imagine energy flowing up from the feet to the head through the center of your body and then down the outside. Breathe deeply as above. Repeat this several times.

Method 6. Shakti Gawain[29] also describes a useful technique of calling upon (invocation) a particular quality, such as strength, confidence, or energy:

"When completely relaxed and energized, say to yourself, *'I now call upon the quality of strength'.* Feel the energy of strength coming to you or arising in you, filling you up and radiating out from you. Experience this feeling for a few minutes. Then through visualization and affirmation, direct this quality towards a particular goal," (requiring this quality).

In addition to improving athletic performance, it does not take a great stretch of the imagination to see how this technique and others above could even be used to improve many qualities and even sexual performance.

Method 7. A simple method that works for me is to lie down in a quiet place, close the eyes and think relaxation. Take about 10 to 20 deep breaths slowly. Inhale slowly, hold the breath for about 2 or 3 seconds and exhale very slowly. The exhale is always longer than the inhale.

Method 8. Mantra chanting as used in Eastern cultures is effective in meditation. Repeat a short word or number, vocally or silently in rhythm with your breathing on each exhale. Focus intently on this word. Also mantra chanting can assist focussing while running[1]. Thus, another state of consciousness is achieved. Select four appropriate words as a positive reminder to maintain good form or to maintain concentration. Repeat these words silently or vocally in rhythm with each step. For example, *"Run light, low arms,"* or, *"Fast relaxed, fast relaxed."*

In one recent 5K race, I found it quite encouraging to repeat, *"This is not fast,"* in the first half of the race. Consequently, I was able to finish strong and fast, passing many runners, in the second half.

Method 9. See the thermometer method to bring prerace tension to the desired performance level under the section later in this chapter on "Overcoming Prerace Jitters/ What to do when nervous"..., number 7.

Summary of Relaxation Methods. You may find your own favorite method or combination of the above methods to relax quickly. After years of practice, I can now relax, without any special technique, fall off to sleep in a few minutes and awake refreshed about 10 to 15 minutes later.

The powerful visualization and assertive statements are discussed in the next sections.

VISUALIZATION

Mental visualization or imagery training is used in a wide variety of sports, such as gymnastics, diving, football drills, hurdling, etc. It is used by nearly all elite runners. Many world champions have used it, e.g., Dwight Stones (high jump), Jack Nicklaus (golf), Greg Lougonis (diving), Chris Evert (tennis), Jean Claude Killy (down hill and slalom skiing), and even the infamous O. J. Simpson (football), to mention a few. As a youth, I used it effectively to practice driving a car as I did not have a car during the time I was taking driving lessons. Some pianists even practice their complicated pieces in their head.

Why is it such a powerful tool? Maxwell Maltz M.D.[30] expresses it clearly, ***"Our nervous system cannot tell the difference between a 'real' experience and one which is 'vividly imagined.'"*** A sports event vividly imagined is known to stimulate the same muscle response as the real experience; this has been proven by the recording of the electrical activity of a muscle by electromyogram (EMG) measurements[14]. Muscles fire in the same sequence as if the athlete were performing the skill. The mental imagery allows a slight firing of the neural pathways that are actually involved in the activity, and so neural pathways for this particular skill are strengthened (deeper grooves) or even corrected. Hence the body believes it is actually practicing the skill visualized.

Purposes of Visualization

Visualization or imagery is a powerful technique that can serve a variety of purposes. Some of the more important purposes are listed below, see Lynch and Scott[1], Orlick[6], Weinberg[28], and Garfield[22]:

1. *To see success in achieving short and long-term goals.*
   See yourself performing correctly and efficiently and achieving the desired goal.
2. *To increase confidence, relaxation, energy and motivation.*
   Before training or competition call up in great detail sights, sounds and feelings during past performances that were highly successful. This results in increased confidence, relaxation, energy, motivation and increased intensity.
3. *To perfect skills.*
   See yourself performing perfect skills on a regular basis. This hastens and reinforces the learning.
4. *To see improvement from a plateau.*
5. *To stay connected to your mystical runner* and feel the ecstasy of a run (see section above on "Harmony of Body, Mind, and Spirit," and Lynch and Scott[1]).
6. *To visualize a race with a risk* and being successful with the risk-taking.
7. *To familiarize with the race or game plan.*
   Imagery can reinforce the race or game strategy to be followed under ideal and non-ideal conditions.

8. *To familiarize with the site of competition.*
   Familiarizing yourself with the surroundings of the competition site, the sounds, smells, weather, and the scene assist to rid the athlete of nerves before the competition. It is now familiar, and he or she now feels they have been there. Normally, the visualization would include the site and the race strategy in the one session.
9. *To refocus.*
   Imagery can be used to refocus when there are internal or external distractions before or during the event. You maintain your composure. See "Refocus" in the "Focus" section below.
10. *To cope with fatigue and prerace jitters.*
11. *To intensify relaxation.*
12. *To help overcome obstacles during a performance,* e.g., a heavy wind, rain, extreme heat or cold.
13. *To achieve the optimum performance state prior to competition, e.g.,* increased energy level or reduced level of anxiety.
14. *To hasten recovery of injuries.*
15. *To cope with pain and injury* by working with drills in the mind when training is not possible.
16. *To correct past errors.*
17. *To visualize immediately before the event,* e.g., before serving a ball in tennis, before a hurdle race, before a dive into a pool, before a golf swing, before a gymnastic exercise, etc.
18. *To prepare for important day-to-day social or work experiences.*

What Are the Essential Conditions to Make Your Visualizations Powerful?

Select a quiet, non-distracting environment. The body and mind must be completely relaxed and emotions calm. Use one of the relaxation techniques described above. In this relaxed state of mind, the central nervous system is most receptive to the mental images focused upon. "Feel yourself to be completely relaxed, confident and in complete control of your body and mental state" (Porter and Foster[3]).

Visualize your perfect performance and following your race plan. If possible, visit the race site beforehand to get the feel of the surroundings; alternatively even a picture of the site will help. Feelings, thoughts, and desires unrelated to the imagery must be set aside. Visualize in great detail and in color. Utilize all the senses: smell, touch, feel, and hearing; above all, feel what you are doing. Also, simulate in pictures also things that could go wrong, e.g., strong wind or rain and with positive reaction to these distractions. The visualizations must be vivid.

Subjective and Objective Visualization

Depending on what you are trying to achieve in the session, there are two different approaches to visualization: **subjective** and **objective**. In the subjective method, you see the pictures from within (internal) and the same muscles are activated as would occur in an actual physical performance. This is the preferable method for rehearsing physical skills, e.g., diving, high jumping, gymnastics, etc.; the athlete gets inside his/her body to experience and feel the sensations involved. In the objective method, you become an observer as if watching a movie of yourself. Both methods should be practiced.

Practice, Practice, Practice

Mental imaging requires practice to perfect the technique. To gain proficiency in it, use it often for all the above situations and others. The more you practice it, the easier it becomes. You need to do it every day, before (in particular), during, and after training. In this way, clarity of the pictures improve.

SELF ASSERTIVE STATEMENTS

Imagine the eight fastest sprinters lined up for the final Olympic 100-meters all with equal physical abilities; then the winning difference is in the thoughts of these athletes. Our "self-talk" and "self-thoughts" can energize and relax, or de-energize and tense up the body.

On the other hand, long-term affirmations extend the present into the future toward a realistic goal. Affirmations are not necessarily true at the time, but have the possibility of becoming true. They say to your subconscious, "You are there already." Your subconscious works on accepting this and eventually this becomes a reality after day-after-day positive "I am..." statements in conjunction with hard work and dedication. After you have gone from make-believe to absolute believing, the subconscious accepts the positive thinking and you act according to the positive belief. (See also the quote by Orlick in the section at the end on "Power of Belief").

Positive self-statements or affirmations are also powerful weapons to combat destructive self-doubts prior to workouts and more importantly during competitions. Affirmations will short circuit the negative talk. "Positive statements before a competition will remind you of excellent preparation, being in control, a goal to be achieved, extending oneself, your plan, and of your readiness" (Orlick[6]).

Autosuggestion is achieved by frequent reading, or repeating these positive affirmations, or playing recorded suggestions to yourself. It is necessary to be consistent in practice for the suggestion to set in.

How to Create Affirmations

- The statement is something you earnestly aspire to.
- Use present tense—act as if it has already happened—generally these will be "I am" statements.
- Be short and specific.
- Use rhyme and rhythm to assist in leaving the impression in the mind.
- Believe strongly in the thought—suspend your doubts for now.
- Use positive and personal statements.
- The affirmations must be realistic and achievable.

Purpose of Long-term or Prerace Affirmations:

- To overcome fears (fatigue, jitters, etc.) or to change negative thoughts into positive thoughts; For example, if you fear your start in a race will be slow, an affirmation would be: *"I enjoy coming out of the blocks, and I feel fast."*
- To achieve goals; For example, if your goal is to run the 1500-meters, with each lap within 1 or 2 seconds of your target times, the affirmation would be: *"I am focused and staying within 1 or 2 seconds of my target times for each lap."*
- To gain confidence, relaxation, energy and concentration.

When and How to Practice Affirmations?

- During deep relaxation, repeat many times over and over.
- Write on cards and display where they may be easily seen, such as on your fridge or on your bathroom mirror.
- Recite when walking, waiting for a bus, before bedtime or upon arising when the mind is receptive, or any other spare moment.
- Record on tape and play in the car while driving to practice or to the competition. (Also, I have found this an excellent method for rehearsing a speech.)
- Read your list of affirmations several times a day, preferably before bed and on arising in the morning.
- Affirmations can be used alone or in combination with imaging.
- Practice only when relaxed with calm emotions.

Performance Cues

Performance cues (to be discussed below under "Focus") are very short affirmations to be called upon during performance. Performance cues or triggers are potent reminders to get you to change muscle tension and focus on concentration, or to create desired physical or psychological feelings before or during performance.

COMPLIMENTS, AFFIRMATIONS, AND QUOTES IN THE TRAINING LOG

Compliments are a form of recognition. Some recognition helps to make the hard training worthwhile. Can you imagine getting a hole in one in golf and not having any witness? Compliments from others can be useful as a source of inspiration. There may be a slight exaggeration or even gross exaggeration, but like affirmations, they are usually close to reality or are real. They can be used to your advantage. You can even sometimes learn from a compliment. Work hard and there will be compliments, although this is far from our purpose in running and competing. People have noticed some worthwhile quality in you or improvement in you. In a way, a personal compliment is also a compliment to your coach.

Write some of these compliments in your training log as they occur: This is not to give you a big head, since you know most are an exaggeration, but there is at least a grain of truth, something to aspire to and boost your confidence and motivation. Some compliments have humor to make you lighten up. What the heck – who cares as long as it makes you run faster. It is well known that greater confidence aids performance; the athlete is more relaxed in mind and body, with more energy and willing to take risks to better his performance.

Also for further motivation, include in your training logs your **affirmations** and **favorite inspirational quotes**. When race time approaches, it is highly advantageous to read over your training log, particularly the night before the race. This gives you confidence since it reminds you of your hard training and preparedness. *The compliments, affirmations and quotes will provide motivation and positive thoughts.*

The following are some examples of affirmations, quotes, and compliments from my training logs; the * indicate a compliment:

1994

- *You move without effort, no unevenness, no up and down and very light.
- I do as much as I can without affecting next day's training.
- I feel I can do more.

1995

- *Perfect form, and economical running (Barry Shepley, Canada's triathlete coach).
- *You run with a lot of poise.
- *You finished the last 100 meters with a smile.
- *You are an inspiration.
- *The greatest race I've seen—without that terrific wind you could have run 2 minutes and 10 seconds.
- *You never take an easy day let's face it.
- *How do you keep young – what is the secret?

1996

- "You have to take it out hard to break the record" (Michael Johnson).
- *How old are you – 45?
- The key is power, not trying too hard. Flow.
- *You are a hurdler.

1997

- It's not pain, it's only discomfort.
- Time or dust will not erase the glory of their deeds.

1998

- *Watching you run was like a concert. (Boston Indoor)
- *I will get out of your way when you lap me. (Boston Indoor)
- *You are very determined when you run.
- *You have improved your body tremendously since six years ago in Trinidad. You look really strong.
- Go out and have fun. Show that you love your sport. Give it your all. (Stirton, Canadian instrumental dancer)

1999

- Learn to let the little things go.

2000

- *You only know how to go fast.
- Train to increase your luck.
- *You are a prancing horse.

2001

- Nothing ventured nothing pained.
- *You are a role model.
- *You are known for your tough workouts.
- *I want to shake your hand. You put on a show.
- Prepare beyond preparation.

2002

- *You are a strong grandfather. (5 year old girl)
- *You must have the wrong health card for a 73 year old. (nurse)
- *I can hit your vein from across the room. (nurse)
- *Looked super smooth.

2003

- *You run like you have wings. [Therefore, my flying foot company logo is appropriate.]
- *Lots of muscle. (Fellow YMCA member).
- "Rejoice oh young man in thy youth." (Ecclesiastes).
  I say rejoice oh old man in thy remaining years.
- "What we do in life echoes an eternity." (*Gladiator*)

2004

- *You are abnormal.
- *You make it look easy.
- "If you lose the race don't lose the lesson." (Barry Shepley)
- *The two most courageous performances I have ever seen. (A younger competitor comments on my W.R. mile and 400m race at Boston Indoor on March 27)
- When injured—turn a negative into a positive. It's time to develop other things.

OVERCOMING PRERACE JITTERS

In July 1989, at the World Championships in Eugene, Oregon, I had a bad case of pre-competitive anxiety during the day of my final 800-meter race. That night in the famous Hayward Stadium, I was to race against the great and likeable Derek Turnbull of New Zealand. I had broken the 60 to 64 age category world record in 2 min. 12.8 sec. a couple of months before, but he lowered it by about 0.2 seconds a few weeks later. He normally wins 5 or 6 gold medals at these championships. This caused me considerable anxiety since this was only my second world championship since Melbourne, Australia. I did not know how to cope with this excruciating mental stress in the long hours before the race. Fortunately, during the warm up my nerves settled. After wasting considerable energy in overtaking the too-fast American, subsequent good friend and truly an iron man, Chuck Sochor, I took the lead at about 350 meters. With about 230 meters to go, the announcer stated Turnbull was in fifth place. This gave me false confidence for he had already run a 5K race earlier in the day having stopped en route to pick up his false teeth and so finished second in near record time. He was human after all. I was feeling energetic and perhaps too confident in the home stretch. At about 60 meters to go, he surprisingly passed me with false teeth intact (the shock effect cost me nearly half a second) and I lost by about 2 meters. I believe the de-energizing jitters (and poor strategy) may have cost me the race or at least slowed me down for the pace was 2 seconds slower than the world record under good conditions.

Now I realize there are effective mental techniques to overcome prerace jitters as explained below. But also, there is nothing like experience in similar races to the above, and hard, consistent training over a long period to build confidence and reduce and control the stress.

Is Nervousness Bad?

"Definitely not" (Garfield[22])! It is normal to feel some nervousness and excitement; this type of readiness is called positive arousal. This causes the adrenaline to be released and works for the athlete rather than against him.

In the World Championships in Buffalo in July 1995, prior to the 800-meter final, age category 65 to 69, on an extremely windy day, I experienced fear of the wind even though I had the world record. The flags were straight out on this dull, dismal day. During my warm up, I imagined a slow painful race fighting this wind as I planned to lead all the way. This brought forth considerably more adrenaline than usual and also sickly nerves. But I had not expected the effect of the huge cheering crowd, and I was at a definite peak. With the wind at my back, I picked it up at 300 meters to go, imagining myself as a big sail and finished in 2 min. 14.33sec.–lowering my world record by nearly 1 second. This was equivalent to a 1 min. 41 sec. 800-meters in the open category based on my dear friend the age-graded tables. Based on this experience and others, I know nervousness is to the athlete's advantage. *"When nervous and confident of your ability this is a sign of readiness" (Garfield[22]).*

What to Do When Nervous and Doubting Your Ability

1. Think of the races when you felt ready and you raced well. Conjure up the same feelings.
2. When there is self-doubt or negative thoughts, focus on things within your control[22]. Put thoughts of the competitors and the outcome out of your mind. *Think of your strategy and race plan*, i.e., what you are going to do. Rehearse it in your mind. Focus on what you can do and should do. Don't think on what you can't do, or what the competitors can do.
3. Use "performance cues" to recall past performances where you raced well. One technique from private sessions with Mark Cummings[26] M.D., sports psychologist, is to think of your best four past races, e.g., in my case **B**uffalo, **E**ugene, **R**aleigh ,N.C., and **Y**ork, University Toronto. This is **BERY** for short. With practice, each first letter conjures up the ideal performance of that race. Now take some deep breaths and relax. Now thinking of the Buffalo race, press thumb and 1st finger together. While thinking of Eugene race, press thumb and 2nd finger together. While thinking of Raleigh race, press thumb and 3rd finger together. While thinking of York race press thumb and 4th finger together. The contacts of the fingers and the key words are the performance cues. This technique has been very useful just before a race and it also gets my mind away from the jitters. See further details on "Performance Cues" in a section under "Focus."

4. Playing of a favorite tune, or inspirational music can have the effect of "psyching up." On the other hand, soothing music can reduce tension.
5. Try to get your mind off the race. Read an interesting book or go to a movie or watch TV. Too much rest and lying around can be detrimental and can lead to fretting and lethargy.
6. Pre-event massage. For an uptight athlete, a soothing relaxing massage (not deep) can be beneficial.
7. Take long, deep, slow breaths emphasizing the exhale. Imagine yourself as a *"thermometer"* where 100% is maximum stress and 0% is no stress[26]. Speaking the word "relax" on the exhale will ensure the proper relaxation. For example, if you think you are at 80% stress and too tense, bring yourself down slowly to zero stress as follows. Repeat 80, 75, 70 etc., slowly to yourself between deep breaths and concentrating on relaxation, and thinking stress is reducing in proportion to the reducing numbers. Eventually bring yourself down to zero stress. Now in this relaxed state, think of your race plan, and/or your past best races (see 3 above). In the event that you feel too relaxed, bring yourself back to a reasonable state of excitement, say 50% stress, for one should not be too relaxed before the race. Based on previous performances, you should know the level of prerace arousal that results in your best performance. Ideally you bring yourself under control to an optimum level of excitement and enthusiasm to go with relaxed loose muscles. (This "thermometer" technique I have found very useful also during the rest period between intense intervals.)
8. Remember, only you can bring pressure and stress on yourself. When you realize this, you can start controlling it.
9. Banish a fear. Isolate yourself in a quiet, peaceful, calm place, where there is no one to disturb you. Imagine you are in a calm peaceful situation. It is useful to recall some peaceful scene, e.g., a calm lake at the cottage or even a calm swimming pool. Smell, taste, feel the visualization. Sit comfortably, relax, and close your eyes. Repeat to yourself a confident statement over and over, which will counteract the fear or self-doubt, e.g., *"I run efficiently; I am confident; and calm; I have trained well; I am ready to do my best."*
10. To boost confidence, read over your training log the night before and the morning of the race. This reminds you of all your hard work and preparedness.
11. Make a list of reasons why you are ready for this race. Normally, if well prepared, it is easy to come up with a list of ten reasons. I have used this before important races to build confidence.
12. Your fears of a competitor are often unfounded. For example, you may fear a competitor who has registered faster times in previous races. But there are several possible factors that could alter the situation:

- He may have been injured or have an injury.
- His training facilities and coaching are not currently as good as yours.
- He started his training only recently, whereas you have a good base and have been training hard for many more months than him. The heats and prelims will therefore be too much for him.
- He has not been able to enter enough prior races for proper preparation.
- Mentally, he could be disturbed with a family problem.
- He may even get injured in the race.

13. *But the most effective technique of all is to constantly remind yourself you are here to* ***perform*** *at your very best, to* ***compete against yourself*** *rather than against your competitors. This can rid you of a lot of tension and pressure. Just go for your current PB (personal best).*

HOW TO STAY MOTIVATED

In your athletic career, you may sometimes lose your enthusiasm for your sport. The following will assist you to stay motivated:

Make workouts fun and purposeful:

- Have a purpose for each workout.
- Try new scenic routes if you are a runner.
- Make each workout a body, mind, soul experience.

Keep a detailed training log:

- Record your daily workouts: it's a kind of ego boost.
- Record your feelings and the beauty all around you.
- Record training tips, quotes, and compliments.

Take a rest when required to recharge:

- Take one or two days rest each week.
- Take additional time off when in a slump.
- Take it easier every third week.
- Take about 10 days off from running after the outdoor season, indoor season, or after a big race.

Change your routine:

- Do cross training on lethargic days.
- Do weight training for variety.
- If you're really stale, have a beer or two with your pals.

Success or improvement is the biggest motivator:

- Establish and meet small goals along the way to the big goal.

Establish regular habits:

- When training is hit and miss, it is easy to skip one or two days without a guilty conscience. But with regular habits established, it is not easy to slack off. Make your good healthy habits and then your habits make you. Success is all about good habits.

Gain inspiration from your age-graded performance:

Using the age-graded tables (developed by WAVA and available from U.S. National Masters News) compare your performance percentage with the approximate world record for your age.

- Compare it to your younger and older competitors.
- Compare your age-graded performance to previous years.

In your five-year age group, you may have finished second, third or fourth, but being older, you could have a higher age-graded percentage; in that case, you are actually the true winner. Also although you are older and a bit slower now, you can find inspiration in the fact that your age-graded percentage has actually improved.

At the World Masters Championships in Puerto Rico in July 2003, I was 74 and at the top on my age group, 75-79, but in my three races 800m, 400m and 300m hurdles I had age graded percentages of 102.3, 98.78, and 99.98 respectively. Although I came second in the 800 and 400, I gained inspiration for the future with my overall average of over 100 percent. You also can find similar motivation by keeping track of your age graded percentages compared to your rivals and your past performances.

FOCUS

Introduction

Mental training can help athletes to focus under high stress and under internal and external distractions. Thus he or she is able to perform to potential. The athlete should have, in addition to a **race plan**, a **focus plan** and a **refocus plan** in case focus breaks down. "The objective of concentration is to focus on what is important while minimizing distractions" (Lynch and Scott[1]).

Examples of Lack of Focus

Track Race

I never knew the extreme importance of focus in a race until I lost it on March 7, 1996 at the Ontario Masters Indoor Championships at York University. In this particular race, I was attempting to lower my 1500-meters indoor world record for the 65–69 age group set the year before in Columbia, Missouri. I was well prepared and confident I could get below the record of 4 min. 47.1 sec. But it all came apart with about 400 meters to go. At this point, I was slightly behind my target but felt I could finish strong and the crowd was very supportive as usual. About this time, I suspected they had put up the wrong lap card for me; then immediately after, my coach at the side of the track gave me a weird signal which confused me; I thought I heard him say, amidst all the cheering, "Four, two, one." This confusion had never happened between us before. I started thinking of these two events instead of concentrating on the lap times. When I came to the point 300 meters from the finish, I had further doubts whether this was 300 meters or 500 meters from the finish. My focus was lost, race plan was forgotten and I finished tired. Without seeing the time, I knew I had missed my target (actually by 2 seconds). This brings up the importance that the ***coach and athlete should have a clear understanding of any signals during a race*, or keep out of the picture entirely. *Confusion causes loss of focus.***

High Diver

Consider the example of a male high diver in a competition who makes two back-to-back dives with drastically different results due to lack of focus in the second dive. He knew both dives well. Before the first dive, he was mentally calm, in control, determined, physically activated and the dive felt like time was slowed down. During this excellent dive, he wasn't conscious of anything at the side of the pool, and just focused on thoughts of his routine. He was on *autopilot*.

Before the second dive, his confidence was shaken by comments from competitors that the wind was now a concern and maybe even dangerous. Now he was mentally uptight due to negative thoughts, a lack of confidence and determination, and with lower physical activation. With these distracting thoughts, he used less mental imagery before the dive. Now he was conscious of the people at the side of the pool, conscious of how he would do in the wind instead of rehearsing his routine in his mind. Result: a badly rushed dive.

Tennis Tournament

Another example of incorrect focus that was far from the ideal state of mind was a tennis tournament I witnessed a few years ago. At first, the pair were evenly matched and both were fine skilled athletes. After one set each, in the third and deciding set, one player grew increasingly frustrated at missing some crucial shots that he normally would make. This resulted in throwing of his racket. It was obvious his thoughts were negative; he was playing too much in his head, causing a draining of energy and lack of focus. Getting down on himself by dwelling about past mistakes was defeating him. If only he had known of these mental techniques. I found this very frustrating to watch, particularly since it was my son.

These examples indicate that ***your mental frame of mind before and during a race is a critical factor in your success or failure in the race.*** Fortunately, there are mental techniques to maintain focus or to refocus as described below.

Types of Focus

Focus can be internal (in the head, e.g., fear) or external (outside the body e.g., crowds) and it can be narrow or broad giving four possibilities[10,1,28]:

- **Broad Internal** (conscious analyzing and planning over a wide range)
- **Narrow Internal** (conscious 'rehearsing': e.g., just before body execution, or rehearsing in gymnastics, dancing, diving, quarterback plays, etc.)
- **Broad External** (overall evaluation of the competitive environment: e.g., assess the entire playing field)
- **Narrow External** (execution of performance: e.g., a quarterback executes the play, or a batter or tennis player watches the ball)

Performing in the ideal zone occurs when an athlete's focus of attention is almost exclusively external (Nideffer[10]). This is *narrow external*, i.e., focused on the performance with external distractions blocked out. A game or race requires predominately *narrow external* focus (Weinburg[28]). Performance is so *automatic* there is very little need to analyze internally. Thus there are fewer shifts from an internal to an external focus. Now time seems slowed down—an advantage in some sports, such as baseball and tennis, since there seems more time to meet the ball. The overall result is a feeling of complete control.

When performance is too *narrow internal* there is too much thinking and analysis causing "paralysis by analysis." During practice is the time to use *narrow internal* focus to correct errors[28].

Choking occurs when attention becomes focused internally; the athlete is unable to shift to external focus[10]. For example, the athlete dwells on a mistake executed moments before and frets about it. Thoughts are negative, fearful, frustrated, etc., or there may be an attempt to search out reasons for poor performance ("paralysis by analysis"). Now time feels speeded up and the athlete feels pressured; the result is increased muscle tension, increased breathing rate and racing heart rate. ***The key to playing in the zone is to find ways of staying out of your head,*** and blocking out external distractions. Thoughts should not be on the portion of the course completed or any past errors. Dwelling on a mistake in a game or race is disastrous. Focus must be on what is coming up. This is accomplished with performance cues, i.e., keywords or phrases to refocus attention.

Focus During Training

In a long training run, or during intense intervals that has become stressful or boring, focus on your running form. Think particularly of proper use of the feet landing correctly and lightly, staying relaxed, and proper use of the hands and arms. Or concentrate on some particular form problem that you are trying to correct. Alternatively, during a long run, I sometimes count left strides on all fingers, ten strides for each digit, that's 100 left strides, 200 total strides or about 250 meters. Some psychologists believe to make the miles seem shorter and arrive invigorated, think less on your body and more about your life (relationships, natural surroundings, job and career, finances, etc.). Of course, the latter would not work in a race or hard interval session where concentration on the effort is required. On a long run on a treadmill or indoor track, I sometimes visualize running along a favorite scenic path in the woods.

The important point is to practice focus in training. If unable to focus in training, you will not focus in a race. Have fun in training but focus.

Before the Race Focus

Days or weeks before the race. Your mental imagery of the race should be one where you remain in focus; this imagery practiced many times for days or weeks before the race, should have conditioned and prepared you to remain more focused. Mental imagery, by making the athlete familiar with the race situation and surroundings, gets rid of a lot of the nerves, allowing the focus to be narrow external rather than negative internal. Many world class tennis players rehearse mentally before the game executing every possible shot successfully[28]. Thus the player feels he/she has already been there and is more confident and ready.

Day of the race. The experienced athlete focuses on his own efforts, and is not distracted by other athletes. His nerves are in control since he has practiced in training with the same mental focus and determination as in competition.

Before the competition, find your own quiet private space, i.e., a time to psychologically prepare. This should be a consistent procedure before all competitions. This is a time to relax completely as possible and put the problems and distractions out of mind until the race is over. Focus is improved when the athlete has high energy and is calm and relaxed; visualize to energize and relax yourself. Now concentrate on your race strategy. Lynch and Scott[1] recommend a visualization procedure, when completely relaxed, whereby attention is successively narrowed in six steps from the whole wide world of sports, to track and field, to your sport, to you, to a part of your body, down to one specific aspect of your performance.

Alex Baumann believes mental imagery got him the world record and Olympic medals (Orlick[13]). Fifteen minutes before the race, he visualized the race and particularly himself; he did not worry about the competition, he imagined every lap and the required split times and how he felt. I noticed the amazing world record holder sprinter and hurdler, Jack Greenwood, in his early 60s doing his mental imagery in Turku, Finland at these World Masters Championships, as he sat beside me.

Focus During the Race

To maintain focus during the race:

- Count strokes, strides, telephone poles or laps.
- In a long distance race, pick out a runner and slowly reel him or her in, then reel in another and another.
- Focus on each mile at a time in a long distance race.
- In a middle distance race, focus on the 3/4 distance from the start; this mentally shortens the distance; the faster finish with 1/4 distance to go uses different muscles.
- Focus on the object or person in front of you[6].
- In a short race focus on the finish line[6].
- Focus on the present; don't let your mind or eyes wander.

The important point is not to let your eyes or ears wander. Also thinking of fatigue, negative thoughts, the past or future will cause you to lose focus and rhythm.

Setting Aside Problems

It is possible that prior to the competition, there is a problem on your mind. Unless you rid yourself of this prior to competition, your performance will suffer since it is an internal distraction. Also thinking on external distractions, past errors, hassles and things beyond your control are de-energizing. Have a method to set the problem aside for now. When the problem springs to mind, say **"stop"** and immediately turn to positive, relaxed thoughts. Take a deep breath and as you slowly exhale say to yourself, *"Relax–it's not worth upsetting myself about,"* or say *"Park it!"* or *"Tree it!"*, i.e., put it in a vacant tree for now (Orlick[6]). Why not visualize putting it in a garbage can and putting a lid on it, or imagine it being flushed down the toilet for now. Stamp it out like a cockroach; stamp your foot and it disappears. One technique is to imagine the problem written on a piece of paper; then the paper is crumpled up and set afire.

Former President Bill Clinton put his distracting personal legal battles in a "small box" (which I suspect subsequently grew into a large box the size of a house). You have to have your own consistent method. **Letting the subconscious solve it for you** is one method of getting rid of a problem days before the competition. Examine all the pros and cons of the problem in detail–then set it aside for a day or so. Your subconscious will work on it in the meantime. In a lot of cases, days later, and often in the morning on awakening, you will know what to do (Murphy[4]).

The Wise Man in the Cave. This is a technique I learned years ago; the reference is lost. You have a big problem that is troubling you and you have all the necessary facts to come to a solution but still there is no resolution. After getting into a relaxed state, and with closed eyes, imagine yourself walking down a path leading to a cave. You enter into the dark cave. At the end of the cave is a wise person of your choice, a highly respected wise friend or relative or even a famous person, alive or deceased. You ask this person the solution to your problem. The solution will come from this person.

Performance Cues

Performance cues are affirmations to be called upon during performance. Performance cues or triggers are potent reminders to get you to change muscle tension and focus on concentration or to create the desired physical or psychological feelings before or during performance. These key words help you to focus on the proper image and to remind you of planned strategy. They should be stated forcefully to be effective, particularly under fatigue. "Repetition of the cue words breaks the train of distracting thoughts or mind wandering" (Dr. Herbert Benson, author of the "Relaxation Response," qtd. in Henderson[21]). These trigger words elicit the desired response and help to gain control over concentration and tension[10]. Since brevity is important during competition, one or two key words are usually used to remind the athlete of one of the following (Weinburg[28]):

- To break bad habits (e.g., "relax face")
- To remind yourself of good form (e.g., "lower arms")
- To initiate action (e.g., "blast off")
- To sustain effort (e.g., "hang in")
- To eliminate negative thoughts (e.g., "stop")
- To relax (e.g., "smooth and easy")

Sam Snead used the word "oily" to assist in a fluid swing[10]. A 400-meter runner could use the word "lift" (rapid high knees) with 100 meters to go. In a 1500-meter indoor race a convenient cue word would be *"lap time"*; this shifts attention to whether pace is too fast or slow. In a strong wind, I have used the cue word *"big sail"* effectively when running with the wind. This focusing or refocusing when concentration breaks down, requires practice, particularly during training and low-key competitions. Preplanned checkpoints and focus are designed to help the athlete perform efficiently and stay on the race plan. In the marathon, triathlon, or rowing races, it is preferable to break the race down into critical parts and to have cue words and/or target times for each part (Orlick[6]); for example:

- At the start
- Middle
- Later
- Nearing the finish

I used this successfully in March 1994 in an attempt at Jim Sutton's world indoor record in the 1500 meters for age group 60 to 64 just a week before going into the older age group. I was able to keep my focus by concentrating on the lap times in comparison to my memorized target lap times. External distractions were blocked out. There were no external or internal distractions, and I broke the record as planned in spite of a crowded track and lapping others, but only by 0.1 seconds.

REFOCUS

The following are four refocusing techniques:

1. Use Cue Words to Refocus

See performance cues above. Use your favorite cue word, such as "stop" or "shift focus," to refocus quickly from negative to positive thoughts, or to regain concentration, relaxation or better form. Repeat "shift focus" several times to shift away from the distracting or negative thought; then focus on your target or immediate goal (Orlick[13]).

2. "Internal Distraction – Learn to Focus Externally"

Dr. Lynch and Dr. Scott[1] explain: When there is loss of control and negative thoughts arise, begin to focus externally to take your mind away from the internal distraction. *Before the race*, if this happens, relax while visualizing some favorite quiet room or calm setting. Then open your eyes and focus on a small simple object; examine it in great detail. "Imagine yourself so small you can hide behind this object." *During a race*, focus externally and intently on some part of the closest runner's body.

3. "External Distraction – Focus Internally"

Dr. Lynch[7] explains: When distracted by weather conditions, crowd noise, etc. *before the race*, go into your quiet place and "visualize your event as the necessary components of a good personal performance." *While competing*, if externally distracted, focus on breathing and form. See also Lynch and Scott[1] for similar discussion.

4. Have a Pre-planned Refocusing Procedure

During the competition, to save precious time, you must have a pre-planned refocusing procedure. Then after refocusing, it should be clear what is the next step (T. Orlick[6]).

Long Term Focus

"For those who set high goals for themselves, and then pursue them with all their energy, life offers possibilities beyond our wildest expectations" (John R. Noe[2]).

MENTAL TOUGHNESS

Before and during competition, positive emotions from mental toughness result in increased energy, improved performance and consistency. The ideal mental toughness would involve all the desirable characteristics of the ideal performance state.

What is mental toughness?

Mental toughness in a stressful situation means:
- Thinking positively, calmly and clearly
- Remaining focused
- Being in complete control of emotions
- Exhibiting many of the other internal ideal state of mind characteristics

Some real examples of mental toughness are:

- A club runner running three distance races in one day and running them hard even though there is no strong competition.
- An aspiring Olympian getting up at 5 a.m. six days a week for years to train intensely in a cold pool.
- Holding down a full-time teaching job, coaching a large contingent of teenagers three times per week, and running 70 miles per week outdoors all bitter winter, running at 5:30 in the morning and again at night after work on country roads (Geordie Farrell, female coach of Saugeen Track Club, Port Elgin, Ontario).
- Derek Turnbull, normally winning five or six gold medals often in world record times, in World Masters Championships in events from 800 meters to the marathon (some events with heats). This is "guts" and oblivion to injury.
- Elvis Stojko, the Canadian skating phenomenon, performing at the 1998 Winter Olympics in Japan with the flu and a painful torn groin muscle, but winning the silver medal.

- One of the greatest examples of mental toughness was Silken Laumann, Canadian world champion sculls rower, who suffered terrible injuries to her leg in a collision of two racing sculls on a busy river in Germany. In spite of broken bones and massive muscle damage, ten short weeks later, she raced in pain in the Barcelona Olympics in 1992 and won a bronze medal. An amazing feat of determination! Silken was a close runner-up to Nancy Greene, world champion skier, for the Canadian female athlete of the century.
- Similarly Reed Oldershaw, world class Canadian athlete in kayaking, in 1978 placed first in the Canadian Trials only two weeks after being released from the hospital, following three operations and a month of rehab to repair a broken hip and femur. He raced with a 2-foot pin in his leg.
- Mental toughness is John Akii Bua of Uganda, world record holder in the 400-meter hurdles in the Munich Olympic Games—running, training for months while wearing a 25-pound vest: running 4 x 1500 metes over hurdles, or twice a day 6 x 600 meters up very steep hills (Moore[11]).

When are you mentally fit?

1. When you use the mental techniques of relaxation, meditation visualization, and self-assertive statements to:
   - Mentally rehearse your race.
   - Stay calm before your race.
   - Concentrate on your race plan rather than the competitors
   - Control the level of arousal prior to a race.
   - Remain totally focused in a race.
   - Mentally see yourself as a smooth, efficient and confident runner.
   - Quickly switch from negative to positive thoughts to achieve positive emotions.

2. For a mentally fit athlete, testing at San Jose State University by psychologists, reported by Joe Henderson[21], indicated 12 important traits, including:
   - Aggressiveness
   - Determination
   - Self-confidence
   - Emotional control

3. You are mentally tough when you make a detailed daily plan (things to do) to achieve success, and stick to your plan. These can be a table of things extra to your training, to give "a winning edge" or a table of things to do to hasten healing of your injury. Check off these items every day. Once the list is made, you are committed, and mentally you know you are doing your utmost.

What Are Some of the Techniques to Build Mental Toughness?

Some of the techniques for mental toughening are described below.

1. To build mental toughness, one has simply to exercise the mind. This is similar to building physical toughness where the muscles must be exercised. Therefore, on a regular basis, engage in challenging mind games and activities, such as chess, bridge, memorize poetry, study philosophy, take a course (computer, language, and memory), etc.
2. Confidence and mental toughness come from consistent discipline in training, racing and lifestyle, such as:
   - Physical toughening: Training mostly every day for years, sometimes in spite of bad conditions (fatigue and adverse weather)
   - A healthy lifestyle of discipline, sacrifice and self-denial
   - Following the coaches instructions in training
   - Many race or game experiences
   - Successfully overcoming many stressful experiences at work, home, and socially
3. Mental toughness is harnessing your negative thoughts, reigning in your negative imagination, and outwardly displaying control and discipline under pressure.
4. Improving your acquired mental skills in visualizing, self-assertive statements, relaxation, meditation and breath control will improve your mental strength. Also have the habit of concentration, the habit of positive attitude, the habit of non-dramatization under stress, and the habit of applying mental techniques. These disciplined, consistent day-to-day mental habits will lead to mental toughness in athletics.
5. Letting go of wrong or negative attitudes (conditioned points of view, bad judgements or outlooks, and unreasonable expectations) will greatly assist in freeing you of tension from negative feelings. To change an attitude, "think-as-if," i.e., think as if you had the desired attitude already. With repetition, your new attitude becomes a habit. This is similar to "acting-as-if" described below under Emotional Control. Positive attitudes make an athlete mentally tough but negative attitudes create stress and de-energize. Get in the habit of using positive thoughts like "I will..." or "I can..."
6. Do the workout you hate to do, the one that hurts; this builds mental toughness. This is the advice given to me from Peter Maher world class marathon runner. "If you are to become a high achiever, go ahead and do what you fear." (J.R. Noe[2]).
7. Realize that you can do more than you think you can. This is positive thinking. The mind is the weak link. This is the advice given to me and other Red Devil track athletes in the early 1950s by our coach Lloyd Percival, founder of the Fitness Institute in Toronto.

8. When you are doing those tough anaerobic repeats, intense workouts or long arduous runs, be aware that these are, to a large extent, for developing mental toughness and tolerance to pain and fatigue. When fatigue comes, think about it as a "good training partner helping you to grow and its necessity on the road to improved performance" (Dr. Jerry Lynch and Dr. Warren Scott[1]). Joe Henderson in "Running your Best Race" states, "Realize that to achieve success competitively, you must experience speeds and distances that are uncomfortable." Percy Cerutty is quoted in "The Herb Elliot Story" as preaching to world champion Herb Elliot: "Walk towards suffering. Love suffering. Embrace it." ***When you know the purpose and the ultimate rewards, the pain or discomfort becomes more tolerable and the workout more beneficial.***

EMOTIONAL CONTROL

If you don't control your negative emotions (e.g., fear, anger, anxiety, worry, self-doubt, discouragement, etc.), they will control your actions. "Fear, sorrow and anger are the three primary negative emotions resulting in psychophysical tension and blocking of motivation" (Dan Millman[5]).

The mind, emotions and body are intimately connected. "Our thoughts produce chemical and physical changes in our bodies" (Bonnar[20]). Also, ***"Every change in the physiological state produces an appropriate change in the mental-emotional state, conscious or unconscious, and conversely"*** (Green, Green and Walters, 1969, qtd. in *Psychology in Sports* by Richard M. Suinn; see also Elmer and Alyce Green in *Beyond Biofeedback*, 1977). This is a very important concept.

All emotions are subconscious or unconscious, and involuntary reactions to our thoughts. Therefore, our emotions appear not easy to control, but there are some effective methods described below.

What Are Some of the Techniques to Achieve Emotional Control?

- The emotional needs are fulfilled and controlled by acquired mental skills such as relaxation, meditation, visualization and affirmations. For example, "Relaxing under pressure, with diaphragmatic breathing, or other relaxation techniques, controls the emotions resulting in optimal performance in sport" (Dr. Charles Garfield[22]). With these skills, the primitive automatic feature of the emotions is thus made less automatic and more controlled.
- "It is nearly impossible to feel anger, fear, anxiety and other negative emotions while the muscles of the body are relaxed" (Maltz[30]). With relaxed muscles, there can be a return to a positive mental state.

- "Maximum emotional toughness requires holding tough beliefs and having the habit of thinking tough" (Loehr[9]). This results in the habit of acting tough since every change in the mental state produces a change in the physical state.
- Good emotional habits (such as confidence, energeticalness, determination, and courage) come from good thought habits. Thoughts control the emotions and emotions cause the body to react or over-react. Emotional toughness is control of negative thoughts since negative thoughts produce negative emotions. Fortunately, we have absolute control over our thoughts. So we must develop positive thought control.
- Practice self-control in your daily life experiences involving stressful situations. Stay cool. Don't be a "hot head." Act in self-control. Learn to shift quickly from negative to positive thinking to avoid over reacting. If you overreact in daily life experiences and during training you will also before and during competition. Emotional toughness and control (the response to stress) is achieved by acts of determination or self-control. You *will* yourself to remain in control of your emotional response. Tell yourself, *"I am determined not to overreact."*
- "As-if" physical acting can cause positive changes in the mental state. Using this simple method, you can trick yourself into feeling a particular positive characteristic, such as confidence. It really works! See also Loehr[9] and Lynch and Scott[1]. By looking and acting happy, courageous, energetic, positive, confident, or relaxed, you will generate one of these feelings. For example, if you lack confidence before a competition, act confidently and you will start to feel and think confidently. Confidence results in positive emotions. "With confidence in your abilities, you are more calm, relaxed and positive under stress resulting in controlled emotions" (Dr. Robert Weinberg[28]).
- Help yourself on the road to growth by creating the Warrior Athlete or Ideal Athlete[5]. Create this model in your imagination. This is another form of acting "as if." Now you have an inspirational model. In any situation, react in the same way as the Ideal Athlete. Think, react and even walk proudly and confidently as your champion model. With practice, you become the Ideal Athlete who has also mastered the Ideal Performance State.
- Maxwell Maltz[30] describes the following: Picture in your mind your desirable end result–dwell upon it constantly, "this will make the possibility more real and the appropriate good emotions will automatically be generated. ***If we picture ourselves performing in a certain manner, it is nearly the same as the actual performance."***
- Non-dramatization of emotional situations[5]: When a stressful situation arises, it is easy "to tie yourself up in knots" and overreact. For example, be patient in your anger; this could save days or weeks of regret or sorrow. Also, you may feel fear, but you don't have to act afraid. Substitute the highly reactive emotional habit with

the non-dramatization habit. Using this technique in minor stressful situations conditions you for the more rare serious stress situations. Non-dramatization means no visible sign of weakness or negative emotion in response; instead, display alertness, calmness, energy, confidence under stress. ***Non-dramatization is self-control.***

- "There is a direct link between muscle states, and mental and emotional states" (John Jerome[16]). Also, "There is a direct link between attitude and muscle. Your emotions affect every cell in your body" (Charles Garfield[22]). The living proof of the above is the poor posture of a person with poor attitude. Therefore, to improve emotions, simply improve posture, walk confidently, relaxed and energetically, and carry yourself like a champion.

Summary of Mental Toughness

The best mental toughener comes from the day to day, week after week, year after year of ***physical toughening from consistent workouts and competitive races.*** Also, mental toughness should be practiced in our daily living experiences. ***Practice the various mental techniques*** to handle stressful situations and to achieve the Ideal Performance State. All these build confidence and the ability to be controlled under stress. In conjunction with non-dramatization of stressful situations, acting "as if," and reacting like the Ideal Athlete, will free you from emotional stress and improve your performance.

THE POWER OF BELIEF, AUTOSUGGESTION AND THE SUBCONSCIOUS

The following excerpts and quotes demonstrate the power of belief, autosuggestion and the subconscious:

- "Practice creative anticipation, the power of positive expectation. We tend to become as we see ourselves" (Vincent Peale[24]).
- Think with deep feeling and desire and enthusiasm of your dream. Keep dwelling upon it. Picture your dream as a possibility, constantly, optimistically. "The appropriate successful emotions will be generated automatically and will make the possibility more real." (Maxwell Maltz[30])
- Terry Orlick[13] stated: Think of your ultimate goal with great feeling and desire. "You must believe, with every fiber of your being, that you can achieve it, and must achieve it, but will achieve it." By self-hypnosis and autosuggestion (e.g., affirmations) absolute belief is achieved. "Once the belief becomes a permanent part of your subconscious thought process, you will automatically behave in accordance with this belief."

- "Whatever your conscious mind assumes and believes to be true, your subconscious mind accepts and brings to pass" (Dr. Joseph Murphy[4]).
- "Always think of what you have to do as easy and it will become so" (Maxwell Maltz[30]).

There are two essential ingredients that in conjunction with all the above will lead to success—hard work and experience. With hard consistent training and race or game experience, the faster race time or the dream is more real, more possible. You now believe it will be even easier and the subconscious has more chance to automatically work its magic.

Final Word

Here's hoping you will have many peak inner experiences ("in the zone" or "sweet spots") in your athletic and non-athletic endeavors. With practice and application of the above principles they will come increasingly more frequent.

REFERENCES

1. Lynch, J., and Scott, W., *Running Within,* Human Kinetics, Champaign, IL, 1999.
2. Noe, J, R., *Peak Performance Principles For High Achievers,* Berkley Books, New York, NY, 1984.
3. Porter K., and Foster J., *The Mental Athlete,* Ballantine Books, New York, NY, 1987.
4. Murphy, J., *The Power of Your Subconscious Mind*, Prentice Hall, Englewood Cliffs, NJ, 1988.
5. Millman, D., *The Warrior Athlete,* Stillpoint Publishing, Walpole, New Hampshire, 1979.
6. Orlick, T., *Psyching For Sport,* Leisure Press/Human Kinetics Champaign, IL, 1986.
7. Lynch, J., *The Total Runner,* Prentice Hall, Englewood Cliffs, NJ, 1987.
8. Elliot, H., *The Mind of a Runner,* American Runner, Spring 1996.
9. Loehr, J. E., *Toughness Training For Life,* A Dutton Book, Penguin Books, New York, NY, 1993.
10. Nideffer, R.M., *Psyched To Win,* Leisure Press, Champaign, IL, 1992.
11. Moore, K., *Best Efforts,* Cedarwinds Publishing Co., Tallahassee, FL, 1982.
12. Pataki, L., and Holden, L., *Winning Secrets,* Published in the USA, 1989.
13. Orlick, T., *In Pursuit Of Excellence,* Leisure Press, Champaign, IL, 1980.
14. Vealey, R. S., Inner Coaching Through Mental Imagery, *Track Technique,* p 3672, 115, Spring 1991.
16. Jerome, J., *The Sweet Spot In Time,* A Touchstone Book, Simon and Schuster Inc., 1989.
19. Singh, L.P.,and Sirisena, *Zen Buddhism,* Envoy Press, New York, NY, 1988.
20. Bonnar, B., Psychology, The Competitive Edge, p18, *Triaction,* June, 1991.
21. Henderson, J., *Think Fast,* A Plume Book, Published by Penguin Group, New York, NY, 1991.
22. Garfield, C. A., *Peak Performance,* Warner Books Edition, Los Angeles, CA, 1984.
23. Loehr, J.E., *Mental Toughness Training For Sports,* Penguin Books, Toronto, Canada, and Stephen Greene Press, Lexington, Mass., 1986.
24. Peale, N. V., *You Can If You Think You Can,* Prentice Hall Inc., Englewood Cliffs, NJ, 1974.
25. Ungerleider, S., Beyond Strength: Psychological Profiles Of Olympic Athletes, *Track Technique*, p3704, 116, Summer, 1991.
26. Cummings, M., *Private Sports Psychology Course,* April, 1989.
27. Hardy, C., and Crace, K., Dealing With Precompetitive Anxiety, *Track Technique,* p3513, 110, Winter 1990.
28. Weinburg, S., *The Mental Advantage, Developing Your Psychological Skills in Tennis,* Leisure Press, Champaign, IL, 1988.
29. Gawain, Shakti, *Creative Visualization,* New World Library, San Rafael, CA, 1995.
30. Maltz, M., *Psycho-Cybernetics,* Prentice Hall Inc., Englewood Cliffs, NJ, 1969.
31. Loehr, J.E., *The Ideal Performance State, Science Periodical on Research and Technology in Sport.* Canada: Government of Canada, BU-1, January 1983.

CHAPTER 3

He was an artist of the track
Every stride a beautiful picture –
Artistry in motion.

RUNNING FORM

Emil Zatopek was not one of the above—he did phenomenally well in spite of his thrashing arms and looking like he was dying or "stabbed in the heart." Perhaps he wasn't aware that faults can be corrected by work on form with or without the supervision of a knowledgeable coach. As form improves, injuries are less likely, running economy (efficiency) and running times will improve and running and training becomes more enjoyable. Running economy can also compensate for VO_2max (see "Running Economy" in Chapter 7).

In my high school and university days, my favorite workout, done a couple of times a week, was to run 100 yards fast at 400 yards pace, walk back, and repeat about 10 or 15 times, while concentrating on good form and relaxation. This was recommended by Lloyd Percival whom I trained with during my university days between 1948 and 1953; he was founder of The Fitness Institute in Ontario and one of Canada's best track and field coaches at the time. I enjoyed these form workouts since I felt I was running effortlessly. After a 33-year layoff, it all came back to me in 1986—just like riding a bicycle!

RUNNING SEQUENCE

One complete running cycle from footstrike to the next footstrike of the same foot (say the right foot) is described below in the following sequence: support phase, driving phase, and forward recovery phase:

- **Footstrike** (first contact with the ground in front of the body)
- **Support phase** (the knee straightens while moving backward)
- **Driving phase** (this phase begins when the support leg moves behind the body weight)
- **Toe-off** (push-off behind the body from fully extended leg)
- **Forward recovery** (the phase between toe-off and footstrike: the knee bends while moving forward, the heel approaches buttock, the knee straightens but never locks out, and the foot descends)
- **Footstrike** (completes the cycle with foot starting to move backward)

In the above cycle, the support and driving phase is about 40% and the forward recovery is about 60%.

Footstrike

At footstrike, the point of contact should be directly beneath the knee and beneath the body's center of gravity. If the foot strikes ahead of the knee, there is braking[5]. Over-striding places the foot too far in front of the body resulting in braking, jarring and promotes heel strike. Therefore, keep the legs under you[4]. Overstriding can be corrected in many cases by dorsiflection (toes pointing upward) of the descending foot: this also decreases foot contact time resulting in increased speed.

All runners land on the outside edge of the foot and roll inward off the big toe as the rolling action acts as a shock absorber. **Sprinters** first contact the ground high on the ball of the foot and do not make subsequent heel contact or contact is slight. The ideal footstrike for **middle distance runners** is to contact the ground on the ball followed by heel contact. The momentary heel contact gives the calf a short rest[2]. Generally, **marathoners** land on the heel rolling lightly to the ball and then to the toes.

Most track runners, elite runners, and runners finishing with a kick use the following: the foot hits gently behind the ball, then immediately after, the heel hits the ground so that the entire foot touches the ground. This is followed by rolling forward off the front of the foot. Only the very fit marathoners use this stride in view of the stress on the calf muscle. Merely by concentrating to run on the toes, the speed increases.

At slow speeds, my footstrike feels like heel to ball or flat-footed but as speed increases in fast interval workouts and in races, I land more forward with ball to heel strike. Of course, with speedwork with spiked shoes on, it is usual to run on the toes. If a cramp develops during a speed workout, I find slowing down slightly and running flat-footed for a few strides will often get rid of it.

The following footstrikes are not recommended:

- **Running on toes for long distances** results in leg fatigue, calf tightness, and Achilles tendonitis[1].
- **Jogging ball to heel at a slow pace** places a stress on the lower leg. This is not recommended for long distances.
- **Running flat-footed**, is also not relaxed or efficient. The flat-footed runner is unable to spring effectively from the feet in view of minimum or limited plantar flexion, so leg drive suffers.
- **Coming down too hard on the heel or too far back on the heel** is inefficient according to the English author Geoffrey Dyson, since it is a pulling action with the foot landing in front of the center of gravity. This type of landing also results in excessive shock.

Driving Phase

As the support leg moves behind the body weight, the "driving phase" begins. This leg reaches full extension in the driving phase.

Toe-Off

With the support leg extended straight back there can be a powerful push-off. The propulsive force results from a combination of hip extension, knee extension, and ankle flexion. This force thrusts the body forward and off the ground. At toe-off from the fully extended leg there is a great advantage in ankle flexibility. Good ankle and hip flexibility results in low angle, 'A' in degrees, between the fully extended lower leg and the ground. This lower angle results in more horizontal power from toe-off; hence the stride is longer. The lower angle results also in lower vertical force component and consequently less vertical displacement of the body (bobbing on each stride). The greater pre-stretch of the calf enables the calf to subsequently generate more power and increased rate of forward swing.

Being an engineer, I prefer to describe and clarify the above by referring to the Newtonian equation: $\mathbf{F = m \times a = m \times dv/dt}$

where **F** = driving force; **m** = mass of body; **a** = acceleration; **dv** = change of velocity; and **dt** = unit of time.

It is seen that if the force is increased there is greater change in velocity. The higher forward velocity of the rear leg results in increased stride length. While running at slower speeds, practice pushing off strongly on toe-off to increase the stride length. But the action has to be smooth, not jerky. After a while, this should become automatic. Running tall will also assist a strong push-off.

Increased stride length is achieved by increased leg strength, ankle flexibility, and hip mobility. The above indicates the advantage of flexible, strong ankles and calves. Every day when you stretch think in terms of reducing the angle between the ground and the lower leg on toe-off. To increase ankle and calf strength, do three sets of 10 toe raises with single leg on a step or floor (preferably) every other day to provide strength.

Forward Recovery Phase

Just after the support foot leaves the ground (toe-off) in the driving phase, the *floating phase or recovery phase* begins and lasts until the other foot makes contact at the front.

In the recovery phase, hip flexor muscles are mainly responsible for moving the limb forward. The hamstrings now contract and shorten (**concentric contraction**) as the knee bends in knee flexion. The heel approaches the buttocks. The heel of the swing leg of a sprinter nearly touches the buttocks. This puts the center of gravity of the leg closer to the pivot point that is the hip joint and greatly reduces the effort and time to swing the leg forward[4]. For middle distance runners, there is still enough heel lift to produce a forward fling. For long distance, this motion would result in wasted energy. The slower you go the less pronounced is the back kick and forward knee lift. Then as the knee moves forward and upward the leg is straightened by contraction of the quadriceps muscles. During this knee extension, the hamstrings are being stretched eccentrically in their relaxed state. The hamstrings then have to work suddenly to slow down the forward movement of the foot and bring the leg backward before the foot strikes the ground. This is an **eccentric contraction** of the hamstrings since these muscles are stretched at the same time as the contraction.

The heel flick (butt kick) followed by high knee of this leg, results in a longer and faster stride. This indicates the importance of the heel flick drill and high knee drill for sprinters, and to a lesser extent, for middle distance runners.

STRIDE ANGLE

The stride angle is the total angle at toe-off between the upper forward thigh and the trailing upper thigh. See the photo of the age 72 author in full flight at toe-off during the US National Masters T&F meet in Orono Maine in 2002 (p. 76). This stride angle is

110 degrees consisting of 70 degrees flexion of forward thigh and 40 degrees of extension of backward thigh, both measured from a vertical line through the trunk. Most competitive runners have a stride angle of 90 degrees and world class runners have at least 100 degrees. Each increase in stride angle of one degree increases stride length by 2%. Unfortunately, aging causes an accumulation of healed up microtears, which restricts movement. Therefore, it is important to maintain flexibility over the years particularly in the hamstrings for retaining flexion, and in the hip region and groin for retaining extension.

RUNNING FORM FOR IMPORTANT BODY PARTS

Hips and Chest

It is very important to be flexible in the hips and to incorporate several hip flexibility stretches into the daily stretching during warm-up and cool down. Hence the hurdle drills are very beneficial even for non-hurdlers.

Run tall with the buttocks tucked in (forward), chest out in front comfortably, and eyes straight ahead. The pelvic region must remain relaxed to get the required flexibility. A perpendicular line from the ground should intersect the pelvis, shoulders and ears[1]. However, one can be too straight; there should be a slight lean. Payton Jordan, head track coach at Stanford University for 22 years, (and a master holding many world records in the sprints) strongly advocates a strong abdomen and obliques for sprinting. This applies to distance runners, too. A strong pelvis keeps you tall, a strong stomach area keeps the back straight.

Upper Body

The following applies to all runners:

- Eyes straight ahead puts head in the correct position, minimizing neck strain, and does not restrain breathing.
- The jaw should remain loose and the mouth open. Practice the loose jaw during your fast formwork and during warm-ups; it soon becomes automatic.
- Neck muscles must not be taut and strained. Fortunately, this is easily taken care of with the loose jaw. (In my high school and university days, tight neck muscles were a fault of mine in running the short sprints but 33 years later I learned of the loose jaw. Now some have even accused me of smiling while racing, something beneficial we practice at times, as well.)
- Shoulders should be relaxed and hanging loosely, with no excessive counter-rotation.
- Chest should be forward allowing increased lung capacity.

Arm Movement

For any movement of the legs, there is an equal and opposite reaction by the arms. Incorrect arm movement can adversely affect the running form of the whole body. Arms too high cause tension in the shoulders and upper back and shorten the stride. Any arm action across in front of the body instead of straight ahead will twist the shoulders resulting in wasted energy, e.g., arms across the body will result in a side-to-side motion and shortened stride. Lower arm movement results in longer stride but less stride frequency. With thumbs up, the arm movement can be straight ahead, but with thumbs turned in, the arms cross in front of the body inefficiently.

The following is an example of poor arm movement. For example, the left arm crosses the body excessively to the right. To balance or counteract this movement, the right leg crosses over to the left resulting in a loss of stride and possibly excess pronation and injury.

Good arm movement involves the following:

- Arms swing freely from the relaxed shoulders.
- Hands should be relaxed but not flopping.
- Thumbs are resting lightly on the index finger.
- The angle at the elbow is close to 90 degrees. The elbows must not be locked; if locked, this would cause the shoulders to rotate, to be tense, and to restrict drive of the arms. With bending and straightening (slightly on the backswing) of elbows on each arm swing, the arms and shoulders are relaxed and as fluid as water.

Differences Between Sprinters and Long Distance Runners. The faster the running speed, the more vigorous the arm movement, the longer the stride, the higher the heel rises toward the hip in the forward recovery phase, and the higher the knee rises in front of the body prior to foot contact in front of the body.

Sprinters. Sprinters swing the arms parallel (i.e., straight ahead). For sprinters, the thumb is slightly turned out to keep the arms close to the body. Arms move vigorously with hands up to the chin and well behind the back. The angle at elbow joint varies on either side of 90 degrees; less than 90 on the forward swing and more than 90 on the backward swing. Concentrate on a strong thrust backward as if you were elbowing someone behind you; this stretches the arm muscles, which results in a more powerful forward arm motion. A powerful arm motion results in a powerful toe-off. And according to Newton's third law of motion, the driving force into the ground will create an equal and opposite counter-force.

Middle Distance Runners. Arms should be nearly parallel, i.e., hands and arms may move slightly across the body, however, straight ahead is preferable. Thumbs are nearly vertical. Arms are less forward and back than for sprinting, but close to the body. Arms are low to ensure relaxed shoulders with hands as high as middle of chest and back to as far as the seam of the pants (or further back for the elite).

Long Distance Runners. Arms generally move slightly across the body in a relaxed, comfortable position. The thumbs point slightly inward with the palms slightly down to allow some arm movement across the body. Arms are lower than for middle distance with less movement. Here again it is preferable to minimize movement of arms across the body.

Do Arms Lead the Legs or Vice Versa? In sprinting and middle distance races, it is obvious that the arms initiate the driving force for the legs. In these events and faster long distance races, the arms lead the legs and have an important balancing and driving function. Also, I have found while running in the deep end in the pool if the concentration is mainly on leg movement then the arms move much less and somewhat aimlessly, and speed is slow. But if the concentration is firstly on arm movement then the legs move along in unison quite efficiently and speed is higher. This has enforced my belief that the arms are the prime mover, the motor.

However, some believe for slower speeds, as for the slower marathoners, that the arms merely follow the legs and arm action is minimal.

BREATHING

Erect posture, chest out, and "belly" breathing will prevent constriction of the lungs and make for greater running economy. Belly breathing is practiced by opera singers and is the proper way to breathe. On inhaling, push the stomach out, and on exhaling, pull the stomach in. This should be practiced when lying down in a relaxed state, or when running slowly, giving you something to think about on those long, slow runs. At faster running speeds, it is impossible to think about this technique but in time it could become automatic if practiced enough.

TOEING OUTWARDS OR ABDUCTION

Toeing outwards on one or both feet can result in reduced stride length and hence significant loss of distance in a race. If you are a competitive runner, a loss of stride of 1.2cm (0.5in) due to "toeing out" (abduction) can be detrimental, e.g., in a mile race:

1.2cm x 1000 steps = 1200cm = 12m or about 40ft. Toeing out on one leg only would result in half of the above loss of distance.

"This faulty style upsets the muscle action and will predispose to injury" (Travers[5]). I have noticed this toeing out from photographs of world class runners. In the four examples below, the toeing outwards appeared to be about 30 degrees from the forward direction and occurred near the end of a race when the body was fatigued.

- Steve Cram, England, in a tight 800-meter race with Sebastion Coe. See Figure 1.11 from Martin and Coe[3].
- Jim Law (the late), phenomenal masters world record holder in 100, 200 and 400 meters, observed at end of a 200-meter race from a private photograph.
- Myself in a close 200-meter race at the USA Masters Indoor Championships in Boston, March 1998. See photograph in May 1998 issue of *National Masters News.*
- Ato Boldon, Trinidad, winning the 100-meter race in an impressive 9.89s but toeing out quite substantially on the right foot in the Commonwealth Games, Malaysia, September 1998.

Do you have this abduction problem? Examine your footprint in the sand or the snow. Do you toe out, as I do slightly on my left foot. This results in a loss of propulsion in the forward direction due to the side component and a reduction in the stride length. To remedy this: formwork, specific exercise, orthotics, or a combination of these may partially correct toeing out.

Distance Lost Due to Abduction. The distance lost in toeing outwards can be drastic in a short or long race. After all, many sprint races are won by inches. For example, if there is 30 degrees of abduction (assuming a foot length of one foot) this can result in about four centimeters loss of forward motion on each step just due to the foot placement. Check this out by placing your foot on a piece of paper and measure the difference in the forward direction due to no rotation and 30 degrees of rotation. Over a distance of 100 meters to the finish, this toeing out on both feet results in a loss of about 2 meters–a whopping amount. This is due to foot placement alone and is believed to be a lower estimate; the lower and upper leg and foot are all in the same plane, therefore the wasted sideways component of the stride should cause a further reduction in the forward direction.

Based on simple trigonometric calculations, the table below shows the amount of distance lost in a mile race due to toeing outward (only) on both feet. The length of the foot (not length of shoe) is an important variable. For convenience ,1,000 steps is assumed or roughly a 1 mile race. For a shorter race, multiply the number of steps by the table value and divide by 1,000.

Table 3.1 • Loss in Distance in Meters due to Toeing Out in 1,000 Steps

Foot length	5 degrees	10 degrees	15 degrees	20 degrees	25 degrees	30 degrees
12"	1.15	4.55	10.22	18.10	28.10	40.8
11"	1.05	4.18	9.37	16.58	25.77	36.85
10"	0.953	3.80	8.52	15.08	23.43	33.50
9"	0.857	3.43	7.67	13.58	21.08	30.15
8"	0.763	3.05	6.82	12.05	18.74	26.80

In training, look for any toeing out particularly when fatigued. Have your coach observe any toeing out. With practice, the correct straight ahead style should become automatic.

DISCREPANCY IN STRIDE LENGTH

Another problem for some runners is a difference in stride length between the right and left leg. Examine in the sand or snow whether one of your strides is significantly shorter than the other. In 1995, I found surprisingly my left stride measured about 3 inches shorter than the right stride. This could make a large difference in any race. This may have come about from running a lot indoors in the counter-clockwise direction; the outer (right) leg has to extend more in going around the sharp bends. However, this could also happen due to less flexibility and/or strength in the right leg since it provides the propulsive force for the left stride. My right hamstring and calf are less flexible than the left side possibly due to past injuries. Also, testing in 1999 during physiotherapy revealed my right calf was about 20% weaker than the left calf. Now I suspect many runners have this similar stride discrepancy unknown to them. Prefontaine had this problem but it obviously did not affect him. As in my case, this discrepancy is probably not apparent to yourself or others, e.g., the stride still appears smooth and even.

What to do about significant stride discrepancy? Testing for strength and flexibility imbalance between the right and left leg is recommended. Also, have a chiropractor check for misalignment in the hip and pelvic region. If the above fails to reveal anything significant, try rotating the hips during running. For example, if the left stride is short, relax the muscles around your hip and swing the left hip forward ahead of the left foot on each left stride. This can be practiced during slow walking and slow running and also when running in the water in the deep end of the pool.

FORM PRACTICE

In practicing form, the aim is generally to become a smooth efficient runner with minimum deceleration on footstrike, more float time, minimum vertical oscillation, and maximum forward motion with each stride. However, some athletes need to correct an overly long stride to gain in stride frequency. Sprinters need to concentrate on toe-up (dorsiflection) prior to foot–strike, minimum contact time and high stride frequency. Remember, practice doesn't always make perfect—perfect practice does. Form should be practiced regularly, and the following should be helpful:

1. Practice form during the warm-up strides and during cool down of each training session; if tired, form training during cool down will not be beneficial. Always emphasize good arm action and relaxed running.
   We usually do five accelerations, about 60 meters, at about 400-meter pace or 90% to 95% speed during warm-up and often during cool down about four or five slow 150-meter runs. The latter runs also aid in recovery.
2. Running downhill, preferably with little slope and on a soft surface (one of my favorite drills), or alternatively running with the wind is beneficial and assists to obtain the objective of free flowing easy relaxed style.
3. During interval training or running at anaerobic threshold concentrate on running lightly and quietly; say to yourself, *I am running effortlessly and as smooth as a deer*, or similar thoughts during your practice. On each repeat have a thought in mind like: *"relaxed, fast arms," "minimum energy," "light, fast, relaxed," "smooth, quick turnover."* Pretend others are watching and you are running impressively.
4. Wearing light shoes will assist to achieve the light feeling.
5. Run with relaxed face, concentrate on a loose jaw (this is most important), relaxed shoulders, running tall with pelvis forward and chest comfortably out, arms not too high, and hands relaxed.
6. Concentrate specifically on remedying one of your weaknesses, e.g., "strong toe-off" rather than reaching out to increase stride.
7. If possible, have a coach or knowledgeable runner watch and comment. However, I have found that form can be improved and even perfected on your own. Ideally, a video of your stride (also during hurdling if you are a hurdler) is helpful for you and your coach to analyze your weaknesses; two heads are better than one.

RUNNING STRIDE LENGTH AND STRIDE FREQUENCY

All serious runners should be interested in how stride length and stride frequency changes with increased speed, and how these change with increased age. A better understanding will indicate what may need to be worked on or improved in your particular case. This can lead to improved speed and/or greater running economy.

Stride Length and Frequency for Distance Runners

At the 1984 Olympics Jack Daniels Ph.D. investigated the stride length and frequency of male and female runners for distance events from 800 meters to marathon. "The fastest turnover rates were among the 800 meter specialists, and the next were the 1500 meter runners, but from the 3000 meters on up to the marathon there was little variation in turnover rate." "The women took only a few more steps per minute than the larger men who had much longer strides." (See page 80 of Daniels' *Running Formula* book.) For the 3000m and longer distances, with nearly constant turnover, the slower speeds are accomplished by shorter strides. In these distance events, nearly all runners have a turnover rate of near 180 steps per minute. Also, at my local YMCA, I checked the steps per minute of five different runners going at different but modera-te rate speeds and all were within a step or two of 180 steps per minute. If turnover is low such as about 160 steps per minute for some beginners, it is beneficial to change with practice to 180 steps per minute. For a given long distance runner, the turnover is essentially the same within a few percent whether the pace is racing at 5 minutes per mile or training at above 6 minutes per mile. Competitors in the middle distance events have considerably longer strides and the turnover may be up to about 220 steps per minute or 110 strides per minute.

For distance runners to increase speed, it is more productive to work on increasing stride length rather than frequency. Increased frequency will result in greater energy usage compared to increased stride length. My experience running in the deep end of a pool confirms the above. In pool running, a longer more powerful arm and leg motion is about 6 percent faster than a rapid arm and leg action. (Note in pool running as in land running, the arms drive the legs.) Or alternatively, to achieve the same speed as in the long powerful arm action, with the faster arm action–the faster arm action is more tiring. Similarly, in swimming, the stroke length is more important than stroke frequency: a more powerful arm stroke will result in more speed with less energy than an increase in stroke rate.

Stride Length and Frequency for Sprinters

For sprinters, as running speed approaches maximum, frequency changes more than stride length. A maximum stride length is achieved and then further speed is achieved by increase in frequency of turnover. Hence to increase speed, sprinters need to work on both stride length and frequency.

Effect of Ageing on Stride Length and Stride Frequency

Dr. Nancy Hamilton of the University of Northern Iowa investigated the effect of aging on running form by video taping runners at the Masters meet in San Diego and the World Masters Championships in Eugene both in 1989 (*Journal of Applied Biomechanics, vol 9,* p 15-26, 1993). She compared the biomechanics of fast and slow, and older and younger athletes. From computer analysis, she learned of ways to preserve specific aspects of running form to slow down the decline in running speed with age.

Facts

The following are some of Hamilton's significant findings for runners:

1. "Stride rate dropped off only a small amount, not statistically significant, after age 55.
2. Runners in their 80s had only 4 to 5% slower stride rates than 35 year olds.
3. Stride length of 35-39 year olds had stride lengths of 4.72 meters compared with 90 year olds of 2.84 meters – a 40% decline. (Note one stride = two steps.)
4. Stride length declined after age 40."

Similarly for walkers: with increasing age, stride rate stays nearly the same but stride length (gait) decreases drastically.

Hamilton's Conclusions

She concluded the decline in stride length and velocity was due to the following in order of importance:

1. "Range of motion of hips during backward motion of the support leg decreased 38% between the ages of 35 and 90. This was most significant after age 50. [I call this 'decline in toe-off angle,' i.e., the angle between the back leg and the ground at push-off.]
2. Range of motion of knees during swing phase or forward return of leg decreased 33% (from 123 to 95 degrees) between the ages of 35 and 90. This was most significant after age 60. [I call this 'decline in knee flexion angle.']
3. With increased age there was increased time spent in the support phase, or time spent in contact with the ground."

Recommendations to Reduce Decline in Toe-Off Angle

- A strong thrust at toe-off also involves powerful calves, quads, hip flexors, gluteus muscles, and ankles. Weight train these areas once or twice per week. Also daily stretching of these areas is essential. Leg squats are recommended to develop mainly the quads, and glutes, but also the hamstrings.

- To strengthen glutes in particular, lie on stomach with legs stretched out; raise one straight leg about 0.3 meters at your foot, and lower to floor. Do 3 sets of 10 reps daily.
- Strengthening the hip flexors will result in a higher knee of the return leg before touchdown. This in turn results in a more powerful toe-off thrust and a longer stride.
- Leg swinging exercises will result in more flexible hips. I have always been a big advocate of flexibility of the hips to assist running form and economy. The leg swinging exercises in Chapter 11 on "Running in the Pool" are recommended also during the warm-up on land.
- The lunge exercise is very useful to increase the toe-off angle. Ensure that the back lower leg is parallel to the ground to achieve a great stretch of the hip flexor muscle.
- Toe raise exercises will result in a far more powerful toe-off.

Recommendations to Reduce Decline in Knee Flexion

Ideally, the knee should be well flexed during forward return so the foot is near the buttocks. This results in a short lever with the center of gravity of the leg close to the pivot point – the hip. Hence the effort to swing the leg forward is much reduced resulting in a fast return of the leg to the front.

- Lighter shoes will assist a faster return since rotating a heavy object at the end of a lever particularly a long one (as in a 90-degree bent knee) is harder work.
- Stretch the quad, hip flexor and hamstring muscles daily.
- The butt kick drill should be done regularly.

Recommendations to Reduce the Contact Time during Support Phase

- The usual recommendation is to dorsiflex the foot (flexed upward) before it strikes the ground. This also assists to have the foot land under the center of gravity (c. of g.) and helps to prevent some possible braking by landing slightly in front of the c. of g.
- The running ABC drills and plyometrics will assist to reduce contact time. Plyometrics, particularly one legged, will build strength and coordination in the foot, ankle, shin, calf, thigh, hip, and will activate the central nervous system as well. With the drills practiced regularly it is possible to save about 0.01 seconds per step. For example, this is a saving of over 1 minute in a 10K race or 2 seconds in a 400 meter race.
- Regular Pilates exercises will improve hip and knee mobility.
- The following typical fast movements: fast feet drill and fast arms drill, punching bag drill, and fast moving of weights will help preserve the neural pathways and the associated fast twitch muscles. This will also result in faster reaction times.

Some Further Useful Exercises

The following will assist stride length and stride frequency:

- Running uphill fast will enhance the dorsiflection of the feet and increase knee lift while building leg strength.
- Running downhill fast or running fast with a strong wind at your back will increase turnover.
- For all runners, strength, flexibility and reaction time are essential to increase or maintain stride length and stride frequency. But for distance runners, a greater oxygen capacity will assist to a greater extent than the above three. This is why elite runners are able to maintain long strides at reasonable frequencies at high speeds–making it look easy. Their superior oxygen uptake allows for the additional energy required for a continuous smooth longer stride. The anaerobic threshold runs, VO_2max intervals and long aerobic runs improve the distance runner's aerobic capacity which in turn allows for a longer stride.

SUMMARY

The following are only some of the important points to remember:

1. Work on form ***regularly*** as part of warm-up and cool down; during warm-up stride (accelerations), you will be addressing the speed component since good form results in speed.
2. Work regularly on ***flexibility*** of knee, ankle, and hip joints and in particular the latter two, during warm-up and cool down stretching.
3. ***Run tall*** with chest comfortably out, thumbs nearly vertical, rear tucked in, and run light and quiet.
4. ***Run relaxed*** with loose jaw and relaxed shoulders.
5. Every other day ***strengthen the abdomen, obliques and back*** to assist in running tall. Stronger lower body and in particular stronger calves, ankles and hip flexors will result in longer stride.
6. ***Practice belly breathing*** until it becomes automatic.
7. ***Practice strong toe-off*** (push-off) regularly until it becomes automatic.

REFERENCES

1. Glover, B., and Shepherd J., *The Runner's Handbook,* Penguin Books, New York, NY, 1978,
2. Watts, D., Wilson, H., and Horwill, F., *The Complete Middle Distance Runner*, Stanley Paul and Co. Ltd / Century Hutchinson Ltd., London , England, 1986.
3. Martin, D., and Coe, P., *Better Training Training For Distance Runners,* Human Kinetics, Champaign, IL, 1997.
4. Coe, S., and Coe, P., *Running for Fitness,* Pavilion Books, London, England, 1983.
5. Travers, P. R., "Injuries Due to Faulty Style," *Track Technique,* No 11.

CHAPTER

4

An athlete without a solid base
is like a house of cards.
Collapse is imminent.

BUILDING A BASE AND HILL TRAINING

Hill training is included in the latter part of this chapter in view of the importance of hill training during the base building phase and cross-country training. In the outdoor season, it is good practice to continue reduced hill training right up to about two weeks before major competition.

BUILDING A BASE

After the competitive season, a rest of about ten days to two weeks away from running but with easy cross-training is highly recommended. Following this, the base building period (with an aerobic emphasis) begins and lasts at least three months and in some countries as long as six months, e.g., in Great Britain. It is an excellent change of pace from the competitive track season and a welcome change for the body and mind. *The good base condition is the foundation on which you build all your future strengths enabling you to do the hard repeats during months of anaerobic preparation and later racing.* According to the renowned track coach, Arthur Lydiard, the base building period is more important than the track training period[1]. An inadequate base will carry the athlete only so far and after a while, the body breaks down. Also, throughout the training year, aerobic training still forms much of the work load both for maintenance and for continuing stimulus for cardiovascular and muscle development.

The base building phase is a welcome change from the competitive season allowing the body to recharge its energies. Therefore, the volume and intensity are both increased gradually. But some speed is incorporated into the workouts so that what was gained in the competitive season is not completely lost. At the end of the base building phase, the athlete can safely and gradually phase into interval and speed training near 100%MHR (maximum heart rate).

Aerobic Conditioning Vs. Anaerobic Capacity Training

It is useful to clarify some of the terminology. Base training is mainly (about 80% total mileage) **aerobic conditioning**; this is below the anaerobic threshold, AT, i.e., about 6% slower than AT speed. The AT varies depending on the experience of the runner but for most it is between 60% to 80% of the maximum heart rate, MHR. **Aerobic capacity** training is to develop the VO_2max. This training is done at about 85% to 95% MHR or about 10K or 5K race pace, therefore, requiring better condition and is more stressful.

What Is the Goal For Building a Base?

Distance runners

For distance runners, the aim is to build strength and general fitness over a period of at least three months to condition the body mainly with aerobic running and hill training. This will enable the runner to withstand the more intense anaerobic interval training and aerobic capacity training to follow.

Sprinters

For sprinters, while building a base, retaining speed from the competitive season is important and mileage is less important than for distance runners. But the basic goal is to condition the body to withstand the more intense speed and speed endurance ("power work") to follow.

What Are the Scientific Advantages of Base Training?

When the following advantages are known then there is more incentive to work hard at the base training:

- Improved oxidative metabolic capabilities in cardiac muscle and skeletal muscle cells;
- Increased blood volume (more red blood cells) and capillary density (tiny blood vessels) to improve oxygen and nutrient delivery to muscles, and CO_2 and waste removal from muscles;

- Increased capillarization occurs in the lungs as well; hence more oxygen is brought in and waste products moved out at a faster rate;
- The heart, muscles, joints and ligaments are strengthened, protecting the athlete from injury. The athlete is able to do more work with less effort;
- The number of sites for energy production (mitochondria) are increased along with increased enzymes that produce energy from fats and carbohydrates in conjunction with oxygen;
- The overall effect is an increase in running economy, strength, endurance, and confidence.

Personal Experience of Benefits and Advantages of Base Training

I have experienced or seen the following benefits of base training:

- I believe the excellent base training I received in cross-country training in the fall over many hills contributed to a large extent to my track success in the past 18 years and particularly my success in the world championships in Buffalo, New York in July 1995 (three world records).
- After the cross-country/base training season of about three and a half months, we normally go inside and start the indoor training in late December, running slow for a few weeks to adjust to the bends of the 200-meter rubber track. One of my training partners was a mid-40-year-old speedster who normally would not have a good base in view of executive work commitments, travel, and family interferences. Although he was a faster runner over 200 meters and 400 meters his conditioning would not normally allow him to keep up particularly in the later stage of the workouts, or to complete the larger number of repetitions ("reps"). This was all due to his lack of base and would often lead to injury.
- I have found after four to six weeks of running hills that I surprisingly can lift a lot more weight, i.e., 15 "reps" easily in the press whereas 10 was my previous limit at the same weight. So it is not only the legs that get strengthened in the hill workouts.
- It is not unusual to see runners run close to their best in the 1500 meters and 800 meters after the base training but before the anaerobic/speedwork training. I have personally seen this in teenage runners. For example, in 1961, Peter Snell, world record holder who was trained by Lydiard, ran a 4:01.5 mile after four months of base conditioning (100 miles per week including Lydiard's favorite hilly 22-mile course) and one marathon. This was before he had started his speedwork training period.

What Are the Ways to Build a Base?

Lydiard's Way

During the base building phase "aerobic runs with speeds near the *maximum steady state* [lactic or anaerobic threshold i.e., no oxygen debt] should produce a pleasant state of tiredness rather than fatigue, i.e., not breathless and struggling otherwise the run becomes anaerobic; you should recover quickly and with the knowledge that you could have run faster" (Arthur Lydiard and Garth Gilmour[1]). These aerobic runs are between 70% to 100% maximum steady state and hence are faster and more effective than implied by LSD[1] [long slow distance]. As training progresses, the athlete can run faster and longer without reaching the anaerobic threshold.

The following is a brief description of Lydiard's[6] aerobic phase and how it fits into the overall schedule: "When we are training for athletics, we don't introduce the specialty exercises until we get into the last 10 weeks (start of anaerobic and speed development) of a training program. Until then, the 800-meter runner does much the same conditioning [aerobic base] work as the marathoner." The aerobic running [base training] is for "as long as possible" or "at least three months." From Monday to Friday, long aerobic running from 30 to 90 minutes would be typical for 800- to 10000-meter runners. The long run on Sunday during the long aerobic running weeks varies from 90 to 150 minutes for 800-meter to 5000-meter runners respectively [and this is reduced during the last four to six weeks before the "first important race"]. "Some hill training is suggested during the aerobic phase to prepare for the intensive four week hill phase which normally follows." The hill phase includes three days per week of "hill springing/bounding/steps running 30 to 60 minutes" with steep hill running also for the 3000-meter steeplechase, 5000-meter, and 10 000-meter runners. "The hill phase includes some short, sharp sprints to prepare for the anaerobic phase which follows when you come off the hills."

"A sprinter should do some training for speed in some form through the whole schedule" (Lydiard[6]). I believe this is good advice also for distance runners to a lesser extent; it is important not to lose all the speed that was gained in the competition season. This view is shared, for example, by David Martin and Peter Coe (Sebastian's father).

Ken Sparkes[7] indicates aerobic running for eight weeks increasing total mileage each week by 10 percent with a lowering of total mileage every third week. Over an eight week period, mileage increases from 38 to 50 miles per week for an intermediate runner. All runs should be at a comfortable conversational pace. In both daily runs and long runs, go 1.5 to 2 minutes per mile slower than your current 10K race pace, i.e., relaxed and slow. Strides twice a week 8 x 100 meters or 200 meters and incorporating hill training or weight training two or three times per week are also recommended. The slower daily runs with shorter strides tighten muscles and ligaments, therefore stretching is recommended before and after each run (Sparks and Kuehls[7]).

Hal Higdon[4] describes an aerobic base building schedule of hard days followed by easy days with total mileage increasing by about 4 miles every two weeks over a 12 week period. He recommends a "steady" long run every week, a midweek semi-long "steady" run, both increasing gradually every two weeks, some easy sprints once per week in the last four weeks, a day off every week, and easy jogging on in-between days.

Achieving More Variety in the Aerobic Training

A steady diet consisting mainly of long continuous aerobic runs day after day as suggested above will not appeal to everyone. Variety can be achieved in the following ways and still achieve the objective.

Aerobic interval training can also be used to develop the aerobic system. This provides variety from the slow long distance runs above and also similar benefits. "Repeated runs at a faster pace over shorter distances with brief rest intervals will achieve the same benefits as long continuous runs" (Costill[5]). Volume rather than speed is the key to successful aerobic interval training; for example, a large number of 300- or 400-meter runs at conversational pace, i.e., below the anaerobic threshold. The repetitions could be done in three or four sets to enable more volume.

Ideally, with this type of workout, I believe the rest interval and number of "reps" should be decided by the athlete and coach and the athlete's current stage of conditioning. The athlete will know when he or she is able to start the next "rep" and fatigue will dictate when he or she had enough. However, it is important to have consistency in the run time and the rest time.

Aerobic capacity (VO_2max) interval training, i.e., 3- to 5-minute repetitions at 5K and 10K race pace. This training, once a week at most, is for more experienced distance runners and could be attempted near the end of the base training phase. Each session should be less than about 8% of the weekly mileage.

Care should be exercised to not overdo the intensity and volume of the long or medium run the day before or after these interval sessions particularly if muscles are sore.

Building a Base with Cross-Country Training

This is my favorite method for building a base. In Canada, with the cooler weather in the fall, the workouts are quite invigorating. Since the workouts after work are on grass or on snow, this sometimes results in running around pylons with lights attached or completing the session before darkness.

Some coaches prefer to concentrate on aerobic repetitions from 300 meters to 1 mile on grass and trails over hilly courses two or three times per week with long easy runs on in-between days and one longer run once per week. The rest between repetitions is usually equal to the time for the run, but preferably when the heart rate goes below 120 beats per minute. This training is usually in preparation for cross-country races. This is the type of base building that I am used to in training with the North York Track Club in Toronto, Ontario, and with the Saugeen Track Club in Port Elgin, Ontario. For sprinters, the hills and distances are understandably shorter than for distance runners. *In all cases, there is a build-up to additional, harder hill work after an initial two or three weeks of runs on the flat.* Normally, with this type of training after the track season of mostly 400-meter and 800-meter races it takes me about six weeks to become a competitive runner in an 8K or 10K cross-country race.

In the fall, my typical base training for two to three months at the North York Track Club on grass and earth trails would be as follows:

- Interval training two or three times a week consisting of one of the following sessions: (1) about 12 to 16 "reps," 60 to 90 seconds, on the flat at about 65% effort normally with short rest, (2) 8 to 10 short fairly steep hills at 85% effort with short recovery run at the top and walk back, or (3) 3 to 4 x 5 minute hill circuits at 75% effort with 2-minute walk rest. All of the above always with about 1.5 to 2 miles warm-up and cool down.
- Anaerobic threshold runs less than 3 miles twice per week and an aerobic conditioning run of about 4 miles once per week.
- Deep water pool running 2 to 3 times per week about 40 minutes per session including about 8 minutes of drills in the shallow end.

The above training equipped me quite well for a winning performance for about 14 years in my age group over 8K or 10K at the Canadian Cross-Country Championships. This indicates that for base training, long, continuous runs mainly are not essential.

For cross-country training, Lydiard[1] recommends time trials near race distance twice per week or a time trial and a race, fartlek (arbitrary-intermittent fast/slow running training), some anaerobic running, and long runs.

HILL TRAINING

When?

A period of hill training in view of its many benefits listed below is essential during base training, and particularly after a good aerobic base. It is the opinion of many coaches that hill training continue into the in-season or sharpening phase but be reduced to once per week and then none within two weeks before a big meet. Start with a low number of repeats and/or shorter hills until the body adapts. In Canada, the winter season rules out hill training (except on the hard roads), however, weight training and stair climbing are good substitutes. During the early hill training phase, the athlete's legs may be tired (similar to early season weight training); this is normal and these effects will be gone within a week or two.

Benefits of Hill Training

1. It amplifies aerobic endurance, leg strength and power.
2. Running uphill improves running form due to increased arm action and knee lift, and increased thrust at toe-off. All of these improve speed.
3. Bounding up hills in particular increases knee lift and stride length to compensate for shorter stride with age, and also to compensate for the shorter strides used during the long-distance base training.
4. It improves strength in the lower body more specifically than weight training. I have found I can lift more weight in weight training after weeks of hill training sessions, so the upper body is strengthened too.
5. It greatly strengthens hip flexors, lower legs and quadriceps in preparation for speedwork.
6. Downhill running teaches relaxation, improves leg speed, and can increase stride length. It gets one into condition quickly with less repetitions than on the flat and without risk of injury. This assumes that the surface is soft.
7. Uphill running is hard work in a short time with reduced pounding compared to distance running.
8. Downhill runs on wood chips, grass or earth trails makes your muscles less resistant to soreness. Research has shown that downhill running on softer surfaces particularly helps to prevent future injuries due to the eccentric contractions (stretched muscles under load).
9. It adapts you psychologically and physically for cross-country.

Types of Hill Training

Hill work is normally below 85% effort; in this case recover between "reps" until the heart returns below about 120 beats per minute. However, for short, steep hills at 95% effort a full recovery is necessary (or at least below 96 beats per minute).

1. **Long distance runs over hilly courses**

These long runs over rolling cross-country terrain develop strength and endurance.

2. **Long hill repeats**

These aerobic repetitions develop running economy or aerobic conditioning at slower speeds but also VO_2max at faster speeds.

To stimulate improvements in VO_2max, run uphill at the same *effort* as a 5K or 10K race pace on the flat, i.e., the same heart rate using a heart rate monitor, or the same perceived effort as on the flat. Jog slowly down and repeat. After the rest, the heart must be at least below 120 beats per minute. Choose a hill that takes between 3 minutes and 5 minutes to run up otherwise you will not be developing VO_2max. Since the effort is the same as on the flat, the number of repeats should be the same as on the flat. With too great an effort you are working in the anaerobic range and fewer "reps" will be accomplished.

3. **Short steep hill repeats**

Short hills are run at faster speeds than long hills. These hard-but-relaxed anaerobic runs, improve running economy and speed. The exaggerated arm, shoulder, and high hip flexor/knee lift actions require added energy resulting in anaerobic energy requirements. For example, an intensive workout used by athletes of Jack Daniels, exercise physiologist, is as follows: on the treadmill 10 times 1 minute at 15% to 20% grade (very steep) at about 9 minute mile pace with 1 minute rest between, jogging off the treadmill (qtd. by Pete Pfitzinger[3]). Since 4% grade is equivalent to speeding up 1 minute per mile, a 16% grade at 9 minutes per mile is equivalent to a 5-minute-per-mile pace on the flat or 75 seconds per 400 meters. A very tough workout.

I have done treadmill workouts similar to the above. On the treadmill, you can devise your own hill workout by setting the speed, the incline, and the other variables. If your treadmill does not have fast enough speed for an interval workout on the flat, you can obtain the equivalent speed by raising the grade. However, I personally find the outdoor air and Mother Nature more stimulating.

4. **Bounding up short hills**

Bounding up hills or "hill springing" is recommended by Lydiard and has been adopted by many coaches. It has the ability to lengthen stride and put spring into the stride.

Hence, running economy should improve over time. The following lists specific advantages in hill bounding:

- The increased dorsiflection of the ankle during push-off increases ankle flexibility and strength.
- The stretch of the calf muscles just prior to contraction loads the muscle with energy providing a more powerful thrust; this results in increased strength and flexibility of the calf.
- The high knee lift required stretches and strengthens the hip flexor and quadriceps resulting in greater stride length.
- Fast twitch muscles are activated.
- This is good plyometrics workout with the advantage of a soft grass or earth surface. By stretching and strengthening tendons and muscles the risk of strains and pulls is eliminated.

Bounding consists of the following: Push hard from the toes of your left foot, with strong arm action, with right knee raised high, with head up and chest out, land on the toes of the right foot. Allow the right heel to sink down the slope below your toes. Continue with alternate feet with a bouncing action and slow momentum up the hill. Start with limited bounding and gradually increase the quantity over succeeding weeks. Bounding is popular with sprinters and is often incorporated into their warm-ups on the track along with other plyometrics. The legs should be strong and well conditioned (normally with weight training) before attempting bounding or other plyometric exercises.

Posture on Hill Training

Keep your chest out, lean slightly from the hips (not the waist) and look forward, not excessively down or up. Basically, this prevents you from leaning too far forward on the uphill, or leaning to far back (braking) on the downhill.

How to Run Uphill

- Lean into the hill (but not from the waist), shorten your stride, concentrate on knee lift, and pump your arms, but not excessively[7].
- Look upward, use a quick, short stride, don't push too hard; when running over the top, quickly resume your pace from the flat[4].
- On steep hills, it is helpful to use very small steps with feet low to the ground. When tired on a very steep hill, fast walking is effective, or fast walking alternated

with running. (The latter would be more popular with older or less experienced runners.)

- Try to maintain the same level of effort and breathing rate that you used on level ground; but generally, there will be more effort especially on steep hills.

How to Run Downhill

- Don't over-stride since this causes extra force in the feet and legs. Over-striding is particularly stressful on pavement as opposed to earth or wood chips.
- Lengthen your stride slightly; for better balance, allow your elbows to rise up and out; and to cushion the shock, land more on the front of the foot rather than on the heels[4]. Keeping the knees slightly flexed on landing will help to absorb the shock.
- Relax, run lightly, and let yourself go. Feel the reduced effort. But letting yourself go can be overdone, so don't be too energetic since it also takes energy to run downhill. Avoid leaning backward. Avoid braking; run with center of gravity over the landing foot. Keeping the chest forward and looking slightly down will assist in achieving the proper pelvic tilt and lean.
- Maintain the same effort and breathing rate as on the flat.

Cross-Country Race Strategy

Firstly, train vigorously for about 6 to 10 weeks on the hills. It helps a great deal to be familiar with the course. Start cautiously but pick up the pace in the second half or last third of the race. But save something if there is a particularly big hill or strong wind against you near the finish. Push harder when you have the wind at your back. Pick off some runners, reel them in.

Although a good strategy on running uphill and downhill is to use the same perceived effort as on the flat, there will be more effort on a *steep* hill—believe me. Don't waste yourself on an uphill as a more even runner will recover faster at the top and pass you. Learn to relax in-control, but with increased speed on the downhills.

Precautions

- Run easily downhill, particularly in training, to avoid injury unless it is on wood chips, grass or soft earth in view of the increased stress and pounding. At 7-minutes per-mile-pace, tests on a steep uphill showed 85% the impact compared to the level and on a steep downhill there was 40% greater impact compared to the level (Higdon[4]).

- To avoid overstressing the legs, do no hills two or three weeks before an important race[7]. [Three weeks appear overly cautious.]
- Hill training twice a week during the base building phase is not unreasonable, but once a week is usually considered adequate during the in-season or speedwork phase. Allow four days between a hill workout and a low-key race since hill training is similar to weight training or water running.

Further Facts

- Note: different authors describe the rise in a hill loosely by percent elevation, grade, slope or incline and these are all synonymous. But, remember that the elevation for **Ø degrees angle = (1.7Ø) %elevation or incline.** For example: 1 degree slope = 1.7m rise in 100m run, or 2 degree slope = 3.4m rise in 100m run (where m = meters).
- Jack Daniels estimated that every 4% grade is equal to speeding up 1 minute per mile[3].
- In a hill with equal gradient up and down, the energy lost on going up is about twice the energy saved in going down.

Alternatives to Hills

- Running uphill in ***loose sand*** (as practiced by Herb Elliott of Australia) is highly effective but not readily available. It is best used by runners who have year-round access since there is a potential problem of Achilles tendon strain or calf strain if too much is done in too short a time. The heel sinks into the sand giving a greater calf and tendon stretch compared to a solid surface.
- ***Stadium stairs or apartment stairs.*** Be careful to start gradually in the first few sessions. Be careful coming down the steps; this puts a lot of stress on the feet and ankles. (I was at a training camp in Trinidad where a young athlete was injured the first day while running stadium steps for the first time.)
- ***Accelerations.*** Fred Wilt states to do repetitions of striding and then running fast for 50 yards to get used to the higher expenditure of hills (qtd. by Higdon[4]). [Similarly, this is good training to simulate the higher energy expenditure in going over steeplechase barriers; but in this case stride fast for only about 10 strides every 80 meters; I call this the "Poor Man's Steeplechase or "Earl's Steeplechase."]
- ***Treadmill*** with elevation feature.

Some Favourite Uphills and Downhills

With some looking around, you can find some favorite hills that are a pleasure to run. To give you an idea the following are trails that I have found, and hopefully there are similar trails in your area. These trails are in and around Toronto, Ontario. All are easy on the legs, mentally relaxing and even uplifting, particularly on a hot summer day or an autumn day since they are in the woods with pleasant surroundings where nature can be enjoyed. There is extra oxygen, too, and it is 10 to 15 degrees Fahrenheit cooler on a hot day. Depending on the weather, my condition, and the type of training I am undergoing, each have their advantages as explained below:

- **150-meter 1.5% gradient earth trail** in Oakville Sports Park Woods:
  Excellent for downhill repeats to practice form, running economy and aerobic-anaerobic workouts; e.g., 16 x run down fast jog back (do 4 repeats in 4 sets). Or 12 x 100 meter run down fast relaxed and walk back for an easier workout when, for example, two workouts are planned on the same day.

- **Hill circuit on wood chips** in Brimley Woods, Agincourt:
  Excellent for a Lydiard type of circuit. E.g., run up approximately 2% gradient 200 meter at fast pace, jog about 2 minutes on the flat to a 200 meter 2% gradient downhill, run down relaxed reasonably fast, recover jog of about 1.5 minutes back to start. Repeat 9 to 10 circuits without stopping. Total time taken is about 45 minutes.

Note: This is less strenuous than the circuit of Lydiard and Gilmour[1] where the uphill is done with bounding and the recovery at the bottom includes sprinting. Lydiard suggests different lengths of wind sprints on each circuit and a mature runner in good condition should spend about one hour on this type of hill circuit session. [I suspect, Lydiard's workout above would be very strenuous for most runners.]

- **One and 1/4 mile rolling-slight downhill wood chip trail** in High Park, Toronto:
  This trail has a good gradient to work on running economy, long stride and gives an aerobic-anaerobic workout. Typically, I run down fast at about 3K race pace and jog back slowly. Repeat two or three times depending on condition.

- **500-meter steep wood chip trail** in High Park:
  Run down fast but relaxed, jog back, rest one minute and repeat 3 to 5 times. This aerobic-anaerobic workout teaches form, running economy and practices downhills for cross-country races. It also helps to prevent future injuries. Many times I

have done this workout about one hour and one coffee after a track workout of fast/short intervals.

- **200-meter steep gradient** on asphalt in Sleepy Hollow:
  This path starts with small gradient and becomes increasingly steeper to about 4% gradient. Usually I run this after a local track workout since it is within five minutes from my house in Mississauga. The emphasis is on relaxation and turnover. It also requires tremendous arm and knee action near the top. It is excellent for training for the 400 meters, particularly a week or two before a 300-meter hurdle race or 400-meter race. Two of these at 95% effort with jog back are usually sufficient when done after a workout. I have also used it as a gauge of my fitness by comparing to times from previous years. This is one advantage in keeping detailed daily logs.

REFERENCES

1. Lydiard, A., and Gilmour G., *Running With Lydiard,* Hodder and Stoughton, UK, 1983.
2. Coe, S., and Coe, P., *Running for Fitness,* Pavilion Books Ltd., London, England, 1983
3. Pfitzinger, P., Reaching New Heights, *Runner's World*, February 1992, p78.
4. Higdon, H., *Run Fast, How to Train for a 5K or a 10K Race,* Rodale Press, Emmaus PA, 1992.
5. Costill, D., *Basics of Sports Physiology,* Benchmark Press, Carmel, IN, 1986.
6. Lydiard, A., *'Running to the Top,'* Meyer and Meyer Verlag, Aachen, Germany, 1997.
7. Sparks, K. and Kuehls D., *Runners Book of Training Secrets,* Rodale Press, Emmaus, PA, 1996.

538
OOSTENDE 2001
COLOR
EPSON

CHAPTER 5

Obey the laws- the laws of running,
to keep out of the court of defeat
and the jail of injury.

26 PRINCIPLES OF TRAINING

The following are important principles and rules that form the basis of training for running. Although the examples pertain to running, the principles also apply to swimmers, cyclists, rowers, and many other athletes.

1 – PRINCIPLE OF BASE TRAINING

A sound base of aerobic training for about three months preferably should follow the outdoor track season and precede the sharpening (competitive/peaking) season. This enables the body to complete the high quality interval training with strength and endurance during the following in-season. A good base also enables you to do perhaps several heats in one day and on successive days at a meet. In North America, this base period normally occurs after the summer track season.

Also after an indoor track season, an athlete should back off for a week or 10 days with little or no running, and do cross-training. Then base training for two or three weeks is again recommended. The same routine is recommended for a road racer or a marathoner after a big race when it's not the end of the season.

An extensive base aerobic training phase, followed by hill training, and then sharpening will produce world shattering results. Arthur Lydiard, the famous New

Zealand coach of Peter Snell and other Olympic champions (his three athletes won two gold and a bronze in the 1960 Olympics), proved that this method (his training philosophy) worked wonders.

Base aerobic training also forms a year round foundation for middle distance and long distance runners.

2 – PRINCIPLE OF GRADUAL ADAPTATION

It usually takes about six weeks for the full training effect to occur; I have even noticed the same workout is easier a week later, but generally you race according to your condition and training in the previous six weeks. Some say it takes even longer for the full training effect to set in. Therefore, a long lead time is required if you are to race well.

It is surprising how the body adapts. At the beginning of the sharpening phase, it is a chore to complete one quarter of the race distance at slower than race pace. Speed has normally been lost in the base building period, but in a couple of months, one can run the whole way at race pace. Over this period, the workouts become increasingly harder, but due to increased condition, the effort remains about the same since the body and mind can tolerate more. There should be no sudden increase in effort between workouts. The workouts should be fun if possible; this can be achieved by variety, e.g., usually a different type of training in the second half of the workout will provide a less mentally taxing session. If the big race you are training for is in the morning and you are used to training in the afternoon or evening, morning adaptation is called for. It is wise to adapt the body often to morning training in this case.

World class athletes normally peak after the third important race. As the body adapts each time the distance is run, the body is stronger, and the athlete more confident and relaxed resulting in faster times if other things remain equal (e.g., weather, lack of injuries, etc.).

Preparation Time

After the base building phase, at least eight weeks and preferably 12 weeks are required to prepare for an important race. In 1997, we moved indoors in mid December after the base building (mainly cross-country) phase. This left one month to prepare for an important 1-mile indoor race. Two weeks were used up in running slow to adjust to the tight bends and harder surface of the indoor track. The remaining two weeks for mile specific training were not long enough for the body to adapt since progress cannot be rapid and the body does not adapt completely in two weeks. Consequently, my time was about 3 percent below my previous September time. On the other hand, in 1993 after the World Masters' Championships in Japan in October, I had over two and one half months to prepare for the same annual race as above. I built on my conditioning for the World Championship in Japan. Hence, in early 1994, I broke both the mile and 1500 meter indoor world record just a few weeks before leaving the 60 to 64 age group. The above indicates the extreme benefit of a long lead time before an important race, providing sufficient time for the body to adapt.

Overload

The body adapts to a higher level of racing if the stress applied is:

- More than the body is used to
- Intense enough
- Regular enough
- Applied long enough (see above)
- Specific to a particular race distance
- Not overdone

This training stress in the hard workouts (or gradually increased mileage) is balanced with easy recovery days. As fitness improves, a greater training load is handled with the same effort. It's a fine line the athlete must tread—always being careful to overload within his or her limits to avoid excess fatigue and/or injury. The degree of stress has to match your fitness level; move forward only when ready. Problems can be avoided mainly by ensuring there is no sudden increase in the stress over a short period of time. Percy Cerutty[8] puts it this way, "Small doses of stress and pain over a long period of time, rather than large doses over a short period of time." In this regard, the use of a heart rate monitor is very beneficial.

Diminishing Returns

This is a very important principle. Progress is rapid in the beginning and slows as maximum potential is approached (similar to a salary vs. years curve). At the highest levels of performance, there is a great deal of work for a small gain, but that is what makes champions. In 1996 and 1997, with my hamstring not completely healthy, my training volume and intensity were often reduced to about 60% of normal. This caused about 1-2 percent slower times in the 400 meters and 800 meters. In other words, the extra 40% in intensity and volume in each week of training would improve my times by about 2 percent only. However, to me the extra effort would be worth it.

In the first 6 weeks of a 12-week sharpening phase with a gradual increase in intensity the athlete can come within about 97% of their target race pace. The remaining six weeks will be required to achieve the final 2 or 3%. (For example, if a runner has a target of 60 seconds for the 400 meters the final six weeks of the 12 week sharpening is required to lower the time from 61.5 to 60 seconds.)

3 – PRINCIPLE OF SHARPENING AND TAPER

Sharpening for middle and long distance runners

The sharpening (peaking) season normally starts after a season of base building and hill training. The sharpening period prepares the athlete to peak in performance in the competitive season. During this period, foundation endurance runs form the backbone of the schedule. There is great emphasis on runs at race pace or faster, hill work, time trials, fartlek, and particularly interval training. In view of the intensity, the total volume of quality training (anaerobic threshold, VO_2max, and anaerobic lactic) should be only about 18% to 25% of weekly mileage for an experienced runner. Also this sharpening season can only be maintained for about 12 weeks as explained below.

Taper

The full training effect would not normally occur two weeks after training. Hence, any hard workout within two weeks of a race may be of little assistance except to build confidence and pace judgement. However, I have found speed can be improved in the last two weeks, particularly in hot weather, which helps to loosen joints and muscles. In fact, Lasse Viren's coach was able to improve Viren's speed further during one occasion a week before the Olympics. But speed should never be left to the last two weeks; it is a good policy to work on speed gradually over the whole sharpening phase. Speed and speed endurance improvement takes many sessions.

Three weeks before a race, one or two workouts can be more intense than normal[4]. After this, with reduced volume but retaining intensity, the body recharges. I have found a low-key track meet one week before a big track meet can be quite beneficial. In the last week, workouts should be light volume but retaining speed. Three days before a meet should not be overdone–two days before, very little. Remember sore muscles often come two days after a hard workout. Also do no water running of any intensity within three or four days of a meet. I made this mistake twice and got tired legs in an important 800-meter race.

Arrive well in advance of the meet so you are not tired from travel. If your race is late in the day, avoid lying around too much; this can make you lethargic and undo all your careful tapering. It's even better to do some easy running.

There is one further aspect to tapering, i.e., relating to the frequency of training sessions. "The athlete should reduce the number of sessions by no more than 30%" (during the tapering period) otherwise the athlete may lose the "feel" for the activity (Houmard and Johns[17]). I have found a long period, e.g., several days without fast running (e.g., 90 to 95% effort) prior to a race would not be beneficial, particularly for the sprints.

Charlie Francis, ex-coach of Ben Johnson, has a good taper for the sprints. See the section "Charlie Francis Sprint System" in Chapter 6. For the marathon see the section "Taper for the Marathon" in Chapter 9.

Rule of 12 weeks

1. Scientific studies have confirmed the efficacy of a 12-week training cycle when starting from a rested or detrained (e.g., return from injury) condition (Sandler and Lobstein[3]). Five examples were listed where a peak occurred shortly after about 12 weeks of training or performance dropped off after this time:
- A weight lifting study;
- A study of six marathon runners;
- A body builder, three-time Mr. Olympia, recommends the 12-week cycle;
- Zola Budd and Joan Benoit Samuelson both had good success 12 weeks after returning from a serious injury.

2. There is also further evidence, reported by Noakes[2], that "Sharpening (leading up to competition) can be maintained for a probable maximum of between 8 to 12 weeks." After this intense training, performance can be expected to fall off:
- "Prokop reported that his athletes usually required 7 to 8 weeks of sharpening training to reach a peak that would last 3 to 6 weeks before their performance would start to fall off" (Noakes[2]).
- Derek Clayton and Ron Hill, world class marathoners, found that running performance improved for approximately 10 weeks and then dropped off (Part 1[1981] and Part 2 [1982] of "The Long Hard Road" Noakes[2]).

3. Many of the Kenyans believe in three months of hard training, followed by easy intervals to keep in shape for the races, usually once per week, e.g., Richard Chelimo, former world record holder in the 10000 meters[14].

4. The 12-week theory coincides with my own experience, i.e., 10 to 14 days active rest (cross-training) after the indoor season, start training again about mid April with about two weeks of base aerobic training, and reaching a peak in mid to late July.

Summary. After the indoor or outdoor season for track and field competitors, or a major race for a marathoner, take an active rest for several weeks, build an aerobic base again, and start another 12-week sharpening phase.

Rules of Ten

- Mileage should not increase more than ten percent per week.
- Train hard for ten weeks, then taper for two before your competition.
- Less than ten percent (one mile in every ten) of your total training should be for racing and race-like tests (race-like effort) (Henderson[11]). [I believe this formula was recommended for long distance training but it is in the right ball park for middle distance training as well; see below "Principle of Balanced Training," which is more specific.]
- Ten days of active rest after the indoor season or outdoor season, or after a major marathon.

4 – PRINCIPLE OF BALANCED TRAINING

An optimal balance between the aerobic and anaerobic capacities is the main target in a training program (Tikhonov[6]). If the athlete overdoes the anaerobic work at the expense of aerobic work, the athlete will not have enough endurance to maintain speed. This is the situation with an athlete who does not build a good base before the sharpening phase. The greater the imbalance, the worse the race times will be. If the aerobic work is overdone with little or no speedwork, the athlete feels unable to maintain the pace if the tempo increases.

An imbalance in an athlete can be determined from actual races or time trials. For example, a middle or long distance athlete who starts fast and can accelerate in a race but then fades near the end is lacking in aerobic capacity.

For myself, the percentage of fast interval training for 300-meter hurdles, 400, 800 and 1500 meters is about 9% to 12% of weekly mileage in the sharpening phase. Up to age 70, this normally involved two to three sessions of mainly short (150m, 200m and 300m) and some long (400m to 600m) interval training per week.

See also Chapter 7 on "General Training Theory for Distance Runners" for recommended maximum percentages of weekly mileage training at anaerobic threshold (10%/session), VO_2max (8%/session), and anaerobic lactic (5%/session). These percentages are based on numbers from Jack Daniels[15]. These numbers are an excellent guide for 1500m to marathon runners, but I believe more applicable to experienced runners. The less experienced and older, particularly above 60 years, should listen to their body and err on the side of less volume rather than more.

The percentages of anaerobic and aerobic energy **used** in the various Olympic race distances are shown in Table 5.1 below. These are based on world record performances up to 1987 for men world record performances up to 1987 for men from Peronnet and Thibauult[20]. The aerobic and anaerobic energies used in a specific race indicate the **quantitative emphasis** to be put on these energies in training. The training must be directed to meet these specific needs.

Table 5.1 • Percentage of Aerobic and Anaerobic Energies Used for Various Olympic Race Distances

Race Distance	% Aerobic Energy	% Anaerobic Energy
100m	8	92
200m	14	86
400m	30	70
800m	57	43
1500m	76	24
3K	88	12
5K	93	7
10K	97	3
Marathon	99	1

Sprinters and middle distance runners would have difficulty in meeting these high **anaerobic** percentages in training. Recovery would not be adequate and injury, sickness, and staleness would result if tempo and recovery runs were neglected at the expense of too much speed training. For example, the usual norm for the average experienced middle distance runner is to do anaerobic intervals once or twice per week with each session representing only about 5% or 6% of the weekly mileage. (See also Rules of 10 under Principle 3, and typical training schedules for experienced middle and long distance runners in Chapter 10.)

However, world class or elite athletes can handle a high anaerobic workload. For example, Martin and Coe[9] in Table 5.9 list the training load for Sebastion Coe (specializing in the 800 meters and 1500 meters) at 18 years over a 39-week training period at an average of 32.5 miles per week as 66% aerobic and 34% anaerobic. The anaerobic percentage achieved by Sebastion is very high. Similarly, in the spring and summer Jim Ryun[12], had a strict regime of aerobic run in the morning and anaerobic interval workouts in the afternoon that would result in a very high anaerobic percentage. Thus these exceptional young athletes were able to approach the figures in the table above for their events.

The different types of training all have a certain fraction of aerobic and anaerobic depending on how close the training comes to the two extremes of pure aerobic (below the anaerobic threshold, AT) or pure anaerobic (all out speed). Some fartlek workouts or hill workouts could have nearly equal anaerobic and aerobic contribution.

5 – PRINCIPLE OF CORRECT MIX IN THE TRAINING SESSION

Aerobic and anaerobic training should generally not be mixed in the main part of the session. For example, it would not be desirable to work both speed and stamina on the same day or the same workout because one would detract from the other. It would be more beneficial to work on speed, flexibility and strength together. This is apart from the warm-up and the recovery runs between repetitions. This is a simple concept that many of us sometimes violate with detriment to the training. Arthur Lydiard and others teach a distance runner not to mix the distance running and speed work together, thus unbalancing the training program[8].

Anaerobic speedwork before longer aerobic running saps the energy and tires the legs resulting in slow or shortened performance in the longer running. Aerobic intervals or a long run before attempting short fast intervals results in much reduced speed and poor form. Just look at your training log for inappropriate training examples. Even long running the day before anaerobic speed work is detrimental to improving speed.

However, there are the following permissible exceptions:

- To build speed endurance, speed is occasionally practiced at the end of a workout. This is to give the athlete the feel of a fast finish when tired, but it is not used to develop *pure* speed.
- Fartlek includes aerobic and anaerobic runs together, but it is for speed endurance, not for developing *pure* speed.
- However, in distance training where *pure* speed is not as important as stamina this principle is sometimes violated to achieve the proper mix in training.

6 – PRINCIPLE OF TRAINING PARTNER

Runners make runners. I am indebted to my past and present training partners usually about 20 years younger (Wayne Cosgrove, Ed Willmott, Dave McLeod, John Pickard, Andre Kocsis, Mark Spielman, Chuck Sochor, John Faulkner, Keith Rodrigues, Ken Glance, Frank Nicholson, Louise Soucy Fraser and Mike Carter, to mention a few). They are nearly as important as a knowledgeable coach.

It's easier *if* you have training partners of *similar ability* to help on those long runs. In bad weather, running by yourself is very difficult and may not be attempted, but in a tight group, all suffer together and it does not seem so bad.

A partner of similar speed makes life so much easier in doing fast intervals. There's company in misery–such as suffering together in doing those hard repeats. In the early "reps," the faster runner instills speed in the runner with more endurance. Later, when the going gets tough, the runner with more endurance has the effect of pulling the faster runner along. Sometimes it is helpful to imagine an elastic band between you and your partner ahead of you. Also there is benefit in following closely (drafting).

Percy Cerruty[8] mentions the "soul power" when a group of athletes train together, resulting in a lot more momentum built up throughout the workout compared to training alone.

However, one can train alone but this requires more fortitude and experience. Your training partner then becomes the stopwatch.

7 – PRINCIPLE OF LIMIT TRAINING

You need a tiring interval workout or tiring long run on your hard days but should not "total" yourself; finish the workout feeling tired but capable of running more. If you are progressing too fast in your training, you are doing too much.

The serious competitor has to go close to the limit to the point where the cool down is a bit of a chore, but still bear in mind, there is always tomorrow. You have to save enough energy for a decent workout the next day, so listen to your body.

In doing speedwork intervals, the approach we prefer is to stop when performance drops off or stop at the first sign of a cramp or sore muscle developing. More could be done but form would suffer and there may be injury. Usually the heart and lungs are willing but remember sore muscles, tendons, and ligaments often come not while training, but one or two days later.

8 – PRINCIPLE OF HARD/EASY

There has to be time for the body to recover and for the training effect to set in. After a hard workout, long run or a race, there are microtears in the muscles that need time to repair. After a hard effort the pH of the blood goes from its normal alkaline range of about 7.3 pH into the acid range of less than 7 pH; time is required for the blood and muscles to return to the alkaline range where the athlete performs best. Also, time is required for the glycogen stores to be replaced. Therefore, an easy day should generally follow the hard day to allow time for recharging. Remember, the easy day is just as important as the hard day. The easy days are like putting money (or energy) in the bank. The all-out efforts are withdrawing it.

Hard days on both Saturday and Sunday could pose a problem[1]; I have gotten around this by taking it easy (active rest) on Friday, then interval train on Saturday and a medium long run on Sunday. Take a nap on Saturday and Sunday. The following Monday is preferably an easy day, e.g., run in the water, or only short, medium fast intervals.

The following are big mistakes in training often with drastic consequences:

- Running a race followed by a long run the next day. (I have done this and suffered severely sore muscles.)
- Two hard workouts in a row or too many hard workouts too close together. This is an invitation for an injury (it happened to me: four hard workouts in five days). Beware of this particularly if there is a recent or chronic weakness in the body. You may even feel all right during the second workout, as it often takes one or two days later for the problem to reveal itself. If you get away with it, it also detracts from the building process.
- Doing your friend's workout (or running pace) rather than your own often leads to trouble, e.g., too much, too soon, too hard. The serious athlete sticks to his or her own schedule.
- Also preferably you must rest *before* as well as *after* long runs, speedwork, and races.

9 – PRINCIPLE OF GOING WITH YOUR STRENGTHS

Your strengths have a lot to do with the amount of fast twitch (speed) and slow twitch (endurance) muscles you were born with. When your strengths and weaknesses are known, a running event should be chosen to match your strengths.

Once you have decided on your specialty race, your training should be directed toward your strong suit. Know your strengths and weaknesses. Working mainly on your strength (endurance or speed) will produce better results than concentrating on your weakness, as the weaknesses cannot usually be greatly improved.

For example, if you were not born with a great deal of fast twitch muscles, you may find your speed is improving only minimally with training. By going with your strength (endurance), you can train with higher mileage and concentrate on longer repetitions. You work on improving your speed over longer distances rather than for a shorter sprint. By building your endurance, you build sustained speed. Herb Elliott (Australian world record holder in middle distance) did not have blazing speed, but with his superior endurance, he was able to start his kick long before others, getting a head start so they could not out sprint him at the finish. Overemphasis on the athlete's weakness can be counterproductive and can easily lead to over-training as the athlete may not have the physical makeup to handle the work demands. For example, there are 800-meter runners who have moved up from the 400 meters. And there are 800-meter runners who have moved down from the 1500 meters or mile. The former should concentrate more on shorter, faster repeats while the latter should concentrate more on longer, slower repeats. In this way, the athlete responds better to the work demands; training is easier and more enjoyable. However, this is not to say the weakness should be neglected; it requires work but not as much concentration.

Jack Daniels[15] states in his *Running Formula*: "In general, strengths should be taken advantage of during the final weeks of training, with weaknesses attended to earlier in the season."

10 – PRINCIPLE OF SPECIFICITY

Training should be specific to the demands of the activity (race distance) to achieve maximum performance. Specific training allows your body to adapt to the specific race stress you will encounter on race day. Train to feel comfortable with the distance and the speed of the race. For middle distances or greater this means adapting to longer distances and at race pace and faster than race pace.

Train for the course environment and terrain you will run for your race, i.e., similar time of day, hills or flat, heat or cold. Even the wind is another important factor; you must be able to run against the wind without concern. (Indoor running eliminates the wind, hills, dogs, and cars.) A good example of the essential requirement for specificity in training is the training for a hurdler. To adapt to the correct stride and rhythm between hurdles the hurdler must train on the correct surface, with the same footwear as in the race, the correct distance between hurdles, and the correct height of hurdles.

Weight lifting should be specific to your race distance: endurance "reps" for middle distance or greater, strength power "reps" for sprinters.

Cross-training should be as specific as possible to utilize the same muscles and heart rate, e.g., cross-country skiing and running in the water simulate running closely. Cycling and swimming (cardiovascular benefits) would be secondary choices for runners. However, downhill skiing, tennis, canoeing and curling would not be specific enough.

11 – PRINCIPLE OF USE IT OR LOSE IT

"Use it or lose it:" *flexibility and strength*! Flexibility and muscular strength are lost gradually each year. One secret to winning is to age slower than your rivals; this is one of my favorite secrets—particularly applicable to master athletes. Offset the loss of flexibility and strength with an everyday stretching program and a weightlifting program every other day. Of course, exercise that all runners are doing is probably the best anti-aging pill. The key word is "stimulation." Exercising regularly in the target heart range as a life long habit (along with a healthy lifestyle) could add two or three decades to your life span; the active person normally has also a healthy diet, good rest, good sex, and does not abuse his or her body, all of which contributes to this wonderful longevity.

While on the subject of anti-aging, don't neglect the following: Supplements to offset the free radical damage are also highly recommended to offset aging, i.e., vitamin E, C, beta carotene, selenium, and grape seed extract. Other magic formulas are reducing stress, maintaining a sense of humor, and eating healthy foods (particularly fruits and vegetables) since nearly all diseases come from the diet. *"The aim is to die young but delay it as long as possible"* (Anon).

12 – PRINCIPLE OF REVERSIBILITY

Once speed, strength or aerobic capacity is developed, these can be negated or significantly lost if they are neglected—even for a week or two later in the season. There is a loss of training effect. The body reverts back toward its original undeveloped state. For example if strength built up in the base building period is neglected in the sharpening period, it will be lost to a large extent. Aerobic capacity can be lost; try running a 5K or 10K without doing long or medium long runs for several weeks. Significant speed can also be lost fairly quickly (a few percent in about two weeks) if you stop working at it.

In the base building period, many coaches omit speed work. Consequently, it takes a long time to get it back. The athlete has to start over again and valuable time is lost. *The best performance is achieved with a long buildup.* During the base building phase (usually the fall), it is important to retain a good deal of the speed developed in the sharpening phase. Inclusion of some speed in the base building period is not pure speed but enough to retain the muscles and neurophysical system so they can respond to a fast turnover. Fast interval training is not necessary during base building, particularly for distance runners–just fast strides during the warm-up, short and medium length hills at fast pace and fartlek. Sustained speed can be worked on in the sharpening (peaking) period.

Martin and Coe[9] are also strong advocates of year-round speed training; they state *"Never venture far away from speed; speed practice should continue, with varied degree, all through a macrocycle* (generally a year or the time to achieve peak maximum fitness)." Arthur Lydiard, the famous New Zealand coach, and the great world champion Ron Clarke were also believers in year round speed training. Charlie Francis, ex-coach of Ben Johnson, strongly advocates maintaining the speed developed in the in-season during the base building phase; see "Sprinting" in Chapter 6.

It takes a great deal of training to build up to a high level of fitness, but it can be lost quickly so beware of too much time off. Maintenance of all variables is essential to success. See also "Principle of Maintenance" below.

13 – PRINCIPLE OF MAINTENANCE

Once a training effect has been reached, it is possible to maintain it with less volume, but intensity must remain nearly the same.

According to Arthur Lydiard, if the athlete has gone through the whole *distance* training program, he will be able to maintain his peak for a two to three month period by just racing about every 10 days and running fast, light workouts in between.

After an optimum of 12 weeks of sharpening, you may still have major competitions a month or more away. Therefore, it is best to reduce volume and the number of track sessions while retaining intensity. This extra period of sharpening is injury prone time. Little can be gained now but much can be lost.

14 – PRINCIPLE OF SUPERCOMPENSATION

Supercompensation is an improved performance phenomenon, i.e., an increase in performance above the original level, which occurs at the optimum time after the athlete is stressed optimally in training then rested. Figure 5 demonstrates optimum supercompensation in an interval training session.

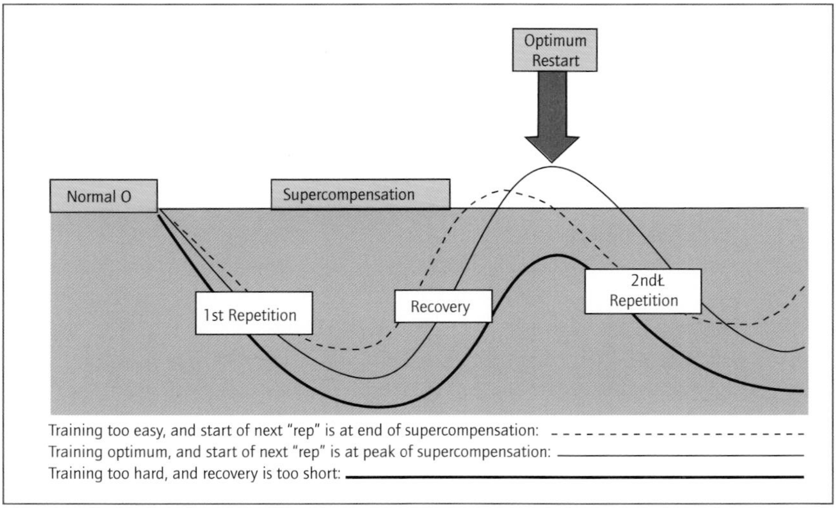

Figure 5- Supercompensation in an Interval Training Session

Supercompensation results as follows: Starting from a performance level "O," the normal biological state, the correct amount of training is applied, which is neither too hard nor too easy. This causes fatigue and a maximum value at the end of the repetition. Proper recovery follows. This is the compensation phase. At the end of this recovery rest period, there is a "rebound"[10] or boost in performance to above the original level "O," the supercompensation zone. Ideally, the next repetition starts at the peak of supercompensation as shown above. Otherwise, if the stimulus comes *too late,* there is a return to the original performance level. Similarly, the training stimulus can start *too early,* i.e., below "O," in which case there is a decline in performance.

There can be optimum supercompensation in a warm-up before a race or competition. However, as you probably know, if there is a long delay between warm-up and the race, supercompensation is lost. Supercompensation is also very much related to the hard/easy training days; an easy day following a hard day allows the body to rebound. This phenomenon also applies to a weekly cycle, or a sharpening period of several months (including the tapering period). Similarly, supercompensation or a rebound occurs at start of the outdoor season after a rest of 10 to 14 days and a short base building period following the indoor track season.

I have used this principle quite successfully in carrying out a second workout about one hour after the first one: another secret of mine. I have found the period of approximately one hour to be sufficient time to recover and be full of energy again. But if the elapsed time after the first workout is too long, e.g., several hours then the energy and motivation is down again.

15 – PRINCIPLE OF PERIODIZATION

Periodization is the division of the training year (a **macrocycle**) to meet the athlete's objectives and to peak during the competitive period(s). When there is one major competitive period over the year, this is called single periodization. If the athlete competes in the indoor and outdoor season, i.e., two major competitive periods, this is called double periodization. The athlete should have a yearly plan, as well as a long range plan, perhaps several years in the future. Martin and Coe[9] outline a detailed long range plan based on projected target times, and designed to work all the energy systems in the correct proportions[9]. See also Chapter 10 herein on "Design Your Own Training Schedule."

Periodization is essentially based on periods up to a few months **(mesocycles)** of hard training, peaking in performance for a brief period, followed by a transition rest period to permit another cycle to repeat. Each mesocycle is divided into one to two weeks **(microcycles)**.

In a periodization scheme, it is impractical to decide in advance the exact details of each week's training on a day-to-day basis for a year in advance. However, certain days of the week could be set aside to work on specific energy systems, e.g., see Chapter 8 and 10. It is best to be flexible as the plan may be disrupted by: injury or illness; faster or slower than expected adaptation; your job; and personal or family-related unexpected matters, etc.[9]

Periodization incorporates a plan for increasingly intense training as the athlete adapts, with a corresponding decrease in training volume. Generally, over a month-period, each week has progressively higher intensity for the first three weeks in the month, with a decrease in intensity in the fourth week. Each successive monthly cycle is harder. This highly recommended approach is similar to hard days followed by easy days but on a coarser time scale.

The following personal experience reinforces the soundness of an easy week. In the summer of 1998, to rest a foot ligament sprain, I reduced training volume and intensity by about 40% for one week. Then I tested my condition on a rolling 2,000-meter wood chip trail where I often trained. Surprisingly, I improved my 3-year-old personal best by an amazing 30 seconds, and with the usual effort.

16 – PRINCIPLE OF INTUITION AND TRAINING FLEXIBILITY

Percy Cerutty, the famous but somewhat eccentric Australian coach and coach of the phenomenal Herb Elliott, was a strong advocate of intuition (listen to your body) and variety in the training. Others who strongly advocated listening-to-your-body were Arthur Newton (the world class ultra-marathoner), and the late George Sheehan (the popular American doctor, runner and writer on the joys of running). Of course, intuition in running works best when one has a good knowledge of training principles. Sometimes I *feel* what particular training my body is lacking.

It is important to have a long-term training goal and related short-term goals, but let intuition play its part on a day-to-day basis. When you are dictated by your "iron-clad" goals, they can occasionally work against you and perhaps cause injury.

There is a need for flexibility in the training schedule. Some days you will feel like doing more or less–train accordingly. The weather may also be a factor that will alter your training plans. Don't force yourself out into the bad weather just because a certain workout was scheduled; better to train indoors, reschedule, or cross-train. Training in icy conditions, extreme cold or wind, can make one tough but can lead to injury or sickness.

A muscle that is sore is a warning; better to reduce your workout or rest. Two easy days can do wonders. Before a groin injury, I had a feeling I should not be training hard after a suspicious sore muscle developed in this area. I disregarded this feeling and ended up with six months of reduced training and physiotherapy. Also if you feel intuitively that you should not do another runner's workout, don't do it; this is normally not a good idea in any case.

Your training program should be flexible to accommodate the weather, your present condition, job responsibilities, and of course the family. In short, when the body speaks, listen to it and disregard your schedule; your subconscious has many years of wise experience.

17 – PRINCIPLE OF CONTINUITY AND CONSISTENCY

Before an important race, do not deviate from your normal routine in any way. Do not vary food, drinks, supplements, sleep, warm-up or normal activities. If you are used to taking supplements spread out during the day, do not take them all at once before your race: bad news I found out, since supplements are acidic. If you are not used to a massage before a race, why experiment? In the marathon, it is important to run in the same training shoes used for long training runs; this is no time to experiment or gamble. I've made a lot of these mistakes before important races—learning the hard way. Usually these mistakes result in sore/tired legs and loss of energy during the race and consequently slower times. For example, in the World Masters Championships in Gateshead in 1999, I walked excessively for two days before my final 800 meters, and before the final 400 meters, I foolishly sat in the stands continuously for about two and one quarter hours watching the exciting events. *In short, avoid anything unusual, such as excessive walking, dancing, continuous sitting, long standing, or swimming in the ocean. In general, follow the same routine as you used in your training.*

18 – PRINCIPLE OF THE 'CHICKEN MIND' BUT STRONGER BODY

The mind is the master, but it can play tricks. The mind is actually weaker than the body. You can do more than you think you can. When the going gets rough in a race and fatigue is nearly unbearable, with the bear on the back and heavy legs, the "chicken mind" says, *"Slow down you and you will feel much better, you can't possibly keep up this pace."* However, if you are aware of the truth that the body is stronger than the mind, then the logical mind can overcome the chicken mind. You have to fight the thought of slowing down or quitting. Then you can press on and even increase the pace, when it counts, in spite of the pain or discomfort. Before a race where you know it's going to hurt, visualize this discomfort and overcoming the chicken mind and the strong temptation to give in and slack off.

The above theory is supported by somewhat similar statements by Lynch and Scott[1]. They list several examples where, *"Fatigue is triggered by the mind before the body actually is ready to become tired."* For example, "Fatigue sets in after an unanticipated hill appears in a race, or you are passed by a runner you knew you could beat." They also state: *"The mental breaking point is tested when the outcome of a race looks dismal; the brain sends messages to throw in the towel."* The negative thoughts turn the body into a less efficient machine, which results in increased energy utilization. In this state of mind, refocus techniques are required to get back on track.

19 – PRINCIPLE OF RELAXATION

Relaxation is the key to running fast and to running economy. Any tension in the body interferes with fluidity of the muscle function—sapping your energy. The ability to relax results in minimum energy expenditure, increased confidence and faster times.

Any anxiety will interfere with relaxed running. Use mental relaxation exercises and techniques to get rid of mental tensions, negative thoughts, and also to free up the mind for positive visualization of your racing. Fred Wilt (*Track and Field News*, 1964) writes, *"Relaxation is achieved by losing one's awareness, especially of the negative aspects of fatigue."*

Bud Winter, author of *Relax and Win,* famous coach of the American sprinters in the 1960 Olympics and coach of several world record holders in the sprints, was a strong advocate of relaxation in running. His famous saying was, *"Faster, looser."* He taught that a runner must first learn to relax at less than 100% speeds, i.e., at about 95% speeds. With considerable practice: training and concentration while running fast, relaxation occurs at higher and higher speeds. In all workouts, the runner must be conscious of relaxation and strive for it. Think fluid, think relaxed, think light steps, think of nothing but how fast relaxed and smooth you can run. It is essential to learn to relax the muscles not directly involved with running, such as the face, neck and shoulders. I have found, a loose jaw is especially important. A smile helps too; some have accused me of smiling while running. Relaxation is the contracting of only those muscles needed at a given instant. While one set of muscles is contracting quickly, the opposing set must relax (loosen). While the hamstrings flex the legs, the "quads" must relax. While the "quads" straighten the legs, the hamstrings must relax. Be sure to concentrate on "faster looser" or "fast relaxed" during all workouts and races.

20 – PRINCIPLE OF LEAST EFFORT

"Your heart, muscles, digestive organs, et al., will always try to get the job done in the least amount of effort" (Ariel[13]). Mother Nature also acts to minimize energy. For example, water running down a hill will take the path of least resistance. In my days of engineering analysis, I assumed the "principle of least energy" in hydraulic calculations to determine the best flow path. In running, least energy expenditure results mainly from perfect form and complete relaxation.

When you run with a slower runner, your stride length and frequency are altered and you run less efficiently, expending more energy. Least energy will be expended in running at your own comfortable pace.

More importantly, you deviate from least energy expenditure in trying *"harder,"* for example, in a sprint particularly after reaching maximum speed. See Principle 19 on "Relaxation."

In distance races, an even pace with no surges (except at the finish) results in least energy expenditure. An even pace or negative split (faster 2nd half) will result in the least effort. When you train say to yourself, *"I am running with minimum effort,"* and believe it. In running up hills or down hills, maintain the same effort as on the flat. Also push harder when running with the wind.

When running or competing in any sport, think *"fluid,"* think *"effortless-effort"*, rather than "push hard," and you will move looser and faster. For example, while running intervals in the pool, I found I moved slower when I tried for extra power (extra exertion) in the arms, but I moved faster with less fatigue and tension when I consciously relaxed the arms.

21 – PRINCIPLE OF REGULARITY

It takes about seven or eight years of regular, consistent running to reach a career peak. A career peak can be measured by a peak in the Age Graded Tables[16] for your gender, age, and event, i.e., a higher age-graded percentage. It is no secret that success comes from years of consistent training at an intense level. Have a long- term plan. Running is an obsession to a serious competitive runner. He or she doesn't have to be cajoled to get out the door to run. They say, " Hey–I get to run again today!"

The training log is a great help to ensure regular training most days or every day of the week. Some days I even write the workout in the log before I do it–then I'm committed. A serious runner hates to see those blank spaces in the log. It is then a matter of pride and an education, too, to look back over the year in the daily log to see all the great workouts. One can also learn a lot from past experiences recorded in the training log; what worked and what didn't; what caused an injury?

Some days you may start a workout and feel this is no fun or you feel stale—not my day for running. On those days, I find I can always run energetically in the water, cross-train, or lift weights, and stretch. No need to take the day off. Remember, two weeks of inactivity could require up to six weeks to get back to your original conditioning.

In summary, *day-to-day perseverance is the key to success.*

22 – PRINCIPLE OF LIVING LIKE A CHAMPION

How we live in the hours away from training has a major influence on our success as a runner. *"Live, train and think like a champion every day."*

The above expression says it all and is good advice. Everything affects how you run and train. Wearing casual running clothes most of the day (when you are not at work) and displaying the medals and trophies in open view around your house will also be a subtle reminder of your running goals. Social activities will compete with your training time and interfere with diet and sleep. You will likely need extra sleep and/or naps. Remember a late night can slow you down for more than one day. Is it worth it? Avoid stress as much as possible. Hopefully you will have an understanding family or partner. The latter is essential; too late if your spouse doesn't agree with the *health* of it after marriage. Of course, your running friends will understand your strict and bizarre behavior on eating, drinking, etc.

Herb Elliott, never beaten in the mile or 1500 meters in his prime, makes the point that running should not encompass your whole life; it should be well rounded. However, to achieve his many world records required great concentration and dedication. For great success, there has to be great sacrifice—for most of us anyway.

23 – PRINCIPLE OF ANTI-SHOCK

Now something *more serious*. This could be the most important advice in this book particularly for older athletes. Structural parts in machines are sometimes subjected to high stresses causing failure when large temperature changes occur suddenly. For example, a part is brought suddenly from cold to very hot or vice versa. However, gradual changes are acceptable. Similarly, the heart undergoes tremendous stress when it goes suddenly from resting to near maximum. For example, a runner warms up for training and there is an overly long delay before starting some intense intervals or a race. The heart suddenly goes from near resting to maximum and the muscles are no longer warm and elastic. The body is put under undue stress. More than likely this was the major problem for one athlete during the relays at the 1995 World Masters Championships in Buffalo after a very heavy downpour of rain lasted over an hour. I suspect the hour wait (or more) in cool, wet weather after his warm-up contributed or bought on his heart attack during his race. He survived by the way, but barely. Another problem may occur when the heart is not raised high enough in an inadequate warm-up. I have noticed these problems taking note of my own heartbeat immediately after intense effort and during recovery. *The principle of anti-shock* involves avoidance of these shocks to the body during training and racing. If there is a long delay between warm-up and training (or a race), it is recommended to do a mini warm-up or at least some stride outs. It is preferable that the first interval in training be slower than the subsequent ones. This is more important in cool weather. It is advisable also to start a race shortly after a warm-up; the time between warm-up and race depends a lot on the temperature of the environment. But the heart rate should be elevated well above the resting rate at the start of the session or race. The nerves and adrenaline supply some increase in heart rate, which is beneficial, however in training, this increase is lacking.

Similarly, Joe Henderson[18] advises against subjecting the body to drastic temperature changes after a race: After a race, cool down slowly. Do not go and jump into a cold pool or cold shower shortly after when overheated, or do not go immediately to a hot shower in cold weather. Either situation invites injury or illness (the immune system is already low from the race). Excess heat will delay the cool down process and will cause the heart rate to increase. A cold shower narrows the blood vessels and may increase blood pressure excessively if taken too soon after strenuous activity. Also it is always good advice to start the warm-up with some walking and start and end the cool down with some slow walking. After a race or intense intervals, it is best to keep moving as the contracting muscles assist the return of blood to the heart. Thus with movement, the heart does not have to work as hard. Immediately after a hard interval or the end of a race, the heart will increase in heart rate for about 10 seconds, and a moving body assists in making less stress on the heart. After strenuous exercise, the heart remains elevated until the oxygen deficit is paid back.

If this all sounds overly cautious, then it is better to be overly cautious. Better safe than sorry.

24 – PRINCIPLE OF NEURAL TRAINING

This is a very important concept or principle for all athletes. But first a short course on the central nervous system is in order.

The brain and spinal cord constitute the central nervous system, which communicates with the muscles via peripheral nerves. Each nerve is a bundle of nerve fibers or neurons either motor or sensory. The motor neurons carry signals (or electrical impulses) to the muscles; the sensory neurons bring information to the brain. Each neuron is associated with many muscle fibers forming a motor unit.

As we age we lose strength and flexibility, so it is wise to do frequent weight training and stretching exercises, but this is not enough. We must also continue to activate the neurons associated with the fast twitch muscles or these neurons atrophy as explained below. Kirkendall and Garrett[7] state the following pertinent facts: "With age the number and area of fast twitch fibers (Type II) decreases. The loss of muscle mass with age is secondary to age- related denervation of muscle fibers, particularly the denervation (non use of neurons) of Type II fibers. With age large numbers of type II motor neurons become nonfunctional; the neural input is disrupted. With reduced demand on skeletal muscle it adapts to the new lower requirement, but with increased demand the declines due to aging can be minimized." Based on the above, the important point I wish to make is that nonfunctional Type II neurons can be reduced by increased demand on fast twitch muscles. This can be accomplished by fast and/or intensive movements on a frequent basis. The demand on the Type II muscles has to be the right type. Many athletes with great strength do not possess the required power to sprint a fast 100 meters or shorter distance; to do so, the specific fast twitch muscles required must be exercised rapidly in a like manner. "Resistance training can improve the central nervous system recruitment [enervation] of muscle, hypertrophy [increase in area of fast twitch fibers], and force output" (Kirkendall and Garrett[7]). However, there must be sufficient intensity and duration over many weeks. For example, endurance type of weight training would have less effect on fast twitch development but is still very beneficial as shown by a study by Heikki Rosko[19]. In this Finnish study, endurance runners showed 8% improvement in running economy and a 3.6% improvement in 20 meter sprints, after 9 weeks with one third of training time devoted to explosive strength training (plyometrics and sprints, but low resistance weights). There is a high rate of activation of fast twitch neurons during sprinting and other competitive/intensive sports; these neurons must be exercised in practice sessions to achieve top speeds and fast reactions.

The following exercises will assist to activate the fast twitch motor units and prevent their atrophy with age:

- Actions that involve split–second decisions
- Plyometrics that involve explosive actions
- Fast feet drills
- Fast arm drills
- Fast step-ups with or without light dumbells
- Fast squats with light dumbells
- Small punching bag exercise
- Tennis ball reaction catching against a wall
- Moving weights fast in weight training and slow intensive (heavier) weight training with sufficient recovery between sessions

- Mental exercises involving fast movements or one of the above
- Sprint training

Note that in the above exercises, it is important to exercise both the upper and lower body. Sprinters show the slowest decline in aging compared to middle and long distance runners. Sprinters are doing a lot of the above, i.e., exercising the neurons associated with the fast twitch muscles. Therefore, all athletes wishing to age slower than normal should do some form of fast movements, preferably explosive, (or similar to the above) on a frequent basis.

This subject of neural training recalls a strange habit or desire I have had for many years, i.e., to slam one fist very rapidly into my other open hand. My friends and relatives looked on this rather quizzically. You might say this was to get rid of some frustrations, but I feel it was my body intuitively saying *"You need some fast powerful movements to keep sharp."*

25 – PRINCIPLE OF TRAINING WITHIN PRESENT CAPABILITIES

Training beyond one's present capabilities and condition, i.e., too fast, too long, or too many repetitions is counterproductive. I call it straining. This leads to tense muscles (in face, neck and shoulders), lack of relaxation, disillusionment, discomfort, and possible injury or staleness. For example, this is the danger of running with those faster than yourself or using someone else's workout. There is a fine line between an optimum workout and one too hard as it is necessary to increase the stress in order to improve. Generally less is better. When the training stress is increased too soon, the maximum training potential is not reached. This is where an experienced coach with a discerning eye is valuable to prevent an athlete from progressing too fast. A self-coached runner, by listening to his body and proceeding gradually week by week, may avoid straining. But a coach is better able to spot problems by observing the form of the athlete. *In summary, straining in training is draining and leads to detraining.*

26 – PRINCIPLE OF SHOCKING THE SYSTEM

An athlete will improve more rapidly in the initial weeks of training, but later, he or she is likely to reach a plateau of no progress. A plateau is likely to be reached after about six weeks in a phase of the training; the muscles have developed a memory by this time. It is then necessary to shock the system to break out of the plateau. This entails a change in the usual routine. It involves an increase in stress by incorporating increased speed, with more or less repetitions and rest. Of course, there still has to be specificity.

REFERENCES

1. Lynch, J., and Scott. W., *Running Within,* Human Kinetics, Champaign, IL, 1999.
2. Noakes, T., *Lore of Running,* Leisure Press, Human Kinetics Publishers Inc., Champaign, IL, 1991.
3. Sandler, R., and Lobstein D., *Consistent Winning,* Rodale Press, Emmaus, PA, 1992.
4. Pataki, L. and Holden, L., *Winning Secrets,* 1989.
5. Anderson, O., Things to do the last four weeks before your marathon, *Running Research News,* Lansing, MI, Vol. 14, Number 5, June-July 1998.
6. Tikhonov, L., The Balance of Aerobic and Anaerobic Capacities, *Track Technique,* Fall, 1993-125.
7. Kirkendall, D., and Garrett, W., The Effects of Aging and Training on Skeletal Muscle, *The American Journal of Sports Medicine,* Vol. 26, no.4, p598, 1998.
8. *Track and Field Review* Fall 1986, Volume 86, Number 3.
9. Martin, D. and Coe, P., *Better Training for Distance Runners,* Second Edition, Human Kinetics, Champaign, IL, 1997.
10. McFarlane, B., Hurdling, *The Canadian Track and Field Association*, Ottawa, ON, 1988.
11. Henderson, J., *Running Your Best Race,* Wm. C. Brown Publishers, Dubuque, Iowa, 1984.
12. Ryun, J., Developing a Miler, *Track and Field Quarterly Review,* Summer 93, Vol. 93, No. 2.
13. Ariel, G., *Movement,* presented at the 1981 European Track Coaches Congress, Venice, Italy.
14. Tanser, T., *Train Hard, Win Easy, The Kenyan Way,* Tafnews Press, Mountain View, CA, 1997.
15. Daniels, J., *Daniels' Running Formula,* Human Kinetics, Champaign, IL, 1998.
16. World Assoc. of Veterans Athletes, *Age Graded Tables*, National Masters News, Van Nuys, CA, 1994.
17. Houmard, J.A., and Johns, A., "Effects of taper on swim performance. Practical implications." *Sports Medicine*, 17, 224-232, 1994.
18. Henderson, J., *Think Fast,* Plume Book/Penguin Books, New York, NY, 1991.
19. Rosko, H., et al, "Explosive Strength Training Improves 5-Km Running Time by Improving Running Economy and Muscle Power", *Journal of Applied Physiology, Vol. 86(5),* P1527-1533, 1999.
20. Peronnet, F., and Thibault, G., "Mathematical analysis of running performance and world running records", *Journal of Applied Physiology, 67*, 453-465. 1989.

SPRINT FORCE
AMERICA
NATIONAL MASTERS
INDOOR CHAMPIONSHIPS
224
2004
SPRINT FORCE
AMERICA
549
2004

CHAPTER 6

Be quick but
never hurry!
John Wooden (famous basketball coach)

TRAINING FOR SPRINTERS

GENERAL

Normally, sprinters are born, i.e., endowed with a majority of fast twitch muscles; but still they have to train to bring out these inborn qualities. These are the more successful sprinters. Sprinters can be developed through all round training (mainly neurophysical) aimed at developing their bodies and every aspect involved in a sprint race.

I believe you can lose 1 or 2 percent of your speed if intensity is neglected for a week or more. Some intense training reduced in volume should be done in two sessions in the seven days before a sprint race. You can even lose your speed and get it back years later. In 1995, I lowered my 400-meter time by 3 seconds from 3 years previous to break a world record (65-69 age group) in spite of aging. This was achieved without pure speed workouts, weights on the legs or plyometrics, also no 100-meter or 200-meter races, but mostly through speed endurance workouts (150 meters and up) and hurdle drills. Of course, there were the usual sprint drills and accelerations during warm-up. This record was about one second faster than the great Jim Law's world record. He had more speed and did a lot of weight training. Therefore, my performance indicates the benefit of speed endurance resulting from 400 meter, 800 meter and 300 meter hurdle training, and frequent races over these distances.

Sprint training involves concentration on the following aspects:

- Strength (weights and plyometrics)
- Flexibility
- Stride rate and stride length
- Acceleration
- Technique (form, relaxation, drills)
- Speed
- Speed endurance
- Reaction time and starting
- Aerobic endurance/tempo (recovery days)

Each workout has some of the above but in the right combination. For example, speed or technique exercises should be done before aerobic stamina or speed endurance. The body must be fresh to work on speed or technique.

SPEED, SPEED ENDURANCE, AND TEMPO TRAINING

In the 100 meter sprint, the alactic (without lactate) or phosphate energy system supplies 70 percent of the total energy; but in a maximum effort of about 45 seconds the phosphate contribution is only about 10% compared to 60% for anaerobic glycolysis (with lactate). Lactic build-up can be minimized by restricting a great deal of the sprint training to less than seven seconds. Since sprinting is mainly an event utilizing the alactic and anaerobic glycolysis systems the training usually involves mainly speed runs of 60 meters or less and speed endurance runs from about 120 meters up to 500 meters (the latter for 400 meter specialists).

A high level of anaerobic conditioning will develop speed endurance and tolerance to acidosis. Some effective means to develop the anaerobic system are:

- Pickup sprints (e.g., walk 50m , jog 50m, stride 50m, sprint 50m, repeat). As condition improves try 60m and 75m instead of 50m;
- Hollow sprints (e.g., accelerate sprint 50m, jog 50m, accelerate sprint 50m, jog 50m, repeat);
- Interval sprints at 95% speed with running start, and full rest between "reps."

Pure speed runs are usually at distances between 30 and 60 meters at 95 to 99% intensity with complete recovery between runs. These short runs mainly develop the alactic or phosphate energy system. Starts are a popular training method to develop reaction, acceleration, and speed.

Speed endurance runs are longer usually from 150 meters to 300 meters. Recovery rests are about three to six minutes for 90 to 95% intensities respectively. At 98% speed, the recovery rest could be up to about 10 minutes. Speed endurance allows the ability to hold speed longer and with less slowing at the end of a race, improves acceleration and results in faster recovery after a repetition or race. To build speed endurance, increase the sprint distance every week and decrease the recovery time.

Tempo runs, continuous, at 65 to 75% max speed are required in between hard days for recovery, to improve the cardiovascular fitness, and to develop capillaries and mitochondria. These runs cannot be neglected entirely, even in the weeks preceding competition considering that the 200 meter and the 400 meter races are respectively about 14% and 30% aerobic.

TECHNIQUE

Sprinting requires particular attention to conditioning the neural pathways and the fast twitch fibers. The correct motion must be executed over and over; incorrect motion confuses and slows progress. Any established incorrect motions may take weeks to correct. Therefore, it is important to work on technique when fresh and not fatigued mentally or physically. Fatigue is counter productive to develop neuromuscular movements. Visualization is also a powerful method to learn the correct motion.
There are several aspects to work on:

- Relaxation
- Start
- Acceleration
- Maintenance of speed after acceleration
- Drills (particularly high knee lift)
- Stride frequency and stride length
- Form (relaxed jaw, shoulders and arms; running tall on balls of feet, with correct arm carriage and action)

FORM

Form improvement can result in increased stride length and increased running economy. Running more upright with chest out and butt in allows a longer stride. In this position, the upright runner can move more freely. At foot contact, after the recovery phase, the runner's center of gravity should be above the foot. Stride length can be increased as long as the foot does not touch the ground ahead of the center of gravity. If there is overstriding, the foot makes contact ahead of the center of gravity and there is braking.

High knee lift is stressed by many sprint coaches. It is important that the knees be lifted as high as you can, but you should still feel comfortable and relaxed. A high knee lift forces the runner to push harder on the rear foot prior to the recovery phase. Conversely, a forceful push of the rear foot causes high knee lift.

Form Drill

The following are medium speed strides over a 50-meter course. Walk back after each run.

1. Run tall and on the balls of the feet.
2. Run with a long stride.
3. Run with high knees.
4. Run putting all the above together.

DRILLS FOR SPRINTERS

Drills for sprinters involve benefits in one or more of the following categories: relaxation and flexibility, form, reaction time, turnover, spring action, injury prevention, strength and endurance. The drills exaggerate the various efficient running movements; hence making it possible to maintain good form automatically throughout the race and particularly at the end when fatigue sets in.

Drills are normally done at a reasonably intense effort but while relaxed. They are normally done during warm-up; since form is being practiced, it is best to do these when well rested. Drills are preferably done on soft surfaces. The high knee, foreleg extension, butt kick, and ankle bounce drill are usually done in two or three sets of about 25 meters in length.

High Knee Drill (A's)

1. The runner *marches* on the balls of the feet with thigh of lead leg lifted high above horizontal. Lower the lead leg to under the body, concentrating on minimum contact time with the floor. Think "hot coals." The minimum contact time works on developing fast neurophysical response, and causes a bounce upward into the high knee position.
2. As above but *running* at a slow pace.
3. *Rapid arm/knee pumping* moving nearly as fast as possible. This improves stride rate[3].
4. *Attach weights* above the knee. March briskly with high knees for about 20 meters or more. Recover. Do several repeats when used to it. Work up to this tough drill gradually, as it puts extra stress on the lower body.

Advantages: This drill builds the habit of high knee action and strengthens the hip flexor muscles required for high knee lift. High knee action lengthens the stride, adds to the force that the pushing leg applies to the ground, and permits the lead foot to be moving faster when it makes contact with the ground. This drill also loosens the hips and hamstrings[1].

Foreleg Extension Drill (B's)

This drill is an exaggeration of normal running. The runner moves at moderate speed while the lead thigh drives high, as in the "A" drill above, and the foreleg is then whipped forward to fully extended. Now the leg is brought through ground contact in a powerful motion with toes up. Some say, "Kill that roach." The toes should be pointed upward to minimize braking on contact with the ground. Brush the ground with the foot. Contact the ground with the ball of the foot emphasizing minimum contact time. The leg now the support leg goes back straight. On the return, the heel approaches the buttock. Then the foot extends outward as the knee is raised high again. Maintain good arm movement. This drill can be done also while standing on land or in the shallow end of a swimming pool.

Advantages: The reach of the foreleg is important to good speed technique because it increases the stride length and in the extended position, it can whip quickly downward and backward. Thus the foreleg is moving quickly when the foot makes contact with the ground resulting in greater speed. It's also a good drill to strengthen the hamstring and to prevent hamstring injury.

Butt Kick Drill

1. Move aggressively and very quickly with tiny steps, exaggerating the swing back of the lower legs such that the heel touches and rebounds off the buttocks on each step. Arms hang loosely at the sides or with short fast swing. The upper legs barely move.
2. As above, but every fourth step is an exceptionally fast butt kick.

Advantages: This drill stretches and strengthens the quadriceps muscles and improves the recovery action of the leg. The driving leg flexes and moves forward after the driving foot leaves the ground. The high foot during the recovery part of the stride enables a short lever and fast return of the leg. Increased flexion causes a speed-up recovery of the leg, whereas limited flexion results in slower speed during the recovery phase and hence lower overall speed.

Ankle Bounce Drill

This is a drill devised by Bud Winter, the famous San Jose State coach. With knees locked, the runner swings each leg forward and moves as in a military type of march, but faster. All leg motion is in front of the body.

Advantages: This movement causes the ankles to flip resulting in the lower leg and ankle doing most of the work, thus strengthening the lower legs and increasing the range of ankle movement.

Quick Feet Drill

1. Take as many tiny steps as possible in a 5 to 8-second interval. Accelerate for about 15 to 20 meters immediately after. Walk back. Repeat. Feet move up and down rapidly, close to the ground, moving in front of the body, and not behind or under the body. The arms move in unison but movement is short. An excellent drill. I can do about 100 steps in 15 seconds; be careful since this can be stressful; I recommend doing warm-up strides first if attempting 100 rapid footsteps.
2. A variation of the quick feet drill is the same as above except the arms hang loosely by the sides; this causes the whole upper body to be super relaxed and the feet can move faster than above. I call this the "rag doll shuffle" (my invention as I have not seen it anywhere). I recommend this before a race to relax the upper body and to fire up (awaken) the fast twitch muscles.
3. Similar to 1, alternate jog and small quick footsteps, about 4 to 6 meters each, maintaining loose arms; go for about 50 meters and repeat (Payton Jordan[1]).
4. Excessively fast feet running on the spot, referred to as "egg shell running" by Payton Jordan.

Advantages: These drills work on improving stride frequency, reaction time and developing fast twitch muscles. Also useful for loosening up during warm-up[1].

Foot Bouncing

Stand on one foot, bounce the opposite foot up and down on the toes as rapidly as possible. The bouncing knee is slightly bent and contact is behind the stationary foot. The bouncing foot barely leaves the ground. ("The Lord of the (River) Dance" has the world record for the number of foot contacts in one second.)

Advantages: Improves stride frequency, reaction time and activates fast twitch muscles. Helps to develop fast feet.

Fast Arms Drill

1. Here is one of my favorite drills. In a standing position, move the arms fast as in sprinting while concentrating on relaxation and form. You will find you can move the arms much faster than when running. (Starting a few weeks before competition I do repeats of 200 meters, 300 meters, and 400 meters in front of a mirror assuming each arm movement represents a 2-meter stride. The heart rate does not go as high as for running so the rest can be much shorter. I can do 200 arm movements (400 meters equivalent) in about 43 seconds ,i.e., less than Michael Johnson's 400 meters world record.

2. Some do this drill with light weights, about three to five pounds in each hand, at a slower rate.
3. Some hurdlers prefer to do this exercise while sitting on the ground followed by lead arm and trail arm action after every three steps (i.e., after every three arm movements).

Advantages: This is an excellent drill to learn relaxation of the upper body during running, and to work the fast twitch muscles.

Single Leg Rotation Drill

Stand facing a low wall or hurdle leaning forward and grasping the wall or hurdle with both hands. Start with right knee high. In a fast, smooth motion go through one cycle from high knee to foot brushing the ground swinging back and returning immediately to the original position. Keep toes pointing up. The foot describes a circular motion as in bicycling. Do about ten cycles on each leg, always stopping after each cycle.

Advantages: This is a speed dynamics drill to improve reaction time.

STRIDE RATE AND STRIDE LENGTH

It is no secret that speed equals stride rate times stride length. For example, 2 meter/step at 5 steps per second = 10 meters per second or 100 meters in 10 seconds. Research shows that overspeed training (see below) for four to eight weeks improves the stride rate and stride length[2].

Note: one stride = two steps

Stride Rate

Stride rate is more important than leg strength. Leg strength increases stride length but greater gains in speed can be achieved by working on stride rate. Stride rate can be improved by overspeed training to condition the nervous system. Some of the popular methods are:

1. ***Downhill sprinting*** on smooth soft surfaces, such as grass, earth or wood chips. This also improves stride length. A hard surface could result in injury so it is not recommended. A slope between one to three degrees is usually recommended. A slope too steep causes braking in the stride and defeats the purpose. Ideally, the downhill portion should be followed by a flat portion of about 20 meters. Completing the run on this flat portion at the same speed,

taking advantage of the downhill momentum, allows the speed effect to further set into the neural pathways; this gives the feeling of running at higher speed on the flat. One disadvantage is the soft surface of grass or wood chips has a slowing down effect. However, I have found that near maximum speed can be obtained on a smooth-packed earth trail of about 1.5 degrees slope (about 2.5m rise in 100m).

2. ***Rubber tubing towing,*** usually on a rubberized track, is often used. Most surgical tubing can stretch to six times its unstretched length and this should not be exceeded (Dintiman, Ward, Tellez[2]). Safety precautions are required. Rubber tubing towing is stressful and is likely to result in soreness afterward so proceed gradually from week to week. In view of the high intensity, do not attempt when tired.
3. ***High-speed stationary cycling.*** It is considered feasible to achieve the equivalent of 5.5 to 7.1 steps per second in stationary cycling or spinning compared to 5 steps per second for a top male sprinter (Dintiman[3]). There are the equivalent of two steps to every revolution of the cycle, so 5 steps per second on the track is equivalent to 150 revs per minute. This is more feasible on a spinning cycle, i.e., with a flywheel in front. Most runners, particularly those not used to cycling and without access to a spinning cycle, would have trouble in achieving this high rpm.
4. ***Standing start and block start.*** These force the athlete into rapid turnover with short stride initially. In the standing start (three point support), it is essential to practically fall over before taking off.

Stride Length

Stride length can be improved by:

- Strength training for the legs
- Plyometrics
- Increased flexibility
- Improved form

Strength training (see Chapter 19) of the legs and plyometrics are the most important methods to improve stride length. For frequency of sessions, see Table 6.1 below.

PLYOMETRICS

Plyometrics should be an essential part of the sprinters training in view of its many advantages including explosive power. See Chapter 18 on Dynamic Warm-up and the detailed Chapter 17 on Plyometrics.

FLEXIBILITY

Flexibility helps to prevent injuries but it also has two other advantages:

1. ***Greater extension of ligaments, tendons and muscles.*** With increased flexibility, the athlete is able to fully extend the hip, knee and ankle joints; and there is greater extension of muscles and tendons. This allows greater acceleration as the driving foot leaves the ground to start the recovery phase. The increased acceleration is from the equation below:

   Force = Mass times Acceleration

   $F = M \times dV/dt$

where V is velocity and t is time

Full extension of the driving leg during the propulsive thrust, F, comes particularly from ankle flexibility (plantar flexion): this results in a small angle between the lower leg and the ground. The smaller angle results in greater horizontal force (greater horizontal velocity and longer stride) and less vertical force (less bobbing up and down). The overall effect of this increased flexibility is faster, smoother running with greater economy.

Sitting on the heels with extended feet pointing backward will improve this particular ankle flexibility[4]; be careful of this initially. Stretching of the soleus and gastronemeus calf muscles stretches the Achilles and ankle at the same time and assists to achieve the above advantages. Also, the greater the flexibility of the hips, the longer the stride will be. I am a great believer in any exercise to stretch the hips. In this regard, the hurdle drills are very beneficial.

2. ***Muscle and joint resistance is decreased.*** With improved flexibility of muscles and mobility of joints, the range of muscular and joint resistance will be decreased and the resultant propulsive force, F, will be higher without any additional expenditure of energy (Tolsma[4]).

REACTION DRILLS

Speed dynamic drills (split second rapid movements) are required to condition the neural pathways. Some sprinters have used the punching bag (e.g., 100 meter Olympic champion Allan Wells of Scotland) to improve reaction time and speed. Other means are quick feet drills and fast arm movement drills described above. See 24-"Principle of Neural Training" in Chapter 5 for more details.

Practicing starts also improves reaction time. Starts from blocks or from a three point stance are the most popular reaction drills. The runner is held for one to three seconds with the coach calling, "Set, go!" If you don't have a coach, a tape recorder with variable delays between "set" and "go" would suffice.

PERSONAL EXPERIENCE TO DEVELOP SPEED

I have found the following very effective:

- Running downhill on a 2- to 4-degree slope to improve both stride length and rate; this is recommended on a smooth earth surface;
- Fast arms running motion in front of a mirror to develop relaxed speed: this can be done much faster than in a race so that in a race, the upper body will be relaxed;
- Fast feet drill; small rapid steps;
- Making a conscious effort to concentrate on turnover, particularly during ins and outs (accelerate, coast, accelerate, coast);
- Running with loose jaw and relaxed neck, and tall on the toes;
- Running lots of sprint races;
- Hurdle drills help to develop strength; speed also comes from strength; 300m hurdle races also helped my speed endurance in the flat 400m races and vice versa;
- Training at a relaxed 95% speed, not 100%.

SEASONAL SCHEDULES FOR SPRINTERS

A year of training is normally divided into three phases: base training, pre-season and in-season. Initially, there is more emphasis on stamina (aerobic endurance) involving long repeats (up to about 800 meters) and hill work. The broader the base of conditioning, the higher the peak of speed work that can be developed later during the in-season or sharpening phase. It is important to retain speed, even in the base building phase where quality training should not be neglected. The overall program progresses from slow to fast, from less intense to more intense, and from quantity to less quantity. The workouts progress from easy to difficult but the athlete should not find it difficult in view of the gradual adaptation. In the early phases, there is more emphasis on strength training, such as medicine ball, hills, weights and plyometrics but gradually these are reduced in favor of more pure speed and speed endurance workouts. These trends are shown in the table below, which reflects the *typical* situation for base, pre-season and in-season phases.

TABLE 6.1 • SEASONAL SCHEDULES

Activity	Base	Pre-season	In-season
	• Aerobic Endurance • Some Speed • Strength	• Speed • Speed Endurance • Strength • Technique	• Speed • Speed Endurance • Less Strength • Technique
	• Quantity • Limited Intensity	• Quantity • Intensity	• Less Quantity • More Intensity
Aerobic/Tempo	• Long easy runs • 3–4 days/week	• Shorter faster runs • 3 days/week	• Recovery on easy days • 2–3 days/week
Anaerobic **Note 1**	Gradual buildup to 3 days/week	3 days/week	3 days/week
Stretching	Warm-up and cool down	Warm-up and cool down	Warm-up and cool down
Weights	• 2 days/week first month. • 3 days/week thereafter.	• 2 to 3 days/week	• 1 day/week Stop 2 to 3 weeks before main race.
Note 7	See the chapter on Weight Training		
Hills/Stairs **Note 2**	• 2 days/week • Increase gradually	• 1–2 days/week	• 1 day/week
Plyometrics **Note 7**	• 1 day/week initially • 2 days/week later	• 2 days/week • possibly 1 day/ week a whole workout including drills	• 1 day/week
Drills	3 days/week	• During warm-up • See above	During warm-up
Speed Technique **Note 3**	Yes	• 2 days/week	• 2 days/week
Medicine Ball	Lots	Yes	Cut back
Speed **Note 4**	1 day/week on soft surfaces	2–3 days/week **Note 5**	2–3 days/week **Note 5**
Starts	Near end of base, if at all	2 days/week	2 days/week
Speed Endurance **Note 6**	No	1–2 days/week	1–2 days/week
Rest	1 day/week	1 day/week	1 day/week
Competition	None	Some low-key competitions	Main competitions

Note 1: Includes hills, speed, and speed endurance intervals. After most anaerobic workouts, slow 100m strides (about four to six) are recommended to break up lactic acid in muscles, reduce soreness and stiffness and to work on technique (e.g., exaggerated arm movement, good knee lift) when the athlete is somewhat tired.

Note 2: Mainly uphill; runs up to about 30 seconds on the hill with short recovery run on top. Some fast downhill running on a slope about two degrees and on soft surfaces is also recommended. No hills on week of race.

Note 3: Includes drills and work on form. Less in base phase.

Note 4: Short runs and accelerations (<60m or less than seven seconds).

Note 5: Includes starts (<30m). Includes overspeed training (e.g., rubber tubing) one day per week.

Note 6: This could be combined after a speed session on the same day if total volume is not overdone and rests are carefully observed. Short sprinters (100m – 200m types) once per week with "reps" of 100 to 300m. Usually 150m "reps" for 100m types, and 250m or 300m reps for 200m types. Long sprinters (200m–400m types) one to two times per week with "reps" of 150m to 500m.

Note 7: Normal sequence: warm-up, plyometrics, running training, weight training, or weights and plyometrics preferably done on separate days if more intense.

Some well-respected coaches use nearly the same routine of speed and speed endurance all year round (apart from an active rest phase), but proceed from slower to faster and with more quantity to less quantity. The Charlie Francis system described below is tailored to retain a good deal of the speed gained in the late competitive season into the following base phase.

Main Training Emphasis

The main training emphasis can be determined by observing the required heart rate during the race and the main energy system involved in the race:

TABLE 6.2

Race	**Heart Rate**	**Main Training Emphasis (Secondary Emphasis)**
100m	100%MHR	Alactic, (Anaerobic Lactic)
200m	100%MHR	Alactic/Anaerobic Lactic
400m	100%MHR	Anaerobic Lactic, (Alactic)

Aerobic conditioning on easy recovery days is still important in sprinting. See Table 1.1 for the aerobic contribution in sprint events.

CHARLIE FRANCIS SPRINT SYSTEM

Charlie Francis, former coach of Ben Johnson, is considered by many to be the top sprint coach in the world. His runners produced 32 world records. In the 1984 Olympics, the Optimists Track Club where Charlie was the main coach, won 8 of 14 medals or almost 80% of Canada's track and field output. Possibly Charlie's greatest strength in coaching was his intuitive ability to be in tune with his athletes, abilities, and their readiness to proceed to increasing loads when healthy and when recovering from injury. This description does not do justice to the overall complexity of the training, and fine-tuning, but nevertheless lists some of his philosophies that have worked so successfully for his world-class athletes. Some of his comprehensive system is described below with his permission and editing:

- For experienced athletes, shorter and shorter periods of general preparation (base training) were practiced at the beginning of each training year. This allowed longer periods of specific training; this also retained the speed that could be lost in long periods of base/aerobic training, thus detracting from speed capabilities already developed the previous year.
- Periodization in training was practiced as follows: Three microcycle (week) series of step-like progressive loadings were followed with the fourth week dropping back in intensity to near the second week. Each month was progressively more intense. He used triple periodization during the year, with the summer divided into two peaks in view of its length. Thus supercompensation training was followed over the month and also during the weekly schedule. (See "14 Principle of Supercompensation" in Chapter 5.)
- Following an emphasis on stamina (general or cardiovascular fitness) there was a great emphasis on *low volume high intensity* central nervous system (CNS) training (intensive accelerations, starts, medicine ball work, weights, and plyometrics)
- Elements of maximum strength (particularly 1/2 squats, bench press, pulldowns behind the neck, and power cleans) were carried out year-round. Apart from fast circuit training, the number of lifts were minimal at near maximum loads. Two maximum strength phases were planned, one before the indoor season and the other before the outdoor season. Intensive weights were avoided following high-speed workouts (100%) but were acceptable following tempo or up to 95% speed workouts.
- A great emphasis was placed on massage and regeneration to enable up to 40% more central nervous system (CNS) "power" training time. Charlie's personal involvement in the massage of his athletes allowed him first hand knowledge of their muscle tone, and hence their ability to progress or back off in their training.
- Speedwork only sessions (never two days in a row) with complete recovery, totaled up to about 2200 meters per week, but only when the athlete was completely fresh. Mostly alactic system work, i.e., full or near full efforts under seven seconds. No overspeed devices were used.

- Tempo runs (65 to 80% max velocity) for recovery, and increased cardiovascular fitness were practiced during the entire year, 100 to 300 meters at least three times per week, totaling about 2000 to 2400 meters per session. These runs often incorporated push-ups, abdominal exercises or other upper body strength work.
- Speed endurance runs (competitive speeds), of 150 to 300 meters, once per week. Usually two "reps" with full recovery between, but shorter distances or none as competition approaches. Speedwork plus speed endurance totaled about 3,300 meters per week.
- The athlete determined what could be handled safely, and if they were prepared and motivated to perform a training element at 92 to 98% effort. Ultimately, they had the final say in their own training.
- After a personal best in intense CNS training, or if performance intensity or form dropped off, this phase of the workout was stopped.
- The training program was flexible depending on what the coach (Charlie) saw, and how the athlete felt and what the athlete was capable of at the time.
- The great importance of peaking before the race was achieved for example as follows: A speed endurance session 10 days before, followed by alternate days of tempo and speed (4x30 meters plus one longer run, both at 95 percent intensity reducing from about 270 meters to 120 meters total per day), with day five and day one before off.
- Charlie Francis emphasizes in the "Speed Trap": for a quick start, the athlete must concentrate on what to do when the gun sounds, i.e., focus on moving the lead hand as quickly as possible in a slight inner rotation. [It is a scientific fact that the arm action precedes the leg action by an imperceptible amount.]

SPRINT TECHNIQUES FROM PAYTON JORDAN

Payton Jordan offers the following valuable sprint techniques and tips plus many others in this reference[1] and others. At 85 (an inspiration to all master runners) with many world age group records in the 100 and 200, he is further qualified as he was Head Track Coach at Stanford U. and the 1968 USA Olympic Track Coach.

- *"Your feet are reactive like a bouncing ball.*
- *Feet and ankles should be tough, quick and elastic.*
- *Push hard with the contact foot to get full extension.*
- *Heel on recovery must be tight (close to buttocks).*
- *Knee lift should not be aggressive, and with no over-reach of stride.*
- *Shoulders must be relaxed and not up, with loose hands and jaw, and thumbs loosely against the outside of the index fingers.*

- *Run loose, fluid, faster but not harder.*
- *Prepare for months ahead of your race. Imagine your race several times before so things are familiar when you get there.*
- *In the start position, the first two spikes are in contact with the track to prevent 'popping up.'*
- *Before the start inhale and exhale fully; on 'set' hold a deep breath, and exhale immediately after the gun.*
- *Think of the starts as an 'explosion' and driving your legs through the top of your head.*
- *In the 100 meters sprint, think 'down hill to the tape' after about 65 meters; it is a positive downhill thinking [a great relaxing idea].*
- *Go through the tape as fast as you can and 10 meters beyond.*
- *Pay strict attention to strong abdominals, obliques and hip flexors in training.*
- *Do 'arm quickies' as fast as possible at the track or in front of a mirror concentrating on relaxed shoulders and face.*
- *Fast feet drills also help to work on improving the speed of the nerve system, e.g., fast in-place running ('egg shell running').*
- *For sprint strength: use hills; carry out a weight program three times a week, usually after running, for maximum results ,e.g., 'half squats' with 50 to 75 percent of body weight, and 'goose stepping' with at least 35% of body weight.*
- *Develop speed with 30, 50, and 70 meter repeats at near full speed.*
- *Successful sprinters have high levels of confidence and self-esteem.*
- *Train first for speed and then endurance."*

Payton says, *"The race is a beautiful note in music; it is like a beautiful piece of writing or poetry. It is a spiritual thing; it is like an artist making beautiful strokes."*

100 Meters

At the start, the force of the forward and upward arm drive dictates the duration and magnitude of the opposing foot's thrust. A powerful quick arm action will be translated into a powerful quick thrust on the blocks by action and reaction. Therefore, the arm movements must be vigorous. This is where upper body strength helps. A common fault is to stand up too soon. Stay low with good lean, not from the waist, and head down for about 20 to 30 meters, drive hard and lift the knees. This good body lean is very evident in watching world-class sprinters during the acceleration phase.

The athlete can only accelerate up to about 60 metes and hold top speed for only about 15 meters. The sprinter's secret is to maintain a relaxed style of running after this without decreasing the force of the drive and not trying to increase speed after reaching top speed. Trying harder at this stage will only result in slower speed. After top speed is reached, the stride frequency can be maintained by slightly reducing the angle between the upper and lower arms. (This technique is useful in the finishing kick of any race.)

Without speed endurance the athlete (although in good condition) will be able to do well only up to about 50 meters. I found this out in a 100 meter race after training only for cross-country during the previous month.

200 Meters

The athlete accelerates to full speed in about 40 to 60 meters, maintains this speed in a coast or float of 100 meters running relaxed as possible after accelerating out of the curve. Without this relaxation there could be a slowing down in the last 30 or 40 meters. Aim to finish strong with high frequency.

400 Meters

The 400 meters is considered by many to be the most difficult and taxing race in the world. In my experience, if one is in great shape, has good pace judgement and has run lots of 400-meter races recently then it can feel no harder than a 200-meter race. This also assumes no gale is blowing. However, too often, runners have poor pace judgement considering their condition. Then he or she runs into excess fatigue near the end of the race; this results in high lactic acid, reduced efficiency, inability to lift the knees, and a much slower pace. Ideally with plenty of training at race pace and race experience, the pace is adjusted to delay fatigue to just before the end of the race.

The 400-meter race is 70% anaerobic and 30% aerobic, which indicates roughly the proportion of time to be spent on these energy systems. Generally, the 400-meter race time is 2 x best 200-meter race time plus about 2.5 to 4 seconds. Therefore, the 400 time improves as the 200m time improves. In the World Championships in Buffalo in 1995, my differential was 3 seconds. Alternatively, in competition, a man can run the 1st 200 meters within less than one second of his best 200 meters without slowing down more than about one second in the 2nd 200 meters. According to past world record holder Lee Evans, ideally the second 200 meters should only be one second slower than the first 200 meters[6]. This is close to Michael Johnson's even world record pace, i.e., less than one second between the first and second 200's.

Strategy:

Have a race strategy. Check your lane before the race for stones, holes, and dips.

The race can be divided into four equal segments all fast but relaxed. Don't strain to pass. Don't panic if passed. Run your own race.

1st 100m – **Burst**

Burst out of the blocks at top speed. Accelerate into and through the curve. In the curve the right arm is swung slightly across the chest. Burst out of the turn. Adrenaline will provide the extra energy due to the initial high speed without loss of physical strength.

2nd 100m – **Glide**

Float down the back straight relaxed with long stride[6]. Think "faster looser." The first 200m is as close to maximum speed as possible without folding in the home stretch.

3rd 100m – **Push**

Pump arms vigorously. Run aggressively. Attempt to pick it up; this is not really possible but minimizes deceleration. You should feel some acceleration as you leave the turn into the home stretch. Run the first 300 meters fast no matter how you feel.

4th 100m – **Lift**

Emphasize relaxation and good form but with speed. Think of good form rather than of your opponents. Exaggerated arm movements with hands up to the eyes will lift the knees and reduce fatigue. Think of high knees, pumping the arms and relaxation[6]. Don't tense up. Normally, the winner is the one who slows down the least in the home stretch.

Training

The champion 400 meter runner has to be in superb condition–an unusual specimen; this involves correct, consistent training; but also a healthy, dedicated lifestyle. He or she has to do almost a double training workload. This includes starts, accelerations, 150's, 200's, 250's, 300's, some 500's and even an occasional 600m. Run as many 250's as possible at 90 to 99% speed staying as relaxed as possible; these are my favorite distance for 400-meter training. This training must involve the usual sprint work, i.e., short sprints up to 60 or 70 meters. Even if you are a 400/800-meter runner, one day a week is recommended on sprint training (about 600m total at 95% speed). Always run at 95 to 99% speed when maximum speed is attempted. The hills, weight training, drills and plyometrics in the table above are essential. Long aerobic runs to build endurance should not be neglected. Two days before a meet, run 30- to 60-meter accelerations about 6 times at about 95% speed. The next day keep off the feet as much as possible.

Concentrate on shorter reps at near race pace from the beginning of the speedwork phase rather than longer and slower reps. As condition improves, graduate from reps of 100m to 150m to 200m and finally to 250m, and occasional 300m, and with shorter rests as condition improves. Always run relaxed at race pace with good rhythm, never straining, as this indicates proceeding too rapidly in the training, i.e., training above one's present level of condition. In latter stages for speed endurance, there is a concentration on 250m reps as longer reps tax the system too much. For example, 4 x 250m is less stressful than 3 x 300m with the same rest, and more relaxed speed and volume can be obtained with 250's. Speed endurance, i.e., sustainable speed also is developed from 200m reps with short rest and many 400m races. It is essential to have good 200m speed and to reach the first 200m at close to one second slower than your best 200m. Practice until you can do this consistently in training.

Ideally, you should be only one or two seconds slower than your target race pace about six weeks before your main race. Run frequent 400-meter races. With each race, confidence and pace judgement builds and the body adjusts to the faster pace.

Typical 400 meter tried and proven workouts we have used (in the North York Track Club), plus a few others are as follows:

All the workouts below are complete apart from five or six 150m slow repeats at end of the workout. There should be lots of workouts at near current 400-meter race pace. The pace below for the repetitions is current 400-meter race pace or slightly faster unless otherwise mentioned. If necessary, adjust the pace and rest so you are not completely exhausted after each "rep" and you can finish the workout without slowing down and still be in good form. Note: beats per minute of the heart = b.p.m.

- 8 to 10 x 100m: Start slower in initial "reps" than 400m race pace and run progressively faster in each "rep," "rep" 4 or 5 is at race pace, end up faster than race pace. Walk back and rest about 30 seconds more after each "rep." Work on relaxation and form.
- 3 sets (250m at race pace, rest until heart rate returns to below 120 b.p.m., repeat) 6 minutes between sets or until heart returns to below 96 b.p.m.
- 3 or 4 sets (250m at race pace, rest 75 to 90 seconds, run 150m at race pace or faster) rest between sets until heart returns to below 96 b.p.m.
- 2 or 3 x 500m accelerations, start below 800m race pace and gradually speed up, ending up faster than 800m race pace in the last 100m.
- 6 to 8 x 150m at race pace or slightly faster, repeat when heart rate returns to below 110 b.p.m.
- 3 or 4 x 300m at race pace with full rest between each "rep".
- 300m at race pace, rest 60 to 75 seconds, run 100m fast as you can, rest about 8 minutes. Repeat 3 times if you can. This is a tough workout; save it for about three or four weeks before major competition. Ideally, there would be at least three sessions of this workout in the last month of the sharpening phase.
- Lee Evans, past 400m world record holder (who trained under Bud Winter), would do up to 3 x 500m once per week starting in February at a fast pace with each month progressively faster. He never liked them[6]. But it paid off.

New 400 Meter Training Workouts

All runs are at 400m race pace unless otherwise specified.

- 80m, rest 1 minute, 100m, rest 90 seconds, 120m, rest 2 minutes, 150m, rest 3 minutes, 200m, rest 3.5 minutes, 250m. The 250m is at 400m race pace; other distances are at between 400m race pace and full speed.
- 100m,100m,150m, 150m, 200m, 200m. Rest between each until heart returns to 90 to 96 b.p.m.
- 100m, rest 75 seconds,100m, rest 2 minutes, 150m, rest 2 minutes, 150m, rest 3.5 minutes, 250m, rest 3.5 minutes, 250m. Alternatively, end up with 250m at race pace, followed by a 200m at faster than race pace instead of 2 x 250m.
- 2 x 50m, 2 x 150m, 2 x 250m. Rest between each until heart rate drops to 90 b.p.m.
- 100m, rest 90 seconds, 100m, walk 4 minutes, 2 sets (250m, walk 100m, 150m), walk 4 minutes between sets.
- 3 x 100m, 90 seconds rest between 100's, rest 2 minutes, 150m, rest 3 minutes, 200m, rest 4 minutes, 300m, rest 1 minute 100m. The 200m and 300m at 400m race pace except 100's and the 150m are slightly faster.
- 4 x100m at faster than race pace, rest 90 seconds between 100's, rest 3 to 4 minutes, 3 x 250m, rest 3.5 minutes between.
- 2 or 3 sets (150m, rest, 150m, rest, 100m). Rest 5 to 6 minutes between sets. In initial weeks of speedwork phase, the 150's and 100m are at present race pace with 1 minute walk rest. In the 2nd set of a session, readjust the 150m time and/or the rest. In the first set: if the 100m was slower than race pace, run slower 150's or increase the rest times; but if the 100m was faster than race pace, run faster 150's or decrease rest times.
- 3 sets (200m + 5 seconds, rest 2 minutes, 200m + 0 seconds). Rest 8 to 10 minutes between sets.
- 3 sets (250m + 7 seconds, rest 2.5 minutes, 200m + 0 seconds). Rest 8 to 10 minutes between sets.
- 4 to 5 x 300m + 5 seconds. Rest 1.5 to 2 minutes between each.
- 3 sets (20m easy, 40m hard, 20m easy). Rest 2 minutes or more between sets. Next do 4 x 100m at between full out and 400m race pace with 1.5 to 2 minutes rest between reps.
- 5 to 7 x 100m with 50m walk rest. It is best to run over the same 100m stretch and reverse directions after each 100m. Some elite runners are able to do 2 sets and go faster on each rep. A tough workout–be careful.
- 4 x 200m at pace between best current 200m and current 400m race pace. Go faster on each of the first 3 reps. The last rep is same speed as the first rep. Rest 6 to 8 minutes between.

- 5 x 200m with decreasing rests of 4, 3, 2.5 and 2 minutes between reps. Good for speed endurance between weeks 2 to 6 before main competition.
- 2 sets (250m, rest 2 minutes, 200m). Rest 8 to 10 minutes between sets.

REFERENCES

1. Jordan, P., Payton Jordan's Sprinting Techniques, Part I and Part II, August 1999 and September 1999, *National Masters News*, Hollywood, CA.
2. Dintiman G., Ward B., Tellez T., *Sports Speed,* 2nd Edition, Human Kinetics, Champaign, IL, 1997.
3. Dintiman G., *How To Run Faster,* Leisure Press, West Point, NY, 1984.
4. Tolsma B., Flexibility and Velocity, *Running Times*, June 1982.
5. Hagerman C., *How to Increase Speed and Agility,* Perigree Books, Putnam Publishing, 1986.
6. Evans Lee, *Planning Training and Racing for Quality 400 Meters,* Presented at the IX International Track and Field Coaches' Congress, Santa Monica, July 30, 1984.
7. Lamb D. R., Basic Principles for Improving Sport Performance, *Gatorade Sports Science Institute,* No 55, Volume 8(1995), Number 2.
8. Chu, D. A., *Jumping Into Plyometrics,* Human Kinetics, Champaign IL, 1998.

CHAPTER 7

"They shall mount up with wings as eagles: they shall run, and not be weary." Isaiah

GENERAL TRAINING THEORY FOR DISTANCE RUNNERS

To know not *how* is to go slow or so-so. But training know-how applied is speed indeed. Enthusiasm and dedication are not enough; without training knowledge, it is like running a marathon in army boots. The general training theory for distance runners is described below.

WHAT IS INVOLVED IN PROPER DISTANCE TRAINING?

- Correct training distances, pace, and recovery between runs
- Correct volume of training, not too much and not too little
- All energy systems worked
- Correct proportion of training time on the five training systems according to the athlete's specific event
- Correct recovery time between training sessions
- Long enough adaptation time

ENERGY SYSTEMS

There are many types of training for distance running, each one varying in intensity and duration and involving different energy systems. Since most sports utilize fuel produced by all the energy systems, training has to expose the athletes to all energy systems, throughout the sharpening/competitive phase. The energy systems occur mainly over the following approximate ranges while undergoing maximum or near maximum effort (except aerobic conditioning and anaerobic threshold training, which are well below maximum):

Table 7.1 • Range of Energy Systems

Main Range:	**Predominate Energy System:**
0 to 30 seconds	**Phosphate or Alactic System**
20 seconds up to 2 minutes	**Anaerobic Lactic Acid (LA) System** (Glycogen without O_2 produces LA)
1 minute to hours	**Aerobic System*** (Glycogen with O_2, no LA produced)

*The aerobic system includes **aerobic capacity** training (VO_2max), **aerobic conditioning** and **anaerobic threshold** training. With these three aerobic systems, there are a total of five *energy* systems, which result in five *training* systems discussed below.

See also Chapter 1 for a more detailed explanation of the energy systems.

INTERVAL TRAINING

The training systems are based on interval training or continuous runs. **Interval training** is a number of repetitions or **"reps"** with rest intervals in-between to recover. To enable a greater volume of work in a workout with less stress, the workout is divided into **sets**, i.e., a number of "reps" per set with rest between sets usually several times longer than the rest between "reps." Interval training is used to develop the anaerobic lactic (speed) system, the VO_2max system, or the anaerobic threshold system.

Some countries, e.g., England, sometimes refer to the fast part (the specified distance) of the interval training as the interval. The North American terminology is used herein: technically, the interval is the rest period between the "reps;" and it is common to refer to "reps" interspersed with rest periods as interval training or "intervals."

Rest Interval

Most of the training effect comes during the rest interval when the heart adapts to the stress of the exercise. When exercise stops, stroke volume is raised beyond the initial value and remains there for about 20 seconds. The greatest stimulus for heart development occurs during the first 10 seconds of the rest interval; this is the reason for the "interval training" terminology by the founder Gerschler of Germany[12]. Perhaps you have noticed immediately after the repeat, the heart rate increases for 10 or more seconds.

To achieve maximum training effect from interval training the rest interval between repeats must be correct—not too short and not too long. Basically, the rest interval must be brief since incomplete recovery develops the energy systems. Complete recovery is used between repeats only in developing pure anaerobic speed.

The rest between sets should not be excessive as the body will cool down too far. For example, cramping of leg muscles may occur (I have found) and could result in injury if the runner continues to run.

Rest Interval Based on Heart Rate

Using the heart rate as an indication of recovery is recommended for short anaerobic-type workouts instead of predetermined rest intervals. The latter requires a very experienced coach who is quite familiar with the capabilities of the athletes under him.

Gerschler of West Germany recommended interval training at 100 meters, 200 meters, and 400 meters with a maximum of 90 seconds between repeats and the heart rate to return during the rest interval to 120 beats per minute in less than 90 seconds, otherwise the intensity is reduced or the practice is concluded. However, in some anaerobic training, rests as short as 30 seconds are used and the heart rate could be as high as about 135 beats per minute at the start of the next repetition. For *short* anaerobic-type intervals, the heart rate is a good method for starting the next repetition.

However, for *long* repetitions, e.g., greater than 800 meters at 3K, 5K, or 10K race pace, starting the next "rep" immediately after the heart drops below 120 or 130 beats per minute (b.p.m.) could result in a rest too short, i.e., too stressful for most runners. In a fit/well trained athlete, the heart could return to about 120 or 130 b.p.m. in less than two minutes (based on my own observations and figures in Martin and Coe[1] and Costill[5]). Now the runner is "heart" ready but perhaps not "mentally" or "lactate" ready to restart. Some mental rest is required, and time is required for lactate and tiredness to subside. Recovery will also be improved in the day or two after the interval session if some additional rest is given after reaching 120 or 130 b.p.m.

But for training at the anaerobic threshold, the rest could safely be based on return to about 120 b.p.m. since these runs are not overly stressful and there is no lactate produced.

Recommended Rest Intervals

Table 7.3 below specifies run times, pace, and corresponding rest times for the different training systems. Alternatively, the following approximate equation and Table 7.2 can be used to determine the rest interval between repeats.

Speed Endurance/Anaerobic Intervals

For speed endurance intervals less than 90 seconds near 100% effort the following equation is recommended:

Rest Interval = 5 x (% of maximum effort/100)^3 x Run Time

The above is an empirical equation. The cube power allows for less rest at lower maximum effort. There is some scientific basis in the equation to account for the percentage of maximum effort since energy used during sprinting is proportional to speed to the 3.8 power (speed$^{3.8}$) from a study by Sargent reported in an article by F. Henry[7].

Slightly below 100% maximum effort is preferred for speed intervals as this is more relaxed and more apt to improve running economy compared to "flat out"; also more repeats can be done in a session and with less possibility of injury.

A rest interval of 5RT (as above) will not give complete recovery. Additional time would be required to clear all lactic acid. For pure speed training, a rest of 8 to 10 minutes may be necessary to achieve full recovery after a nearly all out 200, 300, 400, 500 or 600 meter repeat.

Intervals at Mile, 5K, and 10K Race Pace

The following table of rest time versus run time (RT) was based on my own experience, rest times from workouts of other coaches, e.g., other references[2,3,8,12], and observations and comparison of Table 4.3 by Sleamaker[15], Table 10.5 of Glover and Glover[16], and Table 5.6 of Martin and Coe[1].

Elite runners or the more competitive can take shorter rests. Or start when the heart rate drops below 60% of maximum heart rate.

Table 7.2 • Rest Time vs Run Time

Run Time	Rest Time	Race Pace
RT, minutes	minutes	
1 to 2	1 to 1.5RT	Mile
2 to 4	1RT	5K and 10K
4 to 6	0.8RT	5K and 10K
6 to 10	0.6RT	5K and 10K
>10	0.5 to 0.4RT	5K and 10K

When the run time is near 4 or 6 minutes, take an average, e.g., 0.9RT and 0.7RT respectively.

Intervals at Less than 10K Race Pace

For interval training at a pace slower than 10K race pace, multiply rest time from above by 1.25 x (% maximum effort/100)[3]. The percentage of maximum effort is the percentage of maximum speed while running over the training distance. For example, if the run distance is 800 meters at 80% maximum effort, then run time is best time over 800m (say 2 minutes) divided by 0.8 (i.e., 2 minutes/0.8).

What to Change as Adaptation Occurs?

In interval training, as adaptation occurs the intensity, volume and rest need to be adjusted. To provide more overload, either increase the pace, the number of repetitions, the length of the run, or reduce the rest or a combination of the above. The length of the runs, speed and rest in the late-season sessions build upon the length of the runs and the speed in the early season training sessions. This is a major reason for differences of opinion between coaches on how to proceed as adaptation occurs since the starting base is often different. Also, if the runner's strong suit is his speed or his endurance, the coach will usually favor shorter and longer length repeats respectively.

800 meters: Progress by increasing the speed of the anaerobic lactic runs[9]. This is because the performance at 800 meters is considered mainly anaerobic by many coaches, and it has a close correlation with 400-meter race times[10]. Rest time is also usually shortened as condition improves.

1500 meters: For **VO_2max** training, progress by increasing the length of the run, number of repeats, or if the early season pace was at 10K race pace increase to 5K (or 3K) race pace later in the season. A session at 3K race pace can be too stressful for most runners. Lengthening the run is based on the fact that the 1500-meter performance is mainly aerobic and it has a slightly closer correlation to 3000 meter times than to 400 meter times[10]. The longer runs equate more closely to the sensation in a race, according to Harry Wilson[9].

If the **anaerobic lactic** (speed) runs in initial weeks are below target race pace then it is only necessary to increase the length of the runs and/or the pace.

Generally, for 1500-meter training, it is our custom to start with slower speed, and shorter runs, and less volume and gradually increase volume and intensity (speed) and length of runs over a period of about 12 weeks. As the competition season approaches, increase the speed and reduce the volume.

Jim Ryun[11] recommends the following:

- Begin the season with a reasonable number of repeats at a good pace and short rest.
- At mid season, increase the number of repeats at a good pace and stay on a short rest.
- As the season concludes, decrease the repeats, increase the speed and have a longer recovery between runs.

5K and 10K: Here, aerobic energy is important, so volume is desirable and longer runs equate more closely to the sensations in a race. Therefore, for VO_2max training, increase the number of repetitions and reduce the recovery time, or increase the length of the "rep." (This assumes that the pace is already sufficiently fast, i.e., 5K race pace. In VO_2max [aerobic capacity] training, a faster pace can be too anaerobic).

Volume of a Session

Anaerobic lactic training. The following volumes for an anaerobic interval session exclusive of recovery would apply for an experienced runner in the in-season (sharpening). Elite runners could handle higher total volume per session and beginners much lower than listed below. The repeats are mile race pace or faster, and run time is between 30 seconds and 2 minutes.

For **800 meters**, start slow with about 1600 meters per session, progress up to about 2400 meters in the middle of the sharpening phase and later reduce down to about l200 meters as speed increases and competitions approach.

For **1500 meters**, 3000 meters to 3600 meters per session is a good total for a training session.

For **5K or 10K**, 4000 to 4800 meters is sufficient volume.
See also the last column and 2nd row of Figure 7.4.

Anaerobic threshold and VO_2max training. The volume of an anaerobic threshold (continuous or interval) session, or a VO_2max (interval) session is proportional to the total mileage per week. All this is effectively addressed by Jack Daniels' suggested mileages per session[13]. See the last column of Table 7.3 herein and the energy systems below.

THE FIVE TRAINING SYSTEMS

The five training systems essential to a distance runner are discussed below starting with the highest speed and proceeding to the slowest.

Phosphate or Alactic Training System

Description. The energy from phosphocreatine, PCr, occurs mainly in the first 10 seconds of maximum activity and is essentially depleted after about 50 seconds. For maximum exercise longer than about 30 seconds, anaerobic glycolysis provides the further anaerobic energy production. During recovery, PCr is quickly resynthesized to 50% of the original rest value by 30 to 60 seconds and to about 80% by about 2 to 4 minutes (Lamb[6]). Long rest periods are required to ensure the PCr is replaced completely before the next repetition.

One day in the fall of 1997, my training partners and I trained on a steep hill, 25 to 28 seconds up, intense effort, with a 100-meter recovery run at the top. This type of hill workout was fairly *typical* during our base training phase. The rest between the eight repeats was about 2.5 minutes. This rest was not enough for *complete* alactic recovery. So there was more dependence on the anaerobic lactic system. For the last two repeats, there was a lot of lactic (muscle tiredness or heaviness) at the top of the hill.

Advantages. The intent of this training system is to increase top speed with less effort. Relaxation is the key and requires great emphasis. For a distance runner, this training is valuable to develop a surge or a finishing kick. Also when top speed has been developed in training, the VO_2max intervals will seem easier.

Training. With runs less than about 7 seconds, the athlete's maximum speed is possible and there is no lactic acid produced, but this does not preclude muscle soreness due to muscle cell damage. Although the runs are short, the total volume needs to be restricted in view of the high intensity to avoid injury and allow recovery the following day or two. Total repeats per session should be less than about 600 meters, with 98% to 99% effort (or speed) and full recovery between repeats.

Caution. Full-out speed should be avoided in training to prevent injury, so 98 or 99% maximum speed is recommended.

Anaerobic Lactic Training System

Description. These are repetitions at 95% to 99% speed, i.e., mile race pace or faster. Therefore, the heart rate is near maximum or just below maximum and normally near full recovery between "reps." This is sometimes called ***repetition*** training[2,13] rather than interval training. Runs are normally beyond 150 meters but usually less than 500 meters in view of the high stress and high lactate produced.

Advantages. This training adapts the athlete to tolerate the increases in lactic acid at high intensity speeds, i.e., to run faster with less lactic acid buildup. With this training, the athlete increases tolerance physiologically and psychologically to the prolonged high speed at 100% maximum heart rate (100% VO_2max or greater). The middle distance events, 800 meters and 1500 meters, are run in this range where lactate builds rapidly. This training is also essential for the 3000 meters, 3000-meter steeplechase and 5K since they require a fast pace with minimum lactate accumulation. Also, in all distance races, the finishing kick that wins so many races is ineffective if the legs are loaded with lactate.

Training. To work this system, speed has to be sustained at a level high enough to cause excessive accumulation of lactic acid[3]. Where pure speed training is the purpose of the session, the heart rate should return to well below 100 beats per minute (b.p.m.) between repetitions and long enough to remove most of the lactic acid from the working muscles. Where *speed endurance* is the main purpose of the session, the heart rate could be between 120 and 135 b.p.m. before starting the next repetition. "But lactate levels continue to rise and some lactate remains at the start of the next repetition which is helpful to improve the buffering capacity" (Martin and Coe[1]). At these efforts, the heart rate is maximal or within 10 beats per minute of maximum. These workouts are stressful, however, an experienced runner could do two anaerobic interval workouts per week. Elite runners are able to tolerate two to three such workouts per week.

Jack Daniels[13] states: *"The amount of quality running in a true 'Repetition' session should be up to 5% of current weekly mileage, with an upper limit of 3 miles or 5000 meters; these represent an upper limit and not the required amount."* Daniels calls it **"Repetition"** training, whereas I call it **"Anaerobic Lactic (or Speed)"** training.

Caution. One has to be cautious with the recovery periods otherwise there are critical levels of fatigue and over-training results[3]. The athlete will know from experience when there is excess lactic acid (lead-like legs and difficulty in lifting the legs, often making breathing more labored). It is then necessary to reduce the speed and/or increase the rest interval, or end the session. The interval training also stops when form or speed drops off significantly, or sore muscles or cramps are encountered.

Also, the next rep starting at 120 b.p.m. is most applicable for athletes with maximum heart rate (MHR) near 190 to 200 b.p.m. Therefore this is not recommended for older athletes. See Recovery in Chapter 21.

Vo_2max Training

Training in the range just below VO_2max is called **aerobic capacity** training although there is a significant anaerobic component, as well. When the maximum aerobic capabilities are approached (near 100% maximum heart rate or 100% VO_2max), the VO_2max is developed.

Description. VO_2max is the milliliters of oxygen consumed by an athlete per minute per kg of body weight. It is a convenient benchmark to measure human performance in distance events. The higher the value, the better the performance. However, the true predictor of potential for a runner is the peak running velocity or work load achieved during the VO_2max test, not the actual VO_2max value. See "vVO_2max Training" in a section below.

Increased VO_2max results from improved transportation of oxygen by the circulatory system and increased extraction and utilization by the muscular system. VO_2max corresponds to 100% maximum heart rate (MHR) but the two diverge below VO_2max. For example, to achieve 50% VO_2max you exercise at about 70% of your MHR. It is possible to reach as high as about 130% VO_2max at 100%MHR for less than about 8 to 10 minutes. VO_2max is not usually known unless you have been tested recently in a human performance laboratory, although it can be determined approximately from tables knowing your mile, 5K or 10K race times. MHR is easier to measure (with a watch or heart rate monitor) and put to use. Therefore, the Table 7.4 refers to MHR instead of VO_2max.

Advantages. A high VO_2max enables a runner to use a lower percentage of his/her maximum at a given pace; hence he/she is running more comfortably at this pace than an athlete with a lower VO_2max. "The larger the VO_2max, the smaller the total anaerobic contribution at any given pace or the faster the athlete can run before anaerobic effects impair performance" (Martin and Coe[1]). The runs are stressful, and therefore improve stress tolerance and mental toughness.

VO_2max Workouts. To develop the aerobic capacity or VO_2max, longer runs near 100% MHR would seem to be in order since a one-minute run is only 30% aerobic compared to a three-minute run, which is 55% aerobic (numbers from Lamb[6]). Runs as long as 1600 meters instead of 400 meters are recommended by Pfitzinger[8] to accumulate more time at the effective training intensity. Daniels[13] recommends runs below five minutes. Tudor Bompa[3] states development is best improved with runs of three to eight minutes (or even longer) with heart rate maximal or within 10 beats/min of maximum. Pfitzinger[8] recommends intervals of two to six minutes with heart rate 95% to 98% of maximum. Less experienced runners would prefer shorter runs of about two to three minutes, e.g., 600 meters to 1000 meters at 10K race pace. Experienced middle distance runners may prefer distances of 800 meters to 1200 meters at 5K pace.

The preferable heart rate is about 10 beats per minute, b.p.m., below maximum, otherwise the workout may tend toward anaerobic development rather than VO_2max development. The rest interval is sometimes taken as the time for the heart rate to drop to below about 60% of maximum heart rate before the next repeat, however, note the section above on "Rest Interval."

Jack Daniels[13] recommends: *"The amount of quality running in an 'Interval' session should be up to 8% of weekly mileage, with a 6-mile or 10K maximum."* Daniels calls it **"Interval"** training, whereas I call it **"VO_2max"** training. A total of 30 minutes of "Interval" training (VO_2max training) exclusive of recovery is a good upper limit for a 70-miles-per-week runner[2]. Repeats should be between 3K and 5K race pace or slightly slower. These runs are stressful, therefore once per week or every other week is recommended. Allow an easy day before these workouts and an easy recovery day the following day.

Example VO_2max Workouts

1. One typical workout for the relatively inexperienced would be 3 to 4 of the following: 3- to 5-minute repeats at 10K race pace with recovery equal to run time. Walk and jog or jog all during recovery is preferable to all walk.
2. *Alternatively*, Bompa[3] *suggests shorter* runs (30 seconds to 2 minutes) with short rest (10 seconds to 1 minute) and 4 to 12 "reps" to enable reaching VO_2max. More "reps" are associated with the shorter runs.
3. A three-week training block cycle is recommended starting with shorter (easier) runs initially and ending with longer runs. Also the longest repetitions are one mile to keep roughly within the normally recommended maximum of six minutes for VO_2max runs. Less experienced runners should start with 10K race pace runs. The more experienced should do "reps" at 5K race pace. For example:
   1st week: 5 x 1000m;
   2nd week: 4 x 1200m;
   3rd week: 3 x 1600m;
   repeat the cycle.

As adaptation occurs over weeks of training, the volume of the runs in the threeweek schedule can be increased to 8K or 9K maximum (for the more experienced or marathon runners) total volume in a session. For example:

1st week: 8 x 1000m;
2nd week: 7 x 1200m;
3rd week: 6 x 1400m;
repeat the cycle.

Caution. Training for VO_2max is a tricky business since the pace is so close to 100% anaerobic. Training at 85 to 95% speed (or higher) over the training distance improves the VO_2max and also gets the lactic acid levels high for a reasonable time, since the anaerobic system is simultaneously trained. It is possible if repetitions are too intense and/or the rest is too short, the training will be too anaerobic instead of VO_2max training. This would result in a much shorter workout due to the accumulation of lactic acid. Therefore, the use of a heart rate monitor would assist greatly in keeping the pace at about 10 beats per minute below MHR.

vVo_2 max Training

One of the latest promising training methods is vVO_2max interval training.

Description. Your vVO_2max is your running velocity at your VO_2max. VO_2max alone does not account for running economy, but vVO_2max does. Two runners may have the same VO_2max, but the one with the higher vVO_2max has the higher running efficiency or economy. Refer to the section below on "Running Economy."

A vVO_2max study[17] in 1997 at the University of Lille, France, conducted by Professor Billat indicated several significant advantages for middle and long distance runners, particularly increase in running economy. See also "The Max Factor" article by Ed Keystone in *Runner's World*, December 1999.

Eight trained distance runners underwent the following training for each of four weeks[17]:

- One mid week workout consisting of vVO_2max interval training, i.e., 5 x 1000m in 3 minutes at vVO_2max speed with 3 minutes jog rest between.
- One workout at lactate threshold (2 x 20 minutes), and the other days slower, i.e., 45-minute run (one day), 60-minute run (three days), with one day of rest.

To train at your vVO_2max, it is necessary to determine your velocity at your VO_2max. In the Billat study, this was determined by having the athletes running at VO_2max until exhausted; the velocity is the distance traveled (I call it Dexh) divided by the elapsed time (an average time of 6 minutes for these competitive young middle and long distance athletes). To determine your individual Dexh, I suggest an easier alternative for the less experienced rather than running to exhaustion at VO_2max; in the beginning of the season, this is not a good idea particularly for older runners as one is not yet adapted to near all-out races. It is also not easy to determine when one is running exactly at VO_2max. Instead, Dexh is determined from your estimated 3K race pace for 6 minutes since 3K race pace is close to 100% VO_2max. (Your 3K race time is very close to 57.5% of your 5K race time; See Table 3.1 in Jack Daniels' *Runing Formula*[13].)

Therefore, $Dexh^6$ = (3K race pace meters/minute) x 6 minutes. This would be an underestimate of an actual run to exhaustion at VO_2max but is suggested for the less experienced. I believe the correct pace should be between mile race pace and 3K race pace. Therefore, $Dexh^6$ should be about 3% longer than the estimate based on 3K race pace. The length of the 3 min. "rep" = $Dexh^6/2$.

Advantages. The French study by Billat over the above four-week training period resulted in increased running economy by 6%, increased vVO_2max by 3%, and 4% reduced heart rate at 70% VO_2max. These are all significant improvements over a short period of time. At this fast speed, there would be fast twitch fiber development, central nervous system neural development, increased tolerance to lactic acid, and increased strength.

Recommended Use. I believe these workouts would be quite stressful for most athletes physically and mentally and therefore are not recommended particularly for older athletes or the less experienced:

The 30-30 vVO_2 max Workout

There is an easier alternative to the 5 x 3 minute or 3 x 3 minute workouts. Billat lately has developed an easier method to develop VO_2max and still produce significant improvements. In this new workout, the athlete runs for 30 seconds at vVO_2 max. The rest is 30 seconds at 50% of vVO_2max (actually about 50% of the distance of the run). Continue for as long as possible. This will be about 15 to 20 repetitions normally. As expected, the improvement is less than for the 5 x 3 minute workout since the average time at VO_2max is about 20 to 30 % less than the longer harder workout above. But the 30-30 workout is well tolerated by the less experienced runners and should still produce significant improvements in VO_2max after a few weeks.

I recommend distance runners try the 30-30 workouts to get some variety from the longer repeats (1K to 2K) used in the usual VO_2max workouts. Also sprinters will find these short interval workouts beneficial during the base-building phase.

As indicated above, it is not necessary to run to exhaustion for about 6 minutes to determine the velocity at VO_2max. From above, VO_2max is just a bit faster than 3K pace and a bit slower than mile race pace. Therefore, the velocity at VO_2max is about 3% faster than 3K race pace or 3% slower than mile race pace. If the estimated vVO_2max pace is slightly slower or faster than it need be, this only results in more or less repetitions to exhaustion. For convenience, I have worked out the distance to be run at vVO_2 max in 30 seconds based on a runner's current mile race pace.

Therefore, vVO_2 max pace = 0.97 x mile race pace meters/second.
Distance run in 30 seconds= 0.97 x mile race pace meters/second x 30 seconds.

Table 7.3- The 30 -30 workout at vVO_2max

Mile time Seconds	**Distance run in 30 seconds** Meters
302	155
312	150
322	145.4
332	141
342	137
352	133

After you become adjusted to the above workout, after a month or so, progress to 60 seconds at vVO_2max with 60 seconds jog rest, until exhaustion sets in. In this 60 seconds case, just double the distance run in 30 seconds from the table above. I have found the 30-30 workout very useful at the beginning of the speedwork phase.

Anaerobic Threshold Training

Anaerobic threshold (also named lactate threshold or ventilatory threshold) training and water running training are the two most important training discoveries in the past two or three decades. These were no doubt around before this but have become popular only more recently and taken on great importance.

"For very talented marathoners the performance potential correlates better with the pace at lactate threshold than to VO_2max" (Martin and Coe[1]). This may explain in part why lactate threshold training has received more emphasis in running literature than VO_2max training. Of course, lactate threshold training ("tempo" or "cruise" runs) are more popular with the average runner because they are less stressful than VO_2max repeats.

Description Anaerobic threshold, AT, runs correspond to runs just below the lactate threshold where lactate starts to accumulate rapidly or breathing starts to get heavier. An efficient marathon race pace is generally just slightly below the anaerobic threshold or about six percent slower than anaerobic threshold pace. The anaerobic threshold, AT, as a percentage of VO_2max varies depending on the experience of the runner. AT for a beginner, well trained and elite runner is about 60%, 80%, and 90% of VO_2max respectively. At just below AT, the elite runner is running faster and using more oxygen than an inexperienced runner, but still without accumulation of lactic acid.

At this threshold or just below, the athlete should feel mild distress with speed just slightly faster than that of comfortable feeling[3]. On a perceived effort scale of 1 to 10, from extremely easy to extremely hard, anaerobic threshold running is a 6, being somewhat hard. Conversation should not be difficult. But the best way to determine this threshold is to observe your breathing while running; if you are observant, you will notice at a pace just above the threshold the breathing starts to be somewhat labored. For myself, this is about 160 b.p.m. or about 80% of MHR (maximum heart rate).

Advantages. Anaerobic threshold training causes the following physiological improvements.

- Slow twitch development mainly with some fast twitch development
- Increased heart stroke volume and blood volume
- Increased oxidative/glycolic enzymes which result in increased stamina, an increase in percentage of VO_2max at the anaerobic threshold, increase in VO_2max, and improved running economy
- Increased mitochondria and capillarization, particularly near slow twitch fibers

Training. The recommended pace is 15 to 20 seconds per mile slower than 10K race pace. The runs consist of either a series of intervals (400 to 2000 meter) distances or a continuous run.

In the case of intervals at the AT, the rest between repeats is *normally* less than the time for the repetition or the time for the heart to return to below about 120 beats per minute. However, with shorter runs below marathon pace the rest may be shorter. "Repeated runs at faster pace than for continuous runs and over shorter distances with very brief rest intervals will achieve the same benefits as a long continuous run" (Costill[5]). The rest time between repeats depends on the athlete's experience and condition; the athlete should not at any time be breathing heavily or having difficulty with conversation. If breathing becomes labored, i.e., goes above the lactate/ventilatory threshold, the session needs to be reduced in intensity.

These anaerobic threshold runs are also referred to by Jack Daniels and many other coaches as "Tempo" (continuous) or "Cruise" (interval) runs[2]. Jack Daniels[13] recommends: *"The total amount of quality running for a 'Cruise-interval' workout is up to 10% of your current weekly mileage, with a maximum of six miles for the average runner or eight miles maximum for an elite marathoner."*

Aerobic Conditioning Training

Aerobic conditioning training occurs at a slower pace than anaerobic threshold training. This is much less stressful training than the aerobic capacity training that takes place just below the athlete's VO_2max. Aerobic conditioning training represents the bulk of the distance runner's training. Preferably this should be done as much as possible on soft, even surfaces to minimize the risk of injury.

For a non-athlete, usually 30 minutes three times per week is recommended. This is the key to strengthening the heart and lung (cardiorespiratory) systems.

Description. There are two types of aerobic conditioning for athletes. **One**: slower, shorter runs during warm-ups and cool downs and easy recovery runs. These would be at about 60% intensity or about 1.5 to 2 minutes slower per mile than 10K race pace and lasting about 10 to 30 minutes. **Two**: faster, longer runs to develop endurance. These runs would be at 60 to 70% intensity or about 45 seconds (about 2% slower than marathon pace) to 2 minutes slower per mile than 10K race pace and lasting about 45 minutes to 2.5 hours. During the competitive phase, these aerobic runs must be continued, but at reduced volume and increased intensity (slightly faster).

Advantages. *Develop endurance.* Advantages are similar to anaerobic threshold training. Develop the heart, lungs, neural pathways, enhance muscles physical, chemical and metabolic characteristics, such as slow twitch development, increased metabolizing enzymes, enhanced oxygen diffusion into the blood and increased mitochondria and capillarization. In particular, the long runs could eventually lead to enlarged heart/increased stroke volume, and/or enlarged coronary vessels.

In view of these long periods of running above 30 or 35 minutes (preferably), there is benefit to tolerate stress and to develop energy usage by fat burning.

Training. *Recommended training range for aerobic conditioning.* The pace should normally be below marathon pace, i.e., more than 6% slower than anaerobic (or ventilatory) threshold pace.

It is often recommended that an athlete train in the range of 70% to 80% of maximum heart rate, MHR, for aerobic conditioning[2,14]. The training threshold = RHR +2/3(MHR-RHR) or within 10 beats per minute below, where RHR is resting heart rate. Dr. Kenneth Cooper at the Aerobics Research Institute started millions on his aerobic conditioning program[14] many decades ago. Generally speaking, for women to achieve optimal conditioning the preferred heart rate during training is about 20 beats higher than for men[1].

Walking and Hiking for Aerobic Conditioning Training. If the heart rate during training is less than about 65% of maximum heart rate, MHR, the aerobic training effect is considered questionable[3]. This is the commonly accepted view. However, the following supports *brisk* walking and hiking as cross-training to aid in the performance of athletes.

- Many decades ago, it was the practice for middle and long distance runners, (e.g., in Finland) to supplement their running training with walking at a good pace.
- More recently, Japanese marathoners have also used long walks to assist in their training and while recovering from an injury.
- Fred Foote, ex-coach of world champions Bill Carruthers (silver medallist in the Tokyo Olympics) and Bruce Kidd, stated that fast walking produced significant improvement in his own 880-yard race time over three decades ago.
- Arthur Newton, ultra-marathoner, one of the greatest distance runners of all time (with many world records between 1920 and 1934), believed that a great deal of walking must be done in addition to running training.
- Hiking over hilly and sometimes rough terrain is also a great conditioner. (Starting in 1998, I have hiked briskly for two hours of cross-training about twice/month [except in the winter] with heart rate between 85 and 120 beats per minute.)

Advantages in Walking

I am of the belief that there is a significant training benefit in walking to supplement running training, even though the heart rate is well below 65% MHR since:

- It increases cardiovascular capacity to some extent, increases mitochondria and capillaries, and strengthens legs and ankles.
- Walking can also be used for recovery on days when running is out of the question or on the day off, etc.
- It's beneficial also before warm-ups, before cool downs, between intervals, and sometimes between long runs.

SUMMARY TABLE OF TRAINING FOR DISTANCE RUNNERS

The table below summarizes training for each of the five energy systems. Various patterns of slow and fast running are essential to properly equip the distance runner for competition. However, the training has to be done correctly in terms of distance, pace, and recovery. The table below summarizes the five essential training systems, major benefits, effort required, run time, rest between repetitions, training pace and total volume of the training runs. This table is based on excellent references from world experts: David Martin and Peter Coe[1], Jack Daniels[2,13], and Tudor Bompa[3], and from my own experience.

TABLE 7.4 • TRAINING FOR DISTANCE RUNNERS- 800M TO MARATHON

TRAINING TO IMPROVE:	MAJOR BENEFITS	PERCENT MHR (a)	PERCENT MAXIMUM EFFORT (b)	RUN TIME (c)	REST BETWEEN "REPS"	NOTES, RACE PACE & VOLUME/ SESSION (e), (g)
Alactic System	Speed	100[3] (98–100)	>98	<20 sec	HR<90 to 100 b.p.m.	<600m per session
Anaerobic Lactic System	• Speed • Speed endurance • Tolerate acidosis • Pace judgement • Mental toughness	Near Max[3] >95[2] (95–98)	>95 95–100[1]	30 sec. to 2 min.	HR<100 b.p.m. 5RT	Mile race pace or faster. Maximum 5%[13] of weekly mileage per session
100% VO_2max						
VO_2max	• Speed endurance • Increase VO_2max • Mental toughness • Aerobic endurance	95[2] (90) 95–98[8]	85–95[3] 90–95[1]	2 min. to 6 min.	1RT to 0.8RT	3K, 5K, 10K race pace. Maximum 8%[13] of weekly mileage per session

Anaerobic Threshold						
Anaerobic Threshold System	• Increase • Anaerobic • Threshold • Increase VO_2max • Improve running • Economy	90[2] 80–90[1] (80)	80– 85	90 sec. to 6 min. to 20 min.	Breathing not labored or <120 b.p.m. **(d)** Does not Apply	10K mile pace + 15 sec.[2] Maximum 10%[13] of weekly mileage per session **(f)**
Aerobic Conditioning System	• Increase • Endurance • Tolerate stress • Maintain • Recovery	70–80[1] 75[2] (70–75)	60–70	>5 min. 30 min. to 2 hrs	< 1RT or <120 b.p.m. Does not Apply	10K mile pace + 30 sec. to 2 min.

NOTES:

(a) Referenced values show variation since some are for experienced runners and some are for elite. My recommended values shown in parentheses are for experienced runners.

(b) For those who are unsure of their maximum heart rate, MHR, this column is more appropriate. The higher numbers are for more experienced runners. See also the last column, which lists the training pace based on mile race pace, 3K, 5K, and 10K race pace.

(c) Generally, the middle distance and long distance runners concentrate on shorter and longer runs respectively.

(d) Breathing should not be labored, i.e., not above the ventilatory threshold and conversation should not be difficult. See the "Anaerobic Threshold Training" section above.

(e) Quality (higher intensity) training consists of anaerobic threshold (AT), VO_2max, and anaerobic lactic (S for speed) workouts. The total percentage of quality sessions based on mileage per week varies depends on the experience of the athlete as follows:

Athlete	*Quality Sessions/week*	*% of Weekly Mileage*
Elite	*3*	*28 max.*
Experienced	*2–3*	*13–25*
Less Experienced	*1–2*	*10–18*

Each runner should know his/her own capabilities. To avoid injury, it is better to err on the lower side of the percentage. My total quality percentage per week is about 19% during the speedwork phase. Each runner should concentrate more on those quality workouts that are more pertinent to his/her individual race specialty, e.g., AT for marathon, VO_2max and AT for 10K, and VO_2max and S for 5K. To achieve this the three different workouts can be varied every other week. See Chapter 10 on designing your own schedule.

(f) For anaerobic threshold training, the pace can range from just above or just below the lactic threshold to marathon race pace (about 5% to 6% slower than lactic threshold pace). The training pace is usually 10K mile pace plus about 15 seconds (AT pace) or plus about 30 seconds (between marathon pace and AT pace).

(g) Jack Daniels[13] cautions high mileage distance runners not to exceed the following maximum miles in a quality session: anaerobic threshold intervals session 6 miles (or 8 miles for elite marathoners), VO_2max intervals 6 miles, Speed 3 miles. See a general cautionary note for less experienced and older runners in Chapter 5 under Balanced Training. Also for 800m runners doing anaerobic lactic training faster than race pace, I recommend the volume per session should be in the 2.5 to 4% range of weekly mileage.

Correct Proportion or Balance in the Training System

The correct percentage of each training system depends on the specific event. The emphasis on training for a particular race can be determined by noting the heart rate during the race and the percentage of anaerobic and aerobic used; for example, mostly anaerobic for sprinters and very little anaerobic for marathoners.

RUNNING ECONOMY

Running economy is running with minimum wasted energy and is defined as efficient use of oxygen. Jack Daniels[13] defined running economy as ***"the oxygen required for an individual to maintain any particular submaximal running pace."*** This differs from VO_2max, the maximum aerobic capacity.

Running economy can differ by as much as 25% or more in experienced runners and hence has a major effect on racing times. Running economy can be a better predictor of long distance race times than VO_2max. This indicates its extreme importance.

Two runners with identical VO_2max, body weight and body fat, but with different running economies, running at the same pace will use oxygen at different rates. In this case, the runner with the higher running economy will use less oxygen. Also a distance runner with higher running economy could beat a runner with higher VO_2max. "The more efficient runner will burn less fuel (oxygen per minute) at any running speed, hence can run further on the same amount of fuel" (Noakes[4]).

How Can Running Economy Be Improved?

- *Flexibility, flexibility, flexibility.* More supple joints, tendons, ligaments and muscles result in less resistance and less energy expenditure.
- *Training* should improve running economy, but for some, the genetic factors that affect running economy, such as differences in limb length, body weight distributions, lack of flexibility, and insufficient slow twitch fibers, would enable only small improvements in running economy. Additional training cannot make up for these inborn characteristics.
- *Specificity of training* makes a runner efficient at his/her race pace. When they move away from their specialty, running efficiency or economy suffers. Normally, a marathoner is not efficient at sprinting, and a sprinter or middle distance runner is not efficient at marathon pace. Therefore, training at race pace should improve running economy.

- *Form.* Eliminate the bad habits, such as head bobbing up and down, overstriding, tightness above the shoulders, swaying shoulders due to excessive crossover of arms in front of the body, and run as lightly as possible, gliding along. See Chapter 3 on "Running Form."
- *Optimize stride length.* You may have noticed when you run at a slower than normal pace, e.g., with a much slower athlete, that the pace is not comfortable and is more tiring than expected from this slow pace. You become less efficient due to the shorter-than-optimum stride length. Similarly, if you exaggerate the arm motion causing overstriding, the pace is again tiring and uncomfortable and the running economy suffers.
- *Relaxation.* The more relaxed while running, the more running economy.
- *Low body weight, low body fat; increased strength, flexibility and coordination; lighter clothing and running shoes;* all these can improve running economy.
- *Recovery.* Run when completely recovered from the previous day or previous run, otherwise there is increased oxygen consumption at a given pace.
- *Intensive weight training.* In a 1994 study by exercise physiologist, Ron Johnston Ph.D. at New Hampshire University, running economy was improved by a significant two percent in a group of female distance runners over ten weeks of strength training and usual running routines (Pete Pfitzinger[18]). Running economy can be improved by resistance training if intensive enough and after many weeks since this results in an *increase* in capillary density, oxidative capacity, muscle mass, and in the area of fast twitch fibers (hypertrophy)[19]. "Resistance training can also improve central nervous system recruitment of muscle, hypertrophy, and force output" (Kirkendall and Garrett[19]). These effects would result in less energy expended in running.

It appears controversial whether fast interval training or large volume of aerobic runs is more effective at increasing the running economy. In any case, both are effective but improvement comes only after many months of training.

There have been reports of improvements in running economy with interval training. These athletes are more likely to be middle distance runners since specificity in training is important. Marathoners would likely become most efficient by developing their race-like stride and not by doing fast intervals involving different muscles. Some improvement can be made in economy by middle distance runners in training at the anaerobic threshold and by marathoners by VO_2max training. However, the biggest gain should come in training near race pace for your specialty. By doing so, your body eventually becomes more and more accustomed to the pace and distance, any weaknesses are ironed out and a smooth efficient action results.

For 400-meter and 800-meter training, I have personally found running repeat 100's on a regular basis at about 400-meter race pace working on form and relaxation with a walk back or jog back are very effective to improve running efficiency. This was recommended by Lloyd Percival, one of Canada's most knowledgeable coaches fifty years ago. These repeats I used at high school and university in the late '40s and early '50s. The improved form, greater relaxation, and a feeling of gliding along that I experienced translated into improved running economy. After a 33-year layoff from running, it all came back to me. Lately, fifty years later, I have heard of one other coach recommending the same drill for improving running economy.

HEART RATE MONITORING TO INDICATE PERFORMANCE IMPROVEMENT

Running economy is rarely measured in view of the complexity of testing on a treadmill. But it is possible to measure running improvement using only the heart rate monitor and stop watch as explained below.

Consider the following simplified equations:

- ***Oxygen Consumption per minute = Heart Rate x Heart Stroke Volume x Oxygen Extracted from the blood***
- ***Oxygen Consumption Rate = Oxygen Required Rate***
- ***Heart Rate =*** O_2 ***Required Rate / (Stroke Volume x*** O_2 ***Extracted)***

As seen from the last equation, all the important effects are taken into account when heart rate is measured. Also oxygen required, stroke volume, and oxygen required can change due to the following :

- Oxygen required depends on many changes and adaptations that have taken place, such as:
    - changes in body weight and body fat;
    - increased efficiency of the central nervous system in recruiting more muscle groups;
    - development of slow twitch fibers and aerobic abilities of fast twitch fibers;
    - development of mitochondria, enzymes, and capillaries;
    - improvement in running form.

- ***Heart stroke volume*** can increase with intense exercise due to enlargement of the heart even over a six-month period[1].
- ***Oxygen extracted*** from the blood can increase with training: Costill[5] reports that, "Older runners (men above 60) improve VO_2max after training by extracting more oxygen from blood than by delivering more blood."

GENERAL TRAINING THEORY

Therefore, heart rate is a good indicator of improvement in performance. With improvement over a given distance, the pace is faster at the same heart rate as previously, or at a given pace the heart rate is lower than previously. Alternatively, the improved athlete can run longer at a given pace with a lower heart rate than previously. The time for the heart to return to 120 beats per minute after the repetition is also a good indicator of fitness.

Testing for *speed endurance* with a heart rate monitor would be simply as follows: For example, test for a mile at near race pace, say 6 minutes per mile for 5K race pace (your choice) and take the heart rate just before the end of the mile run and 90 seconds after the run (to determine recovery). Several months later, test again under identical weather conditions, when well rested, and at the same pace on the same track, etc. A lower heart rate during the run or quicker recovery indicates an improvement in endurance performance due to the many combined factors discussed above.

Similar testing can be done to test *speed improvement* during fast repeats. In this case, it is best to take the heart rate only 90 seconds after the repeat; it is too difficult to get the heart rate during the run or immediately after even with heart rate monitor. Faster recovery (reduction in heart rate) after a speed repetition compared to the same speed repetition in previous weeks indicates greater condition or speed endurance. Alternatively, greater speed with the same recovery heart rate compared to previous results also indicates improved condition.

REFERENCES

1. Martin, D., and Coe, P., *Better Training for Distance Runners*, Human Kinetics, Champaign, IL, 1997.
2. Daniels, J., Training Distance Runners–A Primer, *Gatorade Sports Science Institute, Conditioning and Training*, Volume 1, Number 11, February 1989.
3. Bompa, T., Physiological Intensity Values Employed to Plan Endurance Training, *Track Technique,* 108, Summer 1989.
4. Noakes, T., *Lore of Running,* Leisure Press, Champaign, IL, 1991.
5. Costill, D. L., *Inside Running, Basics of Sports Physiology,* Benchmark Press, Inc., Carmel, IN, 1986.
6. Lamb, D. R., Basic Principles For Improving Sport Performance, *Gatorade Sports Science Institute,* Sports Science Exchange, Volume 8 (1995), Number 2, SSE #55.
7. Henry, F., Research on Sprint Running, *The Athletic Journal,* February 1952, 30.
8. Pfitzinger, P., The ABC's of VO2max, *Running Times,* October 1997.
9. Watts, D., Wilson, H., and Horwill, F., *The Complete Middle Distance Runner,* Stanley Paul and Co. Ltd. / Century Hutchinson Ltd., London, England, 1986.
10. Nurmekivi, A., Training Methods in Middle Distance, *Modern Athlete and Coach,* Vol. 19, No. 4, October 1982.
11. Ryun, J., Developing a Miler, *Track and Field Quarterly Review,* Summer 93, Vol. 93, No 2.
12. Higdon, H., Run Fast, *How to Train for a 5K or 10K Race,* Rodale Press, Emmaus, PA, 1992.
13. Daniels, J., *Running Formula,* Human Kinetics, Champaign, IL, 1998.
14. Cooper, K.H., *Aerobics,* Bantom Books, New York, NY, 1968.
15. Sleamaker, R., and Browning, R., *Serious Training For Endurance Athletes*, Human Kinetics, Champaign, IL, 1996.
16. Glover, B., and Glover, S-l., *The Competitive Runner's Handbook,* Penguin Books, New York, NY, 1999.
17. Billat, V. L., et al, Interval training at VO_2max: effects on aerobic performance and overtraining markers, *Medicine & Science In Sports & Exercise,* Volume 31, No.1, pp 156-163, 1999.
18. Pfitzinger, P., *The Weight Debate,* Running Times, May 1996.
19. Kirkendall, D. T., and Garrett, W., E., The Effects of Aging and Training on Skeletal Muscle, *The American Journal of Sports Medicine,* Vol. 26, No. 4, 1998.

35
458
393

CHAPTER

8

Citius, altius, fortius.
(Swifter, higher, stronger).
Motto of the Olympic Games

TRAINING FOR 800 METERS, 1500 METERS, AND MILE

GENERAL

The following are important aspects of 800-meter, 1500-meter and mile training that helped me break several world records, indoor and outdoor, in these events. In addition to the speed and speed endurance training, water running in the pool, anaerobic threshold, AT, and occasional VO_2max runs on the track or trail are highly recommended; these are described briefly below and in more detail in Chapter 11 (running in the pool), and Chapter 7 (AT and VO_2max training). Interval workouts of El Guerrouj and some recent Kenyan world champions are also covered.

Balanced Training. The 800 meters is roughly 50% anaerobic and 50% aerobic. The 1500 meters and mile are roughly 30% anaerobic and 70% aerobic. Depending on your event, specialty training on these energy systems should ideally be roughly in these proportions. However, it is not physically possible for the average experienced runner to attain these high anaerobic percentages; recovery would be difficult and injury and staleness would probably occur. See Chapter 5, Principle 4, and Chapter 10, Table 10.6. The numbers above give only a rough idea of the emphasis to be placed in the training. But neither energy system can be neglected in the training; if either is neglected for more than a week or two before a race, performance will suffer significantly. About 10% to 12% of my weekly mileage is fast anaerobic interval training during the sharpening (in season/peaking) phase; this is a good average for most experienced middle distance runners.

Have a Long Term Plan. It is essential to build a good base for at least 10 weeks, including hills and some speed work, before the sharpening phase, in order to have endurance for the intense interval training. Cross-country training and road racing is recommended during base building. Remember, it takes about six weeks for the body to adapt to the training. Do a lot of race pace training during the sharpening phase. You should be able to predict your lap times closely. Do not train hard for more than 12 weeks. The recovery days are as important as the training days; with more rest or easy days, there is more quality and less injuries. To run 2 or 3% faster may require 40% more work but it is worth it. Be sure to have fun and to taper about one to two weeks before the big race.

Go with Your Strengths. Emphasis in the training should be placed on the development of the dominating performance factors. This means smaller volume and higher intensity for the faster middle distance runners (400/800 meter types), and for those with more endurance (1500m/5K types) larger volume and decreased intensity. The runners then find the training sessions less taxing. See also Chapter 5, "The Principle of Going With Your Strengths." The weaker suit is developed as far as possible but then the strengths are emphasized in training.

Training for the Anaerobic Lactic System. This is done once or twice per week to develop speed, speed endurance, running economy and tolerance to lactic acid. These repetitions normally last between 30 seconds to 2 minutes at about 95% maximum heart rate. For speed development, the rest between repetitions ("reps") is nearly a full rest (e.g., about six minutes or more) or the heart rate reduces below 100 beats per minute. At this speed about 1200 meters to 1400 meters per session are sufficient. See Chapter 7 for more details.

The total volume of repetitions in an anaerobic lactic session should be a maximum of 5% of current weekly mileage based on numbers from Jack Daniels[2,4]. Daniel's book covers training for 1500m to marathon where these sessions are normally carried out at mile race pace. For 800-meter specialists, I believe 5% of weekly mileage is too high when these sessions are done at faster than race pace as is often the case. For example, for 800- and 1500-meter runners with reps about 10% faster than race pace I recommend limiting the volume per session to about 2.5% of weekly mileage. This conservative approach will help to reduce injuries.

Training at the Anaerobic Threshold. Anaerobic threshold (also called lactic or ventilatory threshold) training should be done at least once per week. This is less strenuous than VO_2max training, therefore the safer and easier anaerobic threshold training can be done on days between the intense interval workouts for the 800 meters, 1500 meters and mile. Run mile, 2,000 meter or 2,400 meter repeats at 15 seconds slower per mile than 10K race pace or slightly slower or faster. Choose a conversational pace. If your 10K race pace is 6 minutes and 15 seconds per mile then run at 6 minutes 30 seconds per mile. Rest between repetitions is often taken as the time for the heart rate to reach 120 beats per minute. Alternatively, run for 15 to 25 minutes at the above pace. See Chapter 7 for further details.

The total volume of repetitions in an anaerobic threshold training session should not exceed about 10% of the weekly mileage based on numbers from Jack Daniels[4].

Training to Improve VO_2max. VO_2max (called aerobic capacity) training is important for middle distance and long distance runners. Training to raise VO_2max is suited to develop 3K and 5K race times. To run a fast 800 meters, 1500 meter or mile, the athlete must be able to run a fast 3K or 5K[1]. This will enable one to run longer at a faster pace and with greater running economy. For faster runners (e.g., 400/800-meter types), the repetitions would tend to be shorter (e.g., 400 meters to 800 meters) and with one session probably every week. For runners with more endurance (1500/5K types) or elite runners, the repetitions would tend to be longer (e.g., up to five or six minutes) and could be done every week in the sharpening phase. In the taper week before a major competition, eliminate these sessions. Runs are normally done at 5K or 10K race pace. These sessions are stressful since the heart rate is about 10 to 15 beats per minute below maximum; therefore, it is important not to overdo the quantity or recovery will exceed one or two days. See chapter on General Training Theory for Distance Runners for rest times between repeats and other details.

The total volume of repeats in a VO_2max training session should be less than about 8% of weekly mileage per session based on numbers from Jack Daniels[4]. See a cautionary sentence for less experienced and older runners in Chapter 5 "Principle of Balanced Training."

Periodization. During your 12-week cycle, pre-season or particularly in-season, work progressively harder for three weeks, then back off slightly for one week. After this, start again where you left off at the previous second or third week and so on. Hence each month is progressively more intense. This type of periodization is well documented in many articles.

Run in the Water. Run in the deep end of a pool (river or lake) for recovery, increased flexibility, stamina and overall strength. Wear a vest or belt for flotation, run as naturally as possible, not a "bicycle" (up and down) motion, keep upright, don't bob up and down, and hands should be straight up. Once a week, a hard session of intervals is recommended to improve speed endurance; duplicate the land workout with the same perceived effort, the same length of time for "reps," but rest intervals are much shorter. Do not go hard in the pool within four days of a meet or legs will get tired during the race; several times I made this mistake. In addition, do sprint drills in the shallow end of the pool at least twice a week for at least 10 to 12 minutes. See Chapter 11 for details.

Miscellaneous. Running success also depends to a large extent on low body fat (mine is about 5-6%). Counteract aging with weight training twice per week, stretching every day, and frequent exercises involving fast movements to prevent fast twitch neurons from atrophing with age (see "Principle of Neural Training" in Chapter 5).

TYPICAL WEEKLY TRAINING SCHEDULES

The following two schedules are for the sharpening/speedwork phase (indoor or outdoor season), i.e., after building a good base.

Schedule 1 – More Competitive Runners

This schedule is for highly competitive athletes below 60 years of age, i.e., national caliber and world class athletes above about 85% age graded[3] in their race specialty.

Note: Only two days per week are recommended running on the track; other training days should preferably be on grass or trails.

Sunday:

Long, conversational pace, run (about 20 to 25% of weekly mileage), or occasional low-key 3K or 5K race. If racing on Sunday, omit the Saturday time trial.

Monday:

Run in the water, or 100-meter or 150-meter stride repeats on earth or grass.

Tuesday:

Fast, short anaerobic intervals (e.g., 150-, 200-, 250-, 300-, 400-, or 500-meter repetitions). Over a period of a month or more, progress up to 95% MHR.

Wednesday:

Anaerobic threshold training.

Thursday:

For 800/1500-meter type runners, longer (than Tuesday) fast intervals (70-85% MHR), or VO_2max training on alternate weeks (85-95%MHR).

For 400/800-meter type runners, sprint training: 95% speed, short "reps" totaling about 600 meters only.

Friday:

Rest day or light cross-training.

Saturday: First six weeks

For 800/1500-meter types, sprint training: 95% speed, short "reps" totaling less than about 400m. For 400/800-meter types, fast short anaerobic intervals. For both types, take about one hour rest only and perhaps a coffee. Go to a park for downhill repeats on wood chips or long runs on grass. (Each of the above workouts in volume are about 2/3 to 3/4 of a normal full workout.)

Saturday: Next 6 weeks, not including the taper week.

Each week, run a time trial at race pace. For 400/800-meter-type runners, do one of the following at 800m race pace: a 600m run **or** in later weeks a 600m run, walk jog 200m, followed by 200m run. For 800/1500-meter types do one of the following at mile race pace: 800m, rest, 800m, **or** 1,000m, rest, 600m, **or** 1,200m, rest, 400m. Rest two minutes or until heart rate goes below 60 % of maximum.

Or an occasional low-key 400m, 800m, 1500m or mile race may be substituted for the time trial. This is good advice for both 800 and 1500m runners.

For the more experienced, if possible, do two workouts on most days. This is more feasible for younger retirees who have the training time, and also the time for a recommended nap in the afternoon. The morning workout is normally the recovery workout. One of the two daily workouts is normally a cross-training workout (running in pool, swimming, rowing, or brisk walking) or a weight training plus stretching session. If all this is too strenuous see below.

Schedule 2 – Less Competitive Runners

This schedule is for competitive runners who are above 60 or 65 years of age, less competitive younger runners, or athletes below about 75% age graded[3] in their race specialty. This schedule is also for competitive runners who find they need more rest and a less strenuous week to get good results. For many athletes, Schedule 1 above is too tiring and may lead to frequent injury.

I have noticed that the statistics show running performance after about 65 years of age drops off more rapidly than previously for races from the 100 meters to marathon. For example, this is seen from plotting men's track standards against age from the "Masters Age Graded Tables"[3]. These tables are based on comprehensive data, e.g., including world records for men and women of various ages from below 10 to 100 years. For example, for the 800 meters, the decline in performance changes from 0.88% before 65 to 1.5% after 65. Sprinters show lower decline and marathoners show higher decline than middle distance runners. For one who is exceptionally fit, this drastic decline can occur later than around 65; and it could occur earlier than 65 for the less fit. I have noticed this more rapid drop off in performance after age 70; the great Derek Turnbull from New Zealand told me he noticed the same after 70. I have also noticed in myself and competitive running friends in their 60s that injuries are more frequent. This comes partly from trying to do the same workouts as when we were younger. I now realize I was trying to do too much when I turned 70 in view of the five injuries and many physiotherapy treatments I had in 1999. Injuries take longer to heal at this age, too. Therefore, it is essential to schedule fewer training days at high intensity and more days of rest and cross-training after age 60 or 65. But the quality is maintained as much as possible.

The schedule below mainly for 800/1500-meter types provides an extra easy day and only one workout per day.

Sunday:
Long run at conversational pace (20 to 25% of weekly mileage), or occasional low key 3K or 5K race.

Monday:
Run in the water, or 100-meter or 150-meter stride repeats on earth or grass.

Tuesday:
Fast, short anaerobic intervals.

Wednesday:
Light cross-training or medium long run at easy pace.

Thursday:
Anaerobic threshold training.

Friday:
Longer, fast intervals, or every two weeks VO_2max training or a time trial.

Saturday:
Rest day.

800 METER TRAINING

Ideally, the mileage per week should be at least 35 miles per week including warm-ups, and cool downs and cross-training equivalent miles.

Your speed in the 800 meters depends a lot on your best 400 meter speed. Normally, your 800 meter time equals two times your best 400 meter time plus about

10 to 18 seconds. Therefore, it is important that you work on your 400 meters, too. A good speed reserve enables an athlete to travel longer at a given speed more easily and with less energy. See the 400-meter workouts under "Training for Sprinters" in Chapter 6. The difference between your first 400 meters of the 800 meters and your best 400 meters time is called the "protection time." Mine was about 6 seconds when, in a heavy wind, I broke the 65 to 69 age group world record in Buffalo at the World Championships in 1995. Those runners with less speed and more endurance than their competitors must have a smaller protection time and smaller difference between the first and second lap to be competitive. This indicates the importance of the athlete's best 400 meter time.

You should also be able to run a good 3K and 5K race, therefore some VO_2max training is required. Nurmekivi[1] shows that the faster 800-meter runners have faster 100 meter, 400 meter and 3K race times compared to the slower 800-meter runners; also these race times are impressive. As somewhat expected, the 800-meter race times have the closest correlation to 400-meter times and 1500-meter race times have the closest correlation to 3K times.

Typical 800 Meters Anaerobic Workouts

Note: The race pace referred to in the workouts below is 800 meter race pace unless otherwise specified (e.g., 200 meter repeats at race pace, plus 3 seconds, for 2 minute race pace 800 meters means 33-second repeats). These workouts are each a complete workout but could be followed by slow 150-meter repeats working on relaxation, form, and lactic depletion.

After building a good base, progress gradually in the sharpening phase. At the beginning of the sharpening phase, repetitions should be much slower than target race pace, with more rest and/or reduced number of sets. In the beginning weeks, quantity is stressed rather than intensity. As the body adapts, the training pace becomes increasingly more intense with volume per session reduced. It is important to be running near target race pace about six weeks before the main competition. Ideally, you should train at slightly faster than your target race pace. For example, if your target race pace is 2:12 for 800m, or 33 seconds per 200m, then train at 31 seconds per 200.

In the workouts, instead of a specified rest time between repetitions, it is preferable to start again when the heart rate is between 110 to 130 beats per minute, b.p.m., (or below 60% of maximum heart rate) unless a full rest is called for. Using the heart rate may be preferable since everyone is different and some may not be able to handle the short rests listed below.

- 3 sets (4 x 200m at race pace with 45 seconds between "reps") and 4 to 5 minutes between sets.

- 4 sets (200m at race pace, plus 2 or 3 seconds, rest 30 seconds, run 100m at race pace or faster, rest about 2 minutes, repeat 200m and 100m) and 5 minutes between sets.
- 3 sets (run 250m at race pace, plus 2 to 4 seconds, rest 45 seconds, run 150m fast, rest about 2 and 1/2 minutes, repeat) and 6 minutes between sets.
- 3 sets (200m at race pace, rest 1 minute, 200m at race pace, rest 1 minute, 200m or 300m at race pace) and 6 minutes between sets or until heart beat is below about 110 to 120 beats per minute (b.p.m.).
- 3 sets (3 x 300m at race pace with 75-90 seconds between reps) and 8 minutes between sets. This is a tough workout.
- 2 or 3 sets (4 x 200m starting at race pace + 2 or 3 seconds, each 200m progressively faster with shorter rest ending up at race pace or faster, rest 90 sec., 60 sec, 30 sec. between successive "reps") and 6 minutes between sets.
- 2 or 3 x 500m gradual accelerations, start slow and finish fast, with a total time equal to race pace plus 0 to 3 seconds. Rest about 8 minutes between each rep.
- 2 x 500m runs at race pace, run evenly. Full rest between.
- 4 to 5 x 250m at 400m race pace, rest until heart returns to below 100 b.p.m. between reps.
- 3 or 4 x 200m steep uphill run at 90 to 95 % effort, jog down, rest until heart beat goes down to 100 b.p.m.
- 3 sets (200m at 800m race pace, rest 60 seconds, run 150m at 400m race pace, rest 30-45 seconds, run 100m faster than 400m race pace). Rest 6 to 8 minutes between sets.
- Three time trials: Run one of the following at an even 800m race pace unless otherwise specified. Make sure you are well warmed up beforehand.
  - 600m
  - 600m, walk jog 200m, run 200m
  - 500m, walk 200m, run 200m, walk 100m, run 100m faster than race pace.
- 2 or 3 x 400m between 400m and 800m race pace about five days before a race. Rest until heart is below 100 b.p.m.
- 5 or 6 x 150m at 400m race pace three days before an important race. Rest until heart is below 100 b.p.m.
- 3 sets (500m, walk 1 minute, run 300m). Rest 6 minutes between sets. 500m is at race pace + 5 seconds. 300m is at race pace +3 seconds.
- 4 x 500m or 3 x 600m (run the straights at 400m race pace, stride/jog the bends). Rest between sets: walk 100m + rest 1 minute. This workout is for a 200m indoor track
- 4 x 200m, rest 4 minutes, 3 x 200m, rest 4 minutes, 2 x 200m. The first 100m in each 200m is slow and the second 100 is faster. Pace per 200m is race pace minus 1 to 1.5 seconds.

When you can run four or five 200-meter intervals fairly easily at 800m race pace with a 30 to 40-second rest you will be reaching a peak. Training for 1500 meters will give stamina. Therefore, do also some of the 1500-meter and mile workouts below, and race the occasional 1500 meter or mile.

Typical Aerobic Capacity (VO_2max) Intervals for 800m

During an 800m race the athlete reaches about 140% VO_2max and 100% MHR (the 40% VO_2max extra is due to the anaerobic contribution). Hence, it is advantageous to do VO_2max training several times during the speedwork phase but normally not on the same week as a time trial or a low key race. The following is typical:

- 3 to 5 x 1,000m at 5K race pace. Recovery time is equal to the run time.

1500 METER OR MILE TRAINING

Ideally, the mileage per week should be at least 40 to 45 miles per week including warm-ups, cool downs, and any continuous running in the water, or cycling. I normally consider 7 minutes running in the pool as equivalent to one mile running on land or 10 minutes cycling as equivalent to one mile aerobic running on the land.

Your speed in the 1500 meter depends a lot on your 800 meter speed. Normally, your 1500-meter time equals two times your best 800 meter time plus about 2 to 20 seconds. The 2 seconds applies to extremely well conditioned Olympic (or elite athletes) or those who have exceptional aerobic conditioning in addition to their fine anaerobic conditioning. The fastest 1500-meter runners have faster 400 meter and 3K race times than the slower 1500-meter runners according to Nurmekivi of USSR[1]; so these distances need attention too.

Supplement your training with fairly fast walking, cycling, swimming, rowing or slow running in the water; this all adds to the aerobic conditioning.

Typical Anaerobic Workouts for the 1500m or the Mile

Note: Race pace in the workouts below is current or target 1500 meter or mile race pace unless otherwise specified. (For example, 400 meter repeats at mile race pace, plus 3 seconds, for a 5-minute race pace mile means 78-second repeats). The workouts below are each a complete workout. Many of the 800-meter workouts are also used in the 12-week sharpening phase as described above under 800-meter training.

After building a good base, progress gradually in the sharpening phase. At the beginning of the sharpening phase repetitions should be slower than target race pace, with more rest and/or reduced number of sets, if you need to. In the beginning weeks, quantity is stressed rather than intensity. Over many weeks, keep shortening the rest between repeats and/or increasing the length of the runs, and also increasing the speed of the repeats. As the body adapts, the training pace becomes increasingly more intense with volume per session reduced. But the volume remains higher than for 800-meter runners. It is important to be running near target race pace about six weeks before the main competition.

When you can run the 200s at faster than 1500 race pace then you can move on to do 300s at 1500 race pace. When you can do the 300s at faster-than-race pace then you can move on to do 400s at race pace. Next do 600-meter runs at race pace, then 800-meter runs at race pace. Over a sharpening period of 12 weeks, your body will adjust to these longer continuous runs. Several low-key races are strongly recommended to assist in reaching a peak. There is nothing like the real racing experience to improve race times.

In the workouts instead of time between repetitions, start again when heart is between 110 to 130 beats per minute (b.p.m.) (or below 60% of maximum heart rate) unless a complete rest is called for. This may be preferable for some since everyone is different and some may not be able to handle the short rests listed below.

- 6 to 8 quartermile repeats slower (about five seconds) than anticipated mile race pace with less than two minutes rest. (This is a good workout near the beginning of the speedwork season. As condition improves, the reps are faster and/or with less rest.)
- 4 sets (3 or 4 x 200m at race pace, plus 1 or 2 seconds, with 45 seconds between reps). Rest 5 minutes between sets.
- 4 sets (300m at race pace, plus 2 or 3 seconds, rest 45 seconds, run 100m at race pace or faster, rest 2.5 minutes, and repeat). Rest until heart rate falls below 120 beats per minute between sets.
- 3 sets (500m at 800m race pace, plus about 4 seconds, rest 2 minutes, run 300m at 800m race pace or slightly faster). Rest 6 minutes between sets.
- 75m to 100m steep uphill runs at about 85% effort, recover with 100m run at the top, walk back slowly. Progress gradually, building up to about 8 to 10 over several weeks.
- 1000m at mile race pace, walk 100m, run 200 at 800m race pace, walk 100m, run 100m at 400m race pace.

The following workouts should be done in the following order over a period of about six weeks:

1) 3 sets (4 x 200m at race pace with 45 to 60-seconds walk rest) with 5 minutes rest between sets.
2) 3 sets (3 x 300m at race pace with 75 to 90-seconds walk rest) with 5 to 7 minutes between sets.

3) 2 to 3 sets (3 x 400m at race pace with 90 seconds to 2 minutes walk/jog rest) with about 4 minutes between sets.
4) 2 to 3 sets (2 x 600m at race pace with 2 minutes walk/jog rest) with about 6 minutes between sets.
5) Three time trials: Run one of the following at an even mile race pace except as noted below. Rest until the heart rate goes below 60% of maximum or walk 200 meters. Make sure you are well warmed up beforehand.
   - 800m, rest, 800m
   - 1000m, rest, 600m at slightly faster than mile pace if possible.
   - 1200m, rest, 400m at slightly faster than mile pace.
6) 4 x 400m, rest 90 seconds to 2 minutes between reps, 2 x (300m, rest 45 seconds between reps, run 100m), rest 2 minutes, 2 x (250m, rest 45 seconds between reps, run 150m). Longer reps are at mile race pace; shorter reps are slightly faster. This workout provides some variety, hence mental relief. Normally in practice the 300m + 100m total time and 250m + 150m total time is faster than the 400m continuous time.
7) 3 x 1100m. First 800m easy (aerobic), followed by 300m fast (anaerobic). Rest 3 to 4 minutes between repeats. This develops the final kick to the tape. Less experienced do 2 or 3 x 1000m with 800m easy and 200m fast.
8) 2 or 3 x 400m at about 800m race pace about five days before a race. Rest until heart returns to below 120 beats per minute.
9) 5 or 6 x 150m at 400 race pace three days before an important race. Rest until heart rate returns to below 100 b.p.m. Concentrate on form and relaxation.

If there is time in the schedule, repeat some of the above workouts with an acceleration in the last 100 meters of the repetition to improve the kick. Some of the above 800 meter workouts should be done occasionally plus two or more 800-meter races.

Time Trials

In Schedule 1 For More Competitive Runners, see above, a total of six time trials particularly and/or low-key races is recommended in the latter seven weeks of the speedwork phase. Based on my past experience, I believe this is a sufficient number. In January, February and March 2004, preparation for my successful attempt at the world indoor mile record for age group 75-79, I ran five middle distance races (1000m twice, 1500m twice and one 600m), and seven race pace time trials (e.g., run 1200m, rest 2 minutes, run 400m on three different weeks). This was a total of 11 race-like sessions. In fact, it was far too many as my 1500m in early January (based only on aerobic base training) was four seconds faster than in March. I believe I reached a peak about a month before my mile race as my legs were starting to tire excessively in training after this time. One can be too ambitious.

The renowned distance coach, Arthur Lydiard recommends a total of five time trials (600m to 1200m single long runs) in the last six weeks of speedwork phase for 1500-meter training. Similarly, he recommends a total of five time trials (600m to 1500m single long runs) in the last six weeks of speedwork phase for 800-meter training. On the same time trial workout, the Lydiard schedule includes a 200m time trail. The above frequency and total number of time trials shows Lydiard considers them as valuable training. I agree. But the inexperienced should be careful not to overdo the number of time trials.

Typical Aerobic Capacity (VO_2max) Intervals for the Mile

During a mile race, the athlete reaches about 110% VO_2max and near 100% MHR. Hence, it is advantageous to do VO_2max training several times during the speedwork phase but normally not on the same week as a time trial or a low-key race. The following aerobic capacity intervals will build endurance strength. Endurance strength also results in speed.

- Three to six 1000m repeats at 5K race pace. Recovery time is equal or shorter than the 1000m run time. As condition improves increase repeats to 1200m. See also Chapter 7 for details on rest times. (A 3K race pace is not recommended as it is just below maximum heart rate and very stressful and is apt to be anaerobic since the current pace is not accurately known by most runners).

EL Guerrouj Training for 1500m World Record

El Guerrouj's 1500m world record of 3:28.91 in August 1997 was the result of the very scientific advanced Moroccan training program. His training program in 1997 is summarized briefly below based on information from www.oztrack.com by Marco Velediaz. Miler athletes can learn from his dedicated regimented program and by noting the emphasis on aerobic endurance, the long preparation, etc.

The preparation period started in mid October, 1996 and lasted until mid May 1997. Typically, in a 21-day period, his two-a-day sessions consisted of the following 42 sessions: 23 aerobic endurance (45 min. continuous fast "maximum" run, or, 60 min. recovery run, or 6 x 1K reps, or 4 x 2K reps with 2 min. recovery), 7 strength (typically 4 x 16 reps), 2 physical preparation (stretching, drills, etc), 3 power (e.g., 10 x 300m up-hill reps) and 7 rest sessions.

In February, he broke world indoor records in the 1500m and mile; amazing since it was early in his preparation period. In mid May, he started his "minor competition" phase; a typical 21-day period consisted of the following 42 sessions: 18 aerobic endurance (30 min. maximum run, or 40 min, recovery run, no 1K and 2K reps), 0 strength, 11 warming up, 4 speed (e.g., with surges 10 x 300m in 35 sec., or 6 x 500m), 4 race pace (10 x 400m at 53 sec. with 30 sec. rest), 5 rest. [The omission of strength workouts in this competition phase is noteworthy.]

It is stated the work volume is not large but the quality is high, with not much track work during the year.

THE KENYAN WAY

The following are some typical workouts used by Kenyan world champions from the excellent book by Toby Tanser[5] with permission of the publisher Tafnews Press. I have related these to their personal best race pace for the distance. Using your own race pace should make these workouts possible for the experienced competitive runner. But these are still hard workouts, so the repetitions may have to be reduced and/or the rest times increased, particularly for the older runners. Some of the longer workouts above 3000 meters in volume or repetitions 600 meters and above were placed in the 1500 meter race category herein; although these workouts would be suitable for occasional 800 meter training, as well.

800 Meters Typical Kenyan Training

Race pace is 800-meter race pace for the repetition distance. Recovery is usually a jog rest.

B. Koeck:

PB 800 meters 1:43.17 (World Jr. champion 1992), PB 1500 meters 3:32.9.

Early summer

- 2 x 400m at race pace, + 3 to 5 sec., 1 min. rest between, rest 5 min.;
  +2 x 200m at race pace, 30 sec. rest between, rest 5 min.;
  +2 x 100m at race pace, -1 to -2 sec., rest 5 sec. between.
  =1400m total

July, August

- Accelerations 3 x 400m at race pace, -2 to -3 sec.; +2 x 150m.
- 4 x 300m at race pace, 0 to -2sec.; +2 x 150m full speed.
- 2 x 600m at race pace, 0 to -3sec.; +200m strides at race pace.

W. Tanui:

PB 800 meters 1:43.30 (1st in 1992 Olympics), PB 1500 meters 3:31.20.

Beginning of track season

- 12 x 300m at race pace, + 2 to 5 sec., 3 min. recovery.
- 12 x 200m at race pace, -2 to 0 sec., 3 min. recovery.

J. Kimutai:

PB 800 meters 1:45.63 (2nd World Jr. championships 1994), PB 1500 meters 3:45.
Note the workouts normally total about 2400m.

Spring

- 8 x 300m at race pace, -5 sec., rest 2 min.
- 3 x 600m at race pace, +16 sec., 2 min. rest; +3 x 200m at race pace, -1.5 sec., 1 min. rest.
- 5 x 400m at race pace, + 4 sec.; +2 x 200m at race pace, all 1 min. rest.
- 10 x 200m at race pace , -1.5 sec.; +2 x 400 at race pace, + 5sec., 2min. rest.

1500 Meters Typical Kenyan Training

Race pace is 1500 meter race pace for the repetition distance. Rest by jogging normally.

K. Cheruiyot:

PB 800 meters 1:46.48, PB 1500 meters 3:33.07 (World Jr. champion 1983). He believes 3000m of quality intervals is enough for a 1500m runner.

Summer track season.

- 3 x 800m, 5 min. jog rest.
- 600m at race pace two days before a 1500m race; + 6–8km jogging.
- Complete rest one day before a 1500m race.

B. Koeck:

PB 800 meters 1:43.17 (World Jr. champion 1995)
PB 1500 meters 3:32.9.

Early summer

- 5 x 400m at race pace, 0 to + 2 sec., 1 min. rest; + 5 x 300m at race pace, 0 to-3 sec., 1 min. rest.

N. Kiprotich:

PB 800m 1:43.31 (2nd in 1992 Olympics)
PB 1500m 3:38.76.

- 6 x 300m at race pace, -7 sec., 1 min. rest between; 10 min. rest; + 10 x 200m at race pace, -5 to -6 sec., 1 min. rest.

W. Tanui:

PB 800m 1:43.30 (1st in 1992 Olympics)
PB 1500m 3:31.20.

Beginning of track season

- 3 x 800 at race pace, + 2.5 to + 5.5 sec., 3 min. recovery; + 400m flat out.
- 5 x 600m at race pace, 3 min. recovery.

REFERENCES

1. Nurmekivi A., *Training Methods in Middle Distance Running,* edited by Jess Carver.
2. Daniels, J., Training Distance Runners- A Primer, *Gatorade Sports Science Institute, Conditioning and Training,* Volume 1, Number 11, February, 1989.
3. World Association of Veteran Athletes, "Age Graded Tables," *National Masters News*, Van Nuys, CA, 1994.
4. Daniels, J., *Daniels' Running Formula,* Human Kinetics Champaign, IL, 1998.
5. Tanser, T., Train Hard, Win Easy- The Kenyan Way, *Track and Field News,* Tafnews Press, Mountain View, CA, 1997.

2002
1562
JANUS

CHAPTER

9

What does not destroy me,
makes me strong.
Friedrich Nietzsche

TRAINING FOR 5K, 10K, AND MARATHON

PREPARATION TIME

Gear your training toward a specific event. Allow enough preparation time or else forget it. A proper schedule will have short-term goals (weeks), intermediate goals (months) and a long-term goal (a year). And there should be tests (races and time trials) to gauge whether you are on track. The length of the buildup should be enough to build a proper base (mainly aerobic runs), i.e., at least eight weeks, and preferably three months including lots of hills, particularly in the last few weeks. However, the marathon requires a slower buildup. At the end of this phase, you should be running up to 90% of your target mileage per week during the speedwork phase, which follows[2]. Normally, allow about 12 weeks for speedwork (sharpening), including tapering–longer could result in passing your peak. The marathon may require a few more weeks of sharpening.

The sharpening consists of high quality intense workouts, time trials and/or low-key races and long runs to reach your peak performance and peak speed. This, of course, implies good recovery days. Tapering consists of reducing quality and quantity in the final four weeks for the marathon, and in the final two weeks for the shorter races (see Tables 10.4 and 10.5 in Chapter 10).

TRAINING PACE

Generally, your recent race times for the shorter distances are indicative of what you can expect to achieve at the longer distance. Investigate the charts that list predicted times[6,10]. For example, see Noakes[6], Tables 2.3 and 2.4. However, it is important to realize that these times give a good estimate based on statistics and VO_2max, and can only be achieved with the proper specific training for the longer or shorter event. For example, this does not mean a 5K runner can run the marathon predicted time without submitting to the standard marathon training for several months. By consulting other runners, you can also judge what you should be capable of.

To predict your 10K time from your 5K time, multiply by 2 and add about 1.6 minutes. To predict marathon time from 10K time, multiply 10K time by 4.6. To predict marathon time from half-marathon time, multiply it by 2 and add 9 minutes. The above numbers were deduced from Table 3.1 from Daniels[10]. Also, based on data in Table 2.4 from Noakes[6], "VO_2max vs. Race Times," I found the following relationships for an average runner where AT is running pace at the anaerobic threshold.

- Marathon pace is about 5% slower than AT pace.
- 10K race pace is about 4% faster than AT pace.
- 5K race pace is about 4% faster than 10K race pace.

MILEAGE GOALS

Mileage per Week. The suggested mileage per week for novice to advanced is shown below in Table 9.1. This is based on your target race pace or your actual race pace for your event, or your VO_2max. Most people do not know their VO_2max, but it can be simply obtained using my following formula: VO_2max = 1000 divided by your current 5K race time in minutes. If you fall in-between the three columns below, it will be necessary to interpolate. Mileage for elite runners is not shown as they have a good idea of what produces best results for their body. In fact, every individual should find his/her optimum weekly mileage to produce best results while avoiding injuries as much as possible. But Table 9.1 will put you in the right range.

The mileage per week suggested below should be approached gradually over a month or more. Mileage should be increased no more than 10 percent per week to avoid injury. Also a good plan is to reduce mileage by about a third every third or fourth week to re-energize the body.

Table 9.1 Weekly Mileage Guide

	Novice	Experienced	Advanced
VO_2 max ml per min. per kg	30	38	53
Marathon race pace	4:50	4:00	3:00
!0K race pace, minutes	60 to 64	46 to 52	36 to 39
5 K race pace, minutes	29 to 31	23 to 25	18 to 19
5K runners, miles/wk	15-20	30	40
10K runners, miles/wk	20-25	35	50
Half Marathons, miles/wk	25-30	40	55
Marathoners, miles/wk	30-40	45-50	60-65*

***Note about 65 miles per week** is considered a good upper limit for most advanced marathoners. With increased mileage above 65, the gains in performance are small and have a higher likelihood of injury.

Length of Long Run. For proper performance, the length of the long run and number needs to be adequate. Generally, the long run is 1/4 to 1/3 of the weekly mileage except in the case of the marathon. For experienced and advanced marathoners, it is preferable to increase up to 20 to 22 miles over a period of about four weeks. Similarly, novice marathoners should gradually increase up to 18 to 20 miles. Restricting the long run to about 20 miles reduces injuries. For novice marathoners and even some experienced marathoners, 20 miles will be too long on the feet; the long run should be less than about 3.5 hours to reduce pounding on the legs. (See the Table 9.2 below under Long Runs.) Similarly novice 5K, 10K runners should limit the long run to less than about 1hour 45 minutes.

HOW FAST TO TRAIN FOR LONGER RUNS

The usual rule of thumb for longer training runs is that you should be able to carry on a normal conversation while running. For an average training pace, Henderson[4] recommends:

- 1 minute per mile slower than race pace for the marathon
- 1.5 minutes per mile slower than 10K race pace
- 2 minutes slower than fastest mile [perhaps too fast for most]

A conversational pace and an easier recovery day pace is about 1.5 minutes and 2 minutes respectively slower per mile than your current 10K race pace. Your long run pace for example, should be such to finish tired but not exhausted and without slowing down. Normally, with experience, each individual finds his/her own correct pace.

It is of interest that Bill Rodgers often trained at two minutes slower than marathon race[5], i.e., 6 minutes 50 seconds per mile.

HOW MUCH HIGH INTENSITY TRAINING

High intensity training is taken here to include VO_2max intervals, anaerobic threshold runs, marathon-pace runs, and anaerobic lactic (near 100% maximum heart rate) intervals. See also Chapter 7 for details on these types of workouts. *For 5K and 10K competitors the following high intensity sessions are suggested: one session every other week for novice runners, one to two sessions per week for experienced runners, two sessions per week for advanced/experienced runners, and three per week for elite runners.* Generally, novice runners should not do interval type workouts until after a year of aerobic training. See also Chapter 10 that shows what can be scheduled in practical training weeks for the experienced competitive middle and long distance runners. Generally, for experienced runners, the "quality" sessions (anaerobic threshold, VO_2max, and anaerobic lactate/speed training) total about 20 percent of their total weekly mileage.

WHAT KIND OF HIGH INTENSITY OR QUALITY TRAINING

The correct emphasis or concentration has to be placed on those quality sessions, which are more pertinent to the individual's race specialty. Very simply, the anaerobic and aerobic training *ideally* should be in proportion to the percentage of anaerobic and aerobic energy used in the race. But there are practical limitations in achieving this ideal (see 4-"Principle of Balanced Training" in Chapter 5).

The training emphasis is outlined for the long distance events and some typical workouts are described below. These workouts should be done at most only once per week. Take it easy the day before and the day after. Note that RT equals run time and m equals meters.

5K High Intensity Workouts

In order of priority, emphasis should be on VO_2max, anaerobic threshold, and anaerobic lactate interval sessions.

- 1000m, 1200m, 1400m or 1600m repeats or ladder at current 5K race pace. Rest (jog lightly or fast walk) = 1RT for 1000m and 1200m, and 4 to 5 minutes for mile; see Table 7.2. Volume = 3000m to 6000m depending on experience. Longer "reps" are recommended for the more experienced.
- I have personally found mile repeats even as low as three at slightly faster than 5K race pace are excellent training for the 5K. Alternatively, for a somewhat easier workout, try 5 x 1000m or 4 x 1200m at about 10 seconds per mile faster than 5K mile pace. Rest time equals run time. More advanced runners can reduce the rest after each successive repetition.

- Henderson[4] recommends when concentrating on speed to do just four x 400 meters at slightly faster than your current mile race pace.
- Two times a mile at current 3K race pace with a 4 to 4.5 minute rest between.
- A continuous run after a good warm-up for 2.5K at 5K target race pace will indicate your level of fitness.

You race as you train. The following is based on observation of the training and racing of different athletes. For example, in training, if you can do 5 x 1000 meters in about 3 minutes 10 seconds with a 3 minute rest between, then you should be capable of less than 17 minutes in a 5K race. Or, if you can do 3 x 1 mile at about 5 minutes 50 seconds/mile with a 3 or 4 minute rest, you should be capable of about 18 minutes, 15 seconds in a 5K race.

10K High Intensity Workouts

Emphasis should be similar to 5K training but with slightly more emphasis on anaerobic threshold sessions and less on anaerobic interval sessions.

- 1200m, 1400, 1600m, or 2000m repeats or ladder at 10K current race pace. Rest (jog lightly or walk moderately fast) = 4 minutes for 1200m, and 6 minutes for 2000m. Volume = 5000m to 10000m depending on experience. Longer "reps" are recommended for the more experienced. It is recommended to keep the "reps" below 6 minutes; normally more volume can be done with shorter "reps." Pfitzinger (*Runner's World*, October 1997) and Daniels[10] recommend a maximum "rep" of 6 minutes and 5 minutes respectively.
- Ladder at 10K race pace: 1200m, 1600m, 2000m, 1600m, 1200m = 7.6K total. Rest between reps = 1 RT, 0.8RT and 0.6RT for 1200m, 1600m and 2000m respectively. As condition improves, increase the pace to 5K race pace.
- One of the best workouts (instead of a VO_2max workout) is a 5K race. Alternatively, do two times 2.5K at 5K race pace with a rest between equal to 0.5 to 0.6 of run time.
- Owen Anderson[9] suggests for 10K competitors a quality long run composed of "eight or nine medium miles.and then two miles at 10K speed, followed by a two mile cool down." [The medium miles within a long run should not be too strenuous, otherwise the recovery will interfere with subsequent workouts.]
- 2 x 3 miles at between 5K and 10K race pace. Rest 10 minutes between. Applicable for 5K runners, as well.
- 3 to 5 miles at between 5K and 10K race pace. Near beginning of speedwork phase do only 3 miles. As condition improves progress to 5 miles. This is a tough workout but some prefer this to doing mile intervals as it is more specific to a race situation. Applicable for 5K runners, as well.

Half-Marathon High Intensity Workout

In order of priority emphasis should be on anaerobic threshold, VO_2max, and anaerobic lactate interval workouts.

- Interval training (e.g., 5 to 6 x 1 mile), or continuous for 5 to 6 miles at anaerobic threshold pace, i.e., 10 to 20 seconds per mile slower than 10K race pace. This assumes a 60 mile per week runner.
- For a quality long run, try some easy and medium miles with several miles at goal half-marathon pace in the middle, similar to the quality long run suggested by Anderson for 10K above; see also the third workout below.

Marathon High Intensity Workouts

Emphasis should be on anaerobic threshold workouts primarily and also VO_2max workouts (but less than above), with minimal anaerobic lactate workouts.

- Jack Daniels[10] describes marathon-pace workouts, i.e., from 10 to 15 miles but not to exceed 2 hours of running. Marathon pace is about 35 seconds slower per mile than 10K race pace. These workouts are strenuous and could substitute occasionally for a long run.
- Bill Rodgers had a speed workout consisting of 6 x 1 mile repeats run at marathon race pace, 4:48 in his case[5].
- If you are used to a long run of 20 miles, you will benefit from 18 miles as follows: 10 miles at conversational pace, and then 6 miles at target marathon pace, followed by 2 miles cool down.

WHERE TO TRAIN

A training session should have a *purpose*, i.e., to develop one of the energy systems (see Chapter 7). Normally, this determines the intensity and volume of the workout. Therefore, generally you can train on the road, track, hills, or trails as long as you train in this energy system for the correct length of time, the proper intensity, and volume associated with the energy system. But the track is usually preferred for VO_2max or anaerobic interval/speed workouts.

MARATHON TRAINING

Champion Workouts World class marathoners train 100 to 140 miles per week, sometimes even as high as 200 miles per week, two workouts a day, and quality/speed sessions at least two times a week. For example, in the winter Bill Rodgers ran slow 140 to 170 miles per week on the cold and snowy streets of Boston[5]. At this level, the champion knows what works for him or her since training is individualistic. Frank Shorter[5] said, "I train mostly for the 10000 meters, and just run marathons. If you're training marathon distances all the time, you are so worn down that you can't do the kind of speed training you need to run fast." However, he still ran 20 to 24 miles per day, two workouts per day and three speed sessions per week. Grete Waitz said[5], "I'm a track runner. I don't train for the marathon. I'm not patient enough to train for the marathon. To run more than an hour at a time is boring."

Importance of 5K and 10K type of training. The comments above indicate that in addition to stamina training there is a good emphasis on speed and training for the 10K. This applies to the average marathon runner as well. The long run, in view of its slower pace and shorter length than the marathon does not ensure avoidance of "hitting the wall." The faster paced training for a 10K or 5K will make the marathon pace seem slow. Thus, the VO_2max training at 5K and 10K race pace is of great importance for the marathon. Also, training at vVO_2max, the velocity that corresponds to your VO_2max, is considered by some even better training than the VO_2max training above; however, these are more stressful than VO_2max workouts; see Chapter 7. In summary, your marathon time depends to a large extent on how fast you can do your 10K race or even your fastest mile.

Beginner. The novice competitor should preferably have about two years of running experience before running a marathon. They should also first test themselves with a half-marathon well in advance of a marathon. This gives some indication of readiness and the particular marathon pace to aim for. Speedwork sessions, particularly fast intervals should not be done without a good aerobic conditioning base lasting at least a year.

In order to finish respectably, long runs of at least 15 miles should be done at least five times. In addition, in place of a long run, a half-marathon is recommended about four weeks before the marathon to obtain some feel for the marathon pace.

Those who have difficulty in completing the marathon could intersperse running with brief walking rests. Jeff Galloway at a lecture at the Mississauga YMCA (1996, I believe) advocated that beginners walk a few minutes every mile during the marathon. This would be more popular with those who have only a goal to finish the marathon.

Long Runs

The marathon long run method recommended herein is to vary the length of the long run on *alternate* weekends over a period of 12 to 14 weeks of speedwork/quality training approaching your big race. Namely, the longest long run is followed the next weekend by a reduced length long run (about 15 to 25% less). For the more experienced, and for later weeks in the schedule, there is less difference between the 20-22 mile long run and the reduced long run. This alternate method allows more recovery and provides for flexibility to accommodate marathoners of varying ability. For experienced and advanced marathoners, the reduced length long run may be substituted by a low-key 5K, 10K, or half-marathon race. See the marathon schedule in Chapter 10 on Design Your Own Schedule. However, novice marathoners should have little or no racing or interval training until after a year of training.

Advanced runners should aim for about six to eight long runs of 20 to 22 miles. Experienced and novice should aim for six long runs of 15 to 20 miles. The alternate method above will help to achieve this goal. See also Long Run Pool Method below.

Distance Run In 3.5 Hours

For slower runners, a long run of a given distance unfortunately entails longer time on the feet. "The potential gain beyond 3.5 hours of running (our suggested time limit for runners) isn't worth the risk" (Glover and Schuder[1]). Henderson[4] makes a similar statement. Running form deteriorates with fatigue—leading to increased vulnerability to injury.

The table below shows the miles run during a long run for 3.5 hours at various training paces. The training pace is assumed to be 1 to 1.5 minutes slower than race pace.

Table 9.2 • Distance Run in 3.5 Hours

Marathon time hours:minutes	Race pace minutes/mile	Training pace minutes/mile	Distance run miles
2:37	6.0	7.0	30
		7.5	28
3:03	7.0	8.0	26.3
		8.5	24.7
3:16	7.5	8.5	24.7
		9.0	23.3
3.29	8.0	9.0	23.3
		9.5	22.1
3:42	8.5	9.5	22.1
		10.0	21

The table also indicates why long runs of about 20 miles for most runners are a practical limit in view of the long time on the feet. For example, 20 miles is about

25,000 to 30,000 footstrikes at about three times body weight and much more on downhills. One method for the long run is to limit the length to the target time to complete the marathon but not to exceed 3.5 hours. Water stops are permitted. Also, for the less experienced runner some walking rests are usual.

The method recommended below achieves long runs of 26 miles or more with much reduced time on the feet.

Long Run, Pool Marathon, LRPM Method

In marathon training, the length of the long run done every other weekend and the total number before race day have a large bearing on the final race time. For example, it is known that Jeff Galloway's marathon training program puts a major emphasis on the long run, even exceeding 26 miles. The importance of the long run was also indicated from a study of the Trails End Marathon (in February 1973) by Paul Slovic (see page 320, "Distance Training" in the *Complete Runner*). Joe Henderson reported in *Running Your Best Race*[4] on the drastic slowdown of runners after 20 miles in this marathon. Slovic showed for runners with race times sub 3.00 (14% slowdown), for 3:01-3:30 (22% slowdown), for 3:31-4.00 (27% slowdown), and for above 4:00 (58% slowdown). Typically, the runners with slower race times have much shorter long runs and fewer in number before the big race. The method described below will greatly assist to effectively lengthen your long run, to prevent your "hitting the wall" at about mile 20, and to reduce considerably the drastic slowdown after 20 miles experienced by most runners.

The method I propose is one to achieve the benefits of the 26-mile long run (or longer) while reducing the stress on the legs. I call it the Long Run, Pool Marathon method. A marathon runner runs **a** *total of 26 to 30 long run miles every other weekend with more than half on the roads and the remainder equal to an equivalent amount in the deep end of a pool as soon after as practical: this is the key concept.* A change is as good as a rest. Details are explained below.

Advantages of Supplementing Long Run Land Miles with Pool Miles

- The main advantage is the pounding of the long run on the roads is reduced, therefore reducing the possibility of injury, while at the same time *the effect of a 26- to 30-mile long run every other week is achieved.*
- The pool session following the road run also aids recovery of the muscles, tendons, and ligaments and provides mental relief, as well.
- There is a further advantage, i.e., flexibility in the schedule. Some days you feel like doing more or less on the roads due to: the weather, sore muscles, your workouts during the previous week, stress at work, body biorhythms, fatigue, etc. In the pool, you make up the difference to get the desired total long run mileage. Alternative-

ly, on a bad day, the whole long run can be done in the pool; in this case, some short breaks may be required.

- Pool running builds flexibility, overall body strength and fitness, which are essential for a successful marathon—or even to survive.

Form. Run in the deep end of the pool with a flotation vest or belt (a belt is best). Your running form is the same as on land, except keep the arms straight ahead and straight back. Keep upright with little leaning for good form, good breathing, and for longer stride. It's not a bicycle type motion (up and down); the lower leg reaches out as in running (a longer stride in the pool translates into a longer stride on land). Do not paw the water with your hands; thumbs are nearly vertical. Concentrate on arm movement and the legs will follow; keep arms relaxed and you will travel faster compared to forceful arms. See Chapter 11 for further details.

Perceived effort. When running in the pool with the same perceived effort (exertion level) as on the land the heart rate is, theoretically, 10 to 20 beats per minute lower than on land; the lower value is for an aerobic workout and the higher is for an anaerobic workout. With the same perceived effort road and pool workouts should be equivalent if conducted for *the same time* in the pool as on the land. See Chapter 11 on "Running in the Pool" for more details.

From Chapter 11, I concluded the following for deep end pool running with a flotation belt or vest. The following are based on the same perceived effort on land and in the pool:

- *25 meters running in the pool in "T" minutes feels like 400m in the same "T" minutes running on the land.*
- *100 meters in "T" minutes running in the pool is equivalent to 1 mile in the same "T" minutes running on the land.*
- *For an equivalent pool/land workout, run in the pool 1/16th of the land distance in the same time and effort as for the land distance.*

The above similar statements give some idea of how far you will have to run in the pool to run some equivalent land miles.

With heart rate monitor. Instead of the same perceived effort, more exact equivalence between a land and pool session can be obtained while wearing a heart rate monitor. For an equivalent aerobic workout in the pool compared to the land while wearing a heart rate monitor: *In the pool maintain the heart rate at 10 beats below the land value for the same length of time as for a land workout.*

Running Time and Length in the Pool for the LRPM. Assume you want to achieve the equivalent of a 26-mile long run by combining a land run and a pool run.

- *Pool running time = (26 minus land miles long run) x land minutes/mile = minutes*
- *Total run distance in pool = (26 minus land miles long run) x 100 meters/mile = meters*

Therefore, it is only necessary to substitute into the above equations the number of miles already run on land and the pace (minutes/mile) during your long land run to determine your pool workout running time and total distance of pool run. In the above equations, the total running time in the pool is accurate but the running distance in the pool (based on my experience) is an approximation but will be slightly different for others since everyone has different strength and perceived effort.

Further Details of LRPM Method. This method deals mainly with the marathon long run for marathoners, but other finer details of this program are also suggested. Distance runners other than marathoners can also benefit by increasing their long run and by adopting some of the following concepts:

- After building a good aerobic base with some speed for two to three months the speedwork (sharpening) phase follows. The length of the speedwork period is close to three months maximum if there has been good base training.
- In the first week of the speedwork phase, a marathoner should be able to handle a long run on land between 12 to 15 miles.
- Every two weeks, increase the long run on land by 1 to 1.5 miles (or no more than 10%), but the longest (last) land run is not to exceed 20 to 22 miles or 3 hours.
- On the weekends between the long runs, do medium length easy runs or low-key 5K, 10K, or half-marathon race, a short time trial, or a quality interval session.
- During the week, do easy and medium length runs with one or two quality sessions (anaerobic threshold/tempo, VO_2max, or speed workout) depending on your experience and conditioning (see Chapter 10). The more experienced do more quality sessions.
- For the marathon, the last long run should be four weeks before the race.
- The day or two after the long run should be easy.
- Don't take too long between the long land run and the pool run for best results. Have a coffee on the way to the pool; I know this works. If several hours pass, you will not feel motivated to continue and you will not be warmed up.
- It is important to stretch before and after the pool run.

Advantages of Pool Miles During the Week

- Apart from long run supplementation–running in the water can be done during the week to increase weekly mileage without stress on the body. For those who have time for two workouts per day, one of these can be a pool workout. Aerobic mileage can be increased without shock on the feet, legs, knees, and hips by running in the water with heart rate preferably at least 65% of maximum heart rate minus 10 beats per minute. In the water, when your body adapts to this activity, you will be able to go for a longer time than on land without over-tiring yourself.

- Pool running has further advantages: It improves flexibility. It improves running form. Mitochondrial density and capillaries are increased. Due to the water's resistance, fast twitch muscles are activated. More repetitions in an interval session can be done in the water than on land due to increased oxygen extraction from the blood when submerged in cool water. More calories are consumed in the water than on land – good news for those wishing to lose weight.
- Pool running is also useful for recovery on easy days.

Caution. Although the long run pace in the pool is conversation pace or easier than "comfortably hard," one cannot become pool proficient overnight. It may take many sessions before you can run at this pace for say 90 minutes, particularly after running more than 15 miles on land. Therefore, start getting adapted to pool running during base training. Also, less experienced runners may find the 26 miles total (land + pool) too ambitious and requiring too much recovery. Therefore, in the first few weeks, a total less than 26 miles would be prudent, but land miles should still be greater than equivalent pool miles.

This method may not be suitable for non-swimmers; even with the flotation belt or vest, non-swimmers are not comfortable and relaxed. To get the most benefit, it should be enjoyable.

Summary

This method will reduce injury, build strength and flexibility, improve marathon time by greatly reducing the slowing down in the last six miles, and above all, make the marathon a more enjoyable experience instead of a survival exercise.

Taper for Marathon

An effective taper before the marathon is essential, otherwise the hard training beforehand is negated. The following are recommended during the taper period:

- Start your taper four weeks or earlier before your race.
- The last weekend long run should be four weeks or more before your race.
- Stress intensity rather than volume but both are reduced. The last week has little intensity and volume.
- Decrease mileage gradually (about 20% reduction/week) over the last four weeks; the last-week mileage should be down to about 30 to 40% of peak mileage. Low-mileage runners do not reduce mileage as much.

- During the last four weeks, do the following quality workouts: one marathon-pace run (about 7 miles) three weeks before your race; an anaerobic threshold (AT) run (continuous or intervals) each week, or alternately to an AT workout do 400-meter intervals at mile race-pace for sharpness. Finish your continuous-run workouts with fast strides.
- A 5K or 10K race should be a week away from a marathon-pace run or a long run. A 5K race one week before the marathon or a 10K race two weeks before is permissible.
- Prepare for your race with mental training.
- Two days before your race, rest; one day before take a short, easy run.

THE KENYAN WAY

The champion Kenyan runners are an inspiration to all runners. Much can be learned from their lifestyle and training regime. The following is a brief description from *Train Hard, Win Easy/The Kenyan Way* by Toby Tanser[8] with permission of the publisher, Tafnews Press:

- First and foremost, the training is very hard, often with huge workloads. However, life is hard in Kenya (e.g., cars and TV are rare), providing tolerance to the workouts.
- The athletes are willing to sacrifice.
- Long strolls are a hallmark of their schedule. They are by nature used to walking (and often running) nearly everywhere from an early age.
- Training camps for 8-9 months per year under Spartan conditions enable complete dedication with no distractions.
- Training at altitudes between 1600 meters to 2700 meters, in hot, low humidity conditions.
- Three workouts a day in the training camps starting at 6 a.m.
- Most training camps engage in cross-country training.
- Training with other world-class champions of near equal ability. Promising juniors often train with seniors.
- Tempo training (runs between 45 and 70 minutes) "inevitably turn into a mini-competition at top speed."
- Running lots of steep hills on a regular basis.
- Rest two to three months per year is not uncommon.
- Simple but nutritious diet.
- Lastly, their intense competition within their own country to gain fame and financial success.

REFERENCES

1. Glover, B., and Schuder, P., *The New Competitive Runner's Handbook*, Penguin Books, New York, NY, 1988.
2. Glover, B., and Glover, S-L. F., *The Competitive Runner's Handbook*, Penguin Books, New York, NY, 1999.
3. Compiled and Developed by: World Association of Veterans Athletics (WAVA), Age Graded Tables, *National Masters News*, Van Nuys, CA, 1994.
4. Henderson, J., *Running Your Best Race,* Wm. Brown Publishers, Dubewque, Iowa, 1984.
5. Barret, T., and Morressey, R. Jr., *Marathon Runners,* Julian Messner, NY, 1981.
6. Noakes, T., *Lore of Running,* Leisure Press, Champaign, IL., 3rd and 4th Edition.
7. Bloom, M., *The Marathon,* Holt, Rinehart, and Winston, New York, NY, 1981
8. Tanser, T., *Train Hard, Win Easy, The Keynan Way,* Tafnews Press, Mountain View, CA, 1997.
9. Anderson, O., How Long Should You Make Your Long Run?, *Running Research News,* Volume 14, No. 9, November, 1998.
10. Daniels, J., *Daniels' Running Formula,* Human Kinetics, Champaign, IL, 1998.

CHAPTER 10

A man without a plan is an "also ran".

DESIGN YOUR OWN DISTANCE TRAINING SCHEDULE

"If you fail to plan, you plan to fail" – Anon. A runner without a training schedule is like a house builder without blueprints. Athletes should have a training schedule, e.g., a detailed daily plan leading up to their important meet. However it is very unlikely to find a schedule in a running book that is just right for the individual. Every athlete is different with unique requirements and strengths and weaknesses. If a ready-made schedule for your race specialty is found, it could be too easy, too hard or too long. Also, not every athlete has a coach and even then, most coaches do not provide a detailed schedule.

The following describes how to design a distance training schedule for the average experienced competitive runner based on:

A – The four phases in the schedule.

B – The principles or guidelines to avoid over-training and possible injury.

C – The workouts that have to be emphasized or the correct balance of training for the various distances raced.

With the above information, you are in a good position to design your own schedule since you know your level of fitness, what you can or can't do, your strengths and weaknesses, time available and facilities available. Any special requirements can be incorporated, such as days off to accommodate known family or firm business commitments, courses, days of the week you train with your coach or track team or partner, etc. Also, when you have designed your own schedule, you will be fully aware of the reasons for and benefits of each workout.

Alternatively to designing your own schedules, the detailed example schedules can be used or made easier or harder to suit the athlete; this is explained at the end of the chapter.

QUALITY SESSIONS

The schedules below are tailored to the average experienced competitive runner including master runners and are based on 12 to 13 weeks of quality training (sharpening or fine tuning). The ***quality sessions*** consist of ***VO_2max***, ***anaerobic threshold*** and ***speed*** training. Elite or highly competitive runners may require a more demanding schedule than presented herein. Dr. Jack Daniels, ex-Olympic pentathlete and renowned coach, in the *Running Formula*[1] focuses on distance training schedules mainly for the more experienced runners (I believe) except that his marathon schedules "fit all." This excellent reference provides detailed schedules over a period of 18 weeks of quality workouts leading to the target race. For a particular race specialty and particular phase during the training schedule, Daniels recommends emphasis on ***primary***, ***secondary*** and occasional ***maintenance*** training sessions, which are matched to ***VO_2max***, ***anaerobic threshold*** and ***speed*** training sessions. For example, for 3K, 5K, and 10K runners there is primary emphasis on VO_2max training.

Details of VO_2max (**VO**), anaerobic threshold (**AT**), and speed (**S**) training sessions, the quality sessions, are briefly as follows:

VO: Long repetitions, e.g., 800m to 2000m (shortest for middle distance runners) at 10K, 5K, or 3K race pace. The rest time is normally equal to the run time or shorter; see "Rest Times vs.Run Times" in Table 7.2.

AT: Tempo (continuous) run or intervals at comfortably hard pace just below the lactic or ventilatory threshold (15 seconds slower/mile than 10K race pace). As a rough guide, rest between repeats equals the run time or until the heart returns below 120 beats per minute.

S: Short repetitions, e.g., 150 meter to 600 meter at mile race pace or faster. The rest between repeats is a full rest for a pure speed workout. For a speed endurance workout, or when building tolerance to lactic acid, rest until the heartbeat reduces below 120 to 130 beats per minute.

See also Chapter 7 for more details on these training systems. The above three training sessions should not necessarily occur all in each quality week. For example, Martin and Coe[2] advocate training blocks of 14 days. For middle distance runners:

day 1 and 3 sessions are VO type sessions, day 5, 8 and 10 are S type sessions at 1500, 800, and 400 meter race pace respectively, with distance runs and fartlek (arbitrary fast-slow mixture) between the quality sessions, and a race at day 7 and 14.

Symbols Description

AT	= Anaerobic Threshold training
VO	= VO_2max interval training
S	= Anaerobic Lactic (speed) training
Sr	= Anaerobic Lactic training reduced in intensity: reduced reps and/or speed, or increased rest.
St	= Strides (slower than mile race pace),e.g., 8 x 80 meters.
L	= Long run, normally about 25% of weekly mileage except longer for the marathon.
Lr	= Long run reduced in length
E	= Easy recovery run or easy fartlek
MP	= Marathon Pace. This is similar to AT continuous, i.e., a pace about 5% slower than AT (actually 35 to 40 seconds per mile slower than 10K race pace) but under more controlled favorable conditions of climate, terrain, and measured course. A MP run is 10 to 12 miles. MPr = 6 to 8 miles
TT	= Time Trial usually 1/2 to 3/4 of race distance.
VO/S	= First half VO session, second half S session*
VO/St	= VO session followed by St session
E/St	= E run followed by St session
AT/S	= First half AT session, second half S session*

***Note:** These **S** sessions are to build speed endurance. Normally at least 10 to 15 minutes should separate the two workouts.

PHASES OF TRAINING

The four phases of training are **base**, transition, quality and taper as explained below:

1. After building a good base for about 8 to 12 weeks, the following sharpening phase lasts about 14 to 16 weeks. The **sharpening or speedwork** phase consists of the transition phase, followed by the quality workout phase and the taper.
   There is considerable evidence to suggest that about 12 weeks of quality sessions are about right for sharpening or fine-tuning after a good base of conditioning.

See "The Principle of the Sharpening and Taper" in Chapter 5. This applies also to the marathon after sufficient base training to handle the quality sessions. For example, Ken Sparkes[3] interviewed four elite or world-class marathoners on the length of time needed to train for a marathon. The consensus was about 12 weeks of high mileage including quality sessions are preferred to maintain motivation and to be prepared for the marathon. Prior to this, they are already highly trained, e.g., equivalent to adequate base training.

2. The **transition** phase or preparation period consists of 2 to 3 weeks mainly of Sr, S and AT workouts leading up to the more strenuous primary and secondary quality workouts.
3. The **quality** training phase emphasizes 10 to 11 weeks of primary and secondary quality sessions.
4. The **taper** consists of the following:

- It lasts one to two weeks, but is longer for the marathon;
- Reduced quantity but retaining some intensity;
- A full or increased rest between intervals;
- For middle distance, a time trial or low-key race seven days before the big race;
- For the marathon no long run, L, within the last four weeks, and no 10K race the week before;
- See also "The Principle of the Sharpening and Taper" in Chapter 5 and the section on "Marathon Taper" in Chapter 9.

PRINCIPLES AND GUIDELINES

These guidelines are recommended to avoid over training and allow for proper recovery.

1. Avoid the following on successive days:
    - S and VO sessions
    - S session and race
    - VO session and race
    - L and VO session
    - L and S session
    - L and AT session for half-marathon and marathon training
    - L and race

2. Provide for the following:
    - Reduced L (Lr) or E the day after a race
    - Two days easy (E) before low-key race
    - Three days E before important race

- At least one day E between S and VO sessions*
- At least one day E before and after VO or S sessions*
- After 3K, 5K, and 10K races allow one to two, two to three, and three easy recovery days respectively
- Allow two weeks between 10 mile races and one week between 5K or 8K races
- One (intervals) running session/week in the water at least, but preferably also continuous water runs on some mornings of E days (see Chapter 11 on "Running in the Pool")

Note: More time should be allowed for recovery for the less experienced.

3. Incorporate periodization, i.e., increase intensity gradually for three weeks with fourth week easier.

4. If quality sessions extend beyond 12 weeks reduce quantity but retain intensity of workouts.

CORRECT BALANCE OF QUALITY TRAINING SESSIONS

The correct mix of training must be met for your distance specialty. For your particular running event the amount of relative importance to be put on the aerobic and anaerobic workouts can be seen in Table 1.1 in Chapter 1 and "Principle 4" in Chapter 5. These references show the percentages of anaerobic and aerobic energies used during middle and long distance races, e.g., the anaerobic varies from about 33% for 800m, 8% for 5K, to less than 1% for the marathon. The correct balance of anaerobic and aerobic workouts is obtained by selecting more or less of the following: long runs, easy runs, lactate threshold runs, VO_2max runs, and anaerobic lactic runs.

How much speed (S) training? S (anaerobic lactic) training is obviously of primary importance for shorter middle distances but is only of tertiary importance (next to VO and AT training) for marathon runners. Ideally, the percentage of anaerobic mileage during a typical week would be the same as for the percentage of anaerobic used during the race specialty (as shown in Table 1.1 in Chapter 1); however, there are practical limitations:

- For example, for the marathon, race times depend to a large extent on race times for 5K and 10K; therefore, ideally, the anaerobic percentage of total mileage should approach that for a 10K specialist. But additional S sessions would seriously interfere with obtaining the required weekly mileage for the marathon. Therefore, a compromise is required.

- Also for the average experienced middle distance runner matching the anaerobic training percentage to Table 1.1 is impractical for the following reasons. Normally only two to three quality sessions at most (combinations of AT, VO, and S) are feasible each week when one allows for the long run and easy days in between the quality sessions. To avoid overload S workouts are normally limited to about 5% per session; in my S workouts about 1 and 1/2 miles per session is maximum for about 30 to 35 weekly miles. Therefore, based on the above considerations, the average middle distance runner (e.g., 800m) is able to achieve perhaps 10% only of weekly anaerobic mileage (S sessions) compared to the ideal of about 33% from Table 1.1. However, elite middle runners, such as Sebastion Coe, have reached as high as 33% mileage in anaerobic sessions in a week.

Speed how often? If speed is not worked on for over a week, it starts to deteriorate.

- For 5K events (or longer), a VO workout at 5K race pace will retain speed since this workout is at race pace (or faster). However, the S workout will make the VO workout easier, so this is one reason for not neglecting speed for long periods.
- For events shorter than 3K or 5K a VO workout will build strength (endurance), and strength is speed. Ideally, S workouts should be incorporated every week. The neural pathways forget.
- Strides during warm-up and on days of easy runs assist to retain speed if fast enough but the speed endurance component is lacking in view of the short length. However, strides, e.g., about 6 x 100m or 8 x 80m at about mile race pace are recommended following most long and easy runs.

How much AT, and VO training? The importance of **AT** training increases with longer races. But also it is important for middle distances since it provides quality training with limited stress and aids in recovery (Daniels[1]). AT training is more important to beginners, the less competitive and older runners in view of its reduced stress compared to VO training.

VO training once a week or every other week is sufficient for the average experienced runner in view of its high stress (mental and physical). VO training is mainly done at 5K or 10K race pace so it is of most importance to runners training for events around this pace, e.g., for 10K, 5K and 3K races.

The average distance runner needs to improve his/her aerobic capacity and also to raise the anaerobic threshold with VO_2max and AT training respectively. In view of the above considerations, VO training and AT training are of about equal importance for all events except for the half-marathon and marathon. Also, VO becomes more important than AT training for events around 3K/5K race pace. For the marathon, AT training is more important than VO training.

Summary of Relative Importance of VO, AT, and S Workouts. For shorter distances e.g., 800m there is most emphasis on S workouts and less on VO and AT workouts. Conversely for longer distances e.g., marathon there is most emphasis on AT workouts and somewhat less emphasis on VO and much less on S workouts. In the middle for 3K and 5K events, there is primary emphasis on VO training and secondary emphasis on S and AT training.

The table below summarizes the emphasis on the quality sessions for the various race specialties.

Table 10.1 • Training Emphasis for Various Events

The main training emphasis is put in order of importance, primary followed by secondary and tertiary. The percentage of maximum heart rate, MHR, during the race assists to determine the primary emphasis during training.

Race	Heart Rate	Main Training Emphasis
800m	100%MHR	S, VO, AT
1500m, mile	100%MHR	S, VO, AT
3K	98-100%MHR	VO, AT /* S
5K	95%MHR	VO, AT /* S
10K	90-92%MHR	VO, AT, S
Half-Marathon	Just below AT**	AT, VO, S
Marathon	***	AT, VO, S

The aerobic conditioning training (slower than marathon race pace) is important in all cases and becomes increasingly so as the race distance lengthens.

* The indicates nearly equal secondary importance

** In the case of the half-marathon (and marathon), the heart rate depends on the experience of the athlete. At just below the AT, the beginner is at about 70%MHR, the experienced runner is at about 80-85%MHR and the elite runner is at about 90%MHR.

*** Several heart beats per minute lower than for half-marathon.

EXAMPLE TRAINING SCHEDULES

Based on the above guidelines, the following schedules were drawn up for the average experienced competitive runner:

Table 10.2 • 800m-1500m Sharpening Schedule

10.5VO, 10.5AT, and 15S sessions in 11 Quality weeks and 1 Taper week

SESSION	WEEK	SUN	MON	TUE	WED	THUR	FRI	SAT
Transition	1	L	E	Sr	E	Sr	E	AT
"	2	L	E	Sr	E	S	E	AT
"	3	Lr	E	S	E	S	E	AT
Quality	4	L	E	VO	E	S	E	AT/S
"	5	L	E	VO	E	S	E	AT
"	6	L	E	VO	E	S	E	AT/S
"	7E*	Lr	E	VOr	E	Sr	E	AT
"	8	L	E	VO	E	S	E	AT/S
"	9	L	E	VO	E	S	E	AT
"	10	L	E	VO/S	AT	E/St	E	Race or TT**
"	11E*	Lr	E	Sr	AT	E/St	E	"
"	12	Lr	E	VO/S	AT	E/St	E	"
"	13	Lr	E	S	AT	E/St	E	"
"	14	Lr	E	VO/S	AT	E/St	E	"
Taper	15E*	Lr	Sr	E	AT	E/St	E	"
"	16E*	Lr	E	Sr	E	E/St	E	Main Race

* Easy week. Mileage is reduced by about 15% per week after week 14.

** Assumes **VO** (3K or 5K), or S (800m or 1500m) type of race, or time trial alternately for weeks 10 to 15. Preferably, not a race every weekend; but ideally every other weekend. Preferably, not a 3K or 5K race seven days before the main race, but a low-key 800m or 1500m race or time trial.

Table 10.3 • 1500 -3K Sharpening Schedule

14VO, 12AT, and 10S sessions in 11 Quality weeks and 1 Taper week

SESSION	WEEK	SUN	MON	TUE	WED	THUR	FRI	SAT
Transition	1	L	E	Sr	E	Sr	E	AT
"	2	L	E	Sr	E	S	E	AT
"	3	Lr	E	S	E	VOr	E	AT
Quality	4	L	E	VO	E	S	E	AT
"	5	L	E	VO	E	S	E	AT
"	6	L	E	VO	E	AT	E	S
"	7E*	Lr	E	VOr	E	Sr	E	AT
"	8	L	E	VO	E	S	E	AT
"	9	L	E	VO	E	S	E	AT
"	10	L	E	VO	AT	E/St	E	Race or TT **
"	11E*	Lr	E	VOr	AT	E/St	E	AT
"	12	Lr	E	VO	AT	E/St	E	Race or TT**
"	13	Lr	E	VO	AT	E/St	E	"
"	14	Lr	E	VO	AT	E/St	E	"
Taper	15E*	Lr	Sr	E	AT/S	E	E	"
"	16E*	Lr	AT/S	E	E/St	E or Rest	E	Main Race

* Easier week. Mileage is reduced about 20% per week after week 14.

** Assumes **VO** (3K or 5K), or S (800m or 1500m) type of race, or time trial alternately for weeks 10 to 15. Preferably, not a race every weekend; but ideally every other weekend. Preferably, not a 3K or 5K race seven days before the main race.

Table 10.4 • 5K to 15K Sharpening Schedule

13.5VO, 11.5AT, and 7S sessions in 11 Quality weeks and 1 Taper week

SESSION	WEEK	SUN	MON	TUE	WED	THUR	FRI	SAT
Transition	1	L	E	Sr	E	Sr	E	E
"	2	L	E	Sr	E	S	E	AT
"	3	Lr	E	S	E	VOr	E	E
Quality	4	L	E	VO/S	E	AT	E	AT
"	5	L	E	VO	E	AT/S	E	AT
"	6	L	E	VO/S	E	AT	E	S
"	7E*	Lr	E	VOr	E	AT/S	E	AT
"	8	L	E	VO/S	E	AT	E	AT
"	9	L	E	VO	E	AT/S	E	AT
"	10	L	E	E	VO/St	E	E	Race or TT
"	11E*	Lr	E	VOr	E	Sr	E	AT
"	12	L	E	E	VO/St	E	E	Race or TT
"	13	Lr	E	VO	E	S	E	AT
"	14	L	E	E	VO/St	E	E	5K Race or TT
Taper	15E*	Lr	E	E	AT/Sr	E	E	"
"	16 E*	E	E	AT/Sr	E	E	E or Rest	RACE

* Easier week. Mileage is reduced by about 25% per week after week 14.

Table 10.5 • Marathon and Half-Marathon Sharpening Schedule

4.5VO, 11.7AT, and 4.5S sessions in 11 quality weeks and 1 Taper week

SESSION	WEEK	SUN	MON	TUE	WED	THUR	FRI	SAT
Transition	1	Lr	E	Sr	E	Sr	E	E
"	2	L	E	Sr	E	S	E	AT
"	3	Lr	E	S	E	VOr	E	E
Quality	4	L	E	AT/St	E	E	E	AT
"	5	Lr	E	VO	E	AT/S	E	E
"	6	L	E	AT/St	E	E	E	AT
"	7E*	Lr	E	VOr	E	AT/S	E	E
"	8	L	E	AT/St	E	E	E	Race or AT
"	9	Lr	E	VO	E	AT/S	E	E
"	10	L	E	E	AT/St	E	E	E
"	11E*	Lr	E	AT	E	S	E	E
"	12	MP or, Race	E	E	AT/St	E	E	E
"	13	Lr	E	AT	E	S	E	E
"	14**	MPr	E	E	AT/St	E	E	E
Taper	15E**	Lr	E	E	AT or S	E	E	E or 5K race
"	16E**	Lr***	E	E	AT/St	E or Rest	E	MARA-THON

* Easy week. Between week 4 and week 12, L increases to maximum and then reduces. Ideally, L should increase from about 15 miles (or about 2 hours) to 22 miles (or about three hours).

** After week 13 mileage decreases about 25% per week down to about 30% to 40% in the last week.

*** 10 to 12 mile run, but less than this if previous Saturday was a low-key 5K race.

Table 10.6 • Summary of Quality Sessions (VO, AT and S) in 12 Weeks

EVENT	VO	AT	S	TOTAL VO, AT, S SESSIONS	%Anaerobic* Average/ week	%Quality** Average/ week
800–1500	10.5	10.5	15	36	7.0	22
1500–3K	14	12	10	36	5.1	23.5
5K–15K	13.5	11.5	7	32	3.8	21.9
Marathon and Half-Marathon	4.5	11.7	4.5	20.7	2.2	14.6

Note: In equations below, assume 1VO session is 8% of weekly mileage, 1AT session is 10% of weekly mileage, and 1S session is 5% of weekly mileage. These numbers are based on Daniels[1] recommended maximums. He also recommends maximums of 6, 6, and 3 miles respectively for VO, AT, and S sessions respectively for the average runner.

Method for Estimating Percentages

*% Anaerobic/week

=(Mileage of S sessions + 0.10 of VO mileage)100/Total mileage

=(Miles/wk)x(5%xS sessions + 0.1x8%xVO sessions)/(12xMiles/wk)

Note: The 0.10 above accounts for about 10% anaerobic in VO sessions at between 3K and 5K race pace. Also a race or time trial is considered equivalent to either an S or VO workout depending on the distance.

**%Quality/week

= (Mileage of VO + AT + S Sessions)100/ Total mileage

= (Miles/wk) x (5%xS + 10%xAT + 8%xVO)/(12xMiles/wk)

Conclusion from Table 10.6

- The table shows the difficulty in achieving a high percentage of anaerobic training in a schedule. The reducing percentage for longer events is correct.
- The percentage of quality training is about correct for an experienced runner, i.e., about 20% per week on the average for the shorter distances and reduced for the marathon.

Flexibility of Example Schedules

The following flexibility is built into these schedules to accommodate the various levels of experience and the athlete's condition on the day of training:

1. A reduced long run, Lr, is scheduled the day after a stressful quality session or a race.
2. The easy runs, E, can be either continuous or easy fartlek.
3. For all events except for the marathon and half-marathon, the final six weeks of quality sessions schedules either a low-key race or time trial on most weeks. The less experienced runners and marathoners could consider less races and/or time trials.
4. The anaerobic threshold runs (AT), can be either continuous (tempo) or (cruise)intervals.
5. In the morning of easy days, cross-training (cycling or running in the water) or weights and stretching or a session of strides is recommended. Running in the water for recovery and strength is recommended once a week and preferably more; about 100 meters of water running can be considered equivalent to about one mile of running on the roads if done at the same perceived effort and for the same elapsed time in both cases.
6. Fridays can be an easy running day, a cross-training day or a complete rest day.
7. An easier week is incorporated every fourth week.

HOW TO MAKE THE SCHEDULES EASIER OR HARDER

The above schedules with their built in flexibility should suit most experienced competitive runners. If the schedules are too easy or too stressful for your particular condition or experience, they can be modified as suggested below. At the same time, your special days to train or particular days off can be incorporated.

Easier Schedule

1. Reduce the volume of the sessions or the number of quality sessions per week as below:

Table 10.7 • Reduced Sessions/Week for Easier Schedule

Event	**Average Quality Sessions/Week**	
	Above Schedules	**Easier Schedules**
800–1500m	3	2
1500m–3K	3	2
5K–15K	2.5*	1.5**
Marathon and half-marathon	1.5**	1

* Indicates half the weeks have 3 quality sessions and half the weeks have 2 quality sessions.

** Indicates half the weeks have 2 quality sessions and half the weeks have 1 quality session.

2. For the less experienced or "older" competitor one quality session per week is suggested: a fartlek session, or anaerobic threshold intervals or continuous tempo run, or anaerobic lactic (speed) intervals (mile race pace or greater). Notice that the more stressful VO_2max intervals are not recommended for this easiest schedule. Also the "older" competitor will normally know when the VO_2max workouts are too much for them; one criteria is when it is fun no more, or too painful.
3. Instead of one rest day per week, take two. The latter can include some easier cross-training.

Harder Schedule

For **more experienced competitive runners,** include some or all of:

- Back-to-back quality sessions (this would occur more frequently in middle distance schedules): e.g., AT continuous between S and VO sessions or the day before or after S or VO session; AT continuous or AT intervals preferably can be before or after L.
- For the more experienced middle distance runners, e.g., 800-1500m types where L is less than one hour, an AT or S session can follow L the next day.
- More races and time trials when condition indicates readiness.
- Two a day workouts with an easy session in the morning.
- Instead of a VO (VO_2max) workout, the more experienced competitors can substitute the occasional vVO_2max workout, i.e., intervals at the minimal velocity which produces VO_2max. See Chapter 7 for explanation of these more stressful workouts.
- See also detailed Daniels[1] schedules and detailed Martin and Coe[2] schedules for distance runners.

REFERENCES

1. Daniels, J., *Daniels' Running Formula,* Human Kinetics, Champaign IL, 1998.
2. Martin, D., and Coe, P., *Better Training For Distance Runners,* Human Kinetics, Champaign IL, 1997.
3. Sparkes, K., *Training Secrets,* Rodale Press, Emmaus, PA, 1996.

KITCHENER WATERLOO
137

CHAPTER

11

What is good for thoroughbred race horses
is good for thorough runners, too.

RUNNING IN THE POOL

INTRODUCTION

Cross-training, such as cycling, swimming, rowing, cross-country skiing, and running in the water, can greatly assist your running in several ways. However, the one most beneficial to land running is running in the water. Pool running can also be of great benefit to many athletes besides runners since it builds strength, endurance and flexibility. I, and many others, believe it is probably *the greatest fitness discovery in the past few decades.* Many world-class athletes have used deep-water running as part of their normal training, e.g., Lynn Williams, Steve Scott, Benoit Samuelson, Ed Eyestone, Priscilla Welch, and even Maurice Green, I hear, to mention a few. After about 18 years of this enjoyable activity, I am convinced it has helped me a great deal. For instance, in an 800- or 400-meter race, after proper training, I never get a heavy tired or painful feeling even in a world-record performance; I attribute this mainly to the strength endurance developed through the water workouts.

Initially, most will find water workouts stressful, so start slow, and stop after 5 to 10 minutes. But as the body adapts, longer and harder workouts will be possible until more than than 30 minutes will be feasible. As you become more used to pool running or become more fit, your heart rate will become lower for a given lineal speed in the pool. Later, you may have to remove your flotation belt or vest to maintain a high heart rate.

The following will be discussed here:

- Personal water running experience
- Advantages of water running
- Running form
- Heart rate
- Perceived effort
- Workouts in the deep end
- Workouts in the shallow end
- Precautions

Personal Water Running Experience

From 1986 (when I came out of retirement from running, after a 33-year layoff) until 1991, I did a combination of swimming and running in the water on my easy days. In 1991, I gave up the swimming and used water running about four mornings a week (usually about 30 to 40 minutes) for recovery and generally with one session of hard strength-endurance type of intervals in the deep end. Part of these workouts are in the shallow end with water up to about six inches below the shoulders doing sprint drills (AB's) and plyometrics. When I am in near top shape, I occasionally run intervals in the deep end with no belt and with hands above the water and some fast interval swimming with short rests. Some of my workouts are a combination of deep-water running, shallow-end running and drills, and fast interval swimming. Lately, I have also become a big advocate of intervals with the kickboard and flippers; these provide strengthening of the legs, ankles and the gluteus muscles. Besides, the whole thing is fun.

ADVANTAGES

There are many advantages to consistent water running as follows:

1. Ideal for Recovering from Injuries

In the deep end of the pool, there is no pounding, so this is ideal for maintaining your fitness and speeding recovery as long as the injury does not hurt while running in the water. Also, just prior to returning to running on the land after an injury some running in the shallow end of the pool assists in reconditioning the legs to pounding on the track or roads. This is a trick I learned after a sad experience.

There is an important psychological benefit to the serious athlete when injured; to compensate for the depression of the injury, this activity is mentally satisfying since the athlete knows it is speeding recovery and is maintaining his or her fitness.

2. *Contributes to Overall Fitness and Strength Endurance*

Water running is excellent for developing strength endurance, somewhat analogous to weight training but with a cardiovascular advantage. Unlike weight lifting the whole upper and lower body are strengthened simultaneously. It will also strengthen the "back-up" muscles in your legs, and prevent muscle imbalance. With stronger muscles, you don't need as many muscle cells because each one is stronger. This saves energy and improves your running economy; hence your speed increases.

For middle distance and long distance runners who do pool running, further weight training on the legs is not necessary.

In doing those hard anaerobic intervals, the deep rapid breathing will help to keep your lungs young and elastic and slow down the decline of VO_2max due to age.

3. *Increased Flexibility*

Joints (shoulder, hip, knee, and ankle) become more supple, and flexibility of tendons, and muscles is increased. This is accomplished by good running form in the water, i.e., upright, full sprint type arm motion and legs reaching out with high knee action and tucking the heels under the buttocks. Also, at the end of the workout, concentration on taking your arms and legs through an exaggerated range of cross-country skiing motion ("long stride exercise") further assists in increasing stride length and flexibility.

Due to the buoyancy of the water, the limbs are lighter and it is possible to swing the legs through a much greater range than on the land. This is particularly evident while carrying out drills in the shallow end of the pool.

4. *Running Form is Improved*

Running in the pool allows one to relax and concentrate on running style and, consequently, running form often improves. It helps to make the running motion smoother and more efficient. In the water, you increase your stride length which translates to land running.

5. *Beneficial for Recovery after Land Running*

After a land workout, the cool water and easy pool running for 20 to 30 minutes on the same day or the day after will help greatly to speed recovery. The cool water is rejuvenating, reducing fatigue, muscle soreness and stiffness due to muscle cell damage.

6. *Excellent for Anaerobic Threshold Workouts*

Water running is excellent for improving the anaerobic threshold. The workouts could be continuous runs or interval training (see Chapter 7). For example, in a land workout at the anaerobic threshold, AT, a beginner, experienced, or elite runner is typically at about 70%, 80%, and 90% of maximum heart rate, MHR. At the AT an experienced runner with a MHR of 180 beats per minute, b.p.m., would need to achieve a heart rate of .8 x 180 – 10 = 134 b.p.m. For this submaximal effort, the 10 b.p.m. reduction makes land running and pool running equivalent at the same perceived effort.

7. Improvement of Aerobic Capacity and Speed

The aerobic capacity (VO_2max) or speed can be improved with water running but the heart rate has to be near maximum or, alternatively, the workout has to be at the same perceived effort. For example, an aerobic capacity workout and a speed workout has to be at about 95%MHR-20 b.p.m. and 98%MHR-20 b.p.m. respectively. At these maximal efforts, the 20 b.p.m. reduction makes land and pool running equivalent at the same perceived effort.

For those who can run in the pool in this range, there would be excellent benefits. However, many athletes may have trouble in reaching these high heart rates even without a flotation device. (I found that after 12 years of conditioning in the water my heart rate would not go higher than about 100 beats per minute even with very hard effort. Raise the cadence to raise the heart rate.) But there is still great benefit to run at the *same perceived effort* in the water as on land. The thoroughbred horse trainers are not all wrong. Speed is strength. The water workouts provide strength due to the water resistance and this resistance works the fast twitch fibers. The required perceived effort on the Borg scale of 0 (zero effort) to 10 ("all-out effort") would be as follows for example (quotes within brackets are Borg terminology):

- 6 ("moderately hard") for anaerobic threshold workouts
- 8 ("very hard") for aerobic capacity (VO_2max) workouts
- 9 ("very, very hard") for speed workouts.

8. Adds to Mileage while Preventing Injuries

By substituting water running for some of your runs on the road and/or track, wear and tear on the joints, tendons, ligaments, and muscles is reduced, thus reducing possible injuries. See my "Run Pool Marathon," RPM, method for marathon training in Chapter 9. There are no sore muscles after a water run. Since there is no pounding, soreness and stiffness are virtually eliminated. Also, any lactic acid produced is quickly dissipated after the workout.

For my total equivalent mileage per week, I consider about 7 to 8 minutes of easy aerobic running in the water as equivalent to a mile of easy running on the land. Some say 40 minutes in the pool is equivalent to one hour on land; Joan Samuelson 1984 Olympic Marathon gold medallist says 30 minutes in the pool is equivalent to 90 minutes on land; she must work harder in the water than on land. *But if the perceived effort in the pool is the same as on the land then the running time in the pool is exactly the same as the running time on the land.*

9. Body's Transportation and Extraction of Oxygen Improved

Glenn McWaters[2] states "The blood's capacity to carry oxygen increases when the body is submerged in water cooler than body temperature, and the ability of the body's tissues to extract the oxygen from the blood improves in cool water." This explains to me why it is easier to do more intervals in the water at the same perceived effort. For example, on occasion, I have done as many as 12 hard repeats at two minutes each with a 30-second rest and without a vest or belt; but 12 hard two-minute intervals on land would be an impossibility. Also, I am able to do 20 minutes of continuous sprint drills, AB's, in the shallow end of the pool, once again difficult on land.

10. Mitochondrial Density Increases

The mitochondria are the tiny parts of the muscle cell that change energy in food into ATP energy by interaction with oxygen. Mitochondrial density increases in the appropriate running muscle cells just as in land running due to the specificity (similarity) of pool running to land running; this increased density allows more oxygen to be transferred into the muscle cell and more energy produced. Thus, land running is improved.

11. Tolerance to Lactic Acid is Increased

The water's resistance activates the fast twitch muscle fibers and therefore increases the production of lactic acid. Also, McWaters[2] describes a study at Auburn University comparing treadmill running with pool running at the same perceived effort. During pool running, the same subjects had higher lactic acid levels but these dissipated more quickly than on the treadmill. This indicates to me the possibility of pool running providing conditioning for tolerance to higher levels of lactic acid but only if the workout is above the lactic threshold. If you are above the lactic threshold, your breathing rate is noticeably more labored and conversation is more difficult.

12. Mentally Relaxing

Similar to swimming, pool running, if not too strenuous, is mentally relaxing enabling the mind to drift to problem solving and pleasant thoughts. However, doing fast intervals in the pool requires strict concentration.

13. Indicator of Fitness

I have found, when you are able to go fast in the water this indicates you will also be able to go fast on the land: therefore, water running is an excellent indicator of your fitness level and indicates when you are reaching a peak.

14. Energizing

When one is too tired (or with a cold) to run on land, it is generally possible to do a water workout, since the water is stimulating and you can adjust your pace to suit your energy level.

RUNNING FORM

Running form in the deep end of the pool should be as follows:

- Run upright with only a slight lean forward; leaning forward too much is a common problem restricting the stride length and constricting breathing.
- Run as naturally as possible; concentrate on the exact motion in the water as you would on land except in the pool you can easily exaggerate the stride slightly to increase flexibility (see advantage 4 above); reach out with the lower leg on each stride.
- Hands should not be cupped, pulling the water, but hands (thumbs) should be vertical as in sprinting.
- Keep elbows close to the body and well back on the backward arm motion breaking the surface; and thumbs should break the surface on the forward motion particularly when doing fast intervals.
- Arm movements are straight forward (not across the body) and straight backwards; exert more effort in the backward movement, which stretches the arm muscles and allows more power in the forward direction. This good practice in the pool will carry over to land running improving running form.
- Try to breathe naturally and evenly.
- Concentrate on arm movements and the legs will follow.
- Do not bob up and down.
- Relax the upper body, particularly the arms, to achieve faster speed and conserve energy.
- Do not power yourself through the water: think "fast/relaxed" or "faster/looser." You will go faster this way.

Note: The normal running stride is recommended. However for a hamstring injury the "bicycle" motion (more up-and-down and little reaching out with the forelegs) takes pressure off the hamstring muscle.

HEART RATE

To make intervals or continuous running in the pool equivalent to land running, the heart rate should be equivalent; but consider that in the pool at the same perceived effort, the heart rate is 10% lower than on land. The reasons for this heart rate reduction are the buoyancy of the water and the vest, which reduces the gravitational pull, and the increased pressure of the water compared to air pressure which increases venous blood return and in turn the heart's stroke volume. These effects result in the heart not having to work as hard (McWaters[2]).

It is well known that maximum benefit from training is achieved by training between 70% and 90% of maximum heart rate, MHR. Based on my personal experience on the land, recovery runs (aerobic conditioning) would be between 50% to 60% MHR, anaerobic threshold runs between 70% and 80%MHR, long run interval training (VO_2max) between 85% and 95%, and short fast run interval (speed) training around 95% to 99% of MHR. The above percentages correspond nearly to the percent of maximum effort. However, not all athletes are aware of their maximum heart rate; the rule of thumb of 220 minus your age, or even 200 minus one-half your age for a competitive athlete, can be a gross underestimate for a competitive athlete who has been training hard for years. The latter can prevent the normal reduction in MHR. For example, by the latter formulas, my MHR would be only about 165, but it was actually about 195 beats per minute at age 68. Also, not everyone is wearing a heart monitor. Therefore, the concept of perceived effort is very useful.

PERCEIVED EFFORT

To make pool running intervals equivalent to land intervals, one can also run at the same perceived effort (same level of exertion). Steve Scott, USA Olympic miler, trains in the pool in the morning; one-half of his total mileage of 100 miles/week is in the pool and based on perceived effort (Scott and Samuelson[1]).

McWaters[2] relates the speed in the pool to speed on the track for the same exertion level in both cases, based on calculations. Table 11 below is my personal experience (many timed tests in the pool) of the perceived effort in the pool with a flotation device compared to the same perceived effort on the track. For example, running 25 meters in the pool in 88 seconds feels like running continuous at about seven minute/mile pace on land (i.e., 400 meters on land in 105 seconds). Similarly, running 25 meters in the pool in 65 seconds feels to me like running a 400 meters sprint on the track in about 62 seconds. The data below when plotted in a chart result, surprisingly, in a straight line.

TABLE 11 • Pool Running vs. Track Running for the Same Perceived Effort

Time for 25 meters In Deep End of Pool with Flotation Belt	**Time for 400 meters and Pace per Mile on Track or Land**	
Seconds	Seconds/400m	Minutes/Mile
102	135 approx.	9
96	120 approx.	8
88	105 approx.	7
80	90 approx.	6
71	75 approx	5
70	72 approx.	
65	62 approx.	

Based on the above table I found the following convenient rules for running in the deep end of the pool with flotation belt or vest at the same perceived effort, PE, in the pool and on land:

- To duplicate short distance land interval training for less than about 80 seconds/400 meters at the same PE:
  Time for 25 meters in the pool = time for 400 meters on the track at the same perceived effort.
- To duplicate a long continuous land run at the same PE:
  Pool run distance = (Land run miles x 1609m) x 25m/400m
  = (Land run miles x 1609) /16
  = Land run miles x 100
  = meters

For example, to duplicate one land mile in the pool, run about 100 meters in the pool. (The latter is most accurate for pace less than 5 minutes per mile on land; for slower runs, the above simple formula underestimates the pool run total meters by about 25% or more). Therefore, the above is approximate but to duplicate the land workout, *it is essential to run in the pool for the same time as the land workout and at the same perceived effort in the pool as on land.*

Each individual will have a different concept of perceived effort in the water and on the land, depending on his/her present condition, years of training, and strength/fitness capabilities. By perceiving the same effort of exertion in the pool as on land, one can achieve the same benefit but with the bonus of flexibility and strength training at the same time and without muscle soreness.

WORKOUTS IN THE DEEP END

The normal running stride in the deep end of the pool provides general body conditioning but mainly for the hamstrings, quadriceps, ankles, hip flexors, shoulders and arms. My hamstrings became stronger than my quadriceps (a 1:1 ratio is preferred) mainly from 18 years of water running; the body moves forward in the water due to more power exerted in the backward direction mostly from the hamstrings.

How to make a deep-water pool workout equivalent to a land workout

- Warm-up and cool down, preferably for the same length of time as on land. Be sure to stretch before and after the workout. I recommend the whirlpool or sauna for stretching.
- All repetitions and continuous runs are at the same perceived effort.
- Repetitions and continuous runs are for the same length of time as on land. I found the length of the pool run in meters will be about 6 to 7.5% percent of the land run in meters.
- Recovery time between repetitions is much reduced to about one-third of the land value. But until you become adapted to pool running, you will need more than this amount.
- Preferably incorporate some speed work into all sessions and also some sprint drills in the shallow end of the pool.
- See also the section on "Long Run Pool Marathon" method in Chapter 9.

Running With Flotation Belt or Vest in Deep End

Note: The times quoted are an approximate guide based on my own experience of nearly two decades of pool running. Most of these workouts were done around age 60, hence a younger competitive male athlete should be able to achieve faster times when used to the water training.

It is convenient when timing yourself to base the workouts in the deep end on the time to complete one-half a pool length, L, or 12.5 meters. (The feet start to touch at about 12.5 meters in a standard 25-meter pool.) The following are some of my typical workouts:

- 1L in 37 sec., *, 2L in 1 min. 22 sec., *, 3L in 2 min. 6 sec., *, 4L in 2 min. 56 sec., rest 1 minute. Repeat in reverse, 4L, 3L, 2L, 1L. * indicates 10 to 15 second rest.
- 1 hour continuous run at 47 sec. per L.
- 4 x 10L in 7 min. 30 sec. with 60 sec. rest between sets.
- 10 x 3L in 1 min. 50 sec. to 1 min. 58 sec. with 45 sec. rest. This is hard.

- 1L fast in 37 sec., 1L slow, 2L fast in 1 min. 15 sec., rest 30 sec., keep repeating for 30 to 45 min.
- With a partner, take turns after each repetition alternately leading and following directly in line and close together taking advantage of the easier time in the wake of the leader; E.g., 12 x 3L with no rest.
- 5 x (2L fast, rest 30 sec. followed by 4L kick board). Rest about 60 seconds between sets.
- 4 x 1000 meters on land in T minutes with 2 minute rest followed 15 min. later by 4 x 5L in water in about T min. (with same perceived effort as on the track) with 1 min. rest.
- Steeplechase workout: For steeplechase simulation, do 2 sets x 10L at same perceived effort as in a 2000m steeplechase race with 8 to 10 fast hard arm strokes twice every L to simulate barriers (20 in all). Rest 1 to 2 minutes between sets.
- 15 x 2L at perceived effort of 5K race pace. Rest 30 seconds between 1st and 2nd repetition and reduce the rest by 2 seconds after each rep until before the last rep the rest is only 4 seconds. End the session if speed falls off, i.e., if unable to maintain constant speed for each rep. This workout is for the experienced only.
- For sprint training, it is preferable to attach yourself with a rubber bungee cord to a stationary object at the edge of the pool in the deep end. The following workout should be achievable by experienced sprinters about 40 years old:
  2 to 3 sets of 6 repetitions at 30 seconds each (about 100 arm movements/rep). Rest 30 sec. or 1 min. easy jog between reps and 2 to 4 min. rest between sets. The effort has to be very, very hard to all-out effort based on the Borg scale.
- To improve your running speed time in the water proceed as follows:
  1. If you have been using a flotation device, run without it for about five or six sessions over a period of about two weeks. These sessions include long runs or interval workouts.
  2. After the two weeks, put on a belt or vest and do your usual interval training. Use the same perceived effort as without the flotation device. I guarantee you will be significantly faster—flying in the water. Start this about four weeks before your big race of the year.

Running Without Flotation Device in Deep End. Only do the following when in good condition and thoroughly used to interval sessions with flotation device.

- 3 to 5 x 1L with hands above the water in 56 to 66 sec. with 45 sec. rest.

Combined Swimming and Running in the Deep End. For those who cannot achieve a high heart rate (in the recommended range of about 70% to 90% of maximum heart rate), a combination of swimming and running in the water is recommended to raise the heart rate. Attempt only if you are extremely fit. For example, after a good warm-up, swim 50 meters, immediately continue with a run in the deep end for 25 meters (two half lengths). Take a short rest; rest until you feel ready to go again, then repeat. Since it is not convenient to swim with the flotation belt or vest, the run in the water is without flotation. The number of repetitions you are able to do depends on your condition and your chosen speed in the water. This could be a tough workout, so do not be too ambitious in initial workouts.

Exercises in Deep End. With a different stride or leg movement, the resistance of the water strengthens specific muscles and/or increases flexibility.

1. ***Gluteus muscles strengthening***
   While running in the water, exaggerate the backward swing of the legs. Feel the contraction in the glutes. This will cause you to tilt somewhat forward in the upper body.
2. ***Quadriceps and hamstring strengthening***
   While wearing a flotation belt, lock the knees and keep both legs straight from hips to toes. Swing the legs backward and forward. Feel the contraction in the quads and hamstrings. You will remain in the same spot. The flotation device is required to prevent sinking.
3. ***Increased flexibility with exaggerated cross-country stride***
   Take long strides with long arm movements. Reach forward and stretch backward in the stride as in cross-country skiing. Get full extension forward and backward. You will feel the increased movement in the hip region. This will increase flexibility particularly in the hip region. *A few minutes is recommended for each water running session.*

WORKOUTS IN THE SHALLOW END

Drills and Running

- In addition to the above, I recommend to do sprint drills (AB's) and plyometrics in the shallow end of the pool (water level about six inches below the shoulders) for about 15 minutes or more once or twice a week. Examples of these drills are: high knees, karate kicks, butt kicks, ankle bounce drill, fast high knees, bounding and hopping (hop left foot, hop right foot, hop both feet) and running backward (see Chapter 6 on "Sprinting" for details.). The plyometrics in the pool area is a good way to ease into land plyometrics; the buoyancy will reduce the stress on the legs. Remember, you can do more in the water than on land so eventually work up to 20-minute sessions.
- Also, run fast in the shallow end feet touching the bottom and moving forward, do repeats, e.g., 10 x 1 minute with 15 second rest or 5 x 2 minutes at a slower pace with a 20- to 30-second rest.

- For another variation, attach a bungee cord to your waist and anchor it at the pool's edge. Run against the resistance of the cord. Runs can be continuous or intervals. Running backward against the resistance (facing the support) is also recommended. Aqua slippers may be required as your feet will slip if working hard against the tension. Be careful to work into the intervals gradually as they are stressful on the muscles.

Exercises in Shallow End. Stand at the edge of the pool in the shallow end with water above the chest so that the free leg is always below the surface. Do 12 reps with each leg beginning with one set (taking about seven minutes) and working up to two sets or more after two or three weeks. Your body will dictate the number of sets possible. With experience, speed up the swings of the free leg to obtain more resistance. Always warm-up and stretch before these drills. On land, some of these leg swings can become too ballistic but in the water the resistance acts to prevent problems. These exercises will increase strength and flexibility in the lower body. The motions are smooth and continuous cycles. The movement of the free leg is described below.

1. ***Adductor and abductor muscle strengthening***

(a) *Straight leg swinging sideways:*
Stand sideways to the wall and hold onto the wall with inner hand for support. Swing the free outer leg outward and upward to a comfortable position and back to beside the support leg. Use the same speed outward and back to provide equal exercising resistance for abductor and adductor muscles respectively.

(b) *Leg circles:*
Stand sideways to the pool wall and hold the pool wall for support with your inner hand. Stand on the inner leg. Swing the straight outer leg in half circles. Start with the outer leg well forward and move it straight back to a comfortable position, then outward, then forward and inward back to the starting position. Your foot has then completed a half circle. Do about six cycles in the clockwise direction and about six in the counter-clockwise direction with each leg.

2. ***Gluteus, quadriceps, and hip-flexor muscle strengthening***

Bent leg swinging forwards:
Stand sideways to the wall holding onto the wall of the pool for support with inner hand. The free leg is bent with upper leg at 90 degrees to the lower leg. Swing the free leg backward and forward but with more force and stretch in the backward direction. Feel the contraction in the buttocks region at the end of the back swing. In the forward direction, the thigh reaches horizontal but the lower leg does not go beyond vertical.

3. ***Hamstring, gluteus, quadriceps, and hip-flexor muscle strengthening***

(a) *Straight leg swinging forwards:*

Stand sideways to pool wall holding on with the inner hand for support. With a straight free leg swing it forward and backward. In the forward direction, the leg reaches horizontal then moves backward to a comfortable position while remaining extended. Feel the contraction of the gluteus muscles in the extreme backward position. Concentrate on accelerating in the forward direction to increase the resistance on your thigh and hip-flexor; this will assist to give you a powerful stride on land.

(b) *Exaggerated running motion:*

This is similar to the skipping "B" drill except done standing on the support leg. Stand sideways to the pool wall holding on with inner hand. Start with the thigh of the free leg above horizontal. Execute a karate kick. The free leg is now straight and horizontal. Swing the extended leg backwards. On return, the heel approaches the buttocks. The thigh raises again to above horizontal. Repeat the cycle again in a continuous smooth motion.

4. ***Hamstring, quadriceps, hip-flexor, adductor, and abductor muscle strengthening***

Leg swinging parallel to wall:

Face the pool wall and hold onto the wall with both hands. Swing the free left leg parallel to the wall: move this leg outwards to the left and high to a comfortable position, lower the leg while moving it inward, crossing the body past the support leg, then outward to the right to a high comfortable position. You have outlined the shape of a bathtub or half circle with your left foot. Continue moving back and forth for about six complete cycles. Then exercise the right free leg. This is a favorite exercise on land for hurdlers and many sprinters also for loosening the hips, but with the water buoyancy you can swing much higher increasing your flexibility.

5. ***Abdominal Strengthening***

Straight leg raises:

Position the back against the pool wall with arms fully out to the sides resting on the horizontal top of the pool wall. The arms are supporting the body in the pool. With legs at the bottom of the pool, raise the straight legs (knees locked) slowly until they are horizontal. Pause, and lower straight legs slowly. The resistance of the water provides an excellent workout for the abdominals. Do about 20 leg raises or until you are tired.

PRECAUTIONS

1. Allow four or five days between any water workout and any race since these workouts cause muscle fatigue during a track or road race. I did not know of this in the World Masters' Championships in Turku, Finland, and Durban, South Africa, and had heavy legs near the end of the 800-meters finals.
   A very easy (10 to 15 minute) pool run might be safe within two days of a low-key race, but it is better to stick to the four-day rule.
2. If doing a medium or harder intensity pool run in the morning, your legs could be too tired for running on land at night, I have found. After all, it is "water weights," i.e., the water's resistance simulates weight lifting exercises.
3. If you are injured and it hurts to run in the water then leave these workouts until there is no pain or soreness during water running.
4. Running and hopping in the shallow end of the pool with feet touching the bottom can sometimes result in sore ankles a day or two later. This is particularly so after doing extensive sprint drill (AB's) and/or plyometrics in the water. Since you are not wearing shoes, there is a lack of support. Also, although there is buoyancy to reduce impact, you will find you are on your toes without the support of shoes. Water slippers on the feet help but provide little support. Therefore, it is wise to wear a flotation belt to reduce impact and also to limit the session to about 15 to 20 minutes.

SUMMARY

For runners who like the water, there are many advantages to water running workouts and they are highly recommended by myself and many others to increase flexibility, cardiovascular capacity, and strength endurance in particular while avoiding injury.

REFERENCES

1. Steve, S., Samuelson, J., *Deep Water Running Video Featuring Steve Scott and Joan Benoit Samuelson*, Biogenergetic INC., Pelham, Alabama.
2. McWaters, J. Glenn, *Deep Water Exercise for Health and Fitness*, Publitec Editions, Laguna, CA, 1988.

CHAPTER 12

"A tree that will bend in the wind will not break in a storm."
Anonymous

STRETCHING

A funny thing happened at the Run For the Cure (Cancer) in 1998 in Toronto. I was warming up, stretching before the race with Vince, a new young member of our North York Track club. This was a 5K race with more than 10 000 runners; there were even clowns to cheer up the runners. Vince was lying on the ground with his body in some sort of pretzel shape–a stretch of his own invention. He was new to stretching with his face in a tense grimace of forced determination. A clown bent over him and jokingly said, "Are you all right, sir? Are you in pain?" Vince had not learned that stretching should be relaxed with no strain or discomfort. After the race, the same clown asked, "Are you ok now, sir?"

You can't be too flexible, though some power sprinters may argue otherwise. Normally, I stretch about three or four times per day; not as much as a cat or a dog–they are the experts–continually tuning up all muscles. Stretching is considered essential by most athletes for warming up prior to training or a race to prevent injury, and after to prevent sore and tight muscles. Several times, I recall neglecting to stretch after hard training or a race and suffered the consequences of sore muscles the next day or two later. It always surprises me particularly after a road race to see only a few people stretching and cooling down. Also, stretching should be done before and after doing weight training. This is a common omission. This is even more essential when lifting weights to strengthen an injured muscle. Stretching very gently has to be done after warming up the muscles by fast walking for a few minutes or cycling or running for at least four minutes or so. If available, the sauna or whirlpool is also effective to warm the muscles. I have often started my indoor workouts at the Mississauga YMCA with gentle stretching in the whirlpool for about five to eight minutes; submerging only the legs. I would not recommend this before a race or a hard workout, since it could be slightly de-energizing. Also if you notice any particularly tight or sore muscles during stretching, this is a good time to do some gentle self-massage on these areas.

ADVANTAGES

Stretching has many advantages:

- It ***improves your appearance*** by ensuring good posture and more graceful body movements. This will assist to increase your self-confidence and self-esteem.
- "It ***assists coordination***, makes the body feel more relaxed, increases range of motion of joints, promotes circulation and feels good" (Anderson[2]).
- It ***increases flexibility and elasticity*** of joints, tendons and muscles with the following benefits:
    - Injuries are less likely, mainly from stretching during cool down
    - Also a flexible runner can run more economically and exert more power. About 25 years ago while attending track meet competitions in Ontario, Canada with my two young boys, 8 and 10 years old, I noticed the fastest runners were the most flexible. If you are flexible, you have elastic strength; here is my crude explanation of elastic strength or elastic power: a thin, long (flexible) whip has more power than a thick, short (inflexible) whip.
- It ***assists removal of waste products*** by pumping out old blood and waste material, and bringing in fresh blood. Blood, especially in the veins, is squeezed out on the stretch. As the stretch is released, the muscle returns to its normal size and brings in fresh blood, which serves to cleanse and nourish it. It flushes metabolic wastes, such as lactic acid, from the stressed muscles. Hence, for injuries in particular, this fresh blood brings in nutrients and removes scar tissue.
- It ***compensates for the natural loss of flexibility*** with increasing age (in particular master athletes). As a person ages, the stride length shortens, and the stride frequency also decreases. But frequent and consistent stretching will slow down this deterioration.
- ***"Muscles store elastic energy during a stretch*** giving the muscle more power. A stretch (ideally) should immediately precede the sports competition to take advantage of this increased power. [However], if an athlete warms up and stretches, then stands around for 20 or 30 minutes before the competition, the muscles contract back to their original resting length and the energy is wasted" (Dr. Stark[6]).

- It can ***correct imbalances in the body*** due to differences in flexibility between right and left legs, and between right and left hip region. These imbalances can lead to altered gait in running and result in soreness or injury in other parts of the lower body. (For example, in 1999, I had inflexibility in the region of my left hip flexor that caused right knee problems.)

WHAT TO STRETCH?

Flexibility in the region of the hips is essential to improve stride length and to achieve a smooth stride. Strive for considerable flexibility in the pelvic region, similar to that of a hurdler. Therefore, hurdle drills are very useful and recommended by some coaches. The trail leg drill is also particularly useful. Also, another favorite of mine for the hips is the lunge.

The following muscles must also be thoroughly stretched: Achilles and lower calf (soleus muscle), upper calf (gastrocnemius muscle), quadriceps, hamstring, adductor, abductor, iliotibial band (ITB, upper outside of legs), back, and piriformis muscle (common sore spot in runner's gluteus muscles). See Anderson[2] for excellent reference for these and many other stretches. The ITB and the piriformis stretches are often neglected by many runners; this sometimes results in knee, sciatica and other problems.

Following the above stretches, the sprint AB drills below should be done to condition the ligaments and joints and further prepare the muscles for action, i.e., two or three times about 30 meters of each (see the Chapter 6 on "Sprinting"):

- High knees
- Karate kicks
- "Butt" kicks
- Ankle bounce drills
- Fast high knees
- Fast feet
- Some bounding, particularly if one is a sprinter

Stretching of the prime mover muscle is opposed by tension and stiffness in the antagonist muscle and vice versa. Therefore, it is important to stretch the prime mover muscle and the antagonist muscle (e.g., the hamstring and the quadriceps)in the same session.

DON'T OVERDO IT

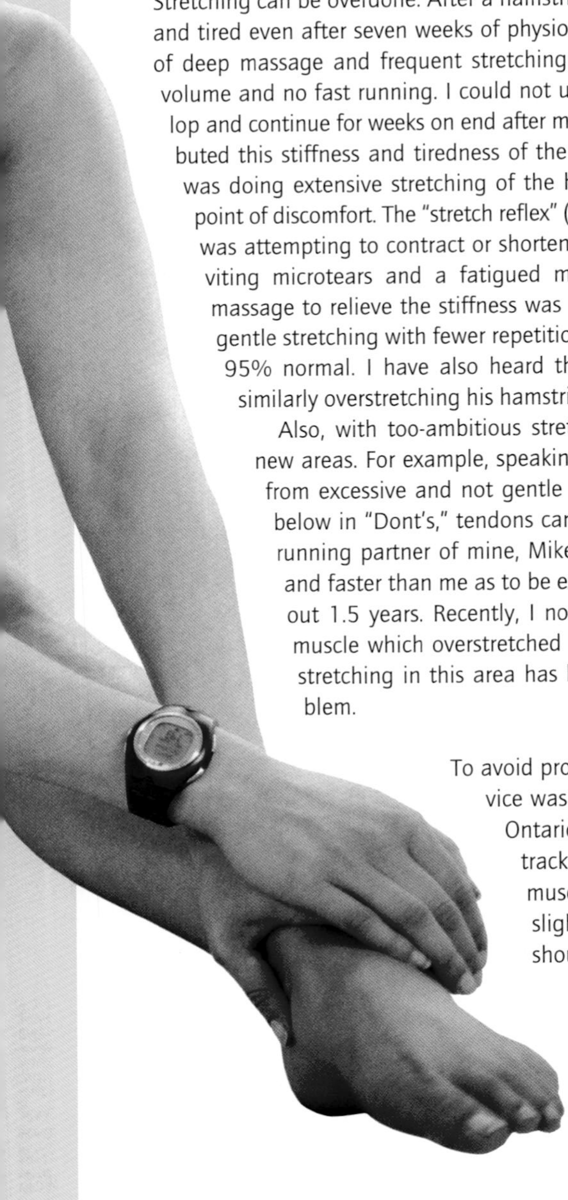

Stretching can be overdone. After a hamstring injury in 1996, this muscle became stiff and tired even after seven weeks of physiotherapy three times a week, many sessions of deep massage and frequent stretching. My training was reduced to about 50% volume and no fast running. I could not understand why this condition should develop and continue for weeks on end after my injury was nearly healed. I eventually attributed this stiffness and tiredness of the hamstring to overstretching this muscle. I was doing extensive stretching of the hamstring two or three times a day to the point of discomfort. The "stretch reflex" (the body's automatic protective mechanism) was attempting to contract or shorten during the stretch. This tug-of-war was inviting microtears and a fatigued muscle due to muscle cell damage. Deep massage to relieve the stiffness was not helping the microtears. When I started gentle stretching with fewer repetitions and no massage, the muscle returned to 95% normal. I have also heard that Jeff Galloway developed sciatica from similarly overstretching his hamstring.

Also, with too-ambitious stretching, sore muscles can develop in other new areas. For example, speaking from experience, a sore back could occur from excessive and not gentle hamstring stretching. Also, as pointed out below in "Dont's," tendons can only be stretched about 3% maximum. A running partner of mine, Mike Carter, 20 years younger (more muscular and faster than me as to be expected) has had bursitis of the heel for about 1.5 years. Recently, I noticed he was over-stretching his lower calf muscle which overstretched the Achilles. I believe that his more gentle stretching in this area has lessened his aggravating, painful heel problem.

To avoid problems of overstretching, some excellent advice was obtained from Dr. Robert Taylor, a London Ontario chiropractor specializing in injuries to track and field athletes: after relaxing the muscle, assume a good stretch, then back off slightly and hold for 15 to 30 seconds. This should avoid the above problems.

STRETCHING DO'S AND DONT'S

Most serious athletes are stretching fairly religiously but some are unknowingly doing more harm than good. There are various stretching problems, e.g., jerking the muscle into position, muscle imbalances, ligament weakening, excessive joint movement, neglected muscles, and overstretching of muscles and tendons.

Do:

- Warm up carefully before stretching to warm up the muscle and to lubricate the joints. This makes stretching more comfortable and effective. However, if the stretch is mild then warm-up is not required, e.g., mild stretching without warm-up can be done while watching TV. Also, warm-up is not essential prior to the Active Isolated Stretch method.
- In addition to the warm-up, some gentle massage for 5 to 10 minutes is beneficial particularly in problem areas, but don't apply any deep penetrating pressure.
- While concentrating on the muscle being stretched, stretch to mild tension using the usual static method, the Stark method, or use the Active Isolated Stretch (all discussed below).
- Isolate and stretch one muscle group at a time. Some stretches stretch the target muscle and other muscle groups, as well. Then you can't be too sure which group is the tightest and needs the most work.
- Breathe deeply as in belly breathing. Always ease gently into and out of the stretch.
- Be patient. It may take months to achieve the desired flexibility in some tight muscles.
- Stretch after training or a race to avoid stiff and sore muscles.
- If stiff at night, stretch again. "Tight at night, sore in the morn," say some of my knowledgeable running friends.
- In the early stages of injury, wait two days before gentle and relaxed stretching. Often an injured muscle is stretched too soon after and too vigorously.
- Keep the back straight while stretching (also in lifting weights).
- Stretch the upper body, as well as the lower body, including legs, arms, back, hips and trunk. The arms and shoulders are often neglected. In fast running, the arms and shoulders are the drivers so these are essential.
- Stretch properly and gently. Improper stretching is worse than no stretching, since it can cause injury.

Don't:

- Don't bounce. Bouncing engages the "stretch reflex." This can cause muscles to tighten rather than extend and can cause tiny tears and sore muscles.
- Don't jerk the muscle into position (ease into the prestretch).
- Don't stretch to force the joints beyond their normal range of motion; this could weaken the joint[3].
- Never stretch a muscle if you experience pain or severe discomfort, and never overstretch a cold muscle.
- To avoid possible permanent damage over time to ligaments, don't position yourself in a stretch that loads the joints and places an abnormal stress on the ligaments; the hurdler's stretch is an example of one to avoid (Dr. Stark[6]).
- Don't overstretch muscles. Dr. Stark[6] states: "Overstretching of muscle places a heavy load on the tendon (e.g., Achilles). Since the tendon is inelastic (the maximum increase in length.can only be 3 to 4%), what often results is a microscopic tearing of the muscle or the bone covering," because the tendon is stronger and more inelastic than the muscle or the bone covering (periosteum).
- Don't stretch an injured muscle or only under the advice and supervision of a physiotherapist. It is difficult to distinguish between a severe cramp and an injury, so be careful.

TYPES OF STRETCHING

There are several types of stretch methods: Ballistic, Static, Spring, Active Isolated, Fraid Nots, and Pilates. The most popular is the static method. These methods are described briefly below:

Ballistic Method

After contraction of a protagonist (mover) muscle, momentum is stopped at the end of the movement by contraction of the antagonist (opposite) muscle. For example, high kicking and running are ballistic movements. In high kicking, the antagonist muscle (hamstring) is stretched by action of the protagonist mover muscle (quad). Also, since the stretched muscle is not held for any length of time beyond its habitual length, the movement fails to stretch the muscle effectively (J. Jesse[1]).

Ballistic stretching is risky without adequate control since injury to muscles and joints is likely as explained below. When a muscle is stretched, there is a basic protection mechanism referred to as the *myotatic stretch reflex* to prevent overstretch and injury. Receptors within the muscle, known as muscle spindles, are stimulated and send a message via the spinal cord to the brain that the muscle is being stretched. In response, a message is sent to the muscle to contract if the muscle is overstretched or stretched too fast. This sudden change from stretching to contraction often causes hamstring injury.

Ballistic stretching was abandoned several decades ago. However, one still sees some uninformed hurdlers doing high kicking. Rapid bouncing in and out of positions can cause muscle soreness and even muscle tears.

Static Method[1, 2, 6]

In static stretching, the muscle is "held" while stretched beyond its usual length. This steadily applied tension conditions the "stretch receptor" nerves to tolerate the new position if the stretch is not overdone.

Active stretching is initiated by the athlete alone. **Passive** stretching or **PNF** stretching involves an external source usually a buddy, coach or trainer. For example, in the hamstring stretch, the athlete lies on his back or her back with the trainer pushing on the leg straight and nearly perpendicular to the floor; the other leg is out straight on the floor. The trainer pushes on the leg for several seconds; the athlete then resists for several seconds, and pressure is then relaxed. The cycle is repeated about three or four times with the trainer exerting increasing pressure on each successive stretch. Be careful with the passive stretch since the stretch is easily overdone if communication between athlete and trainer is lacking. Dr. Stark[6] warns against PNF stretches as more tension is placed on the muscle and it requires a trained assistant. You may find the next day the stretch was too severe; a friend of mine got a calf tear from too intense passive stretching on an already overworked muscle. Using a rope to assist stretches can give the athlete the effect of a passive stretch with the effect of better feedback since the athlete has complete control of the rope.

The **developmental** stretch: Hold the easy stretch for more than 10 seconds, move to slightly more tension for more than 10 seconds. The tension should remain the same or decrease after a few seconds, otherwise back off slightly.

The static method, if not done properly, can cause tightness and injuries since it activates the inherent "stretch reflex" (or myotatic reflex) particularly after a strong rapid movement or after two or three seconds in an overly stressed muscle (e.g., beyond gentle irritation). As explained earlier, the stretch reflex causes the muscle in these circumstances to begin a slow contraction or shortening of the muscle. *If stretching continues while the muscle is trying to contract, this could result in microtears or even worse: injury.*

The Stark Reality Method[6] of Stretching

This gentle stretching method involves five golden rules to avoid stretching problems and injury. See the Credits for permission to reprint selected quotes. *Dr. Stark recommends that each muscle group is stretched twice in succession for more length and power.*

1. ***Isolate the muscle group*** *where you are not putting stress on other muscle groups, ligaments, or joints.*
2. ***Find zero tension*** *where there is no load on the muscle group and therefore no tension in the muscle group.*
3. ***Find the first awareness.*** *Stretch to the point where you start to feel gentle tension in the muscle group. Initially, the relaxed muscles contract (shorten) in response to this loading force. In order for the muscle to relax back to the original resting length, the muscle must not be overloaded. The more gentle the initial load, the faster the muscle group can relax back to the resting length. Then the stretch can start.*
4. ***Less is best*** *as explained above.*
5. ***Allow the loss of tension.*** *The gentle tension must be steady and constant on the muscle group to allow the muscle group to relax and elongate past its resting length. When you cannot feel any tension left in the muscle, the sliding elongation is complete.*

The length of time to hold the stretch varies from individual to individual and depends on the initial load, the amount of warm-up, and whether the muscles are fatigued (shorter and more inelastic). Therefore, holding for 15 to 30 seconds is inappropriate. The stretch is over when the tension in the muscle is gone.

Spring Method

The spring method can also be active or passive. A good example of this method is a person (while standing) bending down with knees straight to touch the floor with fingertips, knuckles and palms. By bobbing up and down, exerting increasing power in the downward direction on each bob, first the fingertips touch the floor, on the next bob the knuckles, and on the next bob the palms, if you are more flexible. By bending the knees, even the less flexible will reach further downward.

However, if done improperly problems could arise; any jerking or bouncing could activate the involuntary reaction of the stretch reflex. Hence, the spring method is not a popular method.

Active Isolated Stretch Method

The active isolated method is an active stretch method that involves three basic principles that produce advantages over the static stretching method.

1. ***Place the body in the best anatomical position to isolate a particular muscle.*** Isolation is normally achieved by sitting or lying down rather than standing up. Most stretches, particularly those while standing, involve other muscles in addition to the one being stretched. For example, see the list of hamstring stretches in this chapter; many of these stretches can produce injury in muscles other than the one being stretched.
2. ***Contract the opposing muscles opposite to the one being stretched.*** According to Sherrington's Law, when a muscle on one side of a joint is contracted (e.g., quadriceps), a neurological signal is sent to the opposing muscle (e.g., hamstrings) on the other side to relax and release. For effective stretching, a muscle should be relaxed.
3. ***Stretch for less than two seconds to avoid the myotatic stretch mechanism.*** When a muscle is overstretched, this mechanism kicks in after about two to three seconds and causes the muscle to contract.

By putting the above three together, one has the active isolated (AI) stretch.

This new method was pioneered by Florida-based kinesiotherapist Aaron Mattes. It is practiced in AI stretching clinics in some major USA cities and used successfully by some world-class athletes (e.g., Steve Spence–a world champion and Olympic marathoner, Michael Johnson world-record holder in 200m and 400m, and many world class tennis players, sprinter Denis Mitchell, etc.) to increase flexibility, range of motion and reduce injuries. Michael Johnson, during his warm-ups used AI stretching for up to 40 minutes with minimal running before his race.

Advantages Compared to Static Stretching

- The active movements activate muscle fibers producing a deep tissue massaging effect. The active massaging routine warms the stretched muscle so a jog before stretching is not essential. Also the massage effect is useful during cool down to remove lactic acid and waste products.
- The massaging effect helps to promote healing of injuries in the latter stages by providing increased blood flow and oxygenation and removal of waste.
- It prevents injuries and soreness of the stretched muscle since the myotatic reflex mechanism is not activated and the gentle stretching periods are short.
- It prevents injury of adjoining muscles since the stretched muscle is isolated.
- It increases or restores range of motion while increasing the elasticity and flexibility of the stretched muscle.
- It takes much less time.
- In static stretching during warm-up before exercise, microtears are likely to occur affecting performance. In AI stretching, this is unlikely due to the short stretch time.

Method

The method is as follows:

1. Put yourself in the correct position to isolate the particular muscle.
2. Bring the isolated muscle into position by contracting the muscle that is opposite the isolated muscle causing the isolated muscle to relax. Continue this contraction during the stretch.
3. Gently stretch the isolated muscle (avoiding any discomfort) using your hands or a rope to enhance the stretch and hold for a maximum of two seconds.
4. Release the stretch before the muscle goes into its protective myotatic reflex contraction.
5. Return to the original position. Relax 2 to 3 seconds.
6. Repeat about 8 to 12 times.

General Considerations

- For the various stretches, the contraction of the opposite non-exercising muscle (resulting in relaxation of the exercised muscle) is normally achieved by bringing the isolated leg into the stretched position.
- Stretches for the upper and lower legs and hip are all done while sitting or lying on the floor.
- Don't use the rope to move your leg into position. Use the rope for the gentle stretch when in the stretch position.
- Exhale on work phase and inhale during the relaxation return phase.
- Each successive repetition can be slightly deeper but should not reach mild discomfort.
- For sample stretches with the rope, see explanation and illustrations in www.aistretch.com/exercises.htm, or Wharton's Stretch Book[4], or books on this subject by the founder Aaron L. Mattes.

Summary

I believe the AI stretching method will gain in popularity with runners since static stretching during warm-up is becoming less popular. In fact, AI stretching fits in well with the dynamic warm-up philosophy, since both stress range of motion exercises. The method below is similar to AI stretching.

"Fraid Nots"

This is a short, simple "Total Body Stretching" method by Tom Drum, using a rope. It was from reading about this method in the "Fraid Nots" booklet, several years ago, that the I became acquainted with the advantages of rope stretching. A few sample stretches ("stretch in slow motion, hold for 6 to 10 seconds") are shown below with the permission from Tom Drum, president of Tom Drum Inc.

For more information on many other stretches for the upper and lower body, see the Web site www.tomdrum.com or phone 888-565-9559.

The president, Tom Drum, mentioned to me the importance of upper body stretches. My personal experience is that good swimmers and good sprinters usually do not neglect these areas, but arm and shoulder stretches are usually not done by most runners; this is in spite of the fact that the arms are the drivers in fast running. For example, a very muscular friend and training partner, Mike Carter, at age 49, tore a shoulder muscle in a 100-meter sprint. No doubt this would not have happened with stretching in this area during the warm-up. This incident convinced me of the importance of upper body stretches. The simple but effective "Fraid Not" routine will assist you to prevent such problems in the whole body.

Pilates

This method, although nearly a century old, is being revived and becoming popular. Brooke Siler, "one of the country's [USA] leading fitness gurus" explains in her excellent book[5] the movements in great detail.

The Pilates method involves[5]:

- Simultaneous stretching and strengthening exercises while visualizing to reinforce the exercise;
- Knowing which muscles, joints and tendons are being worked on, concentrating on this area, and relaxing this area;
- Flowing smoothly from one movement to the next (over thirty in all) to engage all areas of the body;
- Breathing naturally and not rushing or overdoing the movements;
- Exercises that initiate from the "powerhouse or center of the body," between the belt and top of the upper legs.

During a "Rolfing" session (realign the fascia), I learned of the following Pilates-like exercise to strengthen and stretch most of the leg, feet and hip muscles and particularly many of the large and small muscles not normally or overly used in running or other sports. It's an excellent exercise for the hip, adductors, abductors, iliotibial band, hamstring, abdomen, quadriceps, etc. Try the following for a few minutes before getting out of bed in the morning as I do, working alternately on one leg at a time.

1. Lie on your back with knees bent and feet flat on the floor or bed surface.
2. Lift one straight leg to near vertical. Bend the foot in all directions; downward and upward (working the calf and shin muscles), and clockwise and counter-clockwise (working the feet and ankles).
3. With a straight leg pointing upward, swing the leg from side to side.
4. Move the leg in (a) small circles, (b) in waves and figure eights, and (c) in large circles and large sweeping movements. While doing the circles and waves the leg may be straight, bent, high or low. Be innovative.

This exercise is somewhat similar to that developed by Joseph Pilate almost a century ago. The variations I have suggested are different; they just feel good and are very beneficial overall. This is just to whet your appetite: the real exercises are in Brooke Silers book[5] or similar books.

SOME ESSENTIAL STRETCHES

The stretches described below are frequently done using the static method and normally held for 15 to 30 seconds. This length of time is a good idea to release muscle tension, since during the first 10 seconds or so, the muscle may be contracted due to stretching too hard. With rests in-between, the whole session can be done in less than 10 minutes. Some, like myself, sometimes hold for only 2 to 3 seconds to avoid the stretch reflex, then relaxing for a few seconds before repeating about 10 times. Alternatively, I suggest as a possible compromise: stretch easy for more than 10 seconds, ease into slightly more stretch for 10 to 15 seconds (the stretch should still feel gentle, otherwise back off slightly), and gradually apply slightly more pressure for 2 to 3 seconds only, but not to the point of discomfort. (Ask your physiotherapist or trainer about this latter technique, which is an extension of the developmental stretch, before you try it).

Calf Stretch

Gastrocnemius (upper calf)

1. Grasp wall or rail in front with both hands.
2. Front leg is about two feet from wall with knee bent.
   Back leg is fully extended about four feet from wall with knee locked. Feet are flat on the floor and straight ahead. The back is flat.
3. Push the buttocks forward until you feel an easy stretch in the rear calf. Hold and back off slowly.
4. Repeat for the other leg after reversing the feet.

Soleus (lower calf)

This stretch is also good for ankle flexibility and is similar to the above stretch with one small change.

1. Grasp wall or rail in front with both hands.
2. Front leg is about two feet from wall with knee bent.
   Back leg is about four feet from the wall with knee flexed. Feet are flat on the floor and straight ahead.
3. Flex the back knee to feel gentle pressure in the lower calf.
4. Repeat for the other leg after reversing the feet.

   Dr. Stark[6] warns against standing on the *edge of a step and lowering the heel below the step* to stretch the calf; this popular type of stretch "can result in damage to Achilles tendon, behind the knee, gastrocnemius muscle, the heel, or to the plantar fascia."

Outside of Hip

1. This is the same position as the calf stretch above.
2. Same as above with front leg bent and forward, rear leg fully extended and locked.

3. Lean rear leg hip outward, stretching this hip on the outside.
4. Repeat for the other hip after reversing feet.

Groin/Adductors Stretch

1. Sit on the floor with back straight and bottom of feet together.
2. Bring feet close to the body.
3. Bring feet toward the pelvis a little at a time until gentle tension is felt. Do not bend forward.

   Dr. Stark[6] advises against pushing with hands or arms (to increase stretch in the groin) "since the muscles contract against the loading force." He also advises against the standing groin stretch since "the adductors are involuntarily contracted in this position."

Quadriceps Femoris Stretch

1. Lie on your side.
2. Flex your upper knee and hold this leg just above the foot.
3. Pull the leg back with your hand.

   This stretch is preferable to the standing quadriceps stretch. Caution: Do not hold at the foot. This puts too much stress on the ankle joint and the knee joint. (Some days, if your knee feels stiff after having done nothing strenuous the previous day, you may have over stressed the knee by holding the foot.)

Iliotibial (IT) Band

1. Stand sideways about two feet from a wall or rail for support.
2. The "inner" hip and "outer" hip is closest and furthest from the wall respectively. Cross the outer leg over the inner leg. The outer foot is in front now, and this leg is bent slightly, while the inner "target " leg is straight.
3. Lean the hips into the wall. Support yourself with the inner hand against the wall. Nearly all the weight is on the target leg. The inner IT band "target leg" is stretched.
4. Repeat facing in the opposite direction to stretch the opposite IT band.

   Be careful to be gentle with this stretch.

Shin Stretch

1. Squat down with feet flat in front of a rail or post. The buttocks are close to the floor or there is a small angle between the upper and lower legs.
2. Toes point slightly out and heels are about nine inches apart.
3. Pull yourself toward the post or rail, keeping feet flat. Feel the stretch in the shins. Hold and back off slowly.

Lunge Stretch for Front of Hip, Quads, and Groin

1. Stretch out legs: the front leg out in front with rear leg trailing;
2. Lower the front of your hip downward. The rear leg has knee nearly touching or actually resting on the floor. To avoid knee problems, the front leg knee should not be in front of the ankle, and the angle between lower limb and upper limb of the front leg should be more than 90 degrees. The upper body is vertical. Hold for 15 to 30 seconds.
3. Slowly return to standing upright.
4. Repeat with the other leg.

Alternatively, do 12 lunges on each leg alternating from right to left leg and holding each stretch for 2 to 3 seconds.

Hip Stretch #1

1. Lie on the floor face up with both knees bent with legs straight in front.
2. Grasp the left foot with right hand and pull towards right shoulder.
3. At the same time, grasp the left knee with the left hand and pull toward the left shoulder.
4. Feel the stretch in the left hip region. Hold and back off slowly.
5. Repeat for right hip.

Hip Stretch #2

1. Sit in a chair or on a bench with back straight and bottom legs vertical.
2. Lift one leg and rest it on your other knee.
3. Lean forward with straight back to gently stretch the hip region.

Hip stretch #1 can also be done in a sitting position starting with this step 1.

Ankle Rotation

1. Sit comfortably with back straight preferably in a chair.
2. Place one ankle over the opposite knee with the foot overhanging the knee.
3. Rotate this ankle clockwise several times and counter-clockwise several times.
4. Repeat with the opposite foot.

Piriformis Stretch

1. Sit on the floor.
2. To stretch the left piriformis, the left leg is in front and flat on the floor with left foot near the right groin. The right leg is stretched out behind and slightly to the side.
3. Bend over the left leg with straight back to feel the stretch in the left piriformis. Hold for the usual 15 to 30 seconds.
4. Repeat for the right side by reversing legs.

Alternatively, this can be done by lying on a low bench with right foot touching the floor.

HAMSTRING STRETCHES

The hamstring stretch is given special attention here in view of the high frequency of occurrence of stiff and injured hamstrings in runners. Also, it is beneficial to do more than one hamstring stretch in a session to work different parts of the hamstring. There are many hamstring stretches to choose from.

Assume the right leg is to be stretched and for every stretch let yourself relax physically by concentrating mentally on the right hamstring area being stretched. The stretch must be done with no discomfort. Find the hamstring stretches you are comfortable with after trying the ones below. For variety, do several of these in a session, alternating the right and left leg. However, the healthy leg could be stretched for a lesser time.

Many of these exercises stretch other muscles at the same time, so be careful not to overstress these other muscles. Keep the back straight in all stretches. Dr. Stark[6] warns, *"The hamstrings cannot be stretched in any standing position, because they are contracted and expending energy to stabilize the pelvis against the pull of gravity."* This would eliminate a lot of the stretches below.

The following stretches were from various references (since they are popular exercises) but some are shown and explained in more detail with diagrams in Anderson[2]. I have arranged the stretches roughly in order of severity of stretch–easy to hard. Those nearer the bottom are more susceptible to overstretching, which could defeat the purpose of the session.

1. Sit on the floor with both legs straight out in front; bend over from the hips and pull from the toes. Do not dip head.
2. While standing, with both feet together and knees locked, bend over until you feel a gentle stretch in the hamstrings. Holding the hands behind the back assists to keep the back straight.
3. Sit on the floor with right leg straight out, the sole of the left foot placed against the inner thigh of right leg. Now bend forward from the hips.
4. Lie on the back with right leg vertical and left leg bent at 90 degrees, grasp right leg behind the thigh and pull.
5. Lie on the back with left leg straight out, grasp bent right leg behind the thigh and pull.
6. While standing on left leg and leaning against a wall for support, pull the right knee to chest with both hands.
7. While sitting on the floor with legs spread apart, bend over from the hips with back straight and pull the right foot with the hands.
8. While standing, cross the legs with the left in front, bend over with the hands behind the back to keep the back straight.

9. While standing, spread the legs apart, bend over, grasp the right ankle and pull yourself into the ankle.
10. Sit on the outer edge of a raised table or bench, with the right leg straight out in front and parallel to the edge. The left foot rests on the floor. Bend forward to put stress on the hamstring. The back is straight, chest out and eyes forward.
11. Lie on your back on the floor facing the right side of an open doorway. Place the right heel on the right edge of the door. The left leg is straight ahead and passes through the door opening on the right side. Slide the hips closer to the wall making the right leg more vertical and putting more stretch on the right hamstring.
12. Lie on your back, with left leg bent 90 degrees and out directly in front. With a rope (or towel) on right foot and with right leg nearly vertical and straight at knee, pull the rope toward you. For increased stress, the left leg is straight out in front.
13. While standing, rest the heel of your right leg on a table or step (height preferably between knees and hips) with knee locked, bend slowly over with back straight keeping eyes forward to put gentle pressure on the hamstring. Left foot should be straight forward. Rotate the right leg inward to stretch inside of thigh. Rotate the right leg outward to stretch outside of thigh while bending the knee slightly. (This is one of the stretches I do in the whirlpool.) Some experts say to be careful with this stretch since it puts too much stress on the back and the hamstring; although I personally have had no problem with it: but see precautions below.

STRETCHES TO AVOID

Some stretches can increase the risk of injury.

The following is a list of stretches plus some calisthenics exercises to avoid.

1. *Leaning from the waist while standing and twisting.* Rotate the trunk clockwise while bending forward, then sideways to right, then bending backward, then bending sideways to the left. This puts excessive compression on the disks of the lower back. (A much better exercise is with the upper body vertical; rotate the pelvic region counter-clockwise, i.e., rotate the hips to the right, to the front, to the left, and to the back. Repeat several times. Similarly rotate in the clockwise direction.)
2. *High kicks.* This ballistic movement causes over-stretching of the hamstrings as explained above in the "Ballistic Method" section.
3. *Sitting "hurdle" stretch* with trunk bent forward (lead leg straight forward and trail leg behind and to the side bent at 90 degrees). This overstretches the liga-

ments on the inside of the rear knee; to modify, bring the back foot to the inside of the opposite knee (Francis and Francis[3]); see hamstring stretch #3 above, which is the preferable position. (Also, the sitting hurdle stretch with the trunk leaning backward is much worse on ligaments of the knee than the above stretch.)

4. *Kneeling quadriceps stretch* (bending backward slightly). The ligaments of the knees are overstretched[3].
5. *Yoga "plow."* Lying on the back, feet are brought over the head to touch the ground. This causes excessive stress on intervertebral disks of the neck[3], lower back and spine.
6. *Neck hyperextension.* Excessive rotation or bending of the neck backward or forward, places excessive stress on the discs of the neck[3] and constricts blood vessels in the neck.
7. *Touching toes while standing.* This stretches the back and the hamstring while at the same time contracting these muscles. It could lead to injury.
8. In general, stretching with a *rounded back* is to be avoided; it loads the vertebrae of the spine. Keep the back straight.
9. *Hamstring Stretch.* Propping your foot onto a rail in front of you is a problem if the rail is too high, e.g., above the hips. Muscles can be torn. Also with a rounded back in leaning over and with the knee straight there is too much pressure on the back. A lower height with a straight back is safer.
10. Dr. Stark[6] indicates many other wrong positions in stretching that could lead to soreness the next day or injury.

STRETCHING BEFORE A WORKOUT

The latest thinking on stretching before a workout is that it should not be done (or at least minimized) before a strenuous workout or a race. The problem is static stretching, even though mild, leads to some microtrauma of muscle cells and stretching masks pain. Therefore, static stretching immediately prior to training, particularly if stretching is intense and prolonged, could lead to injury if followed by intense or prolonged exercise. Similarly, it is not wise to workout with sore muscles (due to extreme microtears) as it often leads to injury. Also some research has indicated the possibility of decreased performance due to stretching before competition. However, the traditional jog followed by low-intensity stretching before a low-intensity workout could still be retained. Many recent studies recommend a dynamic warm-up instead of static stretching as part of the warm-up. The rationale for this switch to little or no stretching before a hard workout or competition is explained in Chapter 18 on Dynamic Warm-up.

STRETCHING AFTER A WORKOUT

Static stretching is recommended shortly after a workout, when muscles are warm. This provides maximum flexibility, improves recovery and reduces lactate and soreness in muscles, thus helping prevent injury. However, in view of the microtears in muscles after an intense workout, an intense competition, or intense weight training session, it is recommended to wait and stretch two hours later. This gives the microtrauma time to subside.

Static stretching is still very beneficial and needs to be done daily, but at the right time, and always after warming the muscles.

REFERENCES

1. Jesse J., *Running Athletes*, The Athletic Press, Pasadena, California, 1977.
2. Anderson B., *Stretching*, Shelter Publications, Bolinas, California, 1980.
3. Francis F., and Francis P., *Stretching Your Muscles*, Fitness Plus, September 1991.
4. Wharton J. and P., *The Whartons' Stretch Book- Active Isolated Stretching*, Times Books, Random House, 1996.
5. Siler, B., *The Pilates Body*, Broadway Books/Random House, New York, NY, 2000.
6. Dr. Stark, S. D., *The Stark Reality of Stretching*, The Stark Reality Corp., Richmond, BC, 1997.

maxim
LOOK
bollé
2002
IRONMAN
1513

CHAPTER 13

Training also
takes place when you are resting.

RECOVERY

Recovery is necessary to repair microtears in the muscles, to replace depleted glycogen, and flush toxins from the system. It's mental recovery too since strenuous workouts are mentally stressful. You may think there is no need for recovery but after a hard workout, a masseur will find sore muscles you never knew you had; these need rest or they develop into possible injuries.

The heart needs rest, too. Athletes take the heart for granted since it doesn't get sore and rarely causes problems. When it does speak up, it is sometimes too late. Therefore, it is important to realize that the heart needs a rest also, in some cases more than the other muscles. Remember your heart is your best friend; don't neglect it. For older athletes, this could be the most important advice in this book – life-saving advice perhaps. See the section below on "Recovery After a Race."

BEST RECOVERY METHODS

Here are the best methods for recovery between workouts.

1. ***Hard/easy days.*** Always have hard days followed by easy or medium intensity days. Two hard days in a row can lead to injury. Allow at least 12 hours between a hard workout and an easy workout, e.g., this would be an intense interval session on the track or a weekly long run followed 12 hours later on the following day by

an easy cross-training type of workout or easy slow aerobic run. Allow 36 hours at least between hard workouts, and more if muscles are sore or there is fatigue. Ideally, allow 72 hours between hard workouts since sore muscles often come two days after an intense workout.

2. ***Keep moving after a race or intense workout.*** What is the worst thing you can do after a race? Answer: stand around. Don't do this, the blood can pool in your legs. Also, let the heart slow down gradually.

3. With a ***proper warm-up and cool down,*** there is less trauma to the muscles, so recovery is better. During warm-up, muscles can be warmed up in the whirlpool or sauna if available, but don't stay in too long—the heat is weakening. I prefer to submerge only the legs, and to stay only about seven minutes maximum. Stretching can be done in the whirlpool or sauna before a workout; I have done this many times at the local YMCA, but I would not recommend it before a race or a serious workout.

   Start the workout with a slow jog followed by a good stretch session. Following stretching during warm-up, the heart rate should ideally be raised to near the heart rate to be experienced in your race or workout. During your workout, it is helpful to stretch in-between those faster intervals, especially those muscles that are already sore or tight; this assists to prevent further sore muscles or even injury. If you have a trainer, he or she can stretch you between intervals and after the workout. Also, remember the more intense the workout, the longer the cool down.

4. ***Jog between repetitions.*** Research shows that recovery is more rapid between intervals if you jog slowly rather than walk. This helps lactic acid to move out of your running muscles and into your blood so it can be removed more quickly. This enables more fast intervals to be completed. Laboratory testing has shown that the jog should be approximately 3 to 4 minutes per mile slower than 10K pace or 50 to 60 percent of VO_2max for most runners (Pftzinger[1]).

5. ***Recovery strides.*** A slow jog and a good stretch session are necessary for recovery. Some medium-paced strides are also strongly recommended to loosen the joints and ligaments and to get rid of that stiffness, particularly after a long anaerobic threshold or aerobic conditioning workout.

6. ***Elevated legs.*** To get rid of some waste in the legs, lie on the floor with your legs high above the head and resting against a wall for about five minutes. This is a good idea between races on the same day, but it is always a good idea to improve circulation.

7. ***Cold water on the legs*** will speed recovery. Stretch before doing this. If it is summer, walk in a cold lake, river, or stream for about 10 minutes. The colder the better; this is really refreshing and it works. Running in the water in the deep end of the pool at an easy pace will assist recovery. Alternatively, a cold bath with ice cubes has been used by some brave athletes, e.g., Johnston the USA Olympic hurdler used this technique. I've tried it with several trays of ice cubes; it's not too hard to take after the initial immersion. A cold shower on the legs for about five minutes is another way; or apply cold towels that have been wetted and frozen in the freezer.

   A cold shower on the body is effective for recovery on a hot day between events. Also, on a hot day before your first event, a cold shower will lower the body temperature and make the blood more alkaline; hence performance should be improved. On a very hot day before a race, wet your body with a cloth immersed in cold water.

8. ***A hot shower or whirlpool or sauna*** after strenuous exercise is beneficial if muscles are not too sore; if muscles are sore, ice is better. Applying the jets in the whirlpool to the leg muscles but not too close on sore areas is best a day or two after the exercise. The jets on the bottom of the feet are stimulating for the whole body and beneficial if you have plantar fasciitis. But extreme heat or cold immersion too soon after exercise also puts extra stress on the heart; give yourself about 10 minutes to relax after a workout before these sessions. See "Principle of Anti-Shock" in Chapter 5.

   A hot bath, whirlpool or sauna at about 40°C (105°F) for three to five minutes alternated with a cold bath or shower for less than a minute is recommended for recovery. Or try three minutes hot, three minutes cold. At least two cycles are recommended, always ending with the cold bath or shower. By expanding and contracting your blood vessels, waste products are cleared more readily while reducing possible inflammation. Similarly, a relaxing hot shower on the legs for a few minutes followed by a short cold shower to make the blood alkaline is effective to rejuvenate the legs. The cold shower should start below the knees and work upward while rotating the body in a counter-clockwise direction.

9. ***Drink plenty of water after the workout*** to flush wastes out of the system; drink more than your thirst requires; if you lose a pound during the workout replace this with 16 ounces of water.

10. ***Carbohydrate reload.*** Within an hour after a race or workout, drink a sports drink or eat carbohydrates and protein, preferably in the ratio of carbs/protein = about 4/1, e.g., milk and cereal is a good choice. This increases muscle glycogen storage and speeds recovery. The carbohydrates and protein work together to rebuild microtears in the muscle from training. A sports drink is recommended in-between races.

11. ***Massage.*** Within two hours after a workout or race, massage the legs at least 10 minutes. I often do this self-massage using soap or massage oil. Of course, a professional masseur is preferable but not always available. A professional massage once a week is highly recommended. Massage for recovery is most important after a hard fast track workout (especially indoors where turns are tight) or after a 2.5- to 3-hour-long training run.

12. The ***Epsom salt or sea salt bath*** at about 36 to 40°C is a popular way for athletes to relieve sore/stiff muscles, and particularly for persistent stiffness and soreness. This temperature is about as hot as you can stand; keep the water level below the stomach. Use about one or two cups of salts and drink plenty of water. Massage the legs at the same time. After ten minutes or so, you can sometimes feel the soreness decrease, but 10 to 20 minutes immersion is recommended. Shower after to remove the salt.

13. ***Magnetic roller.*** It is claimed that the use of magnetic rollers moved rapidly but lightly over the muscles for a few minutes will also relieve soreness and promote circulation. I have one and believe it helps; it's very handy for travelling; you have your masseur in your pocket.

14. ***Ice.*** If muscles are excessively sore, apply ice: on for 10 minutes, off for 10 to 20 minutes and repeat three or four times. I have found that one application is not nearly as effective. Depending what layers you have between the ice and your skin, 10 minutes may be too short or too long, but never leave ice on till it feels too uncomfortable. The nerves can be damaged with too much exposure.

15. ***NSAID's.*** For excessively sore muscles, take acetaminophen (Excedrin or Tylenol) *not* NSAID's (e.g., aspirin, Advil, ibuprofen, etc., because these can cause many medical problems). See Chapter 16 on "Injury Prevention and Causes."

16. ***Cross-training.*** Get enough rest between training sessions. Cycling, swimming, rowing, or running in the pool eliminates the pounding of running and helps to recover tired/sore legs.

17. ***Walking.*** During the cool down, walking is recommended after jogging and before the stretching. In some cases, if the heartbeat is not brought down gradually, it will stay elevated excessively as happened to an experienced triathlete friend. Hence, the cool down jog should proceed from slow to slower, followed by slow walking, and finally stretching.

18. ***Vitamin E and C and grape seed extract*** taken daily will assist in repairing the tiny muscle tears that occur as the result of training, i.e., about 500mg-1000mg of C (preferably one half in the morning, the other half at night), about 400IU of E, and about 100mg of grape seed extract.

19. ***More frequent rest days*** will result in fewer injuries, more energetic workouts and less muscle fatigue. For example, two days rest per week instead of one is recommended for older masters. A rest day can also be a light cross-training day or hiking, etc.

20. ***Easy activity for recovery.*** Complete rest is not necessary after speedwork or a long run or extra fast medium pace runs. There can be activity the next day but the activity should not cause further damage while recovery is taking place (Henderson[3]) .

21. Also an ***alkaline diet*** will assist in recovery (see Chapter 15).

22. ***Avoid coffee, tea and alcohol after the workout*** since this makes the blood and muscles more acidic (i.e., below pH of 7.0), and to be recovered, the body must return to the alkaline range of about 7.3 pH. If you do have alcohol, satisfy your thirst with water first.

23. ***Periodization,*** i.e., gradual increase in intensity for three weeks and backing off the fourth week is highly recommended by many coaches but rarely followed. Only a small majority are that organized. Studies have demonstrated that this rejuvenation, mentally and physically, results in two to three percent reduction in long distance race times. See Chapter 10, which incorporates periodization in the training schedules.

24. ***Never progress too rapidly*** in your training. Particularly, proceed gradually with speed over a period of weeks on indoor tracks; I learned this through bitter experience. Let the body adapt gradually and you will have much less trouble to recover and with less injury.

25. ***Be flexible in your schedule.*** On a day when you feel sluggish or tired, it is best to do cross-training or take the day off. When muscles are tired, injuries are more likely. Don't be a slave to your schedule. When the body speaks–listen; there is usually a warning of an impending injury, e.g., a sore muscle.

26. ***End of season recovery.*** Allow at least 10 days or more of no running (cross-training instead) after the end of the indoor track season, and a similar rest after the outdoor track season prior to starting cross-country season (or base) training.

RECOVERY IN DAYS AFTER A RACE

One rule of thumb after a race is to take one easy workout day for every mile raced. This is too conservative for an experienced runner. Perhaps it is appropriate for beginners. Jack Daniels[2], renowned USA coach, recommends one easy recovery day for each 3000 meters raced. This is more reasonable. Allow two days easy after a 5K race, three days easy after a 10K race, and two weeks or more of easy days after a marathon.

I have learned that after a race, the heart needs a rest, in addition to the other muscles. Twice in my late 60's, I can recall having a problem due to an interval session the day after a 5K or 10K race. My heart went into an erratic high beat and did not come down for 45 minutes or longer (called atrial fibrilation). In the case of the 10K episode, my heartbeat returned to normal after 45 minutes, but after the 5K episode, the high heartbeat lasted for more than two days. The above indicates the importance for one and all to giving the *heart*, the most important muscle, a rest after a race or strenuous workouts. Of course, as one gets older, this becomes even more important. If you have this atrial fibrilation (tachycardia) problem, it is more likely to occur when tired from a race and/or over-training, when mentally stressed, after consuming caffeine, or a combination of the above. See also a section on the "Heart Irregularities" in Chapter 1.

RECOVERY AFTER A MARATHON

Hal Higdon once ran six marathons in six weeks. Amazing! His recovery methods must have been superb. In his book *Marathon*[4] he discusses some effective recovery methods for after a marathon, i.e.:

- *Keep moving for 10 minutes after but do no jogging;*
- *Drink immediately after and for the next several hours (sports drinks are best but not diet pop);*
- *Elevate legs;*
- *Gentle self massage;*
- *Gentle stretching;*
- *Cool shower (avoid hot baths or showers which increase inflammation);*
- *Rest for one or two hours at home;*
- *Eat a full meal similar to a pre-event meal;*
- *Professional massage after 24 hours;*
- *Easy workouts for at least two or three weeks (twice as long for beginners) with no long runs or speedwork.*

REFERENCES

1. Pfitzinger, P., The Walking Paradox, *Running Times*, October 1996.
2. Daniels, J., *Daniels' Running Formula,* Human Kinetics, Champaign, IL, 1998.
3. Henderson, J., *Running Your Best Race,* Wm. Brown Publishers, Dubuque, Iowa, 1984.
4. Higdon, H., *Marathon*, St. Martins Press, Rodale Books, Emmaus, PA, 1993.

NIKE
NIKE

CHAPTER 14

There was an athletic man and woman who lived in a shoe. They didn't know what to do.
(Firstly, they had the wrong shoe.)

TRAINING SHOES

The right type of training shoes to suit the runner's foot type and foot plant is essential to prevent injury. A running shoe needs to absorb shock and also control the inward-outward movement on ground contact. You should have several pairs of shoes to suit various activities, such as for daily use, for warm-up and cool down, for long runs, for interval training and for racing (running shoes and spikes). (My front hall looks like a shoe factory – 16 pair of various running shoes.)

In 1994, during cross-country training, I tore my plantar fascia on the left foot. This was due to training on steep hills with rough terrain in light training shoes with little or no support. Two years later with daily foot massage prior to getting out of bed, exercise, more massage, lots of physiotherapy, orthotics, and motion control shoes, the problem has fortunately cleared up. Had I been educated on training shoes, this injury would never have happened. Like many other runners, when my feet and knees were healthy, I paid little attention to the type of shoe I purchased. Mainly I looked for flexibility in the ball of the foot, light weight, comfort and price. Does this sound like you? If so, you could be heading for injury (plantar, shin, calf, knee or Achilles). Generally, to prevent problems, runners should choose shoes for training that have sufficient stability rather than shoes too light. Unfortunately, many running-shoe sales people are not much help – they presume the customer is always right. You should know your own requirements, your foot type, whether you ***pronate (roll inward) excessively, or***

supinate (roll outward) excessively, or whether you are without foot problems. Here is a short course on the fundamentals of training shoe selection.

TYPES OF LAST

The last of a shoe has several meanings. Shoe companies build a shoe around a shape (wooden, metal, etc.) called a last. A straight last on the inner side has more stability and a curved last on the inner side has less stability. There are three methods of lasted construction, i.e., **board lasted, slip lasted and combination lasted** as explained below.

A **board lasted** shoe has a flexible cardboard-like material cemented on the lower side of the upper. The board sits under the removable insole) and provides stability and a good platform for orthotics. A board lasted shoe is the most supportive and is considered a *motion control shoe*, which is ideal for excessive pronators[3].

A **slip lasted** shoe has its upper stitched to the midsole and looks like the inside of a moccasin when the insole is removed. This construction provides flexibility and lightness. This allows for better shock absorption. These shoes are classically referred to as *cushioned shoes*[3].

A **combination lasted** shoe is board lasted in the rear foot for rear foot stability and slip lasted in the forefoot for flexibility in the toe area. Some knowledgeable runners look for one of these features. These shoes are usually considered *stable but flexible shoes*, and are for runners who need good mid-sole cushioning *and* support[3].

TYPES OF TRAINING SHOES

One needs to **understand the different types of shoes** and when they are required. The shoes below are listed in order of most stable (heaviest) to least stable (lightest).

- **Motion control shoes** are the most rigid and durable. They are heavy but designed to ***slow the amount of pronation*** with the most medial (outer edge) support and the most support at the heel. The base is often wide. The midsole (between the insole and outsole) is very firm with higher density material. Mostly, they are built on a straight last, i.e., straight on the inner side (arch side). This shoe suits those who pronate excessively, wear orthotics, are a heavy runner, a heavy heel striker, or with *flat feet*.
- **Stability shoes** are stable but less rigid than motion control shoes and usually with a semi-curved last. This shoe suits the mid-weight runner, those who wear orthotics, those without severe motion control problems, or runners with normal arches.

- **Cushioned (or neutral) shoes** are lighter and less stable than stability shoes but more flexible with a softer ride. The midsole is soft, providing more foot mobility. Cushioned shoes have a semi-curved last or fully curved last to encourage foot motion. This shoe suits the runner with *high arches* and a lighter person. Under-pronators do not absorb shock very well and require a cushioned shoe. Injuries due to shock can be eliminated by using cushioned shoes.
- **Lightweight training shoes** are lighter but less stable than cushioned shoes. Most lightweight trainers have no stability and a lot of flexibility in the ball of the foot region. Normally, the last is semi-curved or fully curved. This shoe suits the lighter person without pronation problems for fast training or racing–definitely not for rough terrain where stability is important to protect the feet. On the other hand, there are lightweight training shoes with stability (a straight last); I prefer these for faster training.

Other Features

There are other features of construction to contribute stability, flexibility and cushioning. For example, normally there is more rigid construction on the inner side of the heel and midfoot for pronators; this material is usually a darker color. The overall effect can be tested as follows: Stability or flexibility can be tested by twisting the shoe in the horizontal plane. Place the left hand at the front of the shoe and the right hand at the back of the shoe facing the opposite way and move the hands in opposite directions to twist the shoe and note its resistance. Pulling up on the toe checks for flexibility in the ball of the shoe.

TESTS TO DETERMINE SHOE TYPE

The Wet Test

The wet test will determine your foot type. This will indicate the type of shoe best for you. The wet test indicates the curvature at the inside of the foot or the type of 'last' required. The last is the shape of the shoe (i.e., straight or curved on the arch side). Dunk your foot in water and stand on any surface to leave an imprint of your foot. Test both feet for they may not be the same. As a general rule, the last of the shoe should conform to your wet test shape.

The **flat foot** with low arch leaves an imprint wide at the arch. This imprint usually indicates excessive pronation (rolling inward). Therefore, ***straight last, and motion control shoes*** are best.

The **normal foot** has a normal arch and leaves an imprint with a narrowing at midfoot but not excessive narrowing. There is slight pronation to absorb shock. ***Semi-curved last, and stability shoes*** are best.

The **high arched foot** leaves an imprint with very narrow band at the midfoot. Generally, this is a supinated (or under-pronated) foot – therefore not an effective shock absorber. The best shoe in this case is a ***curved last, and cushioned shoe*** to encourage foot motion and shock absorption.

Test for Pronating or Supinating

Test Number One. The following test from Dr. Mark Klein[3] will determine if you pronate or under-pronate. Stand barefoot in front of a full-length mirror with your feet straight ahead and bend halfway at the knees. If the ***kneecaps remain centerd*** at the midpoint of your foot, then your feet generally function normally, and you should choose a ***stable shoe***.

If your ***kneecaps move toward the big toes,*** or toward the inside of the foot, then your feet ***over-pronate*** and a ***motion controlled shoe*** would be appropriate.

If your ***kneecaps move toward the little toes*** or the outside of your foot, then your feet ***under-pronate*** and a ***cushioned shoe*** works the best.

Test Number Two. Check your old running shoes: Over-pronators will have heel counters tilted inward (from wear) reflecting the motion of over-pronation. Under-pronators will have heel counters that tend to tilt outward. However, heel strikers generally have wear on the outside (back) of the heel. In cases of excess tilt and wear, the shoes need replacement.

SOME USEFUL TIPS

1. **Wrong last type.** From the discussion above, the shape of the shoe on the inner side should correspond to the shape of your foot from the wet test. When the last shape is wrong there is unnatural constraint on the feet, and the feet and/or legs suffer.
2. **Excessive pronation or supination.** People with normal feet and normal pronation are able to wear almost any type of shoe with no problem particularly if the last is correct. The correct shoe becomes essential where there is excessive pronation or supination. Excessive pronation is indicated by excessive wear on the inside of the shoe, and excessive supination by excessive wear on the outside of the shoe. The right shape and type of shoe will help these problems, but the wrong shape will aggravate them.

3. **"Rigid shanks."** Noted sports podiatrist Richard Schuster of New York recommended decades ago, that all distance runners should have shoes with "rigid shanks," i.e., limited flexibility from heel to back of ball of the foot – the metatarsal heads to reduce strain on the arches. You will find nearly all running shoes have this feature except for some light racing shoes. Avoid any training shoe that bends in the middle to avoid excessive stretch of the plantar tendon and consequent injury to the plantar tendon or heel. This is particularly important to those who have had problems in this area.
4. **Flexibility under the ball.** Also the shoe should be flexible under the ball of the foot[1] [forefoot] for easy push off and less energy expenditure. (This is a feature I look for.) If it is not flexible enough, the front and back of the leg take up extra stress, which could injure the Achilles, calf or shin. Test the shoe by bending the toe upward and noting the amount of resistance. The shoe should be flexible in the ball region at purchase; they will not become more flexible later.
5. **Heel counter.** For those who pronate or supinate, the heel counter that cups the back of the foot needs to be firm to provide more support and rigidity. It is important that a rigid heel counter cover the entire heel area. Use the pinch test with thumb and forefinger to check for rigidity of the heel counter.
6. **Too much cushion or too little support** will result in increased pronation if you are a pronator. Too much cushioning causes instability and running inefficiency.
7. **A light shoe in a race can save valuable seconds** – perhaps 10 to 15 seconds in a 5K race. "An 80-gram (three-ounce) orthotic to each running shoe increased the oxygen cost of running by about 0.4 to 1.1%" (Berg and Sady [1985] quoted by Noakes[2]). Also a light trainer shoe compared to a cushioned shoe could be three ounces lighter. Assuming the 1.1% figure from above this could be equivalent to 1% decrease in speed since 1% decrease in VO_2max is roughly equal to 1% slower speed in long distance events. If shoe weight is important then check the literature beforehand, e.g., *Runner's World* surveys. I have some small scales at home where I check the weight of shoes, and I usually take them to the running shoe store when I shop for replacements; then I am satisfied the new shoes are the weight I want.
8. **Space at end of toes.** Some experts recommend 1/2" or more between longest toe and end of the shoe. This is to account for foot swelling, particularly on hot days during running (some say feet could swell 1/2 size but some say the foot only swells widthwise) and also to avoid excess pressure at end of the shoe on downhill running. Sparks[1] recommends an inch of clearance. I personally like the shoes to fit snug (closer than 1/2", perhaps 1/4" on the longer foot). I have met other experienced runners (e.g., the great Ed Whitlock, age 73 [year 2004], Canadian world record long distance runner) who I respect, feels the same – the snug fit feels lighter and speedier. However, some space is required otherwise black toenails will result.

9. **More injuries occur during training than during racing.** The reasons are, the athlete is usually more rested for a race, racing represents a small part of total running, and the volume of a race is much less than a training session. Therefore, it is most important to have good training shoes. During training, I used to wear orthotics (if not too heavy), but during racing, I would remove them and still not suffer reoccurrence of the plantar problem.

   In running outdoors in winter, there is more shock to the body (and possibly more injuries) since running shoes lose nearly half of their cushioning in cold temperatures (such as Canada).

10. **Orthotics correct the position of the foot** so it functions properly, eliminating such problems as over-pronation or misalignment of the legs and other biomechanical problems. An orthotic in a light trainer is not as effective as in a motion control shoe or stability shoe. Therefore, orthotic wearers should spend most of their time in stable shoes. Also, in my personal experience, it is essential that the orthotic sits flat inside the shoe and not cocked. This happens when the orthotic is too wide for the shoe internals and this leads to discomfort, and defeats the fit and purpose of the orthotic. Orthotics should feel comfortable as though they are not there. My first pair never felt right; feeling like a lump under my worst foot. If you wear orthotics, be sure to wear them in training on rough terrain where the foot needs extra support, otherwise injury is more likely.

    Orthotics may cure over–pronation and over-supination, but with *reduced shock absorption* on foot landing. The arch of the foot acts like a spring or shock absorber. On landing of the foot, the arch flattens and the foot lengthens. The arch softens the landing and thus reduces jarring of the knee and hip. An orthotic prevents the spring action and hence the arch cannot absorb shock. (I wonder now whether training in orthotics caused my patella [knee] tendonitis.) Strengthening of the foot muscles by exercises (e.g., toe raises) should be investigated before resorting to orthotics.

    Since orthotics prevent spring action of the foot, the stride length must be reduced. This is another reason (apart from the additional weight) not to wear orthotics during racing.

    When wearing orthotics, it is essential to have the right shoe. Orthotics provide stability and motion control shoes provide stability, as well. If a runner needs motion control shoes and adds orthotics to correct for a mechanical imbalance or other reason, the overall effect may be too much stability. This can lead to problems. In this case, it is advised to change to stability shoes with the orthotics.

    Another problem is the other extreme: putting orthotics in a shoe with too much cushioning, i.e., a cushioned shoe, or light training shoe with little stability. Then the effect of the orthotic is negated and it is like running on an unstable surface like sand.

11. **Replace shoes frequently.** Always discard your running shoes when they get worn to prevent possible injury. Replace your shoes frequently particularly if running on roads or hard tracks. Check your shoes for *hardening, compaction or softening*, which causes loss of cushioning or shock absorption.

    With age, the midsole and heel region *hardens*. The midsole between outsole and upper sole absorbs most of the shock from the foot strike. If it is hard to compress, it has lost its capacity for shock absorption, leading to possible injury. Conventional EVA, the favorite midsole material for cushioning loses 20% of its cushioning after about 300 to 500 miles of use, so beware.

    The midsole may wear out by ***compaction*** (sometimes indicated by pain on landing on a stone). Wrinkling of the rubber at the sides of the shoe also indicates compaction. Compaction can occur on the inside of the heel due to excessive pronation; this could result in injury.
12. **Rotate your shoes frequently.** Be kind to your feet and legs. Always err on the side of more support in training. Change your shoes frequently from one workout to another; this often prevents a problem from developing. The experienced or serious runner should have four or five pair of training shoes, wearing the ones that fit the workout and training surface.
13. **Recovery from an injury** or relief from an injury can be improved with the right kind of shoe. Check with a knowledgeable physiotherapist or podiatrist.
14. **Heel pad.** When training or racing in spikes, I recommend a heel pad about 10mm (0.4") thick. The reason is nearly all training is done in running shoes with a good heel lift. Spiked shoes have little or no heel lift (particularly sprint spikes), hence the Achilles is stretched more and possibly excessively.
15. **Training shoe purchase.** Buy only at a store where clean shoes can be returned if not satisfactory. Take your orthotics with you to try inside the shoes. Never buy through a catalogue unless you are buying the exact same make and size you have used with satisfaction before; otherwise, the chances are they won't feel right.

REFERENCES

1. Sparks, K., *Runners Book of Training Secrets,* Rodale Press, Inc., Emmaus, PA, 1996.
2. Noakes, T., *Lore of Running,* Leisure Press, Champaign, IL, 1991.
3. Klein M., *How to Select the Right Shoes,* Michigan Runner, Vol. 19 No. 2, Summer 1997.

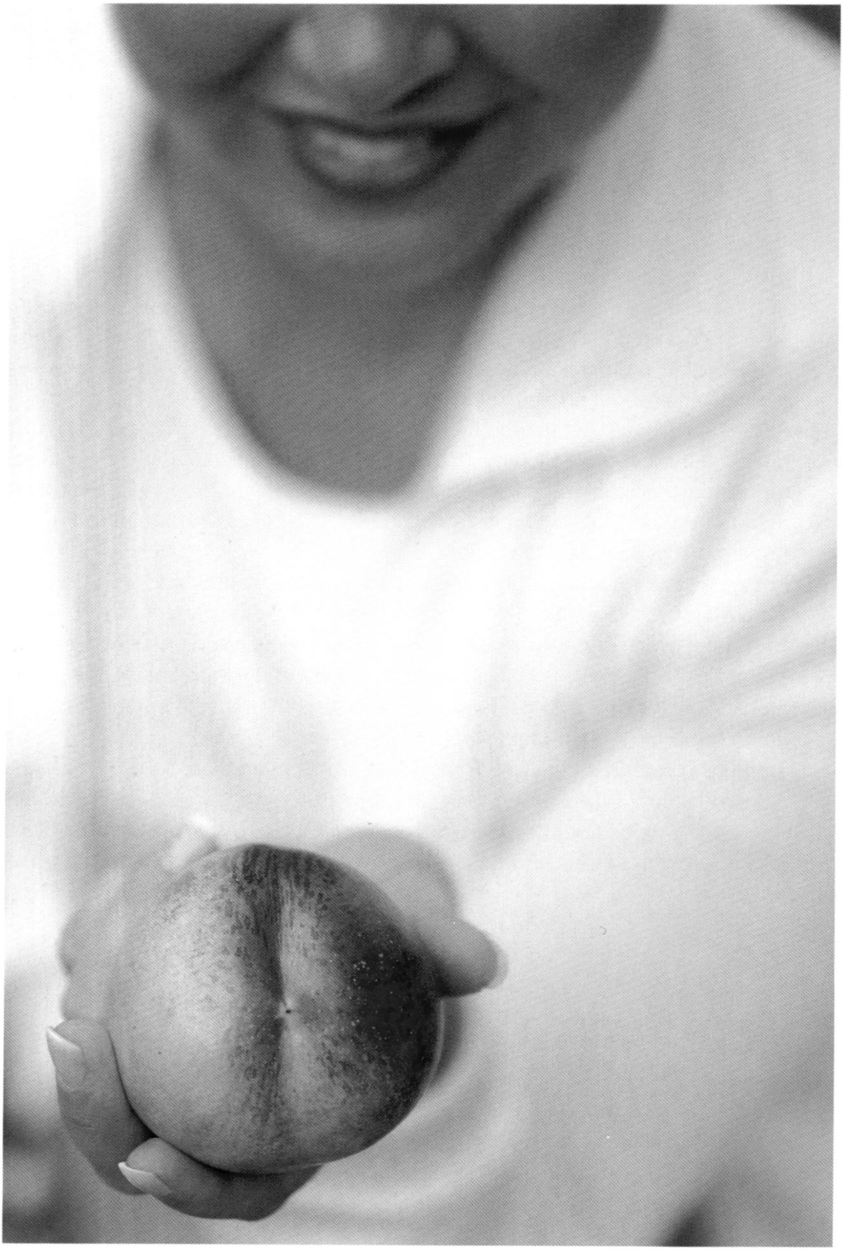

CHAPTER 15

There is food for thought
but more importantly,
have thought for food.

NUTRITION

There are some super athletes who can run nearly full out for 12 to 16 hours per day for 12 to 14 days through the winter snow. If you don't think nutrition is important ask them—the dogs in the Alaska Iditarod dog sled race.

A man phoned in to a radio talk show on nutrition and asked, "My grandmother recommends that I eat six bananas every day. Is this a good idea?" The nutritionist stated that one should listen to grandma, but grandma was correct only in that fruit is probably nature's best food. It was learned that this fellow drove a banana truck delivering bananas. This little humorous story indicates that most people have little or no idea about nutrition and their bad eating habits are literally killing them before their time. It is essential for an athlete to eat properly to achieve the highest performance from their bodies. The following information, particularly for athletes will be discussed below: what you should eat, when you should eat, how much you should eat, food combinations to avoid, high fiber diet, the glycemic index, pre-competition meal, acid and alkaline foods, supplements, including magic supplements.

RECOMMENDED PERCENTAGE OF CARBOHYDRATES, PROTEINS, AND FATS

It is generally agreed that athletes, such as runners, cyclists, and swimmers, should have a high energy diet of 55% to 80% carbohydrates, 10% to 15% proteins and about 10 to 30% fats. In particular, the 10 to 15% for proteins[2,4,7,11,18] seems to be generally agreed upon with (various nutritionists listing) more variation in the amount of carbohydrates and fats.

All serious athletes should estimate their percentage of carbohydrates, fats and proteins in their normal diet. Since normally we tend to follow the same eating habits every day, this is not too difficult to make such estimates using calorie charts, such as in the *Nutrition Almanac*[13], and *Eat To Succeed*[10]. With the same food composition charts, it is possible, with more work, to estimate your intake of the major vitamins and minerals and compare with the RDA (Recommended Dietary Allowances) to determine any deficiencies. For all this, use www.cyberdiet.com.

Total calories per day equals carbohydrates (grams x 4) + protein (grams x 4) + fats (grams x 9). I personally found my normal daily diet was about 3700 to 3800 calories consisting of about 60% carbohydrates, 29% fat, and 11% protein based on two independent investigations.

CARBOHYDRATES

Carbohydrates are the major fuel for sport and exercise. This most efficient food is converted to glucose, stored in the blood, and stored as glycogen in the liver and muscles. Once the storage sites are filled, the extra carbohydrates are stored as fat.

With training, the body adapts and more glycogen can be stored in the body, and with aerobic training, these stores are depleted more slowly. The higher your level of muscle and liver glycogen when you exercise, the longer it will be before fatigue sets in. A high carbohydrate diet ensures greater glycogen storage and longer exercise time. After long exercise, such as the marathon, the body uses fat, glycogen and blood glucose for fuel. The liver supplies blood glucose continuously from its stored glycogen. When muscle glycogen is nearly used up, the runner "hits the wall." This results in fatigue, dizziness, and muscle pain. Now the pace slows dramatically, as only fat provides the fuel. When the store of liver glycogen is used up, hypoglycemia (low blood sugar) occurs, and the brain loses its essential fuel. Disorientation occurs and some refer to this as "crashing."

Your muscles and liver have limited capacity for storing glycogen. Of course, at a slow pace or, for example, an ultra marathon, glycogen stores can last for four or more hours. Therefore, replacement is required during and after exercise. About 1800 to 2000 calories are stored as glycogen in muscles and the liver[8]. Blood glucose is the most readily available source of energy. Also, a marathoner, ultra marathoner or triathlete with 10% body fat should have limitless fat energy even accounting for the 5% of essential fat in the body. After about 30 minutes of exercise, the majority of energy is derived from fat.

The majority of carbohydrates should come from unrefined or complex carbohydrates, breads, cereals, grains, fruit and vegetables. The refined or simple carbohydrates from sugars are devoid of nutrients compared to nutrient-rich fruits and vegetables. Simple carbohydrates should be minimized, particularly if you have a cholesterol problem. However, they do satisfy some cravings and also help to cut down on the volume of carbohydrates an athlete has to consume.

Fruit and Vegetables

Fruit and vegetables supply nearly all the essential nutrients to the human body. They also greatly assist in satisfying the body's requirements for water since their water content nearly matches the water content of our body. It is commonly recommended to eat about four servings of vegetables and about three servings of fruit daily. The following are typical serving sizes:

***Fruit** Serving:*
1/2 cup juice
1 apple, pear, banana, peach, etc.
1/2 cup of cooked fruit
1/2 grapefruit
1/2 melon

***Vegetable** Serving:*
1/2 cup cooked or raw vegetables
1 cup or small bowl of leafy vegetables
1 potato or carrot
1/2 cup juice or spaghetti sauce

Many people, including myself, find it difficult to meet seven servings of fruits and vegetables for healthy living. However, it is permissible to use double servings, although variety is preferable. For example, a typical day for me is 1 large glass of orange juice, 1 cup of cooked vegetables, 1 cup of spaghetti sauce, one banana, one grapefruit or grapes = 8 servings.

Fruit has the following advantages:

- It (and vegetables) satisfies many nutritional requirements.
- It cleanses the body of toxic wastes (therefore, it also improves healing).
- It requires little energy to digest (compared to starches and protein).

- It is alkaline-producing when digested[6] (therefore, it assists recovery after exercise).
- It greatly aids energy[9] (due to high sugar content).
- It reduces risk of cancer, high blood pressure, and constipation.

For best results with fruit, observe the following:

- Best nutrition is obtained, in order of preference from: fresh, frozen, canned (contains excess sugar), and dried fruit.
- Eat only on an empty stomach; i.e., not immediately before, during or immediately after a meal. About thirty minutes before a meal is satisfactory, but after a meal, it is necessary to wait until this previous meal is digested. See the "Food Combinations" section below.
- Fruit juice is a concentrated source of sugar; therefore, it is not recommended in large quantities.
- Fruit alone for breakfast is recommended as it takes little energy to digest, it's rich in fiber and nutrients, and aids in the elimination of waste from the body. For example, in Afghanistan, the workers often eat grapes only for breakfast. However, a big breakfast of starch and protein has the opposite effects and robs the body of energy.

Carbohydrate Loading

All serious runners have heard of the benefits of carbohydrate loading for the marathon and long distance events. If the muscles are fully loaded with glycogen in the days before competition, then the marathoner and long distance runner will run out of glycogen at a later stage and there will be less reliance on the less-efficient fat burning. Fats provide energy at a slower rate than carbohydrates[36]. Glucose provides more calories per litre, L, of oxygen than fat, i.e., 5.1cal/L compared to 4.62cal/L respectively[30]. Also, "hitting the wall" will come later in the race or perhaps not at all with sufficient loading. But some runners may not appreciate that glycogen loading is also of major importance for middle distance athletes before hard anaerobic training and races; for middle distance runners, the greater the glycogen store, the greater the oxygen saving and ATP producing anaerobic metabolism[36]. It is also important to replace the depleted glycogen stores soon after (within a half-hour preferably) the race or training session; at this time, the muscles are more susceptible to storage and they can be loaded above normal levels.

Sugar

Sugar is sweet, but life is sweeter. Excess sugar could be considered as a "poison" particularly in view of its potential for causing heart disease and cancer. An athlete need not be as concerned as a sedentary person, since sugar will be burned off in intense exercise, but here are the important facts to be aware of:

- Sugar (table sugar or sucrose, lactose, maltose, fructose, glucose, honey, maple sugar and corn syrup) is low in nutrients, high in calories and triglycerides (fat molecules). Therefore, sugar is much inferior to complex carbohydrates (starch).
- Glucose is less harmful than sucrose in producing cholesterol. Too much sucrose causes high cholesterol (Davis[24]).
- Sugar before exercise will not produce a "sudden burst of energy" (Coleman and Nelson Steen[30]). Also, Darden[3] states, "Honey, glucose, dextrose and sugar do not seem to improve performance in short term events." Nancy Clark[34] says, "Sugar eaten *during* exercise delays fatigue and is unlikely to cause rebound hypoglycemia ('sugar low')". There is benefit for those in endurance events who exercise for more than an hour. However, sugar slows down fluid leaving the stomach and could result in dehydration. Also excess sugar can cause cramps, nausea and diarrhea[3]. But, a friend ate honey frequently and successfully during a fast 24-hour army route march with heavy pack.
- Fructose sugar has low glycemic index (see section below), i.e., releases its energy slowly. However fructose is known to cause gastrointestinal problems. "You store twice as much glycogen after eating glucose or sucrose compared to eating fructose" (Coleman and Nelson Steen[30]).
- Be aware of hidden sugars (pastry, ice cream, cookies, chocolate, jam, etc.).
- Eating sucrose, lactose, maltose or glucose results in quick absorption and an increase in glucose. This quick absorption results in an imbalance of oxygen or incomplete burning and an acid condition if there is excess consumption (Aihara[6]).

Sugar Disadvantages

Nearly 20 percent of calories consumed in the modern United States are from sugar. However, in her book *Lick the Sugar Habit*, Nancy Appleton, Ph.D., lists nearly 80 health hazards from excess sugar consumption including increased triglycerides, kidney damage, cancers (breast, prostate, colon), heart disease, diabetes, arthritis, osteoporosis, asthma, suppressed immune system, increased total cholesterol, hypertension, and most other common diseases. This is backed up by 78 scientific reports. Hence, it is no wonder that excessive sugar consumption is considered a "poison" by some notable doctors, e.g., Dr. Linus Pauling[27] and Dr. Richard Becker.

PROTEIN

Protein is used for energy only minimally, i.e., supplying only about 3% of total energy[2]. More is used if the glucose store is normally low as in a regular low carbohydrate diet. But protein is essential for building new tissue and repairing the cells broken down through normal living and exercise. We need protein to build muscle (resulting from exercise) and to maintain good muscle tone. Proteins are also essential for the formation of antibodies, the first line of defense against disease, and to keep the acid/alkaline blood content balanced. Excess protein is stored as fat. Many body builders are taking protein powders. However, Williams[28] states, "There are no valid data that protein supplements are more effective than natural protein sources. Strength-trained individuals need 1.5-2g protein/kg body weight–easily obtained from a healthful protein diet."

Amino acids: Protein is made up of about 25 amino acids, nine of which are high quality or complete proteins and the remainder are poor quality or incomplete proteins. These two classes of amino acids are also referred to as essential amino acids and non-essential respectively. The high quality essential proteins have an amino acid composition close to that of animal tissue and human requirements[4]. The high quality amino acids, which our bodies do not produce, come from animal tissues like beef, pork, fish, chicken, eggs and dairy products. Rice and oats and soy are nearly as complete as beef, fish, and eggs although low in one or two complete amino acids[5]. If not enough protein is supplied to fulfil the requirements of amino acids, the body will resort to using body tissue as a source of amino acids. This would be very unusual; in North America ,most athletes consume more than enough protein to cover the nutritional requirements of extra training[8].

Vegetarian diet: With the right combination of nuts, seeds, and legumes (beans, peas and lentils), one can meet dietary needs without meats. (Legumes are the seeds of plants that bear pods). Legumes are an excellent source of protein, iron, calcium and fiber. Because plant sources lack one or more of the high-quality amino acids, it is important to eat the right combination of plant foods. "Protein quality can be improved by combining protein from different plant sources" (Inge and Brukner[2]). Some examples of plant protein mixtures from Inge and Brukner[2] are:

- Legumes (peas, beans, lentils) and cereals;
- Beans and wheat/corn/rice;
- Legumes and vegetables, wholegrain rice;
- Wholemeal bread and peanut butter;
- Brown rice and leafy vegetables.

Preferred meats for runners, swimmers and cyclists: For most athletes, the normal choice is fish or chicken instead of meat. Meat, particularly liver, is more abundant in zinc and iron, and women in particular, need to watch that they are not deficient in these essential minerals. Organ meats are very high in cholesterol, so I usually avoid liver. See the comparison below based on the tables in the *Nutrition Almanac*[13] and *Eat To Succeed*[10] to understand why fish and chicken should be the more frequent choice for an athlete.

Table 15.1 • Meats

	Chicken (No skin)[10,13]	Salmon Halibut Tuna[13]	Beef Steak (Lean)[10]	Beef Steak (Prime)[13]
% Protein by weight	24	25 to 29	30	22
% Fat calories	25	36 to 39	41	76

Note:

- The method of cooking was broiling.
- With fish, there can be wide variation in fat percentage, for example, from 9% for perch to 81% for red snapper. But generally, there are 29% to 39% fat calories and 25% protein by weight. A major benefit comes from the Omega-3 fatty acid in fish, which interferes with the buildup of plaque in the blood vessels[9].
- It is seen from the top row that to get 50 grams of protein, one has to consume about 200 grams of chicken, fish or meat. However, it is obvious that for the same total weight, chicken and fish have much fewer fat calories than prime beef. Beef is rich in zinc and iron. Lean beef has about the same fat as the average fish. Lean ground beef has about 50% to 65% fat calories; however, there is much less if the fat is drained off before including it in meat sauce or chili con carne for example, as I do.
- Note prime beef has the most fat marbling compared to choice lean cuts.

Recommended Daily Intake of Good Quality Protein

The recommended daily intake of good quality protein for the ***normal adult*** is about 0.8 to 1 gram per kilogram of body weight. The above figures are a good average recommended by various countries and nutritionists. However, an ***athlete*** training regularly requires more (than one gram/kg) to make the best of muscle development, and to prevent protein deficiency (Inge and Brukner[2]). More protein is required in the initial stages of weight training or endurance training. The figures below assume that the individual is getting the correct total calories, otherwise the protein requirement increases. The protein requirements for various individuals are:

- 2.0g/kg a day for exercising individuals, i.e., growing children, and adolescents[2].
- 1.2 to 1.4 g/kg/day was suggested for ***active endurance athletes*** and for body builders between 1.1 and 1.7g/kg/day, based on available information from Dr. Peter Lemon, a professor at Kent State University. This was not disputed by the three other physiology/nutrition experts in a roundtable discussion on "Protein Needs of the Active Person."[37] Practically identical figures are also stated by Coleman and Nelson Steen[30] and this range provides 12 to 15% of calories as protein.

Table 15.2 • Protein in Common Foods

The following selective data was taken from the extensive food composition table in the *Nutrition Almanac* by John Kirschmann[13] except where noted. The servings are standard-size servings. The foods listed are mostly high-protein foods except that other common carbohydrate foods are listed as they also add to the protein diet.

Meats	**Grams**	**Serving Size**
Fish, broiled	22 to 30	4 oz.
Tuna, in oil drained	32	4 oz.
Beef, sirloin, broiled	25	4 oz.
Chicken, broiled	27	4 oz.
Hamburger, lean, cooked	24	4 oz.
Dairy Products		
Cottage cheese	22	1/2 cup
Milk skim[10]	8.3	1 cup
Egg	6.5	1 medium
Cheese, hard	7 to 10	1 oz.
Yogurt, partially skim	8.5	1 cup
Vegetable Source		
Kidney beans, canned	7.4	1/2 cup
Chick peas, raw	20	1/2 cup
Lentils, cooked	8	1/2 cup
Navy beans w/pork and tomato sauce	16	1 cup
Potato, baked	2.6	1 medium
Most other vegetables	2 to 4	1 cup
Tofu[34], firm	10	4 oz.
Miscellaneous		
Noodles	6.6	1 cup
Spaghetti w/meat sauce	19	1 cup
Sandwiches	7 to 12	1
Soups	3 to 8	1 cup
Peanut butter	3.9	1 tablespoon
Oatmeal cooked	4.7	1 cup
Corn flakes	2	1 cup
Fruit, four servings	6-8	
Bread, most kinds	1.8-2	1 slice

Table 15.3 • Typical Protein Daily Diet for an Endurance Athlete

In the protein groups, two to three servings in the "milk, yogurt, and cheese group" and two to three servings in the "meats, dry beans, eggs, and nuts group" are recommended[45]. The latter group normally supplies the majority of the total protein in the diet. To satisfy the requirement of about 1.5g/kg, an athlete has to eat twice the servings and/or larger servings compared to a sedentary individual. To reach the required 100 grams of good quality protein for a 70kg endurance athlete, the following is typical. Note that the carbohydrate rich foods make a significant contribution to the protein diet:

Food	Grams	Size
Chicken	27	4 oz.
Spaghetti w/meat sauce	19	1 cup
Peanut butter	4	1 tbsp
Milk	7	1 cup
Yogurt	9	1 cup
Cheese, hard	8	1 oz.
Oatmeal	5	1 cup
Bread protein diet	8	4 slices
Vegetables, four servings	10-12	*
Fruit, five servings	7-9	**

* A serving in this context is one potato or a cup of vegetables.

** A serving in this context is a cup of berries or grapes, or a banana, apple, peach or pear, or one or two cups of fruit juice.

FAT

General Facts on Fat Consumption

- ***Fat consumption.*** The average middle-aged American's diet consists of about 40 percent fat, 40 percent carbohydrates and 20 percent protein[7]. The average British diet is similar (as I have read), and possibly worse as I recall from my three years in England in 1953-56. (I gained about 15 pounds in the first three months from my boarding house meals.) Hence, in view of the high-fat diet, it is no wonder a high percentage of people are often fatigued and die from heart attack.
- ***Essential fatty acids.*** A low fat diet reduces cholesterol and heart attacks and reduces the likelihood of prostate cancer; hence one should be sparing in the con-

sumption of junk food, dairy products and meat. However, Dr. L. Broadhurst (*Alive Magazine #171,* 1996) cautions that many people do themselves more harm than good with low-fat diets. Essential fatty acid deficiencies cause acute, chronic and allergic diseases. There are two essential fatty acids; omega-6 and omega-3, the two families of essential fatty acids found in linoleic acid and alpha linolenic acid respectively. Omega-6 and omega-3 fatty acids are crucial for a strong immune system. Eating these essential fatty acids, particularly omega-3, assists in reducing LDL cholesterol, heart disease, stroke, hypertension, arthritis and depression. Omega-3 also stimulates release of growth hormone and lowers the risk of heart arrhythmias. The common diet is more apt to satisfy the omega-6 requirements from light vegetable oils, fish, nuts and seeds. Alternatively, to satisfy the omega-3 (plaque fighter) requirements, eat flaxseeds daily and fatty fish from cold waters, such as salmon, trout, mackerel, sardines, halibut, and catfish, twice per week . Therefore, in summary it is recommended that you eat fish at least twice per week and consume nuts, seeds, and flaxseed (meal or oil) or fish oil. Get your doctor's OK before supplementing with fish oil because with too much, there is a risk of stroke. Eating fish is the best alternative.

- ***Fat storage.*** When we take in more calories in the form of carbohydrates, fats or proteins than we burn in activities, we store the excess in body fat. Carbohydrates, for example, are broken down into glucose before entering the bloodstream. Nearly all the glucose is re-combined into glycogen and stored in the muscles and the liver as fuel. When the muscles and liver are filled with glycogen, the excess is stored as fat in the body.
- ***Saturated, polyunsaturated and monounsaturated fats.*** Many nutritionists recommend replacing saturated fats with unsaturated fats (e.g., oils and nuts). Saturated fats are linked with cardiovascular disease from clogged arteries and high LDL cholesterol. Darden[11] and other nutritionists state saturated fats are useful if consumed in moderation. Polyunsaturated and monounsaturated fats are sub-categories of unsaturated fats, and both are needed for good health if not overdone. For example, research studies indicate nuts, although high in total fat (about 80%), are very beneficial to reduce cholesterol and to lower the risk of heart disease. Nuts contain these good fats (monounsaturated and polyunsaturated fats). Of course, the effect is greater if nuts are substituted for saturated fats. Peanuts have the most folic acid of all nuts; folic acid helps to prevent cancer and atherosclerosis (narrowing of the arteries). Also, all natural peanut butter has no cholesterol since it is a plant protein rather than an animal protein.

All fats and oils have some percentage of saturated or unsaturated. The following are listed according to their major percentage:

TABLE 15.4 • Saturated, Monounsaturated and Polyunsaturated Fats

Saturated Fats	Monounsaturated Fats	Polyunsaturated Fats
Dairy products, meat, chocolate and coconut	Olives, olive oil, canola oil, peanuts (a legume), peanut butter, nuts, and avocados	Vegetable oils, and fish

- ***Bad fats.*** Be aware of "particularly bad fats" apart from those listed under saturated fats above, such as ice cream, fried foods, french fries, chips, cold cuts, bacon, sausage, hamburger, all other junk foods, baked goods, mayonnaise, salad dressing, gravies, and rich sauces.
- ***Trans-fatty acid*** (*trans-fat* for short) should be avoided in the diet. Trans-fats are created by a process of hydrogenation that turns liquid vegetable oil to solid to resist spoiling. For example, margarine is produced by hydrogenation. There is growing medical evidence that trans-fats are more likely to contribute to heart disease than saturated fats. Some brands of margarine are free of trans-fats, such as Becel (my favorite) and Fleischman.
- ***Burning fat.*** On a slow-long run, fat is the main fuel. As intensity increases, fat supplies less fuel and glycogen supplies more. Above about 95% VO_2max, glycogen supplies essentially all the fuel. On a long run, as the reserves of carbohydrates fall, increasingly more fat is metabolized. The fats are reconverted to glucose and burned as body fuel. This indicates the importance of long runs above about 30 minutes for the marathoner, i.e., to activate and condition the fat-burning process. Training teaches the muscles to use fat throughout the race and reduces the need for glycogen and increases the time before running into the "wall."

Optimum Fat in the Diet

- The American Heart Association recommends no more than 30 percent of calories from fat with no more than 10 percent of these fat calories from saturated fats. This is about 60 grams total fat daily and a 20 gram limit of saturated fats. However, although saturated fats clog arteries, they should not be eliminated; they supply some essential nutrients.

High-Protein/High-Fat/Low-Carbohydrate Diets

Coleman and Nelson Steen[7] also provide a good evaluation of the high-fat diet: "Muscle glycogen is the preferred fuel for high intensity exercise because fat breakdown can not supply energy fast enough. Most athletes train and compete at an intensity that requires carbohydrate for fuel. Performance will be impaired on a high-fat diet."

Achieving the Correct Balance

To achieve the ideal of about 60% to 70% carbohydrates, 10% to 15% proteins, and 15% to 25% fats the following is suggested:

1. It is simpler to count the protein calories than carbohydrate calories in view of the much lower protein percentage; estimated as: % protein calories = (grams protein x 400)/total required calories = <15%
2. Also, by carefully restricting fats to the right kind (monounsaturated and polyunsaturated), it should not be difficult to keep within 15% to 25% of total fat calories.
3. Then by observing the above, the carbohydrates (mainly unrefined and complex) should be close to the desirable range.

TOTAL DAILY CALORIES

The total daily energy required for a mature athlete is equal to the basal metabolism rate, BMR, plus energy required for normal physical activities, and exercise activities. From *Success in Nutrition* by Magnus Pyke[5] the recommended daily intake of calories for a very active adult male of 65 kg is 3600 and for a very active female of 55kg is 2500. Add about 60 calories for each extra 5kg, subtract about 50 calories for each decade past 60 years of age. The above for a very active male agrees closely with my daily calories of about 3600 consumed at age 75 with lean body weight of 66kg.

The calories used per hour for running, cycling, swimming and rowing vary between 600 to 1200 depending on the intensity. To burn 1000 calories in an hour requires very intense activity with heart rate above about 85 % maximum. Athletes use more energy due to intense daily activity.

But, in addition, after working out vigorously for over 30 minutes the "afterburn" causes a significant increase in BMR for several hours or even up to a day in the case of very intense, long activity. I have noticed an increase in heart rate above the resting rate for four hours or more following an intense anaerobic interval workout.

Factors that Affect the Total Daily Calories

The above is a good indication of calories used or required for most athletes, but many people have a more active thyroid gland and hence a higher BMR. The more lively and active, and the more tense usually have a higher BMR than slower moving individuals. Some people are more efficient in carrying out daily tasks, but some have very active daily jobs. And some athletes are energy efficient, so their bodies have adapted to fewer calories. Hence, there are many variables. From the above, it is not surprising that the total daily calories can vary widely amongst individuals of the same lean body weight and age while doing the same activities.

FIBER

It has been found that Africans, Koreans, Japanese and others who eat a fiber-rich diet are almost totally free of heart disease, colon cancer, and diverticulitis (pockets in the bowel) and hemorrhoids, contrary to Westerners who generally have a highly refined diet (high meat, low carbohydrates, high sugar and fat and low-fiber diet). A study in England reported in *High Fiber*[17] by Sharpe compared the average high-fiber, low-sugar, low-meat diet *during* World War II with the low-fiber, high-fat, high-sugar, high-meat diet after the war. The time for food to pass through the digestive tract was one to two days during the war and four days after due to the change in diet.

Fiber can be divided into two broad **categories**: the soluble and the insoluble. We need both kinds for good health. Plants contain some of both. **Soluble** fibers act as a trap that collects certain waste materials and moves them out of the body,[8] thus lowering cholesterol, cleaning the arteries and hence preventing heart attacks. These fibers are found in oat bran, rolled oats, lentils and legumes[8]. **Insoluble** fibers absorb and hold in water. They are non-digestible and cause much shorter transit time for waste in the colon with less bacteria multiplication and consequently a much reduced chance of colon cancer. Insoluble fiber sources are wheat bran, whole grain breads and cereals and many fruits and vegetables[8]. Transit times through the body ideally are within 24 hours with a high-fiber diet, compared to as high as two to four days for the average Western diet.

What Are the Advantages of the High-fiber Diet?

- Waste material in the colon is kept moving at a healthy pace, particularly if fiber is consumed throughout the day rather than at a single mealtime (Inge and Brukner[2]).
- Improved odorless regularity on a daily basis.
- Lowered risk of colon cancer and other cancers, diverticulitis, haemorrhoids, and varicose veins.

- Lowered LDL cholesterol and heart attacks.
- Most foods high in fiber are also healthy for other reasons. They tend to be low in fat calories and sodium, and rich in vitamins and minerals[8].
- "Fiber slows down the release of sugar from food, thereby preventing large fluctuations in blood sugar level; this gives a more sustained release of energy–the key to endurance" (Inge and Brukner[2]).
- Save on bathroom deodorant spray–if you get my drift.

Recommended fiber grams per day and fiber diet. The National Cancer Institute recommends that we obtain 20 to 35 grams of fiber a day from our diet[9]. However, the average American eats only about 10 to 15 grams per day. To increase your fiber intake, switch from refined, processed foods to unrefined like whole grain cereals, switch from white to whole wheat bread, eat plenty of fruits and vegetables (skins on and raw, if possible), rice, brans from wheat rice, nuts and seeds, and legumes[8,9,17]. A high-carbohydrate diet of unrefined complex foods will ensure a high-fiber diet.

To meet your requirement of about 30 to 40 grams per day, the following indicates some examples of fiber-rich foods. It is recommended to space out your intake of fiber throughout the day and vary the fiber sources (Applegate[11]).

Table 15.5 • Sources of Fiber

Each typical serving below equals about 10 grams of fiber from (Inge and Brukner[2]):
• Bran flakes 2 small bowls (60 grams total)
• 5 slices whole-meal bread
• 1 small tin baked beans (130g)
• 3 medium potatoes cooked in skin
• Sweet corn kernels or peas (9 tablespoons)

Genell Subak-Sharpe[17] suggests typical fiber for one day would include "a bowl of whole grain cereal [8g] several servings of fresh or lightly processed vegetables or legumes [20g], two to three slices of whole-grain bread [5 to 7g] and two or three servings of raw fruits, nuts or seeds [6 to 10g]." (I have added in the brackets the approximate grams of fiber associated with these foods.) My brief survey indicates there is much more fiber in vegetables than fruit. For instance, 1.5 cups of vegetables (30g fiber) is equivalent to about 11 raw whole fruits (e.g., apples, oranges, bananas) (30g fiber).

Precaution: Excess fiber may lead to gastronomical distress (diarrhea or constipation[17]) and may interfere with the body's ability to a absorb certain nutrients. Fiber binds with many vitamins and minerals. However, a mineral/vitamin supplement will assist if the diet is too high in fiber. Normally, all that is required is to eat a variety of foods, but the supplement is good insurance.

ALKALINE AND ACID FORMING FOODS

All food is either alkaline or acid. The advantages of alkaline-forming foods for athletes were reported in a paper (Fitness Institute) by Lloyd Percival in the early 1950's. Lloyd was my coach and possibly Canada's best in that era and also the founder of the Fitness Institute in Toronto. He believed that a diet of mainly alkaline-forming foods for athletes was essential, and particularly to assist in recovery after intensive training, i.e., to assist in bringing the blood back from the acid range to the normal alkaline range. Recovery is not complete until the blood and muscles return to their normal alkaline range. Also, an alkaline diet, besides greatly assisting general physical health and recovery, is advantageous for mental awareness and "It can prevent almost all sicknesses, including cancer and heart disease" (Herman Aihara[6]). An alkaline diet is also beneficial for people under stress.

Alkalinity in the blood and muscles: Arterial blood and resting muscles normally have an alkaline pH of 7.4 and 7.0 respectively (where a pH of 7.0 is neutral). With hard, fast running, such as in the 400 meters, blood and muscle pH will drop below 7.0 into the acid range. Of course, this is associated with high muscle lactate, which diffuses into the blood. As a result, the high acidity associated mainly with the sprints and middle distance events limit the muscles' contractile ability, and reduce the speed, running economy and overall performance of the athlete. A heart rate above normal, after exercise, indicates incomplete recovery, i.e., acidity in the blood and muscles. A short recovery between races, for example, about an hour, could be quite stressful particularly for an unfit older athlete in view of the acid condition still remaining.

The alkaline elements are required to change the acid-forming foods into neutral salts. "To be healthy, our body fluid must be kept at an alkaline level (pH 7.4); we must re-supply the lost alkaline elements through the foods we eat" (Ahaira[6]). Presumably, an athlete with pH below normal from eating a lot of acid foods would have a lower blood and muscle pH after exercise, and would return much more slowly to his normal low alkaline pH after recovery, compared to an athlete on an alkaline diet.

Alkaline-forming foods. We may effectively aid the body in maintaining the alkaline condition by eating alkaline-forming foods. These foods contain minerals:

sodium, potassium, magnesium, calcium and iron[6]. (Calcium in the diet is particularly important and too much protein will decrease it in the body). Some foods are acid but in the digestion process, they become alkaline-forming foods, e.g., "Limes contain strong acids but are alkaline-forming foods in the digestion process" (Aihara[6]). This also applies to lemons; lemon juice in water is recommended before a workout or race, between intervals or races and after a workout or race to speed recovery; it is also beneficial first thing in the morning.

Acid-forming foods contain minerals: sulfur, phosphorous, chlorine and iodine[6]. "If one eats a lot of meat, poultry, fish, and eggs, blood oxidation is not so good and leaves much poisonous acid." "Therefore vegetarians live longer and eaters of animal food live a shorter life" (Aihara[6]).

Some popular alkaline-forming foods and acid-forming foods are listed below from Herman Aihara[6] except where noted.

Table 15.6 • Alkaline and Acid-Forming Foods

Alkaline-Forming	**Acid-Forming**
** Fruits, fresh (most)	Flesh foods
Vegetables, fresh (most)	Eggs
Cow's milk	Cheese
Yogurt	Prunes and Plums
Grape juice	Grains (cereals except millet)
Orange juice	Bread
Tofu	Nuts
Salt	Flour, buckwheat
Soy sauce	Sugar (all foods with sugar)
Wine	Beer
Potatoes	Whiskey
Sweet potatoes	Rice, brown and white
Tomatoes, raw[1]	Oatmeal
*Coffee, Tea	Butter
Maple sugar	Tomatoes, cooked[1]
Brown sugar	Drugs
Peas	Spaghetti
Sunflower seeds	Vitamin pills
Vinegar	

Note:

* In the above table, Aihara[6] lists coffee and tea as weakly alkaline-forming, but many other nutritionists describe these as highly acid-forming, particularly coffee. Hatfield[7] states caffeine is highly acid-forming. Murphy[9] also states coffee is acid-forming. Possibly some of these references apart from Aihara are including sugar in the coffee? But my stomach tells me that it is probably acid when I experience stomach irritations when I drink it, particularly on an empty stomach, even without sugar. I was happy to hear Aihara[6], p35, say that wine is alkaline-forming or at least a weak acid, p46[6].

** Cooked and canned fruit supply few nutrients compared to fresh fruit and are apt to be acidic.

Dangers of an Acid Diet

These quotes are from Herman Aihara[6] except where noted.

- Aihara states, "Over-consumption of fats, sugars, white rice, white flour, chemicals added to food, protein rich food, refined foods and drugs leads to an acidic condition." "They not only produce acids; they also use up the body's alkaline-forming elements..."
- "If vitamins are taken too much in pill form, they may cause acidosis." (However, Linus Pauling[27] states, "The vitamins help us to fend off infection and fortify our tissues against the assault of cancer and the auto-immune diseases)." (Therefore moderation is called for; Vitamin C may be an exception.)
- "One of the important causes of cancer, and other degenerative diseases (e.g., heart disease) is the cumulative effect of the acid condition of body fluid." (This should scare most into an alkaline diet.)

Aihara[6] also speaks of the advantages of a cold shower to make the blood alkaline (and to improve judgement, spirits, and reduce stress), whereas hot showers or hot baths make the blood acid. In the shower, proceed from the legs up, front, right shoulder, back, and left shoulder–then head last. Always follow a hot shower or hot bath with a cold shower. I use this routine after a workout to speed recovery, and I recommend it to other athletes.

Recommended alkaline/acid ratio: To maintain the proper alkaline/acid ratio, the diet should consist of 80% to 90% alkalizing foods and only 10% to 20% acid-forming foods[21,22]. The normal diet consists of more like 55% alkaline, 45% acid[22]. When too much acid-forming food is eaten, digestion is problematical even if food is combined well[22]. When acid-forming foods are eaten, they should be accompanied by a considerable quantity of vegetables to balance the meal. Foods rich in water, like vegetables are easy to digest. This preserves the alkaline mineral reserves in the tissues. Hence the diet of high alkaline foods and the balanced diet support each other.

In **summary**, an alkaline diet can prevent degenerative disease, prevent cancer and maintain good health. From the athlete's point of view, alkalinity of blood and muscles is necessary before exercise to enhance performance; also an alkaline diet before and after workouts and races aids recovery. Alkaline-forming foods should be eaten daily in greater abundance than acid-forming foods, or in sufficient quantities to balance acid-forming foods.

Summary of Diets

It may be concluded that there is a lot of commonality in the three diets, i.e., high carbohydrate diet, high fiber diet and high alkaline diet. These three different theories actually support each other. They all have similar characteristics and are recommending the same thing or achieving the same thing in a different way. Therefore, you will find following one of these diets generally satisfies the other two.

PROPER AND IMPROPER FOOD COMBINATIONS

Proper food combinations is not a new subject but too few know the rules. Hence most people are not taking advantage of the benefits of proper food combining. About ten years ago, I first heard about the importance of this from a speech from Peter Maher, a world-class marathoner for many years, who ran for Ireland and Canada. Research over the past eight decades has shown that eating food in the right combination aids digestion greatly. If food is properly combined, it is fully broken down and fully utilized by the body. But in the wrong combination, the body uses more energy for digestion and there can be various digestion problems. To digest your daily meals may require 300 to 600 total calories; energy is saved for other healthy pursuits in proper food combinations. Alternatively, less food is required, also contributing to longevity. Ideally, food is digested completely in the stomach in about three hours and passed quickly through the intestines with none of the above bad effects. The wrong combination can result in undigested food rotting in the body for a day or more–much longer than required.

Important Food Combining Facts

- Each food type (e.g., proteins, starch, fruits, vegetables, and fat) requires different amounts of gastric juice and a different digestive enzyme for digestion.

- Vegetables are "easy to get along with" as they say; they break down in acid or alkaline juices. (Therefore, they can combine with protein or starch.)
- Alkaline foods require alkaline enzymes for digestion and acid foods require acid enzymes.
- Milk combines poorly with all foods; best to take it alone (Dennis Nelson[3]). Milk makes a good mid-morning or mid-afternoon snack.
- The times for digestion are important, too; fruits take less than half an hour to digest by themselves, protein takes four hours or more, and fats take longer still.
- Two or more incompatible foods eaten at the same meal makes for loss of valuable nutrients and inefficient digestion (fermentation, putrefaction, resulting in poisonous substances) due to different juices required for digestion.

Commonly Violated Incompatible Combinations

The following excellent references, i.e., J. and I. Dries[19], J. Dries[22], and D. Nelson[3], recommend to **avoid** the following more common combinations:

- Protein/Starch—e.g., meats, nuts, seeds or dairy products with cereals and grains, potatoes, sweet potatoes, or carrots
- Sugar/Starch—e.g., pastry, fruit with cereal or bread, and sugar dessert on top of starch meal
- Fruit/ Protein
- Fat/Protein—e.g., oils with protein
- Fruit or Vinegar/Starch
- Protein/Protein[19]—e.g., meats with dairy products, meatss with vegetable protein

Nelson[3] also points out, "The tomato is really an acid fruit and should not be combined with starch or protein (with the exception of nuts, seeds and cheese). This is bad news for athletes like myself who frequently eat spaghetti with tomato/meat sauce and often late at night. This bad combination can be confirmed by looking at the "food combination pentagon,"in the Dries book[19], that describes acceptable and unacceptable food combinations; namely, bad combinations are pasta with tomatoes, and meat with tomatoes.

Acceptable Combinations

The following are common acceptable food combinations:

- Protein with vegetables or vegetable salad
- Starch with vegetables or vegetable salad
- Starch with fat (bread with butter)
- Fruit with sugar

Protein with Starch One of the Most Common Combination Violations

Control tests have shown that eating protein and starch at the same time retards and even prevents digestion. This combination takes excess time in the body and excess energy, and results in undigested food finally moving out of the stomach. The problem is that a starchy food requires an alkaline juice to digest it, whereas the protein (meat, fish, chicken, dairy product or nuts) requires an acid juice to digest it. Now these two digestive juices are neutralized. More digestive juices are secreted into the stomach again and again. Finally, this undigested food is forced into the intestines after several hours in the stomach. As a result, the carbohydrates ferment and the proteins putrefy. The nutrients are lost, there is excess gas, indigestion, and it takes many hours longer in the body before this foul waste is emptied. The habit of eating protein with starch is the norm at least in North America and a hard one to break when even a tuna or cheese sandwich, or steak and potatoes is a no-no. It appears that adhering continuously to this food-combining regime may not be practical for many. But all should be aware of the problems of protein with starch and follow the practice most of the time. It is appreciated that at banquets or at family celebrations when one is apt to overeat that this may be difficult. I have found it advantageous to avoid protein with starch, particularly when eating late at night. By eating protein and vegetables (no starch), I sleep much better.

However, protein with starch may be acceptable, if one of the two is much smaller than the other.

Effect of Food Combinations on Digestion and Sleep

"During sleep the body intensifies its assimilation of nutrients into cells and accelerates it's elimination of cellular wastes" (D. Nelson[21]). Hence, if dinner is eaten too close to bedtime, the digestion process interferes with this important function. By robbing yourself of deep sleep, you are contributing to aging, according to sleep researcher Eve Van Cauter, University of Chicago. Also, there is a greater likelihood of food being turned to fat. The times for the stomach to empty (or when fruit can be eaten on an empty stomach) depend on the food combination as follows. The table below also shows how long to wait before eating the next meal or snack, or the required time between the last meal and bedtime. These are approximate times mainly from either Harvey and Marilyn Diamond[1], or Dennis Nelson[3].

- Fruit juice or vegetable juice — 30 minutes
- Fruit [snack] — 20-40 minutes
- Salad or raw vegetables — 1-2 hours
- Fruit meal — 2-3 hours[3]
- Properly combined meal without meat — 3 hours[1]

- Starches 3 hours[3]
- Properly combined meal with meat 4 hours[1]
- Improperly combined meal 6-8 hours

Runners who have to train late in the day and who eat dinner after about 9 p.m. are advised to have their largest meal of the day at noon. However, some, like myself, would find this difficult.

Summary of Food Combinations

1. Follow the recommendations above to prevent indigestion and minimize energy required for digestion.
2. Eat fruit at breakfast with no other food, or between meals.
3. Athletes normally have a high-fiber, high-carbohydrate diet combined with plenty of exercise activity, all of which aids digestion. Hence it would appear that the bad effects of incompatible foods at the same meal could be much reduced. However, since there is no readily available study to support this contention, it is recommended that athletes adhere to the above recommendations (as I normally do).

For those who wish to dig deeper into this important subject, the book by Jan and Inge Dries[19], is an excellent reference.

Unacceptable Eating Habits

In addition to bad food combinations, the following need to be **avoided**:

- Large amounts of water or beverages with meals (dilutes digestive juices and retards digestion)
- Too many different foods at a meal
- Dessert (particularly large desserts) at a meal
- Eating too rapidly
- Eating under stress or when not relaxed
- Meals too large or too late at night

GLYCEMIC INDEX

The glycemic index, GI, for an athlete represents fine tuning of the high-carbohydrate diet. If you are not knowledgeable about the glycemic index, you are missing out on an important training and racing tool. The GI tables were developed mainly to assist diabetics, but these tables are useful to aid athletic performance. They can help you eat for better race and competition performance. The glycemic index is a ranking of carbohydrate foods from near 0 to 100, which indicates whether a food will raise blood sugar (and insulin) rapidly or slowly after it is consumed. Getting glucose into the bloodstream at exactly the right time is crucial to your athletic performance.

During a GI test, a 50-gram sample of carbohydrate food is consumed and the blood sugar level release is plotted vs. time. The GI factor, actually a percentage, is the area under the blood sugar level/time curve compared to the area under the reference 50 gram glucose curve.

Different carbohydrate foods cause glucose levels to rise in the blood at different times after they are eaten. Foods that have a high GI release glucose quickly into the bloodstream. Pure glucose, the reference, has a GI of 100 and has a peak blood sugar level after about 40 minutes and decreases to near zero in less than 2 hours. Foods with a low GI provide a slower steady supply, i.e., up to several hours for foods near the bottom of the list. Using the GI, athletes can plan what to eat before, during and after a workout, race or competition.

Note: In the discussion below, slow digestion results in the slow absorption of carbohydrates and hence slow release of blood glucose with consequent lower GI. The following factors combined affect the GI:

- *Physical form:* Finely processed foods (due to mechanical processing) have fast rates of digestion and high GI. But large particles are barriers to digestion (e.g., pods on beans) that slow digestion resulting in low GI.
- *Fiber:* Foods with high-soluble fiber (e.g., oats and legumes) are viscous (moving slowly) in the intestines and with slow rates of digestion and low GI.
- *Fat and protein:* "Fat and protein slow stomach emptying." "Absorption of carbohydrates, and elevation of blood glucose, occur more gradually when consumed with fats and proteins" (Dr. Janet Rankine[29]). Therefore, fats and protein by delaying digestion cause low GI.
- *Fructose:* High fructose content slows the release of glucose from the intestines and results in only a small increase in glucose. The liver converts the fructose to glucose slowly.
- *Cooking:* Thermal processing or cooking breaks the food down into finer particles for easier digestion and higher GI compared to raw foods. Starch is made more digestible by cooking (e.g., toast); hence the GI is raised.

When to Use Low GI Foods?

Low GI foods have a GI factor less than 50. Some examples are: pasta, milk and yogurt, and nearly all fruits and vegetables (see Table 15.7 below for some important exceptions for fruits and vegetables marked with *). See particularly, foods near the bottom of the list, below GI of about 40, in Table 15.7.

Low GI BEFORE long workouts of strenuous exercise lasting for longer than one hour or more: for example, long competitions and events including marathon or half-marathon running, triathlon or duathlon, long cycling races, and cross-country ski racing. Thus, low GI foods help ensure that a steady stream of glucose is released into the bloodstream during a long event. This allows you to maintain your blood glucose levels and sustain your energy. Low GI foods have shown in research to extend endurance when eaten one to two hours before intensive exercise lasting more than an hour. These are carbohydrate foods that are slowly digested, with glucose released slowly for hours (e.g., 2 or 3) from the small intestine.

Some would find eating one to two hours before is too close to the race. I prefer to eat half-a-breakfast type meal about 3 to 4 hours before a race but this may be too long before to achieve an *optimum* energy release from the small intestine during the whole event. Cyclists could probably get by with eating even one hour before the event.

It is wise to experiment with pre-event meals during training. Normally, one should avoid milk, fat, protein and high fiber (e.g., legumes with indigestible sugars).

Note: Sucrose or glucose or high GI foods taken too close to the race could cause a high and then a low at the wrong time (hypoglycemia). Avoid taking sugars in the 30 to 60 minutes before your event; sugar or glucose just before an event will impair performance[2,29]. Fructose sugar has a low GI but is apt to cause stomach distress. "Glucose (or high GI foods) consumed shortly before an event can cause reactive hypoglycemia and suppression of fatty acid concentration in the blood" (Dr. Rankine[29]). Thus, there is greater reliance on muscle glycogen during the exercise, and it depletes in a shorter time resulting in fatigue and poor performance. You could experience such a situation about 45 minutes after eating pancakes and syrup.

When to Use High GI Foods?

High GI foods have a GI factor above about 70. Some examples are: grains and starches, such as bagel, bread, potatoes, or breakfast cereals (not All Bran). See particularly foods above a GI of 70 in Table 15.7.

1. **High GI DURING long workouts** lasting more than about 90 minutes if exercise is particularly intense. Body glucose can run low anywhere from 0 to 3 hours into a workout when involved in intense intermittent exercise: this depends on your pre-event meal, whether low or high GI and when consumed. If blood glucose has come back to near baseline, e.g., the amount before your pre-event meal then an ingestion of glucose energy will greatly assist. It is best to consume a sports drink

during long events since it is more quickly digested than solid foods during exercise. There is no concern of insulin release in spite of the high GI food since insulin release is suppressed during exercise. Sports drinks also replace water and electrolytes, as well as leaving the stomach quickly. High-glucose sports drinks have higher GI, and sucrose and fructose drinks have lower GI[29]. Fructose with water is a poor choice since it has low GI and could lead to gastrointestinal distress. I personally prefer sports drinks with maltodextrin, the glucose polymer. A fruit with low glycemic index, such as plums or even oranges, during intense exercise would be a mistake. A 591mL of Gatorade (37 grams of carbohydrate) every 45 to 60 minutes is about the correct consumption rate. I recall when my son was a teenager giving him some Gatorade during a tennis tournament; he had been in a hard match for about one and one half hours in the sun and was losing; he was not lacking water. After he received the Gatorade, there was nearly immediate obvious improvement and he went on to win.

1.1 **High GI DURING an interval workout.** Similar to the above, a high GI sports drink (a few mouthfulls) will be advantageous during the rest periods between repetitions, particularly near the end of the session. This will not cause an insulin release in view of the ongoing activity, as explained above.

2. **High GI AFTER a workout, competition or race.** In situations where there is a workout, competition or a race the next day, it is important to replenish the glycogen store in the muscles as fast as possible after the event. This is also particularly important for athletes who train twice a day. High GI foods are best in these cases. Muscles are most susceptible to reloading with glycogen when high GI carbohydrates are eaten within about a half-hour after exercise. It is also generally agreed that some protein with the carbohydrate is beneficial for recovery in the ratio of about 15% protein calories to about 70% carbohydrate calories.

2.1 **AFTER prolonged intensive workout, competition or race** lasting more than about two hours: "Consume a high carbohydrate beverage within 30 minutes of the activity and a high carbohydrate meal 2 hours later" (Coleman and Steen[30]). After a marathon, even more calories may be required in the 24 hours following the race.

2.2 **AFTER short workout or race,** e.g., short swim race, track races, 5 or 10K road or cross country races (less than about 40 minutes). The above advice in 2.1 still makes sense but with fewer calories required at the meal following the event.

Daily Diet High or Low GI?

Dr. Janet Rankine[29] says "A low GI diet is a good choice for athletes and non-athletes on a regular basis since it is more likely to cause lower blood cholesterol and improve appetite control."

Table 15.7 • Glycemic Index For Some Popular Foods

In the table below, I have arranged some popular foods in order of high to low GI based on information in the "International Tables of Glycemic Index" in the *American Journal of Clinical Nutrition* by Kaye Foster Powell and Janette Brand Miller[20]. This excellent reference usually lists GI factors from several references for each food and also the average value of these several references. Note that there is a significant difference in GI factors if the reference 100 is glucose or bread. I have used the average numbers in the glucose column.

High GI 100 to 70	Raisins	Apple juice
Glucose GI=100	*Potato (new)	
Honey	Shredded wheat	***Low GI below 40***
*Potato (baked)	Oatmeal	Baked beans
*Potato (instant)	Ice cream	(canned)
Jelly beans	Bran muffin	Milk
*Broad beans	*Orange juice	Tomato soup
French fries	Rice (brown)	Apple
Rice cakes	Popcorn	Yogurt
Corn flakes		Chick peas
Corn chips	***Low GI below 55***	Butter beans
*Watermelon	Sweet corn	Banana
Bagel	Special K	(underripe)
*Carrots	Potato crisps	Lentils
Bread white	Banana (overripe)	Grapefruit
	Kidney beans	Plum
Intermediate GI 70 to 55	(canned)	Fructose GI=23
Whole wheat bread	Sweet potato or yam	Cherries
Mars bar	Green peas	Peanuts GI=14
Soft drink	Pineapple juice	
*Pineapple	Lentil soup	
Sucrose GI=65	Orange	
Cookies and crackers	Grapes	
(generally between GI	Spaghetti	
55 to 75)	(without sauce)	
Macaroni and cheese	All Bran	

Note: The * indicates some exceptions (above GI of 55) to the fruits and vegetables that are normally below GI of about 55.

WATER

At the World Masters' Championships in Buffalo in 1995, during the cross-country races, there were so many runners collapsing from the extreme heat they ran out of ambulances and eventually cancelled the races. At the same meet, I heard of several athletes who were delirious on the track from dehydration due to the heat wave. I noticed I could not remember which foot to lead with in the preliminary 300-meter hurdles even though I had been sitting in the shade for three hours.

Water, water everywhere but not enough do we drink. This is the case with a lot of people—not enough of the right fluids. "Water is more important to performance than any other single nutrient"[8]; it's the number one nutrient.

Important Facts and Recommendations

We need to be aware of the following:

- ***Water in the body:*** The human body is composed of 60 to 65 percent water with muscle 72 percent water and fat about 20 to 25 percent water.
- ***Advantages:*** Water is essential for control of body temperature, energy production, transport of nutrients and wastes, lubrication of joints, digestion of food, improving the immune system, etc. A study of nine swimmers at Nagasaki University showed that drinking water during swimming intervals improved performance, lowered the body temperature and prevented dehydration (*Toronto Star*, May 15, 1997). It appears that these three advantages would apply even more so for runners, particularly on a hot humid day.
- ***Water comes from*** liquids in the diet, the foods we eat, and from water produced by the metabolism of the food (hydrogen combining with oxygen).
- ***Dehydration:*** "During exercise in the heat, blood that was transferring oxygen to the muscles is diverted to the skin to help eliminate heat" (Coleman and Nelson Steen[30]). Dehydration causes the body temperature to rise and the heart rate to increase. Dehydration of two or three percent (three or four pounds) can result in a three percent reduction in performance in the 1500-meter race and a six to seven percent reduction in performance in 5K and 10 races (from a study by Dr. Fink at Ball State University).
- ***Amount per day:*** Generally six to eight 8 ounce glasses of water should be consumed daily by the sedentary individual. This amount of water is needed if one is not getting the water needed from consumption of other liquids and food. For example, a high-carbohydrate diet with lots of fruit and vegetables would satisfy most of your thirst and some of your liquid requirements. You can also meet some of your fluid needs from other foods and beverages (e.g., milk, juice, herb teas, and soups, but not tea or coffee). Athletes require more than the sedentary individual

and particularly when the air is dry (low humidity promotes sweating on a hot day), or where extreme sweating takes place. Don't rely on your thirst to tell you when to drink.

- ***Before exercising in hot weather,*** drink plenty of water the day before. Also "Drink at least two to three glasses of water up to two hours before an event" (Nancy Clark[34]). This is more than ample time for the kidneys to process fluid, so you will have the opportunity to eliminate any excess before exercising. Eight to 16 ounces is recommended 15 minutes before exercise in the heat; this is called "hyper-hydration"[30]. I concur with both of these recommendations for adults (perhaps less than eight ounces 15 minutes before). At the Nike World Championships in Eugene, Oregon in August 1998, I had no problem in 100-degree F. heat during my 800m (100% age graded) following the above water advice, whereas the silver medallist said he lost at least 10-15 seconds because of the heat. Young athletes would take less than one-half of the above amounts based on the following information. Coleman and Steen[30] recommend for young athletes: "4-8 oz 1 to 2 hours before activity and 4-6 oz 10 to 15 minutes before activity; kids under 10 drink the smaller amount."
- ***During exercise,*** take one-half cup (four ounces) of fluid every 10 to 15 minutes[8]. The American College of Sports Medicine recommends more: 5 to 12 ounces of fluid every 15 to 20 minutes. A sports drink is better, particularly after about an hour of exercise as it supplies some sugar and lost electrolytes.
- ***After strenuous exercise,*** water (more than required from thirst) is required to flush out the resulting toxic by-products. This will effectively reduce soreness and aid in recovery[7]. The fluid lost during a training session should be replaced. Weigh yourself after the event. A loss of 2kg represents a fluid loss of 2 liters, i.e., at least two cups of water for every pound lost. You will find you generally lose one or two pounds after a strenuous workout so two cups or more after a workout is a very good habit to get into.
- ***Total daily water for a highly active person.*** If involved in heavy training or competition, two-thirds ounce of water per pound body weight is recommended[7]. This is 50% greater water requirement compared to an inactive person. The National Research Council recommends one litre of water per day per 1000 calories of food[4]. For a 70Kg runner using about 3700 calories per day, this results in about 3 to 3.7 liters water based respectively on the above references—a lot of water.
- ***Distilled (demineralized)*** *water* is the purest and best choice of drinking water[1,21]. Get into the habit of drinking bottled or filtered water. I got onto this recently after about 10 people died from E.coli in the water in Walkerton, Ontario. Also, the bad taste in the summer turned me off. Besides, who knows the effect of 20-year-old water pipes in your house.

- ***Meals without water.*** Do not drink water with your meal since it dilutes the digestive juices that are breaking down the food. This prevents the meal from being properly digested[1]. This is somewhat controversial. Other experts say water with meals is not detrimental as there is plenty of gastric juice to compensate. Some fluid is normally required with the meal, especially if the food is dry, but not soft drinks or milk.
- ***Maltodextrin sports drink,*** a glucose polymer is the preferred sports drink since it is more rapidly absorbed into the bloodstream from the stomach and small intestine. Thus, the glucose gets into the muscles more rapidly to provide energy.
- ***Water with lemon juice added.*** For athletes on the day of competition, water with lemon juice added will provide some electrolytes and make the body more alkaline, thus assisting to combat lactic acid. Water with lemon juice added makes sense in the morning and during a normal day also.

Electrolyte Deficiency and Dehydration

Exercise in the heat results in a higher lactate concentration and can cause a faster rate of muscle glycogen usage. If the body becomes overheated and dehydrated during exercise, due to lack of fluids, the heart becomes less effective in delivering oxygenated blood to the skin and muscles; this is due primarily to the loss of blood volume. These effects reduce performance.

"If experiencing chills, goose pimples, nausea, headache, faintness, disorientation, or cramping, be aware that these symptoms can lead to heat injury" (Coleman and Nelson Steen[30]). I can add one other symptom: One hot, summer day at age 68 after running an 800-meter race followed only 10 minutes later by a 200-meter race, I noticed the green grass had turned yellow–but I recovered quickly by drinking water in the shade. An athlete should be aware of the following three levels of heat illness:

Heat cramps:

- Due to fluid or sodium deficiency
- Symptoms of stomach or abdominal cramps

Heat exhaustion:

- More serious than heat cramps
- Due to dehydration
- Symptoms of nausea, dizziness and light-headedness, weakness, cramps and shortness of breath

Heatstroke:

- Calamity
- Due to excessive overheating (hyperthermia) and excessive dehydration
- Symptoms of diarrhea, major disorientation, upset stomach, shaking or convulsions and possible coma

Treatment

Depending on the severity, stop exercise, act quickly, get in the shade or air-conditioned room, drink water or preferably an electrolyte sport drink, and in extreme cases, immerse in cold water or ice.

Heat Stroke Formula

If the air temperature, AT, in degrees Fahrenheit, **plus** humidity, H, in %, is **greater** than 150, i.e., **AT(°F) + H(%)** = **>150**, then heat stroke is likely. (My formula is based on scientific data).

Prehydration and Rehydration

Prior to exercise, prehydration is affected by drinking tea or coffee, which stimulates urine production, thus, dehydration is more likely. The ill-effects of dehydration will be prevented if one is well-hydrated beforehand. Nadel[38] states, *"During and after exercise,* rehydration will occur more rapidly when sodium is taken in with fluids." Drinking a sports drink for the electrolytes is essential between events that are two or three hours apart; it is important to rehydrate quickly. Also, the cessation of thirst does not mean you are rehydrated.

PRE-COMPETITION MEAL

You probably already know that the pre-competition meal should be taken about three hours or more before the event, and should be low in calories with low fat, low protein and mainly complex carbohydrates (60% to 80%). But here are some facts perhaps you didn't know:

1. The precontest meal, if mainly carbohydrates, supplies additional energy for athletes for events lasting more than 45 minutes. For shorter events, the pre-competition meal supplies little of the energy needed during the event; this energy comes from food consumed in the two days or week before the event. (Darden[4])
2. For endurance events, eat low glycemic complex carbohydrates (pasta, lentils, legumes, yogurt, baked beans, porridge).
3. Based on my own experience, before a race, eat one of the following depending on the time available:
    - Four hours before (e.g., race at 12 noon or 1p.m.), eat your normal high-carbohydrate, low-fat breakfast: a bowl of cereal or oatmeal with milk, a glass of orange juice and a bagel with jam or peanut butter.

- Three hours before, half of everything above.
- Two hours before, a bagel with jam or peanut butter with a cup of coffee or tea.

The pre-event meal depends on the individual. Learn from your training what is optimum for yourself. It depends also on the intensity of the workout or the race. Nancy Clark[34] recommends: "Allow more digestion time before intense exercise than before low level activity." Thus, there will be more blood available for the muscles.

4. Vitamin/mineral pills should be taken at least two to three hours before a race with a meal. Remember, they are acidic, so don't take too many before a race.
5. Restrict fiber. Bulky foods, such as salads, should be eliminated on the day of the contest. Avoid highly spiced foods. Note: Cooked cereal has only about 11% carbohydrates[4].
6. Avoid glucose, honey or sugar, which draw fluids into the digestive tract for their digestion and absorption leading to dehydration and causing a sudden letdown in energy.
7. Avoid full fat milk or any high fat food. Cereal plus skim milk or low-fat yogurt are good choices two hours before a race. Milk causes phlegm. However, in my experience, a small amount of milk is not a problem even three hours before a race. Milk contains lactose but has a glycemic index of about 30, so it should not present a hypoglycemia problem (sugar rush).
8. Avoid the children's favorites: soda pop and all fast foods, like hot dogs, hamburgers, tacos, greasy pizzas, French fries, etc.
9. Don't choose foods that are not familiar or outside you normal routine.
10. For long events or in the case of two or three races in a day, include some lean protein about four hours before competition to help provide a long supply of blood sugar. However, eat only a small portion since protein may cause fatigue and increased urination.

ALCOHOL AND WINE

In moderation, alcohol is beneficial as it contains flavonoids, which act as antioxidants preventing bad LDL cholesterol from forming plaque in the arteries and also raising the good HDL. However, in excess, it prevents the liver from producing glucose and it can weaken the body and add unnecessary weight to the body. Guinness beer has the advantage of a good source of B-complex. But in moderation, wine (and in particular red) is the best of all. It is rich in iron, B vitamins and minerals, easy on the stomach and with a pH level (amount of acidity) very similar to the pH level of the human stomach (*Complete Book of Longevity* by Rita Aero).

Wine in moderation also has the following advantages: less risk of cancer, heart disease, stomach ulcers and arthritis; reduces or eliminates depression; also it inhibits blood clotting, hence it helps to prevent stroke. The overall effect is much increased longevity, and a happier life, of course. Moderate drinking is less than two glasses per day preferably and recommended with a meal. My habit of one or two glasses of red wine most nights before dinner with peanuts (more B vitamins) is perhaps not a bad habit after all.

Disadvantages for athletes

- Arrhythmias (irregular heartbeat or rapid heartbeat) can be triggered by alcohol.
- Dehydration. After a race, be sure to satisfy the thirst first with water before drinking beer.
- Contains no nutrients but is high in calories, which can be converted to fat.
- Robs the body of many essential vitamins and minerals, particularly B vitamins, magnesium, potassium, and vitamin C and A. In view of this, if taken in excess, it must slow down recovery from injuries.

Therefore, athletes should restrict alcohol to fewer than two drinks per day and not every day and not in days before a competition. This means less than two glasses of wine (5.5 oz), or two regular (or preferably light) beer (12 oz), which are equivalent to three ounces total of alcohol.

VITAMIN AND MINERAL SUPPLEMENTS

The need for supplements for non-athletes. Dr. Hendler in his very complete guide to nutritional supplements[14] (496 pages) states: "My research indicates that it is prudent even for healthy well fed individuals to take a daily vitamin and mineral supplement (properly balanced) to ensure maximum nutritional insurance." Mega doses of 5 to 10 times RDA (recommended Dietary Allowance) should only be taken on advice of a physician, or ideally have a nutritionist check your blood for any deficiencies. Older athletes should be more careful with megadoses. Coleman and Nelson Steen[30] state, "Older individuals may be more susceptible to vitamin/mineral overload and so should be discouraged from taking self prescribed doses of any vitamin or mineral exceeding the RDA." Keeping within the RDA is recommended by many nutritionists, I find, since overdosing on some vitamins and minerals can be toxic. Remember also, supplements are acid-forming in the body. For example, excess vitamin A and D, and excess zinc can be harmful.

The need for supplements for athletes. Many nutritionists say if you eat a balanced diet, you do not need supplements. However, not all athletes are eating properly. For instance, an athlete like myself who requires 3700 calories a day should have the equivalent of about 0.5 cup of milk, 9 servings of fruit, 3 servings of vegetables, and 12 servings of bread or grains in addition to meats, desserts and oil[4]. Fruits and vegetables of the right kind and quantity can supply mostly all the essential nutrients that the body needs. However, I know I and many others are not getting near the recommended fruits, vegetables and milk, etc., so the multiple vitamins and minerals are essential. Most athletes take some supplements for fear of missing out on some important vitamin or mineral. For example, of 28 elite runners surveyed,[23] only one was not taking a vitamin or mineral supplement; more than half were taking a multi-vitamin mineral supplement, 17 were taking vitamin C, 8 were taking vitamin E, and 9 were taking B vitamins. Most had a combination of the above. Surveys have shown that up to 84 percent of world class athletes use vitamin supplements[8].

As long as you are training, vitamin and mineral requirements are higher than normal, and deficiencies can cause breakdown, fatigue, poor recovery, and result in not reaching your maximum potential. Omission of certain foods, and indulgence in others can have drastic effect on athletic performance (and longevity).

Advantages

- Supplements can build stamina and endurance, boost immunity, lower cholesterol, fight colds, allergies, cancer etc.
- Women athletes, in particular, could be low in iron and need to ensure that they have an adequate supply; eating liver once a week will boost iron but it is very high in cholesterol. Women athletes are also apt to have a shortage of calcium and need to supplement their diet with calcium in conjunction with magnesium.
- Many minerals are lost in sweat during training, e.g., potassium and magnesium. Also some vitamins and minerals are lost in the urine when taking diuretics.
- Supplements can provide a boost to athletic performance. The benefits of supplements for marathoners were reported by Dr. Colgan[46], the highly respected USA sports nutritionist. In the study, the supplement group improved by more than 17 minutes average compared to only 6 minutes average by the no-supplement group.

When to take supplements. Preferably, supplements should be taken with meals since these are concentrated doses of vitamins and minerals[12]– [and often megadoses—sometimes causing excessive acidity]. I base this advice also on experience with my own stomach. Acidity can cause cancer cells to form (see "Alkaline and Acid Forming Foods" above). Also just as there are many bad drug combinations, I suspect there are also some bad drug/supplement combinations. Your stomach may warn you, but to be safe, take drugs and supplements at different times during the day.

Some of the more important minerals and vitamins for an athlete are discussed below.

Vitamin C

Vitamin C has many health advantages (Fink[26]): it reduces arthritic pain, cures colds, protects the heart by decreasing cholesterol, strengthens the immune system, protects against aging, aids in absorption of iron, and helps to prevent many diseases including cancer. Linus Pauling[27], Nobel Prize for chemistry in 1954, an expert on Vitamin C and a strong advocate for Vitamin C states, "I conclude that the optimum daily amount for most adult human beings lies in the range 2.3g and 10g." Massive doses of vitamin C seem to be completely harmless; any excess not needed in the body is quickly lost in the urine. Vitamin C can be taken to ward off infections, to heal fractures and muscle injuries[25]. Vitamin C as a supplement is best taken with bioflavonoids (better absorption of vitamin C and speeds healing); this is called "Ester C."

The best sources for vitamin C are potatoes, broccoli, green leafy vegetables, tomatoes, berry fruits, and citrus fruits. Six ounces of orange juice is equal to 90mg of vitamin C compared to the RDA of 60mg. The usual dose for athletes is between 200 to 1000 milligrams; it is recommended to take half the dose in the morning and the other half at night.

Vitamin E

Vitamin E has many similar health advantages to Vitamin C; it stimulates the immune system, relieves muscle cramps, helps prevent delayed onset of muscle soreness (DOMS), helps prevent osteoporosis, protects the nervous system, protects against aging, prevents cancer, protects against cardiovascular disease, and other diseases. The usual daily dose for athletes is 200 to 400IU.

The best sources for vitamin E are wheat germ, vegetable oils/margarine, nuts, whole grain products, soy beans, and green leafy vegetables.

Athletic Benefits of Vitamins C and E

Although vitamins E and C are very popular as a daily supplement for athletes, there is limited evidence that vitamin E and/or C can improve athletic performance, such as endurance.

Many athletes believe as I do in the benefit of vitamins C and E for repair of minute muscle tears after workouts. They are important to prevent or reduce short-term muscle soreness. Because of the chronic muscle trauma some athletes suffer, increased vitamin C may be helpful with chronic muscle fiber damage[2]. Also, Clark[12] states supplements provide repair materials.

I normally take 400IU of E and 500mg of Ester C every day and extra of both when there is extra soreness or when having a cold or the flu.

Vitamins C and E, Beta Carotene, Grape Seed and Selenium for Fighting Free Radicals

Oxygen is both a good guy and a bad guy. In the latter case, it combines with protein, fat, carbohydrates and other elements in the body (normal metabolism) to produce highly reactive, unstable compounds or atoms called *free radicals*. An oxygen atom becomes a free radical when it is robbed of an electron during natural metabolism. This unstable, invalid atom tries to replace the lost electron by raiding stable molecules. When it takes an electron from another molecule, a free radical is created and a chain reaction begins. This slowly leads to irreversible cell disintegration, more rapid aging, and cancer problems. This is similar to damage caused due to "external radiation" (nuclear, X-rays, and environmental radiation), which produces free radicals. In view of the similarity, the processes originating in the body during normal metabolism, etc., are sometimes called "internal radiation". The pollutants, such as carbon monoxide, ozone, herbicides, tobacco smoke, smog, dietary imbalance, and food additives create free radicals. The common antioxidant supplements (C, E, selenium, etc.) are recommended daily to prevent the chain reaction and cell damage by transferring electrons to the free radicals. Antioxidants are in effect anti-aging. And Dr. Haas[18] states, "Antioxidants can reduce the damage from most traumatic sports injuries and minimize the free radical destruction of joint tissues."

In the masters category of athletes, if you age slower, you can run, swim, and cycle faster. You can age more slowly by taking antioxidant supplements vitamins C and E, beta carotene, selenium and grape seed extract to fight the free radicals. The above antioxidants gobble up the free radicals and prevent them from doing their damage; read any of the anti-aging books, e.g., *We Live Too Short and Die Too Long* by Dr. W.Bortz[42]. Exercise causes free radical damage but fortunately the body provides increased protection against this free radical damage.

B Vitamins

B vitamins are concerned with the production of energy from proteins, fats, and particularly carbohydrates–one reason why they are a favorite supplement for many athletes. The B vitamins are essential for normal functioning of the central nervous system; for an athlete healthy neural pathways are imperative. The more you exercise and/or the harder, the more of these vitamins you need. More vitamin B is also beneficial on stressful days and good for the morale. Adelle Clarke[24] cautions that if one or more B vitamins are taken over a long period, this increases your need for all others in the B group. The following cause a loss of vitamin B: alcoholic drinks, very hot days and coffee. However, if you are never tired, the chances are that your intake of vitamin B is adequate[24].

The important B vitamins are described below:

- **B1 (Thiamin)** is essential to several enzyme systems that regulate metabolism of protein, fat and particularly carbohydrates. The more starch or carbohydrates in the diet, the more thiamin is required[5].
- **B2 (Riboflavin)** plays an important role in the metabolism of carbohydrates and particularly protein and fat. It can speed up the repair of damaged muscles and ligaments. Active women may have a shortage of riboflavin[18].
- **B3 (Niacin)** combines with other chemicals in the body to form co-enzymes essential for extracting energy from carbohydrates and fat. It promotes blood circulation and hence aids oxygen transport. Helps lower LDL cholesterol and increases vitality.
- **B5 (Pantothenic Acid)** is the anti-stress vitamin. It enhances stamina and increases vitality.
- **B6 (Pyridoxine)** is essential for conversion of glycogen in muscles and liver into glucose energy. Also it is "necessary for reconstitution of amino acids in food to amino acids in protein of the body"[5].
- **B12 (Cobalamin)** is essential for development of red blood cells, it is important to help maintain a healthy central nervous system and to relieve fatigue. The daily requirement is only 1 to 3 micrograms since the liver stores abut 300 x RDA. Studies on B12 supplementation found no beneficial effect on athletic performance or aerobic endurance[8]. On the other hand, I have met two runners who took B12 supplements (one who took it orally before races and another who took it by injection once a month), and both believed it was beneficial. If B12 is taken orally or by injection, administration should ideally be under the care of a doctor. According to Darden[4], injections of B12 and the B complex would only be of benefit if the athlete suffers from vitamin deficiencies, has been sick, or is in a rundown condition; these injections assist in making a rapid recovery.
- **Foods rich in B vitamins**[2,5]. The above indicates the importance of B vitamins for athletes. Generally, the following are rich in B vitamins: liver, brewer's yeast, dairy products, lean meat, yeast, Bovril, Oxo, brown rice, whole wheat flour, sunflower seeds, whole-grain cereals, and peanuts. As an athlete training daily, I find I have a daily craving for peanuts possibly to replace the vitamin B. Green vegetables provide B6 but vegetables are poor for B3. Dairy products are poor for B3. White rice is poor for B1 and B2.

Calcium and Magnesium

A USA national wide survey in 1980 revealed a huge fraction of the population was deficient in calcium and magnesium, as well as iron and vitamins. Muscles will cramp if calcium or magnesium is lacking; also a lack of either calcium or magnesium or both could result in muscle spasm or twitching[4]. Calcium and magnesium are alkaline-forming when digested[6] – an important further advantage for an athlete.

"Calcium is essential for conduction of nerve impulses, heart function and muscle contractions"(Berkoff[8]). A high protein diet causes excessive excretion of calcium and other minerals. Dr. Haas[18] "recommends active women particularly supplement their daily diet with 1000mg calcium to 500mg magnesium; since with vigorous physical activity especially under hot and humid conditions there is the risk of losing these and other minerals in sweat and urine." Deficiency of calcium will also cause muscles to lose their tone and become sore; they will then be predisposed to injury[25]. Stress fractures are also due to weakened bones caused by a lack of calcium; this is possible in sports involving stress of impact like running. Surveys have shown that calcium deficiency is more widespread than that of any other nutrient.

Two 8 oz. glasses of milk daily will provide about 500 to 600 milligrams of calcium; leafy green vegetables, cabbage, yogurt, cheese, almonds, sunflower seeds, sardines and salmon are also a good source.

Magnesium. The primary function of magnesium is as an activator of certain enzymes in the body, particularly those related to carbohydrate metabolism[4]. Magnesium plays a vital role in converting carbohydrates to energy, controlling heartbeat rhythm, activating enzyme systems, and muscular contractions. (If you have twitching muscles, e.g., trembling calf muscles as I have, magnesium will stop or reduce this problem.) It has also been used successfully for prostate troubles[12]. Magnesium is also especially effective to lower cholesterol in the blood and to relieve nervousness and grouchiness. (However, one rarely meets a grouchy athlete–unless he or she is injured or perhaps a poor loser.) Also "a social drinker who has two ounces of liquor (95% proof) daily will excrete three to five times more than normal magnesium in their urine"[24]. In the latter case, magnesium with calcium supplementation makes good sense. Lack of magnesium could also result in irregular heartbeat and bad nerves[24]. When magnesium is deficient, large amounts of calcium are lost in the urine; also, the more calcium in the diet the more magnesium needed[24].

The recommended daily amount is about 500 to 600 milligrams of magnesium. The following foods provide magnesium: whole-grain products, green leafy vegetables and other vegetables, and fruits.

Potassium

Extra potassium is required for exercise; a deficiency leads to reduced performance. During exercise heat is produced in the muscles and potassium is released into the bloodstream effectively widening the blood vessels. The increased blood flow reduces heat buildup to safe values. The potassium is released as sweat and in urine. Potassium is important in the conversion of glucose to glycogen (stored in muscles and the liver), to maintain the proper alkalinity in the body, and to stimulate nerve impulses for muscle contractions including the heart. It is also important to replace potassium lost in sweat during exercise and/or extreme heat. Potassium must be in balance with sodium; an excess of potassium can cause a serious loss of sodium and vice versa[24].

Foods rich in potassium are: complex carbohydrates (e.g., bananas of course, broccoli, spinach, green peppers, potatoes), sunflower seeds, nuts and fish.

Iron

Iron has several major functions important for athletes in:

- Making of hemoglobin (in the blood) which transfers oxygen from the lungs to tissues
- Formation of myoglobin (in muscle cells), which supplies the oxygen to muscle cells
- Assisting to produce energy by activating enzymes and by transporting fatty acids into the mitochondria.

Every time the feet hit the ground in running, slight trauma occurs causing a loss of iron. When there is a shortage of iron, the red blood cells decrease in number, or red blood cells contain less than normal amounts of hemoglobin. The oxygen-carrying capacity of the blood is then reduced, and the efficiency of all the body processes is impaired. This is called iron deficiency anemia and results in decreased muscular activity and fatigue. Anemia is a worst case scenario. However, milder cases of iron deficiency can cause fatigue particularly in female distance runners. Coffee and tea drinkers, if low in iron, should be aware that heavy consumption can block the majority of iron absorption. Foods rich in vitamins E and C at the same meal enhance the absorption of iron; another reason for athletes to take vitamins E and C. Cooking in iron pots and pans may increase the iron content of certain foods by at least a factor of 10.

Caution: Excess iron can be dangerous. It is advised that you consult your physician for a blood test if you suspect you are low in iron before taking supplements.

Food rich in iron based on various references are: liver, raisins, oysters, sardines, beef, kidney beans, green leafy vegetables, dried apricots, peanut butter, broccoli, peas, and nuts. Poor choices are milk, rice, cheese and fruit. The RDA for non-vegetarian (pre-menopausal) women is 18 mg and 8 mg for non-vegetarian men.

Zinc

Zinc is particularly important for tissue growth, healing wounds and for strengthening the immune system. It is also essential for functioning of the prostate.

Foods rich in zinc are: red meat, poultry, seafood (particularly oysters), whole-grain products, brewer's yeast, eggs, wheat germ and pumpkin seeds. The RDA for zinc is 15 mg. Above 30mg can be harmful.

Chromium

Chromium is worthy of mention in view of its importance in storing glycogen and the many claims that have been made for improving athletic performance. However, the many claims for chromium boosting performance appear to be unfounded.

Nine out of 10 Americans are deficient in chromium, and running increases loss via the urine. Chromium sources are whole grains, meat, cheese and beer and the Recommend Daily Intake is 50 to 200 micrograms (Coleman and Nelson Steen[30]). From Nancy Clarke[34], for example, the following are also good sources: 4 oz. chicken breast (40 micrograms), 1 tbsp. peanut butter (40 micrograms), 1 cup peas (60 micrograms).

"MAGIC" SUPPLEMENTS

There are some magic supplements (performance enhancers) that improve the performance of runners. (However, these are supplementary to hard training.) Some of these "magic bullets" that I have used are discussed here.

Water

Water is the number one magic supplement. This is just a reminder of its extreme importance for an athlete. Make sure you get sufficient water every day, particularly in hot weather.

Grape Seed Extract

Grape seed extract and also pine bark (pycnogenol) are plant bioflavonoids called proanthocyanadins. Both of these have the same beneficial effects. Grape seed extract is growing in popularity since the French, in their ***red*** wine consumption, have shown to have very few heart attacks (the French Paradox) in spite of a fatty diet. I am a big advocate of grape seed, and I normally take 100mg every day; and I suspect there may be advantages in taking an increased dose closer to a major competition as it can increase endurance (see below).

Advantages:

- It is a powerful antioxidant (natural free radical scavenger)–that is 50 times more powerful than vitamin E and 20 times more powerful than vitamin C;
- Helps athletic injuries and helps speed recovery from workouts by reducing muscle damage (lowered free radical damage);
- Works in conjunction with vitamins C and E in the diet (enhancing their activity);

- Improves skin elasticity and smoothness;
- Strengthens capillaries, veins and arteries;
- Improves flexibility of joints;
- Reduces cholesterol by reducing plaque in the arteries;
- There are performance benefits, as well. *Runner's World* (May 1999) reported a study resulting in a 20% increase in endurance on a treadmill test from taking pine bark (200mg per day for a month).

Caffeine

Caffeine can help sports performance but there are limitations to be aware of. One or two cups is well below the IOC legal limit of 9mg per kg of body weight or about 600 to 800mg. I have used a cup of coffee many times about an hour before a workout or a road race or cross-country race, and often black, instead of with sugar to avoid the high and low that could occur with sucrose. I believe it helps. It is also useful to make you lighter before a race since it is a diuretic. On a hot day, I would not recommend it in view of its dehydrating effect. At the World Master's Championships in Buffalo in July 1995, many collapsed from the heat; I avoided coffee close to my races but did indulge at breakfast and had my best meet (three world records).

If feeling tired, never take a coffee and go out for training. The coffee will mask your fatigue. I've made this mistake with drastic consequences afterward. It's like having a sore muscle and taking an aspirin or two before training or a race. You won't know if you are doing harm to your body. *Remember, when young, the body permits many indiscretions and abuses, which in older years may be very serious or fatal.* However, after a workout if not fatigued, have a coffee and you will be ready to go again within an hour with another **slower** workout. This technique I have used many times. But be careful, since coffee can speed up the heart.

Caffeine is absorbed quickly, but it takes a day or more for before it is completely gone from the body. This can be an advantage or disadvantage depending on what you are trying to achieve or avoid. There is good agreement that caffeine is beneficial for endurance events.

There is good agreement that caffeine is beneficial for endurance events. Some sprinters take caffeine to increase contraction of muscles and reaction time. Some advantages below still indicate possible advantages for sprinters. I have experienced sprinter friends who *believe* it works for them. Also, studies have shown that it can improve 1500 meter race time by about four seconds (reported by Owen Anderson, *Runner's World* February 1994).

For a maximum performance effect from caffeine, it should not be used on a regular basis but used only (about 40 minutes) before competition. Alternatively, to non-use on a regular basis, stop consumption three days before a competition.

Advantages:

- Gives feeling of alertness and lessens fatigue;
- Increases motor activity (skillful movement)
- Stimulates the central nervous system, increases release of adrenaline,. and assists muscle contractions by increasing availability of calcium ions.
- Improves reaction time. (This seems to be the consensus, but some studies have shown no improvement.)

Disadvantages:

- Retards feeling of fatigue and reduces drowsiness; hence, if we do not perceive our tiredness, we may push to the point of injury;
- Caffeine is a diuretic and can cause dehydration and loss of electrolytes due to excessive urination;
- Can cause cardiac arrhythmias (irregular and/or fast heartbeat)[7];
- Can cause increased blood pressure, and trembling muscles if taken to excess on a regular basis;
- Causes loss of vitamin B, and blocks absorption of iron;
- Causes significant increase in acid levels in the blood. The extreme importance of avoiding acid-forming foods, like tea and coffee, was explained in *Fit For Life*[1] and also in the section above on "Alkaline and Acid Forming Foods."
- Since it can take 24 hours for the caffeine to be processed out of the body, caffeine could slow recovery.

In **summary**, in my opinion, for athletes, the pros for caffeine outweigh the cons.

Matol

Matol (I believe sometimes called "K" or "KM" in the USA) is a herbal mixture consisting of 13 herbs in liquid form and on the market for more than 60 years. It is high in potassium and magnesium. In the past, it has been used by the Russian hockey team, Edwin Moses and other Olympic athletes. I have used it off and on for the past 9 years and believe it to be helpful in my training. For example, if it is taken before bedtime, you will have difficulty in sleeping because it is energizing. Also, I found after taking it for one week only, I had one of my best indoor meets ever; winning the 60 meter dash, breaking a world record in the 400 meters and running an excellent 800 meters all on the same day. That sold me. A liter bottle of Matol will last me about one month.

It is also used as a daily supplement for race horses to improve the immune system, to improve concentration, endurance and strength. The results have been quite noticeable. The dose is doubled after strenuous exercise or after a race; therefore, it's useful for recovery. Unfortunately, there are no tests on humans.

Advantages

The manufacturer claims the following:

- Purifies the blood by eliminating wastes in the blood; this keeps the blood vessels clean;
- Increases vitality by increased oxygenation (transport of oxygen): oxygen in blood is increased up to 30 to 40 percent;
- Improves general health and slows deterioration of skin tissues;
- Improves concentration;
- High in dietary fiber and can be taken with other supplements.

Disadvantages

- It acts as a diuretic on some people (the same effect as coffee). Therefore, it's best not to combine with coffee.

Creatine

Creatine monohydrate is the latest magic supplement, used by many weight lifters, sprinters, jumpers and middle distance runners. Creatine is produced within the body, and also from digestion of meat and fish. Supplementation can increase creatine within the body by about 20 percent.

Creatine Energy System. It is important to understand how creatine is involved in one of the three main energy systems. Creatine is used in the "phosphagen system or phosphate system" (see chapter on "Physiological Principles") where creatine phosphate (CP) regenerates spent adenosine triphosphate (ATP) in intense activities lasting less than about 30 seconds. The creatine taken up by the muscle (mainly in Type IIb fast twitch fibers) is converted to CP with the aid of an enzyme, and CP refuels the main energy compound ATP. Thus more creatine in the system, if not overdone, means more energy.

Removal of Lactate. Chapter 1 explains in the phosphagen system, H+ (acidic hydrogen ions from lactic acid production) are removed in the process of producing ATP energy from creatine phosphate. In effect, creatine acts to buffer the effects of lactic acid by reducing acidity in short bouts lasting less than about 30 seconds.

Dosage. It is usual to load up with 20 grams of creatine for 5 days in four 5-gram doses per day, and preferably to ingest it with a warm glass of water to assist assimilation and retention. (Recent evidence indicates not to mix it with citrus juice or most fruit juices since they neutralize creatine, creating only waste products.). Alternatively, take three grams daily for four weeks to produce the same creatine loading in muscles. Thereafter, only two grams per day are required for maintenance. Note one pound of beef or salmon contains about 2 grams of creatine, but not all of this is absorbed by the body.

The loading at 20 grams per day for five days started as an expedient research convenience. Of course, the manufacturers love the 20 gram loading myth. Anderson[33] suggests: "If you're thinking of creatine supplementation try six grams per day (e.g., six one-gram intakes) over a five or six day period. After that a 'maintenance dose' of about two grams per day (four half-gram servings)..." This type of reduced loading compared to 20 grams per day was shown in a study (by Roger Harris, one of the original pioneers in this area) to produce "significantly improved performance" compared to no creatine supplementation[33]. I concur with not loading up with 20 grams per day. I always felt intuitively that about four or five grams per day was enough particularly after a physical examination revealed excess creatine in my kidneys. Too large a dose will result in loss of most of the creatine in the urine.

Cycling of Creatine. Some support cycling creatine and some do not. A common cycling routine is to load for a week, take the maintenance dose for six weeks, then stop for two weeks. Cycling ensures the body will continue to produce creatine on its one. Also, it seems perhaps not worthwhile to take it during the off-season.

Some Benefits of Creatine for Athletes

General

- *Lifting Weights and Cycling.* Williams and Krieder[40] report the following significant enhancement of performance after creatine loading: during lifting weights (15% mean improvement in 11 of 16 studies); during high intensity repetitive (normally 6 to 30 seconds) ergometer cycle studies (16% mean improvement in 18 out of 25 studies).
- *Swimming.* A study by C.H. Thompson 1996 quoted by Williams and Krieder[40] indicated no improvement in 100m or 400m swim times after taking creatine, 2g/day for 56 days. Also, in 4 out of 5 studies on swimming there was no ergogenic effect (benefit) due to creatine supplementation[40].
- *Hockey.* In a study of elite hockey players, creatine supplementation made a significant improvement; the usual creatine loading of 20g/day for each of 5 days was followed by 5g/day for 10 weeks before testing (Jones, Atter, and Georg, et al.[39]).
- *Sprint Running.* Passwater[35] quotes Dr. Prevost on some of the following who benefit from creatine supplementation, "Sprinters in the final heat after running qualifiers; an athlete in multiple events..."
- *Middle Distance Running.* Harris, Viru, Greenhaff, and Hultman[41], pioneers in the benefits of creatine to enhance athletic performance, report on a running study involving 300 meter intervals [the anaerobic glycolysis system], and 1000 meter intervals [the aerobic capacity system]. After loading for six days, the creatine group showed very significant reduction in the 300 meter and 1000 meter running times.

Single Sprint

Nearly all studies indicate creatine does not enhance performance in a "single" sprint race, for example:

- *Cycling.* Jones, Atter and Georg[39] report [based on three separate studies], "Three to five days of Cr loading had no effect on power output or total work done in 'single' maximal cycle sprints of 15, or 30 seconds duration [in two separate studies]." Williams and Kreider[40] report similar results in several ergometer cycle studies.
- *Sprint Running.* Williams and Krieder[40] also report, "The ability of creatine supplementation to improve sprint running speed remains controversial." (This statement is for repetitive tests and more so for "single" tests. Also, similar to the Jones study and nearly all such studies, testing was done normally after loading up with about 20 grams per day for about 5 to 7 days. This is the most convenient testing procedure, so there is a lack of *long term testing* normally.)

Therefore, do not expect a benefit in a "single" sprint race shortly after creatine loading for seven days or less. However, since creatine improves recovery and reduces lactic acid, interval training would be enhanced due to increased training quality. In addition, after many weeks of maintenance supplementation, lean muscle mass and strength should be increased due to the creatine. With many weeks of improved interval training due to maintenance supplementation, speed and speed endurance should be improved; and *then*, this should translate into a faster "single" race.

Increase in Lean Body Mass. It is believed by some researchers that creatine supplementation brings in more water to the muscle cells and this indirectly leads to increase in muscle mass by chemical reactions. Researcher Anthony Almada reported an increase of 3.7 pounds in "lean body weight" for men in a study after 28 days of creatine supplementation plus weight training. (Lean tissue is about 50% muscle for men and 40% for women.)

Similarly, I have noticed, on several occasions, a gain in weight of about three pounds maximum after taking creatine five grams per day for only about one week; there was little weight training. In my case, I suspect this is water volume in the muscles, as lean mass may not be developed that fast with little weight training.

Advantages

- Based on the Passwater[35] survey: "The good news about creatine is that it is safe, even when taken in the quantities used by athletes." Williams and Krieder[40] make a similar statement and further state, "Studies indicate no health risk in supplementing creatine up to 5 years."
- It is very easy to digest since it is like a food and tasteless.

- Creatine increases muscular strength, provides energy so that the volume of short exercise can be increased, reduces the effects of lactic acid and accelerates recovery. In particular, creatine improves performance of athletic activities short in nature, i.e., intense activities (less than about 30 seconds) mainly involving the phosphagen energy system. However, there are studies also indicating benefit for longer intense activities; see *Middle Distance Running*[41] in the examples above.
- There is ample evidence of the benefits of creatine supplementation to produce higher quality intensities and to reduce fatigue during interval training and repetitive sprint efforts, particularly less than 30 seconds or even higher. This should translate into improved performance in middle distance and sprint races.

Disadvantages

- Creatine may cause cramps in the muscles. But some professional sport teams on creatine have experienced no cramping. I had three bad experiences by taking it up to one day before a race and unfortunately with very little water; I experienced cramps in the calf in a 60 meter race, a 100 meter race and a 200 meter race shortly after coming out of the blocks. Make sure you take plenty of water with it and be sure to take at least eight glasses of water during the day.
- You may gain about two to three pounds believed to be lean mass or water retention. For long distance runners and swimmers, this additional weight of two to three pounds offsets to some extent the training benefits.
- Long-term effects on the body are unknown. Some health authorities recommend additional research.
- Creatine does not work for everyone. About 20 percent of athletes do not find creatine helpful. Recently I have talked to two sprinters (one John O'Neil, Canadian, world record for 60 meters for age group 70-75) who both stated that the creatine gave them stiff muscles so they stopped taking it.

Health Risk and Injury

There appears to be no health danger or increased risk of injury (apart from cramping). Williams and Krieder[40] state the following: "Available studies indicate no problem in creatine supplementation trials lasting up to five years..." "Additional research is needed to evaluate its medical safety." "Although many groups of researchers have evaluated athletes during intense training, there is no current evidence that creatine supplementation promotes muscle injury." (But I have heard of one elite USA 800 meter runner who *believed* that creatine was the cause of his hamstring injury.)

In **summary**, my assessment is that creatine is the best legal supplement particularly for shorter races if used properly. But it appears not to be advantageous for everyone. Also, long-term effects are unknown.

Glucosamine Sulfate and Chondroitin Sulfate

The following references were used for some of the information below, i.e., "Nutritional Healing"[43] and "100 Super Supplements for a Longer Life."[44]

The super supplements glucosamine sulfate, GS, and chondroitin sulfate, CS, are important in the treatment of several ailments and particularly osteoarthritis. Either supplement can be taken separately for this ailment, but together seem to be the more effective way. Osteoarthritis is a degenerative joint disease involving deterioration (roughening and friction) of cartilage caused by injury, or wear and tear due to aging. It causes tendons, ligaments, and muscles that hold joints together to become painful and stiff[43]; nearly all above 70 are affected, and particularly women. Any athlete with this ailment will be slowed or even stopped in his/her tracks.

This disease could affect all joints, and it particularly affects the knees, hip or back. I include GS and CS here under magic supplements as these supplements are known to bring relief, build cartilage, and even stop the disease–based on hundreds of tests. I have personally heard from at least five individuals (some athletes and some overweight) who have benefited greatly from GS and/or CS. Usually, it is a knee problem. Glucosamine taken orally by athletes aids in the rebuilding of injured connective tissue; for athletes repair and growth of connective tissue is an ongoing process[44].

The usual dose is 1500mg of GS with 1200mg of CS per day.[44] Although there are no toxic effects, a physician should be consulted before taking as there are possible side effects (allergic reactions) for some individuals.

Caution: An interesting fact is that NSAIDs (anti-inflammatories like aspirin) taken for osteoarthritis to relieve pain and repair joints, may actually aggravate the problem.

Whey Protein

Whey protein powder has important advantages for athletes. For example, Maurice Greene, past world record holder in the 100 meters has several protein shakes during the day and particularly after a workout. Whey is a complete protein with the right amount of essential (meaning required from the diet) amino acids that are important to our bodies in addition to most *non-essential* (manufactured by the body) amino acids. The *essential* amino acids are the building blocks for a healthy body. The liver produces about 80% of the amino acids needed by the body. The remaining 20% are the nine *essential* amino acids. Whey is over 95% pure protein compared to meats, which are about 25 to 30% protein.

Advantages of Whey Protein over Other Proteins

- Whey protein has the highest biological value of all proteins similar to eggs. The biological value relates to the amount of protein actually absorbed and used by the body or the nitrogen retention.
- It is easily digestible, soluble, and does not require cooking.
- Topping up your diet with whey protein ensures that you are not lacking in some essential amino acids. Leucine is probably the most important one for athletes since it promotes muscle protein synthesis and muscle growth and aids in growth hormone production.
- Whey contains the highest levels of branched chain amino acids (BCAAs) compared to any natural food source. BCAAs metabolizes directly into muscle tissue instead of the liver like other proteins. Hence BCAAs are the first used in exercise and resistance training. Leucine is also one of the BCAAs.
- Whey enhances immunity. It raises glutathione (GSH) levels by as much as 60% if taken for a couple of months. GSH is important to the immune system and is a powerful antioxidant to fight the free radicals that cause aging and cancer.

Further Advantages for Athletes

- *Increases muscle mass*
- *Speeds overall recovery* (replaces depleted protein)
- Helps to *prevent overtraining* by making up for inadequate protein by reducing muscle deterioration (Bell U study)
- *Causes new cells to grow* thus speeding normal repair of injuries
- *Allows longer and/or more intense training*

Proteins like meats, and dairy products can do some of the above but whey is more easily taken and digested at optimum times before and immediately after a workout. I particularly recommend it to accelerate healing of an injury.

Cautions

Too much protein will cause excess acidity and may cause kidney and liver problems. It should not be taken by those with kidney or liver disease. There should be no long term effects as long as the total protein in food + whey protein does not drastically exceed the recommended total daily protein.

How to Take It?

- Add to pancakes or muffins.
- Add to a fruit smoothie shake (my favorite).
- Mix with fruit juice or milk or add to water (liquids should be unheated).

Dose

If taken in one large dose, then shortly after a workout is recommended. Or take 30 to 45 minutes before or after a meal. Some doctors recommend taking for two months and going off it for two months. Initially, increase the whey protein gradually. Give your body time to adjust.

My recommendation is to base the daily dose of whey protein on the difference between recommended protein intake and your protein intake by food. This ensures that you do not overdose. The recommended intake for competitive athletes is normally about 1.5 grams protein per kg of body weight or about 0.70 grams per pound of body weight. Estimate your daily protein consumption from protein tables (see e.g., Nancy Clark's Sports Nutrition Guidebook). For example, the recommended whey protein/day for a 70 kg competitive athlete = 100 grams – food consumption grams.

Glutamine

Glutamine is the new wonder supplement. It is becoming popular with athletes and may be even more beneficial than creatine. It is the most plentiful free amino acid in muscle tissue and blood. Sixty percent of free-form amino acid in skeletal muscle is glutamine. Strictly speaking, we are talking here of L-glutamine where the L indicates the amino acids more compatible with human chemistry (proteins in animal and plant tissue are made from the L form as opposed to the D form). The big benefits: glutamine aids recovery for athletes, increases growth hormone and lowers lactic acid, while assisting the immune system and also increases brain activity. Details are below.

Glutamine is used in muscles for the synthesis/metabolism of protein. Since it plays a major role in building and maintaining muscle (minimizes the breakdown of muscle tissue), it is used as a supplement by body builders and other athletes. It is a *"non-essential"* amino acid, meaning the body manufactures it, but it is considered as *"conditionally essential"* because after intense exercise, stress, or injury, the body produces insufficient amounts to meet demands. Hence, supplementation is beneficial for the above situations.

Glutamine is used in muscles and in other parts of the body, such as in the brain and nervous system (about (33%) and in the gastronomical tract (about 40%). A stressful situation will reduce glutamine levels by about one-third. Even a common cold will reduce levels significantly. After intense exercise glutamine levels in muscles are reduced by as much as one-half; this was shown in tests on seven athletes following sprinting or long distance running. *Hence, during intense exercise without supplementation, muscles may be robbed by other tissues of glutamine causing muscle cell dehydration and depletion/breakdown (catabolism).*

Benefits of Glutamine as a Supplement For Athletes

- If enough glutamine as a supplement is available before and/or immediately after intense exercise, muscle catabolism can be decreased, muscles remain more hydrated, and recovery is improved. Also over-training is less likely.
- Glutamine increases endurance by replacing glycogen under conditions of glycogen depletion. Glutamine converts to glutamate and produces ATP energy.
- Supplementation with glutamine shows elevated levels of growth hormone. A study of young and old showed even two grams per day of glutamine supplement can increase hormone levels by 400% (1995 LSU College of Medicine). This is a big advantage for athletes. (I am a bit dubious about the 400% claim but still believe it will significantly increase growth hormone levels.)
- Glutamine increases the bicarbonate used to buffer acids like ammonia in the blood. Hence, it is used to balance acid/alkaline levels in the body. During multiple sets of high intensity repetitions, it counteracts lactic acid buildup. Hence, harder longer workouts are possible with less muscle soreness.
- Glutamine is used by the white blood cells. After exercise and particularly after over-training, glutamine levels fall off resulting in reduced immunity. (I have noticed in my own body an increased incidence of colds after a track meet.) Therefore, glutamine supplementation will keep you healthier and reduce training time lost due to illness/infection.

Proper Balance of Amino Acids

If taking glutamine (or any other amino acid), particularly if longer than a month, it is recommended to also take whey protein or the amino acids in the body will become unbalanced. A variety of amino acids is necessary to keep all amino acids balanced. Whey protein has nearly a full compliment of all amino acids and the perfect protein to maintain balance. Also, a low level of one particular amino acid will limit the assimilation of all amino acids. For example, if one amino acid is present at a low level, the assimilation of all will be limited to near the same low level. This leads to a lack of vital proteins in the body. A body in proper balance needs far more glutamine than any other amino acid. Glutamine is the most likely to be depleted after intense exercise so it makes sense to supplement it right after to speed recovery and for retention of general health. Vegetarians in particular must ensure they are not lacking in high quality protein, which will result in lacking some particular amino acid.

Other Glutamine Benefits for General Health

- Improves protein metatbolism
- Combats arthritis, fatigue and impotence
- Helps the immune system in times of stress

- Reduces cravings for sugar and alcohol (I know this works)
- Improves brain functioning (sometimes called the "smart vitamin")
- Stabilizes blood sugar
- Helps the function of heart and intestinal lining

Is it harmful?

Since it is naturally occurring in the body, there are no apparent side effects even with large doses. But it should not be taken by persons with cirrhosis of the liver or kidney problems. Consult your doctor if you have these or any problem that results in an accumulation of ammonia in the blood. Of course, large doses should not be taken; several small doses during the day are preferable to one large dose. This avoids excretion of glutamine due to high dosage.

Recommended dosage

Phil Campbell, in his popular book "Ready, Set, Go! Synergy Fitness"[47] recommends two grams of glutamine before training to facilitate the release of growth hormone during anaerobic training. Personal Best Nutrition (see www.personalbestnutrition.com) recommends two to five grams per day. I personally take two grams right after a workout. Also two grams before would be beneficial. Daily use is recommended. A total of five grams per day is equivalent to one rounded teaspoon per day. I have noticed no adverse side effects.

When should I take it?

Balch and Balch in *Prescription for Nutritional Healing* recommend the following for taking an amino acid complex like whey powder and an individual amino acid like L-glutamine:

- When taking an amino acid complex, it is best to take it a half-hour before a meal or after. If taking L-glutamine or other amino acid, it is wise to take also a full amino acid complex, but at a different time (during the day).
- Take the amino acids for two months and then discontinue for two months. (Some others say take any single amino acid no longer than three months.)
- Do not take large doses for extended periods of time.

See also WholeHealthMD.com for similar recommendations.

Natural Occurring Sources

Fish, meat, beans, raw spinach and parsley, and dairy products are good sources. Glutamine is easily destroyed by cooking.

Growth Hormone

As athletes, we should be interested in aging slower than our rivals. By doing so, we can, in effect, have a younger body and this means increased relative performance, as well as a higher quality life and increased years. Thousands of studies since 1990 have shown that the growth hormone sometimes called "The Fountain of Youth" has a major effect on aging. The American Academy of Anti-Aging Medicine has demonstrated that decrease in HGH (human growth hormone) is a major cause of aging. As we age, the growth hormone in our bodies decreases drastically about 14 percent per decade after age 30, until at 80 it is only about three percent of that in adolescence. HGH has many major benefits, such as improved immune system, improved performance of body organs and glands, and all the benefits of a more youthful body.

One can achieve anti-aging benefits by increasing the growth hormone in our bodies by injection (very expensive and illegal), by non-prescription oral means, or by natural means. Non-prescription oral methods (oral sprays and pills), encourage the pituary gland to secrete HGH. However, they are not normally FDA approved, and more scientific studies are required to determine the effect of age, etc., but nevertheless there have been many favorable anecdotal accounts and some studies indicating benefits. Some experts state the oral sprays are too small a dose to be effective.

I prefer producing growth hormone by natural means as discussed below.

Natural Means of HGH Production

- Intensive anaerobic exercise including intense weight training, and particularly if the lactate production is high.
- Fasting two to three hours before bedtime
- Avoiding alcohol and caffeine two to three hours before bedtime
- Eating low glycemic foods during the day
- Certain supplements can help, particularly L-glutamine and other essential amino acids if taken at the right time of day
- Good sleep

Phil Campbell[47] in his book, *Ready, Set, Go! Synergy Fitness,* outlines the detailed exercise (weight training, sprinting, plyometrics, stretching and drills), and supplements to produce growth hormone by natural means and thus improve athletic performance. Very briefly, to produce growth hormone, he recommends taking two grams of L-glutamine before a bout of intense anaerobic exercise and followed right after by 25 grams of protein. Campbell's methods are backed up by frequent reference to many scientific studies in this area. I was already sold on the use of L-glutamine, whey powder, and intense anaerobic exercise (to stay young and age slower than rivals) before I read his book. For instance, I have observed from age-graded tables of world record running performance that sprinters decline in performance with age much slower than distance runners.

Exercise enhances HGH, and HGH enhances exercise. Following the above routine of 25 grams of protein immediately after intense exercise prevents the stimulation of insulin levels and thus keeps HGH high. However, a sport drink right after exercise would cause a drastic rise in insulin levels. To maximize the HGH release "Don't take sugar for two hours after training."(Campbell[47]). But if rapid recovery is more important, e.g., between races only hours apart, then to ensure rapid replacement of glycogen in blood and muscles, take a carbohydrates/protein mixture of (4/1 ratio) within two hours of exercise.

One of the exercises in the above book the "reverse karate kick" reminds me of a funny experience (but not the ha-ha variety). I was competing at the Boston National Indoor championships in March 2004. I was on my way to the 400 meter final in about 20 minutes and feeling sluggish after my world record in the 75-79 age group mile 2 hours earlier. Suddenly I experienced first hand, accidentally, the reverse karate kick of another athlete right in the most sensitive part of my lower body. I was no longer sluggish, thank you–woke me up all right. After about 7 minutes of icing, I forgot about it in the race–another world record, fortunately. It seems there is an advantage to every disadvantage.

REFERENCES

1. Diamond Harvey and Marilyn, *Fit For Life,* Warner Books Inc., New York, NY, 1987.
2. Inge, K., and Brukner, P., *Food for Sport,* W. Heinemann Australia, Richmond, Australia, 1986.
3. Nelson, D., *Food Combining Simplified,* Santa Cruz, CA, 1988, Based on "Food Combining Made Easy," by Dr. Herbert Shelton.
4. Darden, E., *Nutrition and Athletic Performance*, The Athletic Press, Pasadena, CA, 1978.
5. Pyke, M., *Success In Nutrition,* Richard Clay (Chaucer Press) Ltd., 1975.
6. Aihara, H., *Acid and Alkaline,* Ohsawa Macrobiotic Foundation, Oroville, California, 1986.
7. Pesmen, C., *How a Man Ages,* Ballantine Books, New York, NY, 1984.
8. Berkoff, F., Lauer, B., and Talbot Y., *Power Eating,* Communiplex Marketing Inc., Montreal, Que., 1989.
9. Murphy, J., *Keys To Nutrition Over Fifty,* Barron's Educational Series Inc., Hauppauge, NY, 1991.
10. Haas, R., *Eat to Succeed,* Onyx Book- Penguin, New York, NY, 1987.
11. Applegate, Liz., "Eating to Win- Essential Nutrition For Runners," *Runner's World,* Rodale Press Inc., 1995.
12. Clark, L., *Know Your Nutrition,* Keats Publishing Inc., New Canaan, Connecticut, 1973.
13. Kirschmann, J. D., *Nutrition Almanac,* McGraw Hill Book Company, New York, NY, 1973.
14. Hendler, S. S., *The Doctor's Vitamin and Mineral Encyclopedia,* Fireside Book, Simon and Schuster, New York, NY, 1990.
15. Broadhurst, C. L., "You do Need Fat," *Alive Health Magazine,* #171, 1996.
16. Mindell, E., *Mindell's Vitamin Bible,* Warner Books Inc., New York, NY, 1985.
17. Subak- Sharpe, G., *The Natural High Fiber Diet,* Tempo Books, New York, NY, 1976.
18. Haas, R., *Eat To Win, the Sports Nutrition Bible,* Rawson Assoc., New York, NY, 1984.
19. Dries, J., and Dries,I., *The Complete Book of Food Combining,* Element Books, Boston, MA, 1998.
20. Foster-Powell K., Brand Miller, J. B., "International tables of glycemic index," *American Journal of Clinical Nutrition,* 1995;62:871S-93S
21. Nelson, D., *Maximizing Your Nutrition,* D. Nelson, Santa Cruz, CA, 1988.
22. Dries, J., *The New Book of Food Combining,* Element Books, Rockport, Mass., 1992.
23. Sparks, K., and Bjorklund G., *Long Distance Runner's Guide to Training and Racing*, Prentice Hall.
24. Davis, A., *Let's Eat Right To Keep Fit,* Signet Book, New American Library, Scarborough, ON, 1972.
25. Watts, D., Wilson H., and Horwill F., *The Complete Middle Distance Runner,* The Anchor Press Ltd, Tiptree, Essex, 1974.

26. Fink, W., in Haskell, W. (Ed), *Nutrition and Athletic Performance,* Palo Alto, CA: Bull Publishing, 1982,52.
27. Pauling, L., *How to Live Longer and Feel Better,* Avon, Broadway, New York, NY, 1986.
28. Williams, M.H., "Nutritional Supplements For Strength Trained Athletes," *Gatorade Sports Science Exchange,* 47, Volume 6, Number 6, 1993.
29. Rankine, J., W., "Glycemic Index and Exercise Metabolism," *Gatorade Sports Science Institute,* 64, Volume 10, (1997), Number 1.
30. Coleman, E., and Nelson Steen, S., *The Ultimate Sports Nutrition Handbook,* Bull Publishing Co., Palo Alto, CA, 1996.
32. Bauman, A., "Master Your Metabolism," *Runner's World,* September, 1998.
33. Anderson, O., "Why Your Creatine Consumption Is Costing Too Much," *Running Research,* Vol. 14, No. 7, September, 1998.
34. Clark, N., *Sports Nutrition Guidebook,* Human Kinetics, Champaign, IL, 1997.
35. Passwater, A., *Creatine, Good Health Guides,* Keats Publishing, Inc., New Canaan, Connecticut, 1997.
36. Newsholme, E., Leech, T., Duester, G., *Keep On Running,* J. Wiley & Sons Ltd., West Sussex, England, 1997.
37. Lemon, P. et al, "Effect of exercise on protein requirements," *J. Sports Sci.* 9:53-70, 1991.
38. Nadel, E. R., "New Ideas for Rehydration During And After Exercise In Hot Weather," *Gatorade Sports Science Institute,* Volume 1, Number 3, June, 1988.
39. Jones, A. M., Atter, T., and Georg, K.P., "Oral creatine supplementation improves multiple sprint performance in elite ice-hockey players," *J. Sports Medicine & Physical Fitness,* 1999; Vol.39-No.3:189-96.
40. Williams, M. H., Kreider, R. B., *Creatine – The Power Supplement,* Human Kinetics, Champaign IL, 1999.
41. Harris, R. C., Viru, M., Greenhaff, P.L., Hultman, E., "The effect of oral creatine supplementation on running performance during maximal short term exercise in man." *J. Physiol* 1993;467:74P.
42. Bortz, W., *We Live Too Short and Die Too Long,* Bantam Books, New York, NY, 1991.
43. Balch, J. F., and Balch, P. A., *Prescription for Nutritional Healing,* Avery Publishing Group/ Penguin Putnam Inc., New York, NY, 2000.
44. Murray, F., *100 Super Supplements for a Longer Life,* Keats Publishing/Contemporary Publishing Group Inc., Lincolnwood IL, 2000.
45. *The Food Guide Pyramid,* prepared by Human Nutrition Information Service, U.S. Department of Agriculture.
46. Colgan, M., " Effects of multi- nutrient supplementation on athletic performance. Proceedings of the 1984 Olympic Scientific Congress.
47. Campbell., P., *Ready, Set, Go! Synergy Fitness,* 2nd Edition, Pristine Publishers Inc. USA, 2003.

192
NUS

CHAPTER 16

Rule of Too's:
Too long, too hard,
too much, too soon.
Anon

INJURY PREVENTION AND CAUSES

In training remember the above quote (the major causes of all injuries), and particularly remember: In all things "gradualness."

At the world masters Championships in Eugene Oregon in 1989, I asked a friend and competitor if he had any problems with his legs. He rattled off about four or five current problems. Then I felt much better with only the one problem, a hamstring.

All runners will get injured eventually. For example, Paul Slovic reported in the "Complete Runner" results of his survey of the 1973 Trails End Marathon, that nearly one-half of the 184 respondents experienced injury or illness during their training for the race. Therefore, all should be aware of how injuries happen, how to prevent them, and how to deal with them when they do happen. Injuries are predictable and avoidable[13]. I find it is often easy to predict injury in others who do not train sensibly, employ erratic training, or too rapidly increase in mileage, intensity, or speed.

Staying injury free should be a major priority of all runners. Many great runners have been sidelined for good, particularly by knee injuries, but with more knowledge, coupled with patience and oftentimes common sense, this could have been prevented, e.g., by cross-training, not training through an injury, and more rest. As competitive runners, it is a fine line we tread, for to succeed in a race, training must be done at race pace or faster and this often leads to fatigue when injuries occur. Be especially careful when you are nearing a peak; one tends to feel more and more is possible in view of the extreme fitness. An injury-free athlete can make significant gains on a frequently injured athlete. The winner is very often the careful athlete who has avoided injury in training.

This chapter lists the causes of the major injuries, precautions to reduce injuries, general treatment of an injury, best treatments for an injury, and some important lessons I learned from personal injuries.

PERSONAL INJURIES AND LESSONS LEARNED

My personal injuries in the past 12 years are discussed since there are important lessons to be learned from them. One can learn from another's mistakes and avoid serious demoralizing problems.

Only those injuries that took about six weeks or more (except as noted) for recovery are discussed; e.g., three sprained ankles are not discussed. In most cases, I did pool running and with less serious cases, land running with reduced volume and intensity, while taking physiotherapy.

The following information was from my detailed training logs; this indicates the advantage of keeping good training records to show what worked or was a mistake, and hopefully to prevent similar mistakes in the future.

2004

- **Left hip, followed by right hamstring, followed by right hip flexor.** *Cause:* Too many starts from blocks and hurdles during a TV commercial resulted in little running training for three months, except for cross training. *Lesson 1:* Too early in the season, early April, for these activities. Good preparation is required for these strenuous activities. *Lesson 2:* Once there is an injury, it is very likely to be followed by another later due to overcompensation, or starting back too soon.

2003

- **Back sprain.** *Cause:* A neighborly hockey game in the previous December after 50-year-layoff restricted proper running stride for about five months.
- **Achilles.** *Cause:* Two sprint races early in the indoor season. Insufficient accommodation to running in spikes.

2002

- **Left adductor.** *Cause:* Running training six days in a row. *Lesson:* Need to do cross training in-between running days, particularly at age 73.

2001

- **Right adductor, followed by lower left hamstring, followed by upper right hamstring.** *Cause:* All overuse injuries. The initial problem started due to a hard interval workout the day after an 800-meter indoor race, which resulted in the above problems over a three-month period. *Lesson:* Once there is an injury, it is very likely to be followed by another due to overcompensation, i.e., not running properly on recovery.

2000

- **Broken small toe.** *Cause:* Household accident. *Lesson:* Be safety conscious (walking in the night, lifting, etc.) around the home.
- **Plantar fasciitis** (plus hardening of the plantar tendon). *Cause:* Running in light training shoes with little support. *Lesson:* An old injury can return; strengthen the injured area; massage the plantar tendon to compensate for the stiffening and hardening that occurs with age.
- **Overuse of calf.** *Cause:* Fast intervals on the outdoor track with spikes; the first session on the outdoor track since about 12 weeks. *Lesson:* (This painful condition on running only lasted a week but prevented participation in the US Masters Outdoor meet.) Proceed gradually into fast track workouts in spikes.
- **Hip strain.** *Cause:* Running fast intervals indoors; the first session in three months. *Lesson:* Proceed gradually when training indoors on tight turns.

1999

- **Various tendon and ligament problems.** *Cause:* Training twice a day often three times per week on the track at age 70. *Lesson:* Less is better above age 65; strengthen ligaments and tendons with plyometrics to prevent these problems.

1998

- **Inflammation of the plantar fascia.** *Cause:* Fast running in spikes with hard orthotic inserts. *Lesson:* Avoid the above.

1997

- **Adductor tear.** *Cause:* The first session of hurdle training in April; a minor problem developed into a major problem due to neglect; the injury returned three months later after a 14-hour plane ride to South Africa. *Lesson:* Make sure to rest the minor problems to prevent developing into major problems later; proceed gradually in hurdle training; strengthen the muscle to prevent reoccurrence.

1996

- **Hamstring tear** (reoccurrence). *Cause:* Four hard workouts in five days; insufficient rest after the competitive track season. *Lesson:* Easy days should follow hard days; take 10 days or more rest after the track season before the base training season; strengthen the muscle to prevent reoccurrence.

- **Hamstring tear.** *Cause:* The first hurdle practice in April. *Lesson:* Proceed gradually in hurdle training, particularly with drills for several weeks before serious jumping.

1994

- **Plantar fasciitis.** *Cause:* Training for cross-country on steep rough hills with light training shoes (little stability). *Lesson:* Wear proper shoes with good stability while training on rough surfaces.

1992

- **Right calf tear** (reoccurrence). *Cause:* Running slowly five weeks after a prostate operation. *Lesson:* Muscles have to be reaccustomed gradually to pounding on a track; also, once a weakness, always a weakness unless strengthened with weight training.

1991

- **Hamstring tear.** *Cause:* Overuse due to 3 hard days in a row. *Lesson:* Avoid 2 hard days in a row; must take alternate hard and easy days.
- Patella tendonitis (right knee). *Cause:* Running sharp turns in the clockwise direction. *Lesson:* Know your weaknesses and strengthen the quadriceps.

1990

- **Right calf tear (reoccurrence).** *Cause:* Brought on by favoring a sore right quad muscle. *Lesson:* Favoring sore muscles can lead to strain in other muscles.

1989

- **Right calf tear.** *Cause:* Circuit training (hopping, skipping, step-ups without proper warm-up; a one and only session. *Lesson:* Avoid any unusual exercise or work up to it gradually over several sessions; legs should be strengthened by weight training before attempting plyometrics.

1987

- **Right calf tear.** *Cause:* Trying to accelerate when tired, during fast intervals. *Lesson:* Do weight training to prevent injuries.

CAUSES OF SPECIFIC MAJOR INJURIES

Knowing the causes of injuries can assist to prevent injuries.
The following indicate the major causes of the most frequent specific injuries:
Inflamed **Achilles** Tendon

- Too fast too soon
- Running and hurdling in spiked shoes on hard surfaces
- Tight calves, bad footwear, excessive speedwork, and hills[3]
- Hurdling on hard track
- Over-activity, hurdling, long jump, triple jump, and high jump, also prolonged over-use of tendon[10]

- Shoes that put pressure contact on the heel or the tendon, buildup of speed session too rapidly, and change of usual running surface, e.g., from grass to hard road or vice versa[8]
- Weak feet (Dr. George Sheehan), improper warmup
- Excessive stretching

Sprained **Ankle**
- Running on uneven surfaces, i.e. cross-country
- Running in place on hard surface when tired[4]
- Stepping on roots on a trail or in a pothole or uneven surface (inside track rail)
- Weak feet (Dr. George Sheehan), improper shoes
- Severe camber on road or beach

Torn **Calf** Muscle
Causes have a lot of similarity to Achilles injuries
- Hill running
- Accelerating when muscles are tired and tight, sudden change of direction[4]
- Hard running on steep hills especially in cold weather, too much speed work without experience or proper warm-up, and running on slippery surfaces[8]

Inflammation on Top of **Foot (Tenosynovitis)**
- New shoes or ridge inside shoes

Compartment Syndrome[3]
Swelling calf muscles are restrained by the fascia, resulting in the shutting off of the blood supply
- Too rapid an increase in mileage

Groin/Adductor
- Sprint starts, and slippery surfaces[8]
- Hill running, when knees and feet are turned out to get shorter stride in going uphill, particularly when tired and in mud[6]
- Too rapid a progression to fast repeats on an indoor track
- Hurdling when muscles are not properly conditioned to the activity

Hamstring Tear
- Excessive sprint work without gradual adaptation
- Acceleration in sprinting (particularly when tired), missed footing (e.g., on ice), insufficient warm-up or muscles cooled down after warm-up, ballistic stretching[4]
- Slippery surfaces[8]

- Insufficient warming up, common in explosive events involving sprinting[6]
- Inflexible hamstrings, hamstrings weak under eccentric load, or hamstrings less than 60% of quads strength
- Hurdling and hill training

Hamstring Tendonitis[4]
Injury at back of knee
- Overuse, running hills, especially downhill, when muscles are tight
- Running in shoes with little heel (e.g., spikes) causing the hamstring to over stretch

Bursitis of the **Heel**
Inflammation of the bursa, the sac of fluid that cushions or lubricates movement of the Achilles tendon where it meets the heel bone
- Poor conditioning and inadequate warm-up, and exposure to cold weather[10]
- "Ill fitting shoe whose heel counter rubs up against the back of the heel"[16]
- Excessive stretching of the Achilles

Hip Strain
- Too much too soon
- Tightness or recovery from injury in other areas of the lower body causes uneven stride and consequent hip problem
- Running tight turns of indoor track without gradual buildup

Iliotibial Band Friction Syndrome
Pain above and below the lateral side of the knee
- Excessively worn shoes or prolonged running on a sloped surface road camber[3]
- Overuse (in quantity and intensity) in runners with awkward running styles[6]
- Excessive supination; running on circular track or uneven surface; inflexible calf, glutes, outer thigh; worn shoes
- Insufficient stretching of IT band
- Knee strain
- Step-ups carrying excess weight
- Running too many miles on hard surfaces, or wearing inappropriate footwear[3]
- Excess mileage too quickly
- Banked road[2]
- Weak quadriceps, change in training running surface, change in running shoes, and squat weight training with too rapid a progression[4]
- Full squats, duck walks, and sitting with pressure against fully flexed knees[11]
- Sharp turns at high speed

Medial (inside of knee) Ligament Strain

- Too long too soon
- Severe wrenching of knee[6]
- Excessive pronation, running on road camber or uneven surface
- Fast running on tight turns of indoor track

Lateral (outside of knee) Ligament Strain

- Wrenching of knee[6]
- Excessive supination, running on road camber or uneven surface

Runner's Knee

Improper tracking of the kneecap

- Weak vastus medialis muscle (lower inside of quad), weak feet (Dr. George Sheehan), excessive supination or excessive pronation

Osteoarthritis

Degenerative joint wear and tear (hip, knee or foot), particularly in older runners, causing stiffening, pain, and sometimes swelling

- Overuse in conjunction with a postural fault, e.g., short leg, etc.[2]
- Repetitive joint injury, hereditary, diet lacking in minerals and vitamins

Plantar Fasciitis

- Flat footed runner
- Running spikes with no arch
- Running with tight calves in shoes with little heel support and no arch support[3]
- Sudden turn, shoes with very stiff soles; also caused by feet that pronate (roll inward)[5]
- Sudden stop, start, or turn, particularly when tired[4]
- Training on rough hills in running shoes with no motion control or stability
- Fast intervals wearing hard orthotics or heel pads with no taper at front of heel
- Too much speedwork in spikes

Torn **Quadriceps** Muscle

- Excessive weights on quads and running with tired quads.
- Too much too soon
- See Hamstring tear[4]
- Weak quadriceps, plyometrics

Sciatica

Nerve down the buttock and back or side of the leg down to the foot

- Jarring foot strike forces transmitted to the back often coupled with structural abnormalities such as flat feet, high arches, knee problems, and knee length discrepancies[9]
- Lack of flexibility and strength in lower back[9]
- Degenerative disease in older runners[5]
- Inadequate or no stretching in the gluteus area

Shin Soreness
Pain in muscle or tendon along inner or outer edge of shinbone; and may be accompanied by stress fracture

- Overuse[4]
- Change of stride due to favoring some other part of the body[4]
- Change in speed, terrain, surface, or change in shoes[4]
- Resuming training too quickly after layoff[4]
- Rapid mileage increases, hard surfaces, bad footwear, and excess pronation[3]
- Running and jumping on hard surfaces and sudden stops[11]
- Running on sidewalks or roads with light running shoes or worn running shoes
- Downhill running on hard surfaces, insufficient recovery, and excessive running
- Lack of stretching of shins

Spurs of Heel
Causes are similar to those for plantar fasciitis

- Excess on hard roads
- Poor fitting shoes or shoes with little support
- Tight calves, poor footwear, excessive speedwork, and hills[3]

Stress Fracture of the Foot
An X-ray will show a crack only after about 3 weeks (due to formation of a callus over the crack

- Too much too soon
- Calcium deficiency[10]
- Improper, light shoes and unsupported high arch[5]
- Running on hard surfaces

Stress Fracture of the Lower and Upper Leg

- Sprinting or hurdling on hard surfaces with spikes
- Too much too soon; also, jumping[4]
- Calcium deficiency[10]
- Excess mileage on hard surfaces with inadequate shoes
- Weak feet (Dr. George Sheehan), excessive supination or excessive pronation
- Running on pavement in worn shoes

Stress Fractures General

- See above causes

SUMMARY OF CAUSES OF INJURIES SURVEY

The above specific injuries were examined in total to determine the relative importance of the causes of injury. These causes are listed below in order of importance. Note the same number indicates equal importance.

1. **Training too hard too soon or training to excess**
2. **Unsuitable shoes:**
   - Too worn
   - Too rigid or too flexible
   - No arch support
   - Poor fit
   - Heel cup rubbing or little heel support
   - Overuse of spikes
   - Change of shoes or overuse of same shoes
2. **Running surface:**
   - Camber of road
   - Slippery
   - Hard surface
   - Change of surface
3. **Accelerations and decelerations:**
   - Accelerating when tired
   - Excessive sprinting
   - Sprint starts
   - Sudden change of direction
   - Sudden stops
3. **Weak feet**
4. **Hills:**
   - Overuse of uphill or downhill training
4. **Pronation:**
   - 75% over-pronation cases and 25% over-supination cases
5. **Overuse of weights:**
   - Doing squats, step ups, and toe lifts, etc
   - Excess weights for weak muscles
6. **Imbalanced muscle strength and structural abnormalities:**
   - see Note A and B below.
7. **Inadequate warm-up:**
   - see Note C below.
8. **Stretching:**
   - Ballistic
   - Overstretching
   - Inflexible
9. **Plyometrics**
10. **Diet or lack of fluids**

Notes:

A. *Lack of balanced strength[2, 5]:*

It is important to develop an optimum level of strength around the knee and ankle joints. When muscle imbalance occurs, the stronger opposing muscle can overpower the weaker antagonistic muscle thereby causing damage to its fibres and tendons. Constantly over-stretched muscles on one side of a joint due to imbalance created by the stronger muscle on the opposite side, result in weakness and loss of power in the stretched muscle. For example:

- If the quad muscle is more than 1.5 times stronger than the hamstring, injury is likely. The treatment for this muscle imbalance is to strengthen the hamstring and continue with stretching, after the muscle has healed.
- Similarly, shin splints can occur from muscle imbalance due to calf muscles being proportionately stronger than shin muscles. The treatment for shin splints is to strengthen the shins (e.g., by running up stairs) and to stretch the calves.
- Dr. Sheehan[7] stated, "In thigh, groin or back injuries, weakness is often noted in the hamstrings or abdominal muscles."

B. *Structural abnormalities*

Structural abnormalities, such as short leg, knock knees, bow legs, leg alignment, postural and foot faults, etc., put extra stress on muscles, tendons, bones, joints and ligaments[2, 5].

C. *Improper warm-up*

Internal temperature of muscles is often not raised high enough during warm-up. Russian studies have indicated that power (strength) exercises for the hamstring muscles in warm-ups prevent the rupture of muscle fibers by raising the temperature of the muscles[2]. Exercising with rubber tubing could be used effectively to raise the temperature of muscles.

IMPORTANT CAUSES OF INJURY

- ***Poor mechanics (form):*** errors in technique such as in hurdling[2].
- ***Fatigue:*** Most sprains and strains begin when fatigue sets in and lactic acid accumulates. "Momentary un-coordination: this is due to fatigue or tight muscles or cold muscles and the sudden inability of antagonistic muscles (e.g. hamstring) to relax while opposing (quad) muscles are moving the body" (Jesse[2]).
- ***Mineral deficiency:*** Lack of sodium, potassium, magnesium and other minerals cause cramping and lead to injury by making the athlete weak and tired especially in extreme heat[2, 5].

- ***Weak feet:*** Rotate and massage the feet every day. (I do this every morning.) This will help to prevent injuries. Cross-country training and racing, and hiking strengthens ankles and feet. The greater strength and flexibility in the feet will also increase stride length and speed.
- ***Weak quadriceps:*** The quads need to be strong to provide shock absorption and to help prevent knee injury.
- ***Previous injury or stiffness in other parts of the body*** cause compensating injuries elsewhere.
- ***Running fast indoors always in the same direction.*** Usually, the inner leg develops a problem (e.g., the inner hip or the knee are likely candidates). It is highly recommended to reverse directions on the track on different training days if possible. If this is not possible, proceed gradually over several weeks in picking up the speed.

PRECAUTIONS TO PREVENT INJURIES

The following precautions will prevent or reduce injuries.

1. *Don't over train.* Remember the "Rule of Too's."
2. *Recovery.* The importance of recovery cannot be over emphasized. Back off every three weeks in your training; cool down properly; follow easy days with hard days; epsom salts baths, iced towel, or cold shower on the legs after a hard workout for sore muscles; carbohydrates plus protein within one hour after the workout; use vitamins E and C to aid repair of muscles; whirlpool and frequent massage (even self-massage).
3. Participate in a *long-term stretching, conditioning and strengthening program.*
4. *Avoid running downhill fast on hard surfaces.*
5. *Correct training shoes.* Purchase the right kind of shoes to suit your particular needs and your style of running. Have several pairs of running shoes since some may aggravate in a particular spot. Change shoes regularly (some say after about 300 miles) and do not wear worn shoes or old shoes with rubber that is too hard or too soft. Check inside of shoes for ridges.
6. *Do not train in spikes too frequently.* For example, restrict their use for speeds faster than 95% speed and certainly wear them no more than twice per week. In preliminaries or semi-finals, wear running shoes if it is certain you can qualify this way.
7. *Run safely.* Do not put yourself in a dangerous situation, e.g., running in exceptionally cold or icy weather; if running outdoors at night, wear white clothing. Also, from personal experience and experience of a close friend, in very hot, humid weather particularly when dehydrated, there could be lack of concentration that can lead to being hit by a car. Do not train alone in very hot weather.

8. *Do your own workouts.* Do not use another person's hard workout unless it is on your hard day and you are used to the type and intensity of the workout.
9. *Know when to stop a workout.* Always stop intervals when form starts to drop off or before. Remember, many injuries occur when the athlete is tired; when the muscles are fatigued, normally unused fibers are called into play. Also, stop immediately when there is any local tenderness or localized pain or cramping.
10. *Gradual progression in training.* Beware of any sudden change in the training or any new exercise involving different muscles; there has to be a gradual progression. Also, increase mileage gradually, but not more than 10% per week.
11. *Stretching* may be the most important injury preventive. Stretching following the workout is considered by some as more important than the warm-up stretching. However, over-stretching to the point of discomfort can cause injury too.
12. *Home accidents.* Beware of lifting heavy objects around the home or at work; (this is "homicidal") unless used to it. It seems that a finely tuned athlete is more susceptible to injury of this type.
13. *Indoor track.* Fast interval training on an indoor track is stressful due to the sharp turns and running in spiked shoes. At the beginning of the season start slowly and increase speed gradually over several weeks to enable the legs to adjust. For the same reason, massage of the legs is more essential during the indoor season to prevent injury and hasten recovery.
14. *Do not neglect your feet.* Your feet are your best friend. To assist in preventing plantar fasciitis, massage the bottom of the feet daily: stretch the longitudinal arch with some deep applied pressure. Strengthen the feet every other day with about 15 or more toe raises, preferably not on the edge of a step. Also, rotate the ankles clockwise and counter-clockwise daily to increase flexibility and to guard against ankle strains. To assist in preventing hamstring pulls, occasionally run down hills on a soft surface.
15. *Run on grass or forest park trails* (free of roots), as much as possible, rather than hard asphalt or even harder sidewalks. On the track, run in the opposite direction occasionally or during warm-up.
16. *Plyometrics.* Before incorporating intense plyometrics (hopping, jumping from boxes, etc.) into your training, start with a program of weights to condition the legs. Do these only under knowledgeable supervision and preferably on grass or a rubber mat.
17. *Weights* strengthen the legs and prevent injury. Strengthen your weak areas and correct any imbalances, e.g., between the hamstrings and quads. A once-pulled muscle is susceptible to the same injury in the future no matter how good the healing job. However, muscle strengthening will make this much less likely.

18. *Avoid any unusual exercise,* or proceed gradually over several sessions. Avoid "bunny hops," sometimes called "frog jumps" (jumping from a squat position); these can result in injured knees or very sore muscles, and, in any case, do not simulate the running motion.
19. *Know when to stop regular training.* You can train with some sore muscles if the workout is not overdone; it is not unusual to have some soreness. However, abnormal soreness or even a slight pain or cramp is a warning, so back off on the training or skip that planned race unless it is an essential race. Running a race with sore muscles will make them more sore afterward and could lead to serious injury. Take two or three days off, as many as necessary, take extra vitamins C and E, and cross-train (any activity that does not aggravate or cause further discomfort). For less severe problems, running could be continued with reduced intensity and volume until the problem is cleared up sufficiently. Normally, a slow run the next day preferably on a soft surface or a run in the water will assist in getting get rid of the soreness. These precautions are preferable to a month or more of no training to recover from a serious injury. George Sheehan put it correctly, "Run with an annoyance, but never in pain."
20. *Frequent chiropractic checkups.* A serious athlete is advised to have frequent (once a month roughly) checkups as I do with a sports chiropractor to detect if any imbalances or mis-alignments have developed in the body. These could lead to serious injuries if neglected. Also, after injury, a sports chiropractor can in many cases identify the cause of the injury and provide remedial attention to avoid the same problem in the future. In some cases, chiropractic treatment has solved the problem, preventing the use of surgery.
21. *Cramp or injury?* Be careful of anything that feels like a bad cramp; it could be a tear since the feeling is sometimes very similar. Don't run on cycle on it.
22. *Go easy after an injury.* When an injury feels better, be careful to progress gradually in training since the injured area is still weak. Now is the time to strengthen the injured area. Avoid two hard workouts on successive days.
23. *Don't run through an acute injury.* You will start favoring the injury and cause inappropriate stresses elsewhere. "The athlete inadvertently substitutes other muscles for the injured muscle group causing pronounced weakness to occur in the injured group and more injuries in the future" (J. Jesse[2]).
24. *If training with a chronic injury* keep the injured area warm and apply a heat liniment beforehand, particularly in cold weather. Apply ice after training.
25. Finally, *listen to your body.* As an athlete, you are already super-sensitive to any aches or pains. Better to be over-cautious. There is nearly always a warning. Remember a few days off is better than six weeks of recuperation and physiotherapy later.

TREATMENT OF INJURY

The athlete can treat minor injuries without the need for physiotherapy with RICE (Rest, Ice, Compression, and Elevation). Compression and elevation are used generally for the first one or two days. After this, movement will assist to provide circulation and hasten recovery. During recovery for minor or serious injury the advice in books such as that by J. G. Garrick[4], M. Read[6], and H. W. Griffith[10] are very useful to aid in quicker recovery. For more serious injuries (you will know), e.g., where there is pain in walking, a sports physician and physiotherapy will be required.

Prior to the doctor's visit for an acute injury (or a less serious injury), the following should be done to speed healing and reduce scar tissue:

1. **Rest** to reduce bleeding, inflammation, swelling and to prevent further tearing.
2. **Ice.** Immerse injured part in ice water or apply ice packs to stop bleeding, prevent swelling and to reduce pain.
3. **Wrap** with an elastic bandage to prevent swelling. Do not restrict circulation; this is avoided with firm, comfortable wrapping or using a sponge or rubber pad on the injury site to concentrate the pressure.
4. **Elevate** the injured part to reduce pressure on the injured area; this prevents further swelling.
5. Ice packs can be applied over the injured area. Alternatively, ice packs can be applied under the compression bandage. In this case, remove the bandage and ice every 15 minutes or so to warm the area before reapplying the ice and bandage.
6. Leave the compression bandage on and apply ice packs for the next 24 hours[11] usually [or up to 48 hours].
7. Avoid weight-bearing[11] and resistance movements.
8. "After swelling subsides, remove the compression bandage, and as discoloration and discomfort disappear, very gradually return to action" Morehouse and Gross[11].

In subsequent days and weeks, physiotherapy may be required. Whether "physio" is required or not, do the following to speed recovery. Self-massage (usually cross friction), gentle stretching (e.g., about 10 times 20 to 30 seconds per day), followed up by ice at least twice (about 10 to 15 minutes on and 10 to 15 minutes off). Light weights or rubber tubing exercises can be done after an injury is nearly healed.

Ice vs. Heat

It is sometimes confusing and controversial whether to use ice or heat. However, after 48 hours, there is generally more preference for ice. Ice and the whirlpool are my favorites in that order. I personally have had much better success with ice than with heat.

Ice is an anti-inflammatory; it constricts blood vessels, thereby preventing swelling and internal bleeding; it also reduces bruising and promotes healing. Therefore, it is applied immediately after sprains (ligament tears), strains (tendon and muscle tears) and bruises. The less blood collecting, the shorter the healing time. Ice also reduces muscle spasms (cramps).

Ice should be applied three or four times a day, 15 minutes at a time[10]. I have found for deep tissue injuries, one application of ice on a chronic injury is not effective; for best results, at least three applications are required, with about 10 to 15 minutes during the off period, to produce good results the next day. I usually put a paper towel next to my skin with the soft gel pack over it, and 10 minutes seems long enough. When it gets too uncomfortable, it's time to remove the pack. However, a better method is to massage the area with ice in a styrofoam cup. Ice should never be left stationary directly on the skin; there is a danger of frostbite. There have been cases of damaging the nerve endings. Ylinen and Cash[1] warn about the use of cold sprays on acute injuries since they may freeze the skin before penetrating to deep tissue if used improperly; it is preferable to use an ice pack wrapped in a wet towel. They also recommend only 10 minutes cold application time for injuries near the surface.

Heat can be used 48 hours after an injury *if it feels better than ice.* (Some say not until after 72 hours[12].) Within these times, heat increases bleeding and swelling. After 48 hours, heat increases blood flow and healthy nutrients to the injured area and removes debris from the injured area. The heat also causes muscles to relax, bringing greater freedom of movement.

Use heat lamps, hot soaks, hot showers, heating pads, or heat liniments and ointments[10]. Moist heat is best. I have found the whirlpool beneficial if the jets are not too close to the injury. Heat liniments are not highly recommended by some coaches. The following methods are effective[12]:

- A wet towel put in the microwave and then wrapped in a dry towel. Apply for 30 minutes (or until the towel loses heat) four to six times a day.
- A hot water bottle wrapped in a wet towel.
- Hot bath 10 to 20 minutes with epsom salts preferably.
- Hot shower directed to the injury. I have found a hot shower directly on a sore neck brings relief.
- Whirlpool, but avoid a forceful jet on the injured area, which will chase away healing blood flow[12]. On the other hand, in later stages, a jet not too close should assist in ridding the injury of scar tissue.

Alternate Ice and Heat. If you have the patience, the best treatment after 48 hours is to alternate heat and cold packs. Consult your physiotherapist for recommended times between the hot and cold. If you have access to a whirlpool next to a pool, you can go from one to the other for about five to seven minutes in each.

Exercise and Weights

It is important to start exercising and weight training again "as soon and as actively as your injury allows, but, after a serious injury, first get clearance from you doctor" (Griffith[10]). Muscle building should not be started until you are nearly back to your previous level. To speed recovery, Garrick and Radestsky[4] recommend find a motion (e.g., a daily activity) that activates the muscle, and gently repeat it to keep the muscle stretched and active. On recovering from injury, I have avoided any particular exercise if it hurts, but I can see the benefit in the above philosophy if the movement is gentle. Early mobilization of the tissue, if not painful, will accelerate healing.

Exercise. During recovery, when there is no pain to walk, jogging can be attempted; jog until there is discomfort and then walk, repeat this cycle. Alternatively, swimming, cycling, rowing or running in the water can be done as long as the activity does not cause discomfort. When there is discomfort stop right away. The above mild activities will promote circulation and hasten recovery as long as the activity is not overdone.

Weight training: In regard to weights on recovering from injury there is great benefit in eccentric weight exercises (the muscle lengthening while contracting). The eccentric movement should be done slowly. See also Chapter 19 on "Weight Training" (section on "Training Principles"). For example, a Swedish study by Alfredson et al.,[15] showed that eccentric calf muscle training cured 15 runners of Achilles tendonitis whereas 15 others with the same problem using conventional methods required surgery. The training was briefly as follows: Stand with balls of feet on edge of a step, lower the body slowly on the "unhealthy" leg, raise the body on the "good" leg. Do three sets of 15 repetitions with straight unhealthy leg and three sets of 15 with bent unhealthy leg. There was no concentric work (the muscle shortening while contracting) on the bad leg. Continue with weight being added gradually up to 12 weeks. Start initially with one set only.

Stretching

For soft tissue injuries, a good deal of stretching is required, since the muscle shortens on healing. Without this stretching, the shortened muscle will be more easily injured in the future. One muscle specialist told me that the stretching was more important than the physiotherapy. Be sure to warm up beforehand. It is important to hold the stretches for at least 15 to 30 seconds; stretch to the point of gentle discomfort. Stretching overdone will cause the muscle to shorten. Alternatively, to avoid this possibility use "Active Isolated Stretching", i.e., two or three seconds stretch, relax two or three seconds, repeat.

Mental Imagery

For faster recovery, mental imagery can be used. The technique has been widely taught. See for example the book *Healing From Within* by Dennis Jaffe, Knopf, 1980. First you have to believe it works. Imagine tiny blood cells bringing new oxygen in, and all the bad blood and wastes moving out. Visualize white light surrounding the injured site, bringing warmth and healing and energy. Conjure up your own mental picture (e.g., tiny boats in and out) while in a relaxed state for a few minutes per day; the subconscious will work on the healing in the meantime. See also the "Visualization" section in Chapter 2 herein on "Mental Training."

BEST TREATMENTS FOR INJURY

After 18 years of competitive running and more than 30 major injuries, my two favorite treatments for injury are active release technique, ART, and laser treatment. I believe these two treatments will rapidly grow in popularity among athletes in view of their rapid healing of injuries. I have found both treatments very effective and to result in fast recovery from a wide variety of injuries. I would have a preference for ART over laser if my injury resulted in a noticeable loss of range of motion. When used together, they are a powerful healing combination.

Nearly all my running injuries were from overuse. Generally, an injury limited my running range of motion, strength and speed necessitating a reduction in training volume and intensity. Usually, running training never stopped, or at least involved cross training.

Since I addressed these problems early on – in many cases after about four to six treatments, I was able to return to running training at reduced intensity and volume. Unfortunately, one has to expect healing time to increase with age. With proper preventative maintenance (stretching, Pilates, strengthening) these problems usually do not reoccur.

Type of Problems Treated

ART and laser treatment are both simple and effective for pulls and strains in muscles, tendons, ligaments, nerves and fascia; collectively known as soft tissue. For example, they can cure and relieve back pain, neck pain, knee pain (runners knee), rotator cuff; wrist pain, shin splints, plantar fasciitis, bursitis, arthritis, sciatica, etc.

Active Release Technique

ART is relatively new to the general public but has been popular, for more than a decade, with world class sprinters such as former 100m world record holder Donovon Bailey. ART is becoming more popular and is being practiced by chiropractors, physiotherapists, and massage therapists.

How does it Work?

ART can break up and remove scar tissue (cross fibers and adhesions), which limits motion, strength, and speed. The certified ART doctor identifies the scar, usually a tight area with altered texture. The patient is instructed to move the body part in a specific direction to lengthen it. To cover the range of different injuries, there are over 300 specific movements to be learned by the certified ART practitioner. An assistant is sometimes present to help move the body part into unusual territory. During these precise movements, the doctor with magic fingers and thumbs moves the tissue to a fully elongated position while moving longitudinally over the scar, creating tension and breaking down the scar tissue. These combined patient and doctor movements are repeated several times. There is some brief discomfort and possibly tears to the eyes but there is the consolation that you are on the mend.

In many cases, the patient has decreased pain and greatly increased range of motion after the first treatment. The number of sessions to resolve a problem could vary from three to ten depending on the severity. Of course, it is always preferable to address any problem early (as I do) to shorten the sessions.

Advantages of ART

- Provides rapid return of normal range of motion and fast recovery compared to other methods.
- In some cases, an ART treatment would enable one to compete a day or two later whereas otherwise it would not be possible.
- Gets rid of scar tissue, frees up trapped nerves and increases oxygen and blood circulation in the problem area.
- Success rate for injuries is normally 80 to 90 percent.
- Enhances performance and also prevents injuries by lengthening muscles and increasing range of motion.

Laser Treatment

Laser stands for Light Amplification by Stimulated Emission of Radiation.

There have been countless studies demonstrating the effectiveness of low level laser therapy, LLLT. For example:

- In a study of 4,000 subjects with a variety of arthritis, muscle pain and tendonitis, more than 80 percent found marked relief.
- A survey of 116 physiotherapists in Northern Ireland who used LLLT regularly for a wide variety of problems ranked LLLT first on the basis of effectiveness when compared with four other common electromagnetic methods including ultrasound.

LLLT is called the "cold" or "soft laser." Professional sport people were among the first to recognize the benefits of LLLT. It is also especially popular in treatment of thoroughbred race horses and racing greyhounds.

How It Works

Light has a healing effect as evidenced by the healing effect of the sun on surface injuries. The low-level light beams of laser produce physiological and chemical (photochemical effects) when applied over the problem area and immediate surroundings. The concentrated light of LLLT, although non-thermal, works similarly to the action of sunlight on vital processes in plants. The laser beam consists of photons of a single wavelength. These little packets of energy produce changes in injured cells but are not destructive to healthy cells. Basically, the concentrated photon energy is absorbed in the mitochondria and converted to chemical energy within the cell in the form of ATP energy. This energy causes significant metabolic and biological effects in the cells. There is stimulation in the nerve, immune, lymphatic and blood vessel systems, and enzymes are activated. The resulting increased blood flow carries increased nutrients and oxygen into the damaged tissue, and toxins are taken away more readily. The result is an accelerated healing process.

While taking this treatment some mental pictures will further hasten recovery. Visualize the photons bombarding the injured site, the nutrients sailing in tiny, gleaming, white boats, and the toxins being pushed out in tiny, black boats.

The dose (energy) and intensity (power per unit area) differ for each injury and depends on the injury type, depth, location, and laser type (type of wave length), all of which is predetermined by computer program.

Advantages

- Accelerated recovery compared to other methods results in an earlier return to training.
- Promotes blood and oxygen circulation and revives the tissue.
- It raises white blood cell counts and thus improves immunity.

- Decreases pain, swelling and inflammation.
- Increases nerve regeneration.
- Can be used immediately after injury (preferably within four hours).
- No known side effects.

THE GOOD AND BAD OF ANTI-INFLAMMATORY DRUGS

A serious athlete often has sore muscles and minor injuries and many athletes are taking anti-inflammatory drugs for relief. Many athletes take aspirin or coated aspirin or Advil during initial injury stages. It is essential to be aware of the pros and cons of these and prescription anti-inflammatory drugs since they can lead to medical problems if not administered properly. For instance, I developed an ulcer (a short-term) from taking prescription NSAIDs incorrectly without food.

This type of drugs are called NSAIDs, which means nonsteroidal anti-inflammatory drug. They are used to treat arthritis, and other conditions, and to relieve pain and inflammation. Typical popular NSAIDs are aspirin (Bayer), naproxen sodium (Aleve), and ibuprofen (Advil and Motrin). These drugs curb production of prostaglandins resulting in less pain and inflammation. But prostaglandins protect the stomach lining, so there is a possibility of an ulcer or kidney damage from NSAIDs with improper or long-term usage.

Advantages of NSAIDs:

- Pain relief within an hour that lasts for about 7 hours[14]
- Relieves inflammation in the long term (see below)

Disadvantages of NSAIDs:

- With regular dosage the anti-inflammatory effect takes several days to a week or more, to become apparent and possibly longer to reach maximum effect. Therefore, dosage for one or two days only has minor anti-inflammatory effect. However, the effect of ice is immediate.
- Medical problems could develop, such as muscle cramps, stomach irritation, stomach ulcers, gastrointestinal bleeding, heart palpitations, rectal bleeding to mention a few, and particularly in older adults. (I can vouch for the ulcers and muscle cramps). There are about two dozen possible problems.
- There is increased risk of infection since the intestines are less effective in preventing bacteria entering other parts of the body.

Important Advice:

The *Pill Book*[14] advises:

- Take with food and a full glass of water.
- Check with a doctor if taking any other medication, as well.
- Avoid alcohol while taking NSAIDs.
- Don't lie down for 15 to 30 minutes after taking.
- Do not take aspirin with other anti-inflammatories.
- Never take a double dose to make up for a missed one.

Further Advice:

- Avoid taking anti-inflammatories at least 24 hours before longer races, such as a marathon, to avoid bleeding in the stomach and urine. NSAIDs also mask any pain; hence, you could be making your injury worse. Play it safe. Use this advice for other shorter races and workouts.
- It is always good advice to take only one drug at a time; hence, alcohol does not mix well with NSAIDs.
- Acetaminophen (e.g., Excedrin and Tylenol) relieves pain and fever but not inflammation. However, they are relatively non-toxic and may be taken without regard to food14. They are recommended for very mild injury or muscle soreness since there seems to be controversy regarding how quickly NSAIDs become effective as an anti-inflammatory–some say two or three days and some say a week or more. So take one of the above if you intend to take only for pain–good advice, which I follow for short-term problems.
- Some athletes may be interested to learn that two glasses (about a five ounce size) of wine before dinner is also an effective pain killer and good for morale, too, if one has an injury.

DELAYED ONSET OF MUSCLE SORENESS

Delayed onset of muscle soreness, or DOMS, for short, is the phenomenon of soreness appearing usually about 24 to 48 hours after intense or prolonged exercise. The soreness usually does not last more than one to two days and is usually the result of one or more of the following: too much, too hard, too soon, or too far. This soreness is mainly due to microtears in muscles, plus inflammation and swelling. However, if pain occurs before 18 or 24 hours after exercise this may indicate injury. Some soreness the next day is not uncommon. Soreness is good if mild and is part of the adaptive process to strengthen the muscles. DOMS may also be due to excessive eccentric exercise, such as in downhill running when muscles are stretched on landing of each foot strike. However, if downhill running is not overdone, it can be beneficial; after the muscles recover from the damage, the muscles are more resistant to soreness and damage for a month or more.

With a bad case of DOMS, it is best to reduce training intensity and quantity for a few days to let the body repair the damage. Slow running will help to eliminate or reduce soreness. Also I have found it is best to stop training right away when sore or fatigued muscles develop during a workout. And in weight training, don't train to the point of muscle burn until any soreness has gone away. These recommendations could avoid injury.

LESSONS LEARNED DURING RECOVERY

A healthy body can tolerate neglect but not an injured one. Therefore, a body recovering from injury is more sensitive to any excess stretching or excess weights or any exercise overdone.

The following are **facts and precautions during recovery** from an injury, information your physiotherapist may not tell you, and learned by careful observation and mistakes made during recovery:

- *Reduce mileage by 50%.* While recovering from an injury, the mileage run should preferably be reduced to about 50% with much reduced intensity.
- *Go easy after physio.* On a day of physiotherapy, particularly after extensive electrical vibrations or fairly extensive weights on the legs, go very easy on any workout the same day or preferably do no workout that day.
- *Adequate stretching.* If weights are done to strengthen legs, make sure to stretch legs before and after, and warm-up legs beforehand by jogging, cycling, fast walking, hot shower or heating pad. Many neglect to stretch after. Strengthening of the injury is best done after the muscle feels healthy again and on easy running days.
- *Water running and weight training don't mix.* On a day of running in the water, do no weights on the legs; this is a double weight workout. Similarly, on a day of swimming, it is preferable to do no weight workout on the arms.
- *Massage can do damage* and produce sore muscles. Be careful on an injury. It's best to stick to the masseur you know. Also, do not massage near an injury too soon after being injured. Professional massage, even self-massage, should be done within two hours of a workout for maximum benefit.
- *Rest after deep massage.* On a day of deep friction massage do no workout after or simply walk. After a "Rolfing" session (deep massage to align the fascia) do no workout that day and go easy the next day.
- *Always use ice after the workout* while the injury is still not completely healed.

One might say some of this is too cautious, but it is better to learn from another's mistakes than your own. Be over-cautious during recovery to avoid setbacks.

REFERENCES:

1. Ylinen, J., and Cash, M., *Sports Massage*, Stanley Paul, London, England, 1988.
2. Jesse, J., *Running Athletes*, The Athletic Press, Pasadena, CA, 1984.
3. Larkins, P. A., *Common Running Problems–Sports Medicine*, Produced by the Australian Sports Medicine Federation Ltd, Canberra, Australia, 1987.
4. Garrick, J. G., and Radetsky, P., *Peak Condition*, Harper and Row Publishers, New York, NY, 1986.
5. Mirkin, G., and Hoffman, M., *The Sports Medicine Book*, Little, Brown and Company, Boston/Toronto, ON, 1978.
6. Read, M., *Sports Injuries*, Arco Publishing Inc., New York, NY, 1984.
7. Sheehan, G., Medical Advice, *Runner's World*, 1972.
8. Coe, S., and Coe, P., *Running For Fitness*, Pavilion Books Ltd, London, England, 1983.
9. The Editor's of Rodale's Runner's World Magazine, *Running Injury-Free*, Rodale Press Inc., Emmaus, PA, 1986.
10. Griffith, H. W., *Sport's Injuries*, The Body Press, Tucson, AZ, 1986.
11. Morehouse, L. E., and Gross, L., *Maximum Performance*, Simon and Schuster, New York, NY, 1977.
12. *Prevention Magazine*, April 1992.
14. The Pill Book Company, Inc., *The Pill Book*, 7th Edition, Bantam Books, New York, NY, 1986.
15. Alfredson, H., et al, Heavy-Load Eccentric Calf Muscle Training for the Treatment of Chronic Achilles Tendinosis, *American Journal of Sports Medicine*, Vol.26, No. 3, p360-366.
16. Pagliano J. W., Heel Bursitis, The Foot Beat, *National Masters News*, September, 1998, Eugene, OR, USA.

CHAPTER 17

Jack be nimble, Jack be quick, Jack jump over the hurdle stick.

PLYOMETRICS

Plyometrics has gained wide attention in recent decades but has been used by track and field athletes in Europe since 1920. About 15 years ago, my ex-coach, David Welch, wanted me and two other master athletes to do rope skipping during our warm-up. At the time, I didn't know of the many advantages of plyometrics and had heard that one needs a solid base of weight training before doing plyometrics. I was afraid of injuries. So we didn't take it up. A mistake. Actually, for low-impact plyometric exercises, gradually introduced, a base of intense weight training is not essential for an experienced runner with reasonable strength as explained below under Preparation.

Plyometrics for the lower body involves hopping, skipping, bounding and jumping to assist in developing speed. Plyometrics develops strength and power (work per unit time or force times velocity) in muscles and tendons involved in sprinting. It also develops the explosive power required in starting and improves neural response (quickness). After one is used to plyometrics, the strengthening of muscles, tendons and joints will assist in preventing injury. The objective is to improve the athlete's ability to generate maximum force in the shortest time, namely explosiveness. The focus is on speed of contraction rather than the magnitude of the force (as in weight training).

THEORETICAL EXPLANATION

The distinct method of training to develop power or explosiveness is called plyometrics. Power is a combination of speed and strength. Hence, it is advantageous to work on plyometrics and weight training but not necessarily on the same days. The main aim of plyometrics is to decrease the time for muscles to contract.

There are three types of muscle contractions:

- ***Eccentric contraction:*** muscles lengthen under load. It is used to decelerate the body or normally precedes a maximum effort like a golf swing or striking a ball.
- ***Concentric contraction:*** muscles shorten under load. It is used to accelerate the body or move an object.
- ***Isometric contraction:*** muscles loaded while stationary. For example, two hands pushing against each other.

For effective plyometric training, an eccentric contraction is followed immediately after by a concentric contraction to produce a powerful force. The initial rapid stretch loads the muscles with energy. The immediate switch from eccentric contraction to concentric contraction results in an immediate deceleration of the mass and a powerful reflex reaction force causing a rapid acceleration of the mass in the opposite direction. A more powerful reflex force is achieved by:

- A more rapid initial stretch. You can generate more power in any muscle group by first starting a rapid stretching movement in the opposite direction.
- A shorter time between the eccentric contraction and concentric contraction, i.e., between deceleration and acceleration. There must be no hesitation.

In the following examples picture the rapid load pre-stretch, rapid change of direction, and subsequent explosive reflex force:

- A doctor taps your knee cap causing your leg to jerk; this is the *myotatic stretch reflex*. The rapid stretching of the muscles activates the myotatic stretch reflex causing the muscles to contract fast as a safety mechanism to prevent over-stretching.
- An athlete jumps down from a box: the stretched muscles on landing load the muscles dynamically with energy. The potential energy (height times body weight) on landing is stored in the muscles and released immediately in the rebound. If there is not too much give (sinking) on landing the energy from the bent legs is immediately released in an opposite reaction and results in a powerful force and upward spring. The rapid stretching of the muscles activates the myotatic stretch reflex, stimulating the muscles causing them to contract faster with more power if there is minimal delay after the stretch.
- An athlete sprints, skips, hops, or bounds: the rapid prestretch on landing and immediate change of direction generates a powerful force similar to the above.

- In the arm press weight exercise. A rapid lowering of the weight (eccentric contraction) lengthens the muscles and the immediate upward lift switches to concentric contraction, shortening of the muscles, producing more power than realized with a slow down-up movement.
- A golfer in winding up and follow through to the ball
- A batter in winding up and reversing toward the ball.

Advantages

Plyometrics is not just for sprinters. It can improve running economy (oxygen utilization at a given pace) in distance runners by several percent if practiced regularly for about six weeks. With regular plyometric exercises all runners can improve strength, ankle mobility, stride push off, stride length, and reduce injuries. Sprinters can also improve their explosive start.

After studying many references on plyometrics, I have concluded/discovered five basic or major advantages of plyometrics.

1. Central nervous system (CNS) activity:

There is an extremely high degree of CNS activity involved in skipping, hopping, and jumping in addition to the explosive muscular contractions. These percussive shocks are felt throughout the entire body and the CNS. Hence, plyometrics can help retain the CNS neural pathways and associated fast twitch muscles which decrease every year as we age. Without such intense activity, many of the neural pathways die out as we age taking the associated fast twitch cells with them. These inactive muscle cells are turned to fat cells. Hence, plyometrics is anti-aging. One Internet reference I consulted said: "Plyometrics is not for people over 60." In my opinion, those over 60 have a lot to gain from plyometrics in view of the above. It can help all masters to stay young mainly since the neural pathways are well activated and retained. It is even possible to reactivate fibers, which have suffered from disuse.

2. High G (gravity) forces:

The forces generated are a factor of about 10 higher than those normally used during weight training. In plyometrics the forces generated on landing can be as high as three to five times body weight (3 to 5 G). However, in weight training for leg extensions or leg curls, for example, the weight is only about 0.3 to 0.5 times body weight for most runners.

3. Advantage of eccentric contractions:

The plyometric contractions involve an initial lengthening of muscles under these high percussive loads. It is these eccentric contractions in running which gives sore muscles and muscle fatigue. But during normal weight training, it is the concentric contractions (shortened muscles under load) that are mainly exercised. Hence the high load eccentric contractions during plyometrics condition the muscles to prevent sore muscles and injuries during running.

4. Specific to running:
Specificity is imperative. Ideally the movements in plyometrics should match or duplicate, as nearly as possible, the movements in your sport whether it be basketball or running. Plyometrics is very specific to running since the body is vertical as in running and the forces developed are very similar.

5. All body parts exercised:
Plyometrics involves all body parts since the forces generated travel through the whole body. However, in weight training, only one specific muscle is exercised at a time.

Summary of Plyometrics Advantages

- Increases running economy
- Increases upper and lower body speed
- Increases jump ability
- Increases explosive leg strength and explosive reaction
- Produces the greatest strength gains in the shortest time
- Builds coordination, balance and posture
- Improves mobility of ankle, knee and hip joints
- Improves muscle response time
- Tones muscles
- Increases muscle flexibility
- Increases elasticity of tendons and ligaments
- Reduces injuries
- Neural pathways are activated more so than in weight training
- Anti-aging

EXERCISES FOR LOWER BODY

There are countless varieties of plyometric exercises. This chapter concentrates on exercises which are related to or will benefit running. I have chosen some of the ones more popular and useful to runners and easier to learn. The legs receive the most stress during running, so these exercises are targeted. Single leg plyometric exercises are more specific to running. See also an excellent reference by Donald Chu, PhD, *Jumping Into Plyometrics,* for many illustrated exercises. This comprehensive book[8] pictorially describes the various plyometric exercises specific to 25 different sports, i.e., jumps-in-place, standing jumps, multiple jumps, box drills, bounding, depth jumps, medicine ball, etc.

Preparation

Start gradually with low jumps and build slowly. In this way, it is as safe as any other exercise. Usually a sound weight training program is recommended before doing plyometrics training. However, lower impact plyometrics can be implemented by experienced runners with good strength without a lot of intense weight training beforehand. For instance, I have little weight training on the legs and can easily do the low and intermediate plyometrics without problems. But it is essential to start gradually and limit the number of foot contacts. For the more advanced plyometrics, like jumping from boxes and over hurdles, the usual recommendation is that the athlete should be able to squat with a weight 1.5 times his body weight. A larger and stronger muscle from previous weight training will be able to generate more force during the plyometric exercises and will be less prone to injury.

Plyometric exercises in the shallow end of a pool are a good preparation for land-based plyometrics. In the pool with water level at mid chest, the body bears only about one-third of normal weight. However, in the pool, I have found the contact time between eccentric stretch and concentric shorten is longer compared to the land. Hence, plyometrics in a shallow pool are useful to reduce load but not as effective because in the water it is difficult to minimize foot contact time. The concentric contraction is not as powerful. It is recommended to wear some aquatic shoes to avoid slipping. Be knowledgeable about the drills on dry land before doing pool drills.

Another form of preparation for plyometrics is eccentric stretch and hold. For example, drop from a box and freeze rather than continuing immediately with a jump up.

Form

- Maintain an upright position.
- Land lightly with knees slightly flexed. The legs act as a shock absorber.
- Perform at maximum speed for most effect.
- Aim for quality rather than volume. When form deteriorates–stop.
- For the experienced, the foot contact is ball-heel-toe.
- Swinging and throwing your arms up as you jump or bound pulls your body up, and thus decreases the weight you push off the floor (called the reaction force).

General Considerations

Since all exercises are explosive with high G loads, each exercise should take less than 10 seconds. The exercises are usually done over 10 to 30 meters and repeated two or three times depending on experience. For the inexperienced a session should last only about three to five minutes, and for the advanced about 12 minutes.

LOWER IMPACT ALTERNATIVES

Recommendations:

- About 40 to 60 foot contacts per session (note a two legged landing is two foot contacts)
- One to two minutes between sets

Two-legged ankle hops in one spot. While remaining in one spot, stand with feet shoulder-width apart and body vertical. Using the ankles only, hop up and down rapidly with minimum foot contact time on floor.

Two-legged small hops. Stand tall and move forward with small quick hops. Move the arms together. As arms move forward hop forward. As arms move backward, hop forward again and repeat for about 10 meters. This feels good.

Two-legged big hops. Stand with knees slightly flexed, and jump forward as far as possible with a strong swing of the arms from behind as in a broad jump. Repeat several times.

South-West-North-East two legged jumps. Start with feet shoulder-width apart, knees slightly bent and land always on the balls of both feet. Bound forward to south and bound back to the center. Bound sideways to the west and back to the center. Bound backward the north and back to the center. Bound sideways to the east and back to the center. Repeat at least twice or until tired.

Step-ups and step-downs. This is a low-intensity plyometric exercise recommended when beginning plyometrics or for someone injured. Three to ten minutes is recommended at 20 to 45 steps per minute for an easy to high intensity session respectively[5]. To exercise left leg only: step up with left foot, up with right, down with left, then down with right. Repeat. To exercise right leg only: start with right leg up, left leg up, right leg down, then left leg down. Repeat.

Fast feet. Run on the spot on the toes with feet barely leaving the ground. Knees are slightly bent. Arms move rapidly but movement is short in view of rapidity of steps. Another variation is to move over a distance of about 20 to 30 meters with very short steps and then suddenly accelerate into a fast running stride.

Sprinting. Sprinting is a form of plyometrics. Each foot strike loads the legs with two to three times body weight and is immediately followed by a concentric contraction. Do five to six reps about 50 meters during warm-up.

Trampoline. Trampoline exercise is totally plyometric. It applies to all the advantages above and more. In addition, it builds balance, stabilizer muscles and reflex muscles to a greater extent than many of the other exercises described here. One Internet reference (Dr. Morton Walker 2003) lists 30 advantages of rebounding including: cleansing of the lymphatic system, and slowing down aging. The trampoline is believed by many to be the best way to stimulate the central nervous system. In view of the wide range of gravity experienced by the body, all cells in the body are stimulated. Since all cells are activated, the associated neural pathways are also activated. See advantage 1. Lack of intense activity causes many of the neural pathways and associated fast twitch cells to die out as we age. Compared to other plyometrics the trampoline produces high impact benefits with low impact forces; it is not strenuous on joints. There are also impressive aerobic advantages if carried out long enough and intensely enough. Like other plyometrics exercises all muscles are involved particularly, ankles, calves, quads, gluteals, hamstring, lower back, abdominals, and spine, in addition to ligaments and tendons. This is contrary to weight training which develops each muscle separately. Even a few minutes per session a few times per week is recommended since it's highly beneficial. However, some warming up beforehand would be necessary or start very gradually.

Rope skipping. This is another good plyometric exercise for beginners.

INTERMEDIATE IMPACT ALTERNATIVES

Recommendations:

- About 80 to 100 foot contacts per session
- Three minutes between sets

Single leg hopping on spot. While remaining in one spot, hop up and down on one foot using only the ankles and calves.

Single leg hop forward. (a) Hop for 10 meters on left leg. Hop for 10 meters on right leg. (b) Alternately hop forward four times on left leg and then four times on right leg. Repeat for about 10 to 15 meters.

Two-legged hop to and from box. Stand facing a box about 0.30 to 0.46 meters (12 to 18 inches) in height. Swing both arms forward to jump up to top of box with both feet. Immediately swing both arms backward to jump back down to start position. Repeat until fatigue starts.

One-legged alternate bounding for height. This is like an exaggerated skip with oversized strides to spend more time in the air. Push off from the right leg. Raise the left leg knee high as possible and with an exaggerated swing of the right arm. Land lightly on the left leg. Continue on alternate legs. Usually five to eight bounds per set. Maximum distance about 20 meters. Do one or two sets depending on experience and conditioning. This is a fine muscle builder; the muscles that drive you forward (calves, glutes, and ankles) become more powerful and effective, thus contributing to a longer stride. Bounding up a grass hill is also recommended.

One-legged bounding for speed and distance. As above but concentrating on speed and distance not height. With long strides and exaggerated arm motion bound forward fast for about 20 meters. Emphasize the hang time in the forward direction. Continue bounding quickly on alternate legs. Try to keep the head level. This is also a very popular exercise that improves stride length. Uphill bounding on a soft surface would be less stressful than on the flat.

HIGHER IMPACT ALTERNATIVES

Recommendations:

- Athletes should be able to squat 1.5 body weight and bench press body weight.
- These are for highly competitive athletes who are advanced in the use of plyometrics, i.e., after being accustomed to lower impact exercises for about six weeks and after a good base of intense weight training.
- Limit to 120 to 150 foot contacts per session. Less for heavier athletes.
- Six to eight minutes between sets since these exercises are more intense.

Lateral step-up. Stand in front of a box 0.20 to 0.30 meters (8 to 12 inches) high meters). Place one leg on top of the box with the other leg on the floor. Use the box leg to raise up the body quickly until the box leg is straight. Lower your body quickly until the other leg touches the floor using only the box leg for support. The leg on the box is the support leg at all times. Repeat until the support leg is somewhat tired but not overly tired. Repeat with opposite leg. It is helpful to put the box next to a wall and place hands on the wall for support.

Drop jumping. Drop, not jump from a box of about 12 to 18 inches (0.30 to 0.46 meters). Feet are shoulder width apart. On landing on both feet with flexed knees, immediately jump up high (explode) with a double arm forward swing. The drop pre stretches and loads the leg muscles (eccentric contraction) and the intense upward drive shortens the loaded muscle (concentric contraction). The very advanced may land on two legs with dumbell weights or on one leg. These are not recommended here.

Research studies at universities in Sweden and Indiana concluded that two-legged box jumping is no more stressful than running if carried out sensibly. Two-legged box jumping increases bone density and hence reduces stress fractures.

Box to box jumps. Several boxes (at least three) are placed about a meter or more apart. Proceed as above: drop from a box and land on two legs with flexed knees. Immediately jump (explode) onto the next box using a double arm swing, landing on both legs. Continue. The difficulty is increased as the box height is increased and/or the distance between boxes is increased. Therefore, initially start with lower spacing and height. For additional difficulty, the hands are held behind the head throughout.

Hurdle to hurdle jumps. Similar to the above but use hurdles instead of boxes. This is more convenient as hurdles are usually more readily available and the height can be easily adjusted. Scissor hurdles are preferable to solid hurdles as they come apart when hit. Start with low hurdles until experienced. Make sure you do not land on top of the hurdle as this could cause injury. Use a double arm swing and raise the knees high and together in going over the hurdle. Alternately, cones can be used and are safer, but without the flexibility of height adjustment.

MEDICINE BALL EXERCISES

Medicine ball exercises target the abdominals, back, and torso (i.e., not the legs). These exercises emphasize movements, not individual muscles. Hence, normally the whole body as a unit is involved. Medicine ball exercises ensure that the upper body, abs and back are not neglected in plyometrics training. There are three basic movements: pass, throw and side spin.

Some safety considerations. Always keep the back straight and knees bent; this is particularly required when picking up the ball from the floor. In the backward throw the ball should not be too far behind the head. Start with a light ball and proceed to heavier in later weeks. Do not catch the ball in front of your face. Do not exercise after intense activity.

Repetitions and sets. For strength and muscular endurance, do 6 to 12 reps. For muscular endurance, do 12 to 24 reps. Usually 2 to 3 sets. A normal session would take about 15 minutes involving 6 or more exercises.

Ball size. This depends on the athletes condition, experience and particular goals. For example: for endurance, balance and flexibility (lighter), and for strength (heavier). Considerations:

- Heavy enough to slow down your movement
- Light enough for accuracy and range of motion
- Err on lighter side than heavier
- Beginner size: about 2.7kg (6 pounds)
- Intermediate size: about 4.5kg (10 pounds)
- Advanced size: 5.5kg (12 pounds)
- Normally 5kg for men and 3kg for women.

Some typical more popular exercises:

Chest pass to wall. Start with ball at mid chest. Throw ball toward a solid wall. Stand an appropriate distance away to let the ball bounce on the floor before you. Catch the ball on the rebound from the floor and throw back immediately to the wall. Alternately, omit the bounce from the floor.

Exercise abdominals with partner. Lie on the floor with knees bent and lower back in contact with floor facing up towards your partner standing up in front of you. The partner drops or throws the ball toward your chest. Catch the ball (eccentric contraction) and immediately throw it back (concentric contraction). Repeat about 24 times. Do two sets if possible.

Exercise obliques in side swing. Stand sideways to a solid wall about 2 meters away; right foot closest to wall. The feet are always solidly planted and shoulder-width apart. Rotating at the waist clockwise throw the ball at the wall. Catch the ball on the rebound while moving in a counterclockwise direction. Without losing momentum throw the ball back to the wall by rotating at the waist in a clockwise direction. Repeat. Alternatively throw to a partner.

Miscellaneous general exercises with partner.

- Chest pass: Start with ball at mid chest.
- Underhand throw: Start from full squat with ball between legs and raise straight up. Alternatively without partner, throw for height.

- Backward throw: Start from half squat with ball between legs, stand up with knees slightly bent and release ball from behind head.
- Overhead throw: Start with ball behind the head, take one step forward and release ball. Alternatively without partner, throw for distance.

Workout Sequence

Sequence of workout: warm-up, plyometrics, running tempo or intervals or speed training, and finally strength training. Normally plyometrics should not be the very last session in your practice day (when muscles are tired) in view of the stress involved. However they could be done after a lighter workout session. Alternatively plyometrics and/or weight training is done in between running days. See Safety section below for more details.

RECOMMENDED FREQUENCY

Two to three times (for lower volumes) per week during the base training phase (off-season). Two times per week during the speedwork phase. One to two times per week during the competition phase. It is also recommended to reduce the intensity in the competition phase. Once only (or not at all) on week of a race, but with reduced volume and not within four days of the race. With lower volumes, plyometrics can be used more frequently during warm-ups.

SAFETY

- Athletes must be in excellent physical condition and have good strength level.
- Complete a dynamic warm-up (see the chapter on Dynamic Warm-up) before doing the plyometric exercises.
- Heavier athletes above 90 kg or 200 pounds should not perform depth jumps exceeding about 0.46 meters (18 inches). The force in a drop jump could be three to five times body weight. Therefore, heavier persons need to be more cautious since they experience higher loads through the ankle, knee and hip joints.
- Grass surface or rubber mat or Tartan track surface is necessary in view of the shock to the whole body. The surface must be non slip and firm, but allow a slight give on landing.
- Shoes should have good support to protect the plantar fasciitis tendon, Achilles tendon and the knee. Never practice in bare feet or in spiked shoes.

- Start gradually with low jumps and build slowly. Increase the number of sets and contacts over a period of weeks.
- Take plenty of rest between plyometric workouts; two days between sessions is recommended for more intense plyometric sessions.
- Stop when ground contact time increases or when fatigue sets in. Quality and good form are stressed rather than quantity.
- Do not exceed the foot contacts per session specified in the exercises above. Take fewer foot contacts for the more intense exercises and fewer foot contacts for heavier athletes.
- Avoid plyometrics when tired or muscles are sore as these are normally when injuries occur.
- Avoid intensive lower-body weight training on days when intensive lower-body plyometrics are used. Similarly, avoid intensive upper body weight training on days when intensive medicine ball exercises are used.
- Those inexperienced in plyometrics should not practice plyometrics the week of taper before competition.
- Less is best. The bottom line is: degenerative joint disease can occur from repetitive high impact exercises. So be careful.

RECOVERY

- The greater the intensity, the longer the recovery.
- Walk back slowly after a repetition and start the next rep when rested.
- Take several minutes between sets as required. See recommendations under Low, Intermediate and High Impact Alternatives above.
- Increase the number of hops each week and/or the distance covered over a period of weeks. Similarly, increase the number of medicine ball repetitions over a period of weeks.
- It is always better to do less. Listen to your body. Everyone is different. So stop before overly tired. Hence the number of reps and sets are not iron clad, and if specified herein this is only a rough indication.
- See also Recommended Frequency above.

CHAPTER 18

Soldiers prepare for combat with war-like activities.
Likewise, athletes should prepare for competition with a running-like dynamic warm-up.

DYNAMIC WARM-UP

Lately, many running coaches, including myself, have begun to realize that there is a much better way of warming up for training or competition than the traditional (jog, static stretch, and perhaps some strides). This new way uses exercises that mimic running and is called the dynamic warm-up. A dynamic warm-up involves ABC sprint drills (described below), leg swinging exercises, fast strides, and plyometrics, but with little or no static stretching in view of its several major disadvantages during a warm-up.

An ideal warm-up increases muscle and joint temperature by one or two degrees, and simulates actual running movements, which stimulate the central nervous system, cardiovascular, psychological and physiological systems. The dynamic warm-up does all of these more effectively than static stretching. The rationale for this switch to little or no stretching *before* a workout or competition and the advantages of the dynamic warm-up are explained below.

DISADVANTAGES OF STATIC STRETCHING BEFORE TRAINING

Recent research trials and literature surveys indicate the following disadvantages:

- Static stretching does not warm up muscles sufficiently. The warming up during jogging is often lost during the long static stretching session, usually 10 to 15 minutes. This is particularly the case during cold outdoor weather.

- There is little similarity or specificity between static stretching and the rapid lengthening (eccentric contraction) and shortening (concentric contraction) of muscles under load while running when injuries occur.
- Static stretching even though mild leads to some microtears in muscle cells and stretching masks pain. Therefore, static stretching immediately prior to training particularly if stretching is intense or prolonged could lead to injury if followed by intense or prolonged exercise.
- Possible decreased performance. Research shows stretching within 60 minutes before the start of competition or training leads to decreased force output. Peak force and rate of force may be reduced by a few percent. Strength decreases slightly up to an hour after long static stretching. Hence performance is decreased in endurance and speed events.
- Many recent trials and literature surveys indicate static stretching before exercise is not beneficial to prevent injuries: for example, notably an Australian study of 1538 Army recruits doing intense exercise (Pope et al, 2000), and a review of 138 sport science articles (Shrier, 1999). However, I believe it is impossible to be conclusive on this point since there are many variables to consider: e.g., elite vs. recreational athlete, young vs. old athlete, flexible vs. inflexible athlete, intense exercise vs. non intense, and type of sport. In fact the risk of injury appears about even in favor of static stretch, or not at all before a workout; this would be a fairer statement.
- Static stretching is not a central nervous system activity like running or a dynamic warmup.
- There is no similarity to actual running since most of the stretching is done while stationary and while sitting or lying down.
- Static flexibility deals with structure and maximum range whereas dynamic flexibility as in running deals with the central nervous system and "easy range of motion (McHugh, 1977).
- Compared with the dynamic warmup there is less blood flow to muscles.
- In some events, such as sprinting, too much flexibility can be detrimental.

Summary of Above Disadvantages of Static Stretching Before a Workout

In view of the above disadvantages, stretching *before* a strenuous workout or competition is not recommended. Instead, a dynamic warm-up is recommended. However, the traditional jog and gentle stretch before an *easy* workout could still be retained.

ADVANTAGES OF DYNAMIC WARM-UP

- The movements result in increased muscle temperature compared to static stretching, hence muscle contractions are more rapid and forceful.

- The movements are specific to actual running. The movements reinforce and teach the good running form movements that improve running performance. Hence, running form/technique can be worked on and improved during the warm-up.
- By simulating actual running movements the athlete is better prepared physiologically and psychologically for training or competition compared to static stretching.
- By substituting dynamic movements for static stretching the muscle microtears can be avoided.
- Consistent ABC drills practiced for about six weeks could result in reduced stride contact time by about 0.01 seconds. This is a significant improvement: for example, about one second in a 200m race or over a minute in a 10K race.
- Joint mobility is improved to a greater extent compared to static stretching.
- The cardiovascular system is worked on at the same time as the muscles and joints.
- The activities normally include fast movement plyometrics (jumping, hopping, bounding) which result in forces of five to 10 times body weight through the whole body and central nervous system. These exercises will improve reaction time, strength, explosive power, and stride length; also running economy in distance runners can be improved by four to six percent.
- A dynamic warm-up involving plyometrics activates the neural pathways of the central nervous system in movements mimicking running movements. The plyometric exercises will help to retain the neural pathways. This is particularly important to older athletes who tend to lose neural pathways and associated fast twitch fibers due to lack of fast resistive movements in training.

RECOMMENDED DYNAMIC WARM-UP SEQUENCE

1 Sprinters walk or jog for 400 meters. Distance runners jog for about a mile.

2 Leg swinging to exercise all parts of the lower body except the calves. See the chapter on "Running In the Pool" (shallow end) for details of eight exercises if not familiar.

3 Sprint ABC's drills. Good form is essential. Do 2 x 30m of each with brisk walk back. (See the chapter on Sprinting for details of the following drills if not familiar):
   - A: High knee marching
   - B: Foreleg extension marching (exaggerated running motion)
   - C: Butt kicks
   - Ankle bounce drill
   - High knees running
   - Sideways running while alternately criss-crossing the legs
   - Quick-low-short steps drill for 15 meters then accelerate for 15 meters
   - 12 lunges

4 The following drills are done on the spot

- Feet bouncing for 30 seconds (stand on one foot, bounce the other foot rapidly)
- Fast arms drill for one minute sitting or standing

5 Plyometrics

Start in initial weeks with double leg hops, about 20 foot contacts per session and work up to one legged hops and a total of 60 foot contacts per session after a month. Progress to bounding after about three weeks. See the chapter on Plyometrics.

6 Sprints

Do 5 x 50m at 90% effort with walk back. First and last reps are slower.

7 Walk 400 meters and start the training or competition.

Some of the above steps may be omitted. Not counting the walks a shorter version of the above should take only about 25 minutes. In this time, a mild perspiration and increased heart rate should be achieved.

CHAPTER

19

Build skeletal strength before
cardiovascular fitness to avoid injuries.
When fitness exceeds strength,
injuries come.
Robert de Castella[9],
former world record holder in the marathon.

WEIGHT TRAINING

When I discovered that stride frequency hardly changed with age but stride length decreases drastically with age (see Chapter 3 on Running Form) I realized the great importance of strength training for all runners. With greater strength, a runner exerts more force to the ground and stride length increases. Even a few more centimeters per stride is a tremendous advantage in any race distance. Also, I learned that Steve Spence (world-class U.S. marathoner) in 1990 increased his step length at marathon race pace from 70 to 73 inches (a 7.6 cm increase) from weight training. Now I am even more convinced of the many benefits of weight training. Overall fitness is cardiovascular fitness, flexibility and strength. Many club runners neglect flexibility and strength in their training. The many advantages of strength training listed below are more than sufficient reasons for an athlete to include strength training, by lifting weights during his/her weekly schedule. The compliments alone and your increased well being, self-esteem and confidence make it worthwhile, but there are further compelling reasons to embark on a weight training program.

It takes only a short time to realize the benefits. Ten machines, two sets x 10 repetitions/set per machine, can be done in less than 20 minutes. With a program of only five to six sets every other day there are "substantial increases in strength" (McAlpine, *Men's Health*, February 1990). Less than a few minutes every day or every other day will maintain your muscles and even increase strength; thus, it is advantageous to have weights in your home. I find about five to seven minutes of some weights or rubber tubing exercises; some lunges, squats, without weights; etc., in my bedroom before bed, most nights, keeps my muscles in good tone.

There are other methods to increase strength, such as hill training, running in the water and plyometrics. See Chapter 4, Chapter 11 and Chapter 17 respectively. Intense plyometrics tend to induce more severe, longer-lasting muscular soreness and should only be started after a weight training program to prepare the muscles. Also, if you have no weights at home or are travelling, a lot can be accomplished with rubber tubing or your own body weight: for example, deep-knee bends, lunges, step-ups, toe raises, dips between chairs, chin-ups and sit-ups.

Before You Start

Areas of the body to work on:

- If you are going to take weight training seriously, you need to know the names of the various major muscles in the body and the exercises that develop these muscles. Look in the mirror and pick out those body parts that you think might need some extra training. Then you simply do a disproportionate amount of training for that area. There is no need to over develop those muscles already fully developed; maintenance only is required. However, as distance runners, we do not want to be muscle bound. Our main purpose is to develop strength and power without carting around extra muscle.
- The strength of the upper and lower body needs to be balanced.
- The strength of opposing muscles needs to be balanced.
- Strengthen those muscles that are particularly important for your sport, e.g., jumping, hurdling, cycling or running.
- It is recommended that you consult a good sports chiropractor for an appraisal of any biological imbalances or muscle weaknesses so that these weak areas can be addressed with specific weight and stretching exercises.
- It is important to strengthen those muscles that have been injured in the past to prevent reoccurrence; these are normally a weak link.

ADVANTAGES

- It strengthens bone, and builds muscle and helps correct muscle imbalance. Muscle fibers get larger (hypertrophy). It makes tendons and ligaments stronger. All this helps prevent strains, tears and fractures. Hence, the athlete does not get injured as often. It's the weak link that usually gets injured. After an injury, one realizes the importance of weight training to build back strength and to guard against future injury. Also weight training, within limits, during injury recovery has a positive psychological effect since you are doing something helpful to substitute for the running.

- Coordination between the central nervous system and muscular system is enhanced.
- For sprinters, it is essential. Strength is speed and power. Increasing the power of each step increases speed.
- With increasing age, the stride rate (and also stride length) decreases. Ken Sparks (a master's world record holder at 800m and 1500 meters) found from treadmill tests his stride rate slowed down over the years. To compensate, he does leg presses to work on the fast twitch fibers (see section on "Muscle Fiber" in Chapter 1). Sparks also emphasizes his arms, shoulders, and chest during weight training to maintain his posture in running and to prevent fatigue (qtd. by M. Bloom, *Runner's World*, May 1998). Also, for the same reasons as above, strength in the abdominals and lower back are essential for runners.
- Upper body strength (e.g., arms, shoulders, abdominals, back) enables you to maintain running form. Upper body fatigue causes deterioration of form and more expenditure of energy. With proper form (running tall with hips forward, chest out), breathing improves and stride lengthens.
- For middle and long distance runners, and cyclists it improves endurance. Studies have shown at least a 10% increase in time to exhaustion after more than two months of weight training.
- A study in 1994 by Ron Johnson, PhD., exercise physiologist, showed more than a two percent improvement in running economy for female distance runners after 10 weeks of leg, "abs," and arm weight training (Pfitzinger[1]). "Almost every elite runner today incorporates some sort of weight training into their weekly schedule" (Ken Sparks[2]). Also weight training conditions the muscles and joints and thus assists to avoid injury during the intensive interval and speedwork sessions.
- Weight training will result in loss of fat and increase in muscle, reducing your body fat percentage, making you faster.
- Range of motion is improved; in the negative phase (return) of each weight training exercise the muscles that were used in the positive phase are stretched. This stretching adds to the flexibility from your everyday stretching exercises. Any training exercise that produces a lengthening of the muscle group will increase flexibility. When muscles are worked through their full range of motion, they remain flexible.
- For master runners in particular, weight training is highly recommended to counteract the loss of muscle, which occurs with aging. With weight training you will age more slowly.

OFF-SEASON AND IN-SEASON TRAINING

For track runners, a typical season is divided into base training, indoor season and outdoor season. For distance runners, a typical year is the off-season, pre-season, and in-season.

Off-season. The greatest benefit of strength training is gained during the off-season with the highest volume of sets and reps. In the off-season (base training phase), more weight training can be done as the running training is not as intense. Two weight sessions per week is typical for the first month; at this time, do more reps to condition the body gradually. In the following weeks, the sessions can be increased to three times per week. For sprinters, it is a time to build strength, with less reps, for the in-season intense workouts. For distance runners, it is a time to build muscle strength but mainly muscle endurance with more reps. Increase the weight as the weeks go by, e.g., an increase of 5% to 10% per week. For older runners and the less competitive, two times per week with more reps per set is recommended to save the joints.

During the **in-season** and as the competition season approaches, running workouts are more intensive so the weight training has to be less intensive (less weight and less sets) and less frequent. During the in-season, strength is maintained with 1-2 sessions per week and once per week on weeks of a low-key race and weeks of exceptionally intense workouts. Dintiman, Ward, and Tellez[3] state: "One workout weekly during the in-season will nearly maintain off-season gains."

About two or three weeks before your big competition, weight training should be stopped to prevent draining of precious energy. Similarly, there should be no running in the pool within four days of a race, since this is like weight training and can tire the legs during a race—as I know from several bad experiences (e.g., Turku, Finland and Durban, South Africa). It is essential to have fresh legs before the race.

Steve Spence, world-class marathoner, recommends shelving the weight training even a month before your marathon and doing push-ups, sit-ups or dips instead ("Master the Marathon", *Runner's World*, September 1997). He says, "The greater the intensity of my running the less intense my weight training" (Ken Sparks[2]).

In the fall (base training phase), I often do only two sets of 10 "reps" (endurance weights) at each of 12 to 14 machines two or three times per week. This is not too stressful to continue once or twice a week in the in-season as long as it is not close to a race.

Elite and Olympic-type athletes

Elite and Olympic-type athletes (particularly sprinters) lift weights more frequently (than less-experienced athletes), but under well-supervised and controlled programs. The body adapts to the high frequency. For example, the following frequencies of training are fairly typical in the off-season for world class sprinters:

- Weights on arms one day followed by weights on legs the next day throughout the week.
- Weights on arms in the a.m., and weights on legs in the p.m.; three times per week; one day rest between weight training days.

The above allows the particular body parts to rest and recover over 48 hours. This recovery results in more rapid strength gain and allows muscle fibers to repair. In the examples above, in order not to interfere with the 48 hours of recovery, any speed and speed endurance running training ("power training") should be done *before* doing weight training on the legs, i.e., the same day; this makes sense since the weight training sessions for elite athletes are normally intense (see also "Recuperation" below). In the example above, if power training is done on the day between weight training, there is only 24 hours or less of recovery. Charlie Francis had his athletes doing weights on speed and speed endurance days with "abs" and push-ups, for example, on days when "power" work was not emphasized (e.g., on tempo days).

RECUPERATION

Running and weight workouts should preferably be separated by three or four hours or more; however, this is normally not too practical unless you are a full-time athlete. If weight training is done on the same day as running training, it is preferable to run first. There should be, definitely, no intense weight workout before intense running[5]. Dintiman[3] also recommends that weight training be left to the end of the workout, but before cool down. Speed training should be done before weights, otherwise running form is affected due to fatigue. It is particularly important for sprinters to be fresh during the sprint sessions; a skill cannot be learned when the athlete is tired.

Studies have shown that normally about 48 hours rest in between weight sessions is required to give muscle fibers time to rebuild. Enough time must be allowed for recovery and growth. However, many coaches recommend doing weights on the easy endurance days of training[5]; (this would be a satisfactory time if the weight workout is not too intense). If intense weights are done on the evening of the easy day, there would be insufficient time (24 hours or less) for recuperation of muscle fibers since the following day is often a hard day for runners. If weights are done on the morning of the easy day, and the intense running workout is done on the evening of the following day, this is nearly 36 hours of recovery, which should be satisfactory. When weight training is done is more important for sprinters who are lifting heavier weights with more torn fibers. Sprinters who are doing long-intense weight sessions should do these shortly after (or several hours after) their speed training.

FREE WEIGHTS vs. MACHINES

Machines are safer, easier to use and quicker to use than free weights. With machines, I find I can get sufficient endurance weight training in about 20 minutes (about 12 machines and 2 sets of 10 reps each).

Free weights develop the main muscles and the balancers (the little muscles that often get injured). But a training partner is often required for safety. However, for maximum performance gains in strength and flexibility, use free weights. It is usually recommended to graduate to free weights after one becomes well conditioned and stronger after exercising on machines.

RUBBER TUBING EXCERCISES

The resistance of rubber tubing lends itself to endurance type of weight training. Exercising the legs and ankles with rubber tubing has the following advantages:

- It provides weight training with movement while simulating the running motion better than during squats, leg presses, lunges, leg extensions and hamstring curls.
- It can be done anywhere, providing weight training without the necessity of free weights or machines.
- It is beneficial for recovery from injury and can be done easily in the home.

Procedure for Leg Exercises Attach a loop of rubber tubing about two meters in length to a rail or leg of heavy furniture. Loop the tubing around the ankle so that it is secure while moving this leg backward and forward. Always return slowly to the unstretched tubing position to provide optimal exercise during the negative phase; this is eccentric muscle work (stretched while contracted muscles). Exercises are normally done in two to three sets of 15 to 20 repetitions. The movement of the target leg is described below.

Facing the support:

Exercising the *hamstrings*:

- With a straight leg, move the leg backward from the vertical to about 30 degrees from the vertical and then forward more slowly to beside the support leg again. Repeat.
- Start with leg straight in front. Move the leg backward while bending the knee to about 90 degrees. Return the leg slowly to the front while unbending the knee. Repeat.

Facing away from the support.

Exercising the hip *flexor*:

- Start with target leg about one foot behind support leg. Raise the target leg until the upper leg is parallel to the floor, and the lower leg is vertical. Return slowly to the rear while straightening the leg. Repeat.

Exercising the *quad*:

- With a straight leg, move the leg forward from the vertical to about 30 degrees from the vertical and then backward more slowly to rest beside the support leg again. Repeat.

Standing sideways to the support.

Exercising the *adductors (groin)*:

- Attach the tubing to the ankle of the leg closest to the support. With a straight leg extended away from the body, move this leg toward and slightly across the body (away from the support).

Exercising the *abductors (outer thigh)*:

- Attach the tubing to the ankle of the leg farthest from the support. With a straight leg starting at near the body, move this leg away from the body and the support.

TRAINING PRINCIPLES

The following training principles will result in maximum gains in strength in the shortest time. You will notice that weight training has a lot of similarity to running training.

- Consult an instructor at your health club, or your coach before starting to learn the right way for the various exercises with machines or free weights. Of course, there are numerous excellent books[5,6,7,8,10] on weight training to also guide you. The books more related to athletes[5,6] rather than body builders are more useful for runners.
- In view of the similar intensity to plyometrics and weight training, they could be in conflict if done during the same workout. "Avoid lower–body weight training on days when lower-body plyometrics are used" (Dintiman, et al.[3]). (A plyometric session and weight training session may be acceptable on the same day if one or both are not too intense with reduced volume.) Also, a hard water workout is similar to weight training so weights should not be done on the same day.
- Warm up aerobically (cycling, running, skipping, even fast walking) and stretch before the session.
- Another way to warm up the muscles is to start with a whole set of light repetitions, e.g., about 25% to 33% lighter than for the sets to follow.

- Alternatively to the above, start with lighter weights and work up to heavier weights in each set. It is usual in each set to lift a fixed-load for a fixed number of reps, e.g., 110 pounds x 10 reps. However, it is important to have variation in the training; the body needs to be shocked for maximum gains. This is achieved by increasing the load in each set and while reducing the reps. For example, for set 1, 2, and 3: 110 pounds x 10, 120 pounds x 8, and 130 pounds x 6, respectively. This is only convenient on a machine where loads can be changed quickly since rest between sets should be brief to achieve a cardiovascular conditioning effect. However, the rest between sets is increased as the load is increased.
- Train first for volume and later for intensity[5].
- Never hold your breath when you lift; this decreases the blood return to your heart and could cause fainting. Exhale when exerting the greatest force and inhale on the return or negative stroke.
- Get in shape gradually and do not overtrain. Overload enough for gradual adaptation but not enough to produce extreme soreness.
- Begin with the larger muscle groups of the legs and hips before the smaller muscles of the arms become fatigued. Smaller muscles fatigue more quickly (Dintiman[4]).
- Alternate muscle groups to avoid exercising the same group twice in succession. However, this is not always possible in a busy health club or YMCA.
- Cycle (vary) the volume and intensity of your workouts[5]. Vary the reps and the weight. Perform particular exercises more intensely in one workout than another. For example, Monday light weight, Wednesday medium weights, and Friday heavier weights with fewer reps. Some days you will feel stronger or weaker; vary the intensity accordingly. See also periodization below. These variations lead to maximum gains. Similarly, a runner will not improve by running at the same pace every day.
- For speed improvement, raise explosively and lower slowly, e.g., raise in 1 second and lower in 2 seconds (Dintiman[4]).
- Maximum strength comes quickest with few reps (1 to 3) and heavy resistance 90% to 100%. However, this could lead to loss of some flexibility in a distance runner.
- For strength endurance training, Jim Ryun[13] recommended the following to build upper body endurance:
  - Work with light weights (what you can easily lift 20-25 times) to avoid building bulk.
  - Work weights three times per week unless competing.
  - Discontinue the weight program during the last 2-3 weeks.
  - Avoid deep knee exercises at all times.
- Periodization is recommended in weight training, as well as in running training. Usually, there is a four-week schedule with the initial three weeks having progressively more sets and/or intensity. The fourth week has reduced sets and intensity below the initial week. During an individual week, it is best to vary the intensity on

the weight training days, e.g., light, medium, heavy. Also, normally there are three sets in a session with the first, second, and third set at about 60%, 70% and 80% of maximum respectively. The cycle repeats in the following month, but with increased intensity (weight).

- Always stretch after doing weights to prevent sore and stiff muscles the next day or two days later. I find a lot of serious lifters do not do this.
- To increase strength or endurance, the muscles must experience more intensity and/or volume gradually applied over a period of weeks and months (usually about six weeks), e.g., a combination of the following:
  - Increased load
  - Increased number of repetitions
  - Increased speed of movement
  - Increased duration of session
  - Decrease of rest interval
  - Increased frequency of training session

  Once again, there is a great similarity to running training.
- Work to improve any imbalance in opposing muscle groups. For example, a quadriceps muscle that is too strong, e.g., twice as strong as the hamstring muscle may result in hamstring injury. A runner needs strong quadriceps, but ideally, the strength ratio should be quadriceps/hamstring = 3/2 or smaller. Charlie Francis, ex-coach of Ben Johnson, believes the ratio for sprinters should be at least 1/1. Strong quadriceps (and hip flexor muscles) enable a 400 meter runner to maintain high knee lift in the final 100 meters of the race. In addition to weight training, hills and stairs can help to achieve the correct balance between hamstrings and quadriceps.
- For maximum gains in strength, pause when the muscle is in the fully contracted state. This is called the "peak contraction" technique and can be used in the leg extension (quadriceps) exercise or the leg curl (hamstring) exercise. Also lowering slowly in the negative phase is beneficial; see paragraph below. For more reps after fatigue sets in, some body builders use the "slipping" technique, i.e., remove some weights after each set of reps.[8] (Similarly, the great Zatopek would do 200 yard repeats when he tired of 400 yard repeats.)
- The negative phase in weight lifting is an eccentric contraction whereby the muscle contracts as the muscle *lengthens*. In a concentric contraction, the muscle *shortens* as it contracts against gravity or a resistance. Examples of eccentric contractions are:
  - In the calf muscle in the toe raise exercise (standing with toes on the edge of a step) when the heel drops below the step
  - In the quadriceps muscle in the reverse (backward) direction of the leg extension exercise
  - In the hamstring in the reverse direction (downward) direction of the knee flexion exercise
- Eccentric strengthening. The slowing down in the reverse direction (negative phase) against gravity or a resistance has an important benefit for injury protection

and injury recovery. It is the eccentric contractions in running that cause the sore muscles since less muscle fiber is involved in eccentric contractions compared to the concentric contractions. Therefore, the eccentric contractions in weight lifting condition the muscles to prevent sore muscles and injuries during running. This is the main reason for the usual recommended practice of lowering (in negative phase) the weight slowly in four seconds and raising it in two seconds.

- When joints of the arms are stressed under load, it is important to not lock out the joint of arms (i.e., fully straighten) to prevent possible dislocation or tearing of the joint. For example, this could occur in the chin-up exercise.
- Always lift with good form. Do not use momentum by not pausing between the lowering and lifting phase. This cheating reduces growth of muscle. However, there is the following exception. See Power Boost below describing explosive lifting mainly for advanced sprinters to develop explosive strength by stimulating the fast twitch muscles.
- Taper in the weeks before competition.

See Dintiman, Ward, and Tellez,[3] who list detailed daily strength and power programs for beginners, intermediates and advanced athletes.

Power Boost

Strength by itself will not result in speed. To have speed, you must have power, i.e., work done in unit time or force times distance per second. Power comes from neuromuscular (fast twitch muscle) development as opposed to hypertrophy (bulking up). Hypertrophy is increase in muscle size due to high intensity low reps weight training: working to near failure or absolute failure in some cases. Neuromuscular development refers to stimulation of the central nervous system to recruit fast twitch fibers. This can be accomplished by sprinting, sprint drills, fast hill running, plyometrics, and explosive lifting of weights. See two examples in the table below.

There are two methods of explosive lifts both with explosive positive phase, or *lifting as rapidly as possible*, after lowering the weight in one to two seconds:

1. Using momentum, i.e., with no pause between negative and positive phase.
2. Not using momentum, i.e., with a slight pause between negative and positive phase, but not "bouncing" the weight.

The momentum method is more apt to lead to injury due to higher loads. The no-momentum method is safer. But both require excellent form. Explosive weightlifting should be done only by experienced lifters with a good base in view of the risk of injury.

To run fast, train fast; similarly, lifting weights fast will assist you in running faster. Moving heavier weights fast has similar advantages to plyometrics. First the muscle is stretched under load, storing energy, and immediately it is contracted (shortened), producing a maximum force. For example, in the bench press arm exercise as the weight is lowered the muscle is stretched; then without pause at the bottom the weight is lifted explosively causing shortening of the muscle. This results in the greater number of muscle fibers called into action and simulates closely the situations like sprinting, high jumping and long jumping. The stretching during the lowering stimulates the nervous tissue within the muscles. To take advantage of this favorable stimulation and to achieve maximum force, do not pause between the stretch of the muscle and its shortening contraction phase. Do the quick movements in the lifts that involve the same muscles and movements used in your sport. Do some of your repetitions with lighter loads and maximum speed to warm up. To develop maximum power for sprinters, move weights as heavy as the speed of movement will allow. Exercising fast with light weights does not develop as much power but is safer.

NUMBER OF REPS, SETS, AND LOADS

Feel the Burn

You will be developing muscle if you feel a burn in the muscle exercised. The burn is caused by an accumulation of lactic acid and hydrogen ions in the fatiguing muscle. Therefore, for good results, feel some discomfort in the targeted muscle in one or more sets for each exercised muscle. More progress comes with more discomfort. Advanced or elite sprinters often go to *muscle failure* or exhaustion where another rep is impossible. But results can be obtained with little or no discomfort. There may be some soreness the next day, particularly in the beginning of the season. Train again when soreness has gone away. But soreness reduces each time you work out.

Number of Sets/Week and Volume/Session

There is only a small gain of a few percent in doing three sets instead of two, or in training three times per week compared to two. But the more competitive may feel the extra effort is well worth it. This is the law of diminishing returns. A similar effect must exist when doing running repetitions.

The volume or total number of repetitions in a weight training session can vary between 60 (small) and more than 100 (large).

Number of Repetitions in a Set

The number of repetitions (reps) in a set depends on the objective whether it be strength, power, or endurance. See the table below for nine different objectives. Hence, reps could vary between about three and 30. The lower reps are for elite sprinters and the higher reps are for long distance runners. The usual for most runners is 10 to 15 reps in a set. Older athletes should do fewer reps per set and only two sets, to save the joints.

The table below shows the reps, rest between sets, and the load as a percent of one single repetition maximum (1RM) depending on the specific objective, or what is meant to be developed. The number of sets is not defined as this depends on the individual and their experience, energy, etc., but there are normally two or three sets. The %RM is approximately correct as this varies somewhat for each exercise. For details on fast twitch type IIa and type IIb, and slow twitch type I fibers see the chapter on Physiological Principles. Basically, the slow twitch are activated at the beginning of the set and as the muscle fatigues, the fast twitch IIa are activated and lastly the super fast twitch IIb fibers.

Table 19.1 Weight Training for Specific Development

Develop	# of reps	Rest between sets	% RM	Train to
Olympic lifts, speed squat, speed press, etc., (explosive strength)	2-4	3 minutes	95-90	Muscle failure*
Type IIb fast twitch fibers (Jacob[11])	4-6	2 minutes	90-85	Muscle failure*
Type IIb and IIa fast twitch fibers (Jacob[11])	6-12	1-2 minutes	85-70	Muscle failure*
Strength and muscle size	5-8	2 minutes	90-80	Muscle failure*
"Speed strength" (McFarlane[12])	6 -10	1-3 minutes	90-75	Muscle failure*
Power (explosive)****	8-12	3-5 minutes	40-50	Muscle burn
Strength and muscle toning**	10-12	1 minute	60-65	Muscle burn
Slow twitch type I fibers and strength endurance*** (McFarlane [12])	12-20	45-90 seconds	70-50	Muscle failure*
Slow twitch type I fibers and strength endurance***	12-20	30-60 seconds	60-35	Muscle burn

* Train to failure or exhaustion in at least one set. These lower reps, high load sessions are normally for elite or advanced sprinters.

** A good range for middle distance runners to work in.

*** For middle and long distance runners.

**** Usually up to five sets for more experienced lifters.

Typical reps per set for sprinters, middle and long distance are as follows:

- A typical four months in the off-season for competitive sprinters, training to muscle burn, is as follows:

Table 19.2 Off-season Weight Training for Sprinters

Month	Reps per set	Sets	%RM
1	10	2	65
2	8	3	70
3	6	3	75
4	5	3	80
4	3-4	3	85 advanced or elite sprinter

- 800 meter runners should exercise in the range of 8 to 12 reps per set to build speed power. Milers should exercise in the range 16 to 20 to build speed endurance.
- Long distance runners would benefit from exercise in the range of 20 to 24 reps per set to build speed endurance.

Generally, most athletes with the purpose to build strength should exercise at 10 reps per set and two to three sets. In the beginning, when starting weight training, choose the amount of weight that you can lift 10 times while feeling some fatigue at the end of the set. Initially it is a matter of trial and error. After a few sessions, when you can lift 12 of the same weight, add a few pounds and start again at 10 reps. Continue with this procedure. After a month or less, progress to eight reps if the main purpose is to build strength.

Athletes with the purpose to build endurance should start above 14 or more reps per set and every week increase the number of reps.

NUTRITIONAL SUPPLEMENTS FOR STRENGTH TRAINED ATHLETES

Melvin Williams[14] stated in 1993,"There is little or no scientific evidence supporting positive effects on muscle growth, body fat reduction, or strength enhancement in strength-trained athletes for the following supplements: arginine, lysine, ornithine, inosine, choline, carnitine, vitamin B12, chromium, or omega-3 fatty acids. However, with creatine supplementation preliminary research indicates increased power in short-term, high intensity exercise; and increased weight gain, either contractile or water."

IMPORTANCE OF ABDOMINALS AND BACK MUSCLES

Ideally, the abdominal muscles should be exercised every day. At least 25 to 50 (in sets of 25) crunches are recommended by many coaches. It is the quality that counts. I have found a total of about 4x20 reps on the abdominal machine and 2x15 reps on the back machine about three times/week will maintain my strength. Some serious runners are doing up to 350 reps of various forms of abdominal exercises to work all areas. The abdominal muscles support your posture during running and help prevent back problems and other injuries. With strong abdominals and lower back, you can run tall and hence your stride is longer. Herb Elliott, the famous Australian runner, used to say, "You run from your stomach [meaning abdominals]." You rarely see a fast runner with a paunch.

If your back gets tired during the normal crunches, use the following pelvic tilt exercise: Lie on your back with hands at your side, with knees bent and feet flat on the floor. Press the small of your back into the floor while contracting the abdominals. This, at the same time, exercises the lower back. Hold briefly; this is your good running position. Relax and arch the back gently, keeping the buttocks and shoulders always in contact with the floor. Repeat until tired. You can do a lot of these without tiring.

POPULAR WEIGHT TRAINING EXERCISES

Specificity of exercise is important. Some of the more popular exercises are listed below followed by a brief explanation and some precautions:

All exercises are important but the essential ones for runners have bold numbers.

	Exercise	**Main Muscles Developed**
1.	Hanging leg raise	Lower abdominals, hip flexors Alternatively, support yourself on your for arms on the parallel bars apparatus.
2.	Leg raise	Lower abdominals, hip flexors
3.	Crunch	Upper abdominals
4.	Sit-ups	Upper abdominals, hip flexors, lower back
5.	Twists using pole	Obliques
6.	Side bends	Obliques
7.	Squats	Thighs, hips, maximus gluteus, maximus medius, lower back, calves
8.	Leg press machine	As for squats
9.	Lunges	Thighs, hip flexors, gluteus muscles, calves
10.	Step-ups	Thighs, hips, calves
11.	Toe raises on edge	Calves, Achilles of step

12.	Knee extension	Quadriceps machine
13.	Knee flexion	Hamstrings machine
14.	Dumbbell running	Biceps, tricepsmotion
15.	Chin-ups or pull	Biceps, chest, shoulders down machine
16.	Bench press	Chest, shoulders, triceps
17.	Bicep curl	Biceps
18.	Upright rows	Trapezius, upper back, biceps
19.	Bent-over row	Biceps, forearms, upper back, shoulders
20.	Straight-back, stiff-leg deadlift	Gluteus maximus, adductors, hamstrings
21.	Parallel dip	Triceps, chest, shoulders, back
22.	Six other popular machines	For hip flexor. For adductor. For abductor. For back. For abs. For seated or standing calf, raise.

Some brief explanation and precautions are given below for these exercises. For more details, refer to strength and body building books, such as[5,6,7,8,10].

1. While hanging from a bar, bring knees up to the chest and return to vertical. Alternatively, raise straight legs together, or one leg at a time. Alternatively, support yourself on your forearms on the parallel bars apparatus.

2. Lie on your back on the floor or on an incline bench. Grasp a stationary object from behind. Raise legs to nearly vertical position and lower slowly. Legs should be slightly bent at the knee to protect the back.

3. Lie on your back on the floor, arms crossed on chest, with knees bent, feet flat on the floor, or rest lower legs on a bench. Bent knees prevent lower-back strain. Raise your head and shoulders slowly from floor with back stationary. Lift only until you feel the abdominals contract. Hold for one or two seconds. Lower slowly. Crunches done properly do not strain the back. When you can do two sets of 12 to 25 slow crunches, consider holding a five pound or heavier weight on your chest.

4. As for crunches above, but raise head and shoulders toward knees until arms touch knees. Pause, when sitting up to prevent bouncing. Return slowly. Alternatively, exercise the obliques by twisting on the way up so left (right) elbow touches right (left) knee. For those with a weak back, try the pelvic tilt. See the section above on "Importance of Abdominals and Back Muscles".

5. Stand with feet shoulder-width apart. Place a pole on shoulders behind the neck, with hands on the pole, and rotate trunk first to the left and then to the right while keeping the hips stationary.

6. From a standing position, lean over to the left as far as possible and then to the right. Dumbbells can be used hanging from the arms.

7. Perform squats with weights on the shoulders or held at the front or with dumbells held with arms hanging. Feet are shoulder-width apart. Keep feet flat on floor. Keep torso as upright as possible. Slowly lower until upper and lower legs form about a 110-degree angle. Squats can be hard on the knees; never go into a full squat. Do half squats. Quarter squats are the least stressful. Also do not bounce at the bottom since this can lead to injury of the back and/or knees. Wear a weight-lifting belt when lifting more than 75% of your body weight to protect your lower back and abdomen from injury. A bar on the base of your neck is not recommended as it presses down on the spine; it is preferable to use dumbells in the hands. Exhale on rising. Many body builders stop just short of lockout of the knees. Alternatively, the leg press machine (#8 below) is safer all round. At night in my bedroom, I often do one-legged half squats or quarter squats with or without dumbells; this is a great exercise and convenient.

8. The leg press is safer than squats and produces less stress on the back but is slightly less effective. Don't bounce. Some trainers and coaches say don't lock the knees in the extended position. Do this exercise instead of squats when back or knees are sore. Male Olympic sprinters can do about 5 reps of the leg press (or half squat) at two and a half times body weight (2.5:1). Female and lower caliber sprinters push much less, so be careful.

I have heard that the leg press relieves some stress on the periformis after running.

9. Lunges are one of my favorite exercises; they feel good, increase strength and flexibility in legs and hips, improve balance and increase stride length. With a bar resting on shoulders, or with dumbells in each hand, step forward with front leg bending until the thigh is nearly parallel to the floor and front knee is over big toe (not beyond); the front thigh should never be parallel to floor. The back leg is bent with back heel off the floor. Keep your back and head as vertical as possible. Eyes look slightly up. Hold for 2 to 4 seconds. Return to upright and step forward with the other leg. All motions are smooth and controlled. Do 10 to 12 "reps" with each leg. Initially, in training, start with no weights. Do this exercise also without weights to improve flexibility. I often do about two dozen (12 on each leg) alternating legs and without weights.

Note that dumbbells are preferred to the bar on the shoulders since they are easier to balance. The bar is also uncomfortable and stressful on the spine.

10. With loaded bar resting on shoulders or dumbbells in hands (preferably) step up on a box with right foot then left foot. Pause at the top. Step down on left foot followed by the right. Repeat starting with left foot and continuing the sequence. That is one rep. Do two sets of 10 to 12 reps. Initially, for a few sessions start with no weights.

Note that dumbells are preferred to the bar on the shoulders (see above).

11. Do toe raises with dumbells in each hand. Stand with toes on a step. Raise up on the toes, hold for 2 seconds and lower slowly. To work all calf muscles do reps with toes straight ahead, then with feet turned out and then with feet turned in. This is also a good exercise to strengthen the feet and prevent plantar fasciitis. Initially, for a week or two start without weights or with light weights.

The above can more safely be done on the flat as there is a possible problem in over-stretching the Achilles on a step; see Chapter 12 on "Stretching".

12. Raise the legs slowly and smoothly. Lock the knees when the legs are fully extended. Pause to give complete control during the slow negative movement. Don't bounce or kick the weight. If there is pain in and around the knee during the exercise or days after, stop and consult the experts[5]. Some trainers say don't lock the knees in the extended position.

As an alternative for those with a knee injury, the straight leg/knee locked lift while lying on the back, is recommended to avoid stressing the knee. Attach a weight to the ankle and lift the straight leg while sitting or lying on your back.

13. Curl the lower leg close to the buttock. If this is difficult then the weight is too heavy. Don't use momentum. Pause when the hamstring is fully contracted. Lower slowly.

14. With feet shoulder-width apart and with dumbbells (5 to 10 pounds) in each hand, duplicate running arm motion in a fairly fast motion. Arms move straight ahead and straight back. Do about 30-40 arm movements (20 per arm) without weights-less reps for heavier weight. Also, a fast-relaxed arm action is recommended *without* weights particularly for sprinters; do intervals with exercise time equal to race time. The latter has been around for many decades but few are practicing this valuable exercise. It is very effective to learn perfect form and relaxation at a fast pace and also to prevent arm fatigue. (I learned of this in the early 1950's from Lloyd Percival, founder of the Sports Institute in Toronto). With or without weights, these are both excellent exercises for runners.

15. The chin-up, and pull-down machine are equivalent[6]. For the chin-up: grip the bar with palms facing away from the body; start and finish each rep with arms nearly fully extended but not quite (i.e., no locked joint). For the pull-down, grip the bar with palms facing away from the body; pull the bar down until it touches the top of your chest; return the bar until arms are nearly fully extended.

16. Vary the flat and incline position with each workout to broaden the muscular adaptation[6]. Plant feet firmly on floor. Hands are shoulder width apart. Press the bar up until arms are nearly fully extended. Lower slowly.

17. Stand with feet shoulder width apart. Grasp the bar with *palms facing outwards*. Start with the bar hanging at arms length in front of you. With elbows stationary lift up the weight until it is at shoulder level. Concentrate on contracting the biceps while curling smoothly upward. Pause. Slowly lower until arms are nearly fully extended. If you have to "jerk" the bar up, the weight is too heavy. Repeat.

18. Upright rows are somewhat similar to the above. Stand with feet shoulder-width apart. Grasp the bar with *palms facing inward* and hands about six inches apart. Start with the bar hanging at arms length. Lift the bar straight upward to shoulder level keeping the back as straight as you can. Pause at the top. Lower slowly. Repeat.

19. Place your right knee and right hand on a bench keeping your back horizontal. The vertical left arm holds the dumbell. The left leg supports nearly all the weight. Lift the dumbell straight upwards. Lower slowly. I use a 35-pound dumbell.

20. Grasp weighted bar with overhand grip. Stand with feet shoulder width apart with bar hanging from straight arms. Lower bar to the top of the feet by bending at the hips and bending knees slightly. Keep arms and back straight throughout. Lower bar until a mild stretch is felt in the hamstrings. Various sources vary on how far to lower the weight. To protect the back, it is best to bend no further than 30 to 45 degrees from vertical. With knees still bent lift the bar by extending at hips until standing upright. Extend knees at top if desired.

21. Grasp the parallel bars firmly and push up raising the body until the elbows are nearly locked out. Lower the body slowly as far as possible between the bars. Repeat until fatigued.

22. Most good weight gyms have these machines. Exercise on these machines is highly recommended for runners. Consult your local trainer for their use.

PREVENTATIVE MAINTENANCE WEIGHTLIFTING FOR DISTANCE RUNNERS

For distance runners who do not have access to a gym, or prefer to exercise in their home, the following preventative maintenance weightlifting is recommended. All the major muscles are exercised and will assist in preventing injuries. You will be surprised how much you can achieve in 10 minutes.

- *Start with lighter weights and/or less reps* in initial weeks. Use low weight and high reps. Two sets normally two or three times per week.
- *Squats.* With light dumbbells, do 20 to 30 reps. This is most conveniently done with the large Swede ball between your back and a wall. Or do 12 to 15 single leg half squats.
- *Calf.* Use your body weight or light dumbbells and lift off the floor with your toes, or if the Achilles tendon is healthy stand on the edge of a step and lift your body. Stop before the muscles get overly tired. Weak calves often are the cause of Achilles tendonitis.
- *Lunges.* With light dumbbells, do 12 to 24 lunges.
- *Adductor and abductor muscles* can be exercised with rubber tubing attached to a solid leg of a bed, chesterfield or dresser. This works well with high reps as the load is relatively light. See the section on Rubber Tubing Exercising.
- *Leg extension and leg curls* are recommended. At home, you can do these with rubber tubing or a 5- or 10-pound weight strapped to above the ankle. Do at least 20 reps. To exercise the quad, the straight leg raise while lying on the back is preferable to the leg extension sitting in a chair, as it is easier on the knees.
- *Dumbbell running motion.* See exercise 14 above for details.
- *Crunches or sit-ups.* See exercises 3 and 4 above.

STRENGTH EXERCISES MORE SPECIFIC TO RUNNING

Regular strength training with weights has many advantages for runners, but it can be shown that most of the usual exercises are not specific to running. For instance, nearly all are done while sitting or lying down. To be specific, the body should be vertical and the angle between the lower and upper leg should be small when the load is applied since this is the case in running. The Olympic lifts, the snatch, power clean, and jerk, are close to being specific and have the advantage of being explosive. But they are too complex for the average runner, hence with more possibility of injury, and also very time consuming to learn properly. Plyometrics is a much more practical alternative to develop speed and power.

Owen Anderson in an excellent article from *Peak Performance* titled, "Weight Training For Runners: be more specific," recommends some strength exercises that are specific to running, i.e:

- One-legged hops in place (I recommend no more than 2 sets of 12 for beginners)
- One-legged squats (use the big Swede ball; quit when legs are tired)
- Speed bounding (emphasizing the horizontal component)
- Hill training (this works nearly all muscles)

These are good recommendations. I would add the deadlift (see number 20 above), rubber tubing exercise for the quadriceps and hamstrings, and speed bounding for height as well.

REFERENCES

1. Pfitzinger, P., The Weight Debate, *Running Times*, May, 1996.
2. Sparks, K., and Kuehls, D., *The Runners Book of Training Secrets,* Rodale Press, Emmaus, PA, 1996.
3. Dintiman, G., Ward B., and Tellez T., *Sports Speed,* Human Kinetics, Champaign, IL, 1998.
4. Dintiman, G. B., *How To Run Faster,* Leisure Press, New York, NY, 1984.
5. Fahey, T. D., *Basic Weight Training,* Mayfield Publishing Co., Mountain View, CA, 1989.
6. Sprague, K., *Sports Strength,* Perigee Book, New York, N.Y., 1993.
7. Schwarzenegger, A., *Arnold's Bodybuilding for Men,* Simon and Schuster, New York, NY, 1981.
8. Sprague, K. and Reynolds, B., *The Gold's Gym Book of Bodybuilding,* Contemporary Books, Inc., Chicago, IL, 1983.
9. Sandrock, M., *Running with the Legends,* Human Kinetics, Champaign, IL, 1996.
10. Dobbins B. and Sprague K., *Gold's Gym Weight Training Book,* Berkley Books, New York, NY, 1981.
11. Wilson. J., Muscle Fibers- An In Depth Analysis Part 2, www.abcbodybuilding.com/magazine/musclefiberspart2.htm
12. McFarlane, B., Hurdling, *Canadian Track and Field Assoc.,* Ottawa, ON, 1988.
13. Ryun, J., Developing a Miler, *Track and Field Quarterly Review,* Summer 93, Volume 93, No. 2.
14. Williams M., H., Nutritional Supplements For Strength Trained Athletes, *Gatorade Sports Science Institute, 47,* Volume 6 (1993), Number 6.
15. Lopez, V., An Approach to Strength Training For Sprinters, *Track Technique,* Spring 1991, 115.

USA
65
704
USA
65
334
5

CHAPTER 20

Don't look back! Something might be gaining on you.
Satchel Paige

TACTICS

GENERAL

On the dull windy day of the 800 meter finals at the 1995 World Masters T and F Championships in Buffalo, the flags were flying straight out. Hence, in nearly all age groups, there was great reluctance to take the lead; this resulted in very slow times. These bad conditions gave me a bad case of nerves–a lot of adrenaline. My race strategy was to take the lead all the way, and I stuck to this in front of the huge roaring crowd. My main competition in this 65 to 69 age group was Unto Matteson from Finland. If one was afraid of size, then he would strike fear into the heart. He hung on close behind until 500 meters, making a courageous effort in spite of the fierce wind on his large frame (see photo on the left). Here, I made an extra effort to sail with the wind and pulled away to break the only 800 world record of the day in 2:14.33. But here is the interesting part of this story. At the South African Worlds two years later, he sent me a message with one of his Finnish friends, "Tell Earl I was dead at 400 meters." We had gone through the first 400 in 64 seconds. He had not followed his race plan or his race plan was faulty.

Even world-class athletes and world record holders can get foiled in their favorite event–getting boxed in, etc. Sebastian Coe in the 800 final at the Munich Olympics was the fastest in the world in this event and in superb condition. Coe hung at the back of the field sometimes running out in lane three. Around the final turn, he was at the back of the pack. Ovett sprinted into the lead but Coe was too far back in spite of passing four runners with his famous powerful kick, finishing in a humiliating second to his rival Ovett.

Many of the recommended tactics are common sense, but in the heat of a race, they are often forgotten due, initially, to excess adrenaline, or later in the race, from fatigue, which dulls the mind.

The best tactic is to be well prepared with a solid amount of training. Your body must become accustomed to the race distance and race pace over a long period of time. Hence, training is more important than tactics. But have a race plan, rehearse it mentally, and stick to it. Also, avoiding some of the mistakes in tactics can often make the difference between victory and defeat.

PLANNING

Plan ahead. Decide on your race strategy well in advance of the race. Never leave the planning and strategy until after the race starts. In an important indoor mile race in front of a large crowd, a good friend and I agreed just after the start of the race to take turns on each 160m lap. In the end, he out-kicked me. In retrospect, I should never have ventured into this sharing of the lead, for at the time, I suspect I was probably in better condition.

Planning your tactics requires evaluation of the answers to the following important questions.

From Paul Schmidt[1]:

- *"What is the level of the athletes own performance capacity?*
- *What is the estimated performance level of the rivals?*
- *What are the tactics normally employed by the rivals?*
- *If there are heats what is the estimated time to qualify for the next round?*
- *If split times are to be called out what are the split target times?"*

From Harry Wilson[2]:

- *"Which are most dangerous in a short fast finish?*
- *Which prefer a fast pace from start to finish?*
- *Which are best with a long finishing burst?*
- *Which runners will never lead and like to come from behind?"*

In addition, how does the race strategy change depending on adverse weather? Also if your coach is to attend what are the signals, if any, from the coach? This is important because if there is any confusion in the signals, this leads to confusion and loss of focus as happened to me in an important race. If you do not have information on your rivals' favorite tactics then learn as much as possible from observing them in the preliminaries.

Visualize to realize. Once the race plan has been decided, this should be mentally rehearsed for many days ahead. I found this useful also for the long hurdle races, e.g., which lead leg over each hurdle. During the warm-up, the athlete should be undisturbed to warm up alone. You may have to say, "Sorry I'm concentrating on the race, please talk to me after." At this time, review and visualize your final race strategy. Make sure split times, etc., are super clear because with fatigue there could be confusion, as I have found.

Tactical Rules For Sprinters

- ***Running the curves.*** A sprinter should "sling-shot" out of the curve (accelerate) particularly in the 200 meters. As much as one or two meters can be gained on the curve over a runner inexperienced with this technique.

TACTICS FOR MIDDLE DISTANCE RACES

- ***Break from lanes.*** In the 800 meter race, after the break from lanes, at about 100 meters from the start, cut in gradually. Cutting in sharply lengthens the race by several meters.
- ***Running the curves.*** Always try to accelerate slightly on coming out of the curve; this is particularly effective in the indoor 200 meter or smaller tracks in view of the sharper curves. In the early 1990s, I watched Eammon Coglan run, or should I say float the indoor mile on the 11-lap wooden track at the Copps Coleseum in Hamilton, Ontario. He is truly the master of the boards and not long after, he broke the mile world indoor record for 40-year-olds in 3 minutes 58.3 seconds. I noticed a slight acceleration as he came out of each curve. This tactic can result in fractions of a second gained on every lap. There are the following reasons why this is so effective:
  - There is a natural tendency to slow down on the curves as there is extra effort involved in overcoming the centrifugal force. Also the inner stride is now shorter.
  - By accelerating slightly out of the curve the runner in the lead widens the gap between those strung out behind since they are still going slower on the curve.

Be aware of this tactic to gain valuable distance. If you follow behind the leader who uses this tactic, you too have to accelerate out of the curve to maintain close contact. If you are the leader then this tactic is most useful. Therefore, whether a leader or a follower, practice this acceleration during training. Be prepared. However, it is a slight acceleration, not a surge that wastes energy.

- ***Passing on a curve.*** Always pass on the straight to save energy.
- ***Running wide*** in the second lane or even the third lane to avoid being boxed in should be avoided. "The difference between running in the first lane and lane two is about seven meters in an 800-meter race" (Schmidt[1]).

- ***Surging.*** Any sudden acceleration before the final straight will detract from the finishing kick and results in early energy drain. An unexpected move could throw the opposition off but this should only be done if it is practiced during training. I have even seen elite runners make the mistake of a surge in mid race, to come up from behind to pass the leaders. This acceleration is like accelerating in a car; it takes extra energy to accelerate. Save your surge for the final kick.
- ***Taking the lead*** when there are runners of equal capabilities in the field will drain your energy more than those who follow. Unless the leader is in a class of his or her own, i.e., far superior, they will rarely win. "It is worth about 1 to 1.66 seconds per lap (400m) to follow closely behind your rival in a middle distance race" (Chester Kyle (1979) quoted by Noakes[3]). "In middle distance track events, about eight percent of the runner's energy is used in overcoming air resistance" (Dr. Griffiths Pugh quoted by Noakes[3]). This is quite believable: I have noticed a big advantage (a saving in energy) in a race or in training in following about one meter behind. There would be even greater advantage in windy conditions. If you can be so fortunate as to have a competitor of nearly equal ability and pace then it is wise to follow closely behind and save yourself for the finishing kick. This indicates the great advantage of a "rabbit" in a race. However, to avoid a slow race and possibly being outsprinted in the final straight or being boxed in the superior runner has to take the lead.
- ***Pace judgement.*** Beware of a runner who doesn't know the pace and takes off too fast. If you know your rival's capabilities, you shouldn't get sucked into following. If it's an unknown athlete, just remember you know your pace–stick to it. Training with the watch develops pace judgement.
- ***Maintain race pace.*** When following a competitor at your target race pace, do not linger behind if they slow down. Maintain your target pace. (I have been fooled by this a couple of times.)
- ***Shadowing.*** Remember that some runners who are used to leading by a large margin could get distressed with someone shadowing them (following close behind).
- ***"Break away*** from the strong finishers preferably before the last third of a race if you do not have a strong finish" (Wilson[2]).
- ***Avoid losing contact*** with the leaders–leaving too much to make up in the finishing kick. Hold a position where you can respond quickly.
- ***"Avoid looking around for rivals"*** (Schmidt[1]). This reminds me of the mile race of the century between Landy and Bannister in the Empire Games in Vancouver in 1955. Landy made a classic blunder in looking back to his left while Bannister passed on his right.
- ***Have a strategy based on your strengths.*** For example, avoid setting a slow pace when those behind have a much faster finishing kick.
- ***Run close to the rail.*** If leading after rounding the final curve, do not leave a space between you and the rail for an opponent to sneak through. (I nearly had a

bad experience in an U.S. Masters Indoor Championship 800 meter race against the great Jim Sutton of the USA in April 1992. Coming off the final bend after leading the whole race, I had a slight lead and started to run out from the rail (a bad habit). He started to move into this opening. I didn't know he was there but fortunately, I moved back to the rail, which forced him to go around. This negated his usual devastating famous finishing kick, and I won by 0.02 seconds (by a nose you might say).

- ***Avoid being boxed in*** particularly in the back straight, with less than 300 meters to go and in the last curve for home (Schmidt[1]).
- ***Passing.*** A good place to pass is just before the final curve; this forces any rival to run wide to pass you before the straight. However, you may have to pass here if your rival is running too slowly, but only if you can maintain a fast pace to the finish.
- ***The run for the tape.*** "Once the athlete sets off on a long run for the tape he or she must not let up" (Wilson[2]). This means knowing your capabilities well. Most athletes cannot maintain a fast kick with more than about 150 meters to go.
- ***In event of a strong headwind***, if possible avoid being the lead runner. When running alone, you will automatically be working hard against the wind; when the wind is with you, increase the effort and you will fly. I have used this strategy successfully in cross-country and other races; see for example the opening paragraph. When the wind is with you imagine yourself as a big sail and step up your efforts. A small increase in effort at this time will result in big gains. Another way to look at it is to maintain an "equal effort" when running with or against the wind.
- ***Think fast but relaxed.*** If friends urge you during your race to "relax" this does not mean to slow down. Think relaxed *but fast*. (This comment has confused me in the past to my detriment).
- ***The unexpected tactic*** is probably better left to the Olympic athletes, like suddenly picking up the pace midway through the race, or with 500 meters to go in a track race or wasting energy with frequent surges.
- ***The finishing burst*** in the home straight is essential with a strong arm action and must be decisive. If you can pass a rival decisively by surprise in the final straight this is worth about 0.5 seconds in shock value. There is a momentary pause equal to about two steps advantage before your opponent can react. Or conversely, you can get about two steps behind if someone suddenly does that to you. It is the one who reacts first who has the advantage. This I learned from bitter experience. However starting your kick too soon will negate any advantage.
- ***"Use active arm action"*** in the home straight (Schmidt[1]). But, aim for rapid turnover rather than long strides; this means shorter and slightly higher arm stroke.
- ***Run through the finish line.*** Do not reduce speed before the finishing line; run through it for at least five meters.

TACTICS FOR LONG DISTANCE RACES

- ***Know the course*** well to perform well. Visualize the course as much in advance of the race as possible; the course will seem shorter. Without knowing the course, it is difficult to plan your strategy. Mentally rehearse your strategy before the race over this terrain. Your strategy should also account for weather conditions.
- If nothing else, ***know the last kilometer*** or mile and for the marathon the last few miles. From there, it is possible to eke out your remaining energy to arrive with little or no energy left at the finish and to maintain your focus. I have found it most disconcerting if you are confused about how far it is to the finish. If someone passes you near the end, you should know if there is enough energy left to fight off your rival in the remaining distance.
- ***Use your stop-watch*** to guide you as to how far you've gone and how far to go to the finish.
- ***Conserve energy***. You will need extra energy if near the finish there is a big hill, or you will be running against a stiff wind. You need to save something extra for this or your time will be extra slow over this portion of the course.
- ***Hill train***. If you know weeks before the race that the course is hilly, it is important to do some hill training to prepare. But no hill training the week of the race.
- ***A mile (or landmark)*** at a time. When the going gets tough think of short-term goals – concentrate on running to the next hill, to the next block, the next landmark, or run each mile one at a time. This will help to divert your mind from fatigue.
- ***Never start too fast***; this is particularly important in the marathon. In the middle distances, the common rule of thumb is: two seconds too fast in the beginning will result in about four seconds slower overall time. Common sense must overcome the adrenaline burst. Pick up the pace in the latter part of the race.
- Be aware that ***mile markers are sometimes inaccurate.***
- ***Hill strategy.*** Run uphill and downhill with the same effort or breathing rate as on the flat. I have found this strategy works well on moderately steep hills but not in the case of very steep hills.
- ***Wind strategy.*** When running with a heavy wind at your back, imagine a sail on your back. Think, "This is a lot easier now." This is the place to pick up the pace and to pass other runners. Rehearse this strategy in your mind before the race. See discussion under **strong headwind** in the section above on Middle Distance Races.
- ***Use different muscles when tired.*** When tired change your form to use different muscles. I have used the following technique when tired: Run for 100 meters or between telephone poles with slightly increased stride. For the next 100 meters, use a quicker slightly shorter stride. The next 100 meters, use a combination of the previous with a slightly longer and quicker stride. Then repeat the cycle. This is also useful to relieve boredom.

- ***Relieving boredom*.** Also to relieve boredom and get your mind off the tired feeling, try the following: It is a good strategy in distance races and very encouraging to pick off slower runners along the way. Reel them in. Set your sights and concentrate on the next approaching landmark or the back of a runner you are reeling in. Alternatively, count ten steps of your left leg on each finger; after going through ten fingers you have eaten up roughly 250 meters. Then repeat the process.
- ***When fatigue sets in*,** concentrate on good form. Concentrate on your foot placement, then your stride, then your arms, your shoulders, neck and face. Think relaxation and good form into all these areas.
- ***Company*.** Run with someone of your own pace. Misery likes company. Run preferably behind someone (the bigger the better) to save energy on wind resistance. But don't dally if they slow down.
- ***Catch-up strategy.*** What to do if you encounter a surging competitor and you want to stay with him or her? When you pull up to your rival, he or she takes off again. Never respond immediately. You can use less energy than your rival if you catch up more slowly than they took off. For example, say your rival creates a gap of 10 meters in 10 seconds after his surge. You should make up this 10 meters gap in a slower time, say 15 or 20 seconds. Never try to catch up on a hill. However, if you catch up to your rival at the bottom of a hill, he or she might make the mistake of surging on the hill.
- ***No wasteful surges in mid race.*** Be careful not to waste energy on a sudden acceleration, passing on a hill, or just after reaching the top of a hill. Generally, it is best to save your move to near the end of the race if you have the speed.
- ***Passing.*** Catch up to a competitor over a long distance but always pass decisively. A runner not to be feared can be passed at an even pace.
- ***Keep close*.** Do not let your opponents get such a big lead that it cannot be made up.
- ***Mantra chanting.*** To maintain focus on a run repeat a phrase to yourself. The phrase should coincide with your running step. Each syllable or word should be associated with a leg movement. For example each word is uttered with a step in the following; "Relax, smooth, breathe easy," or "I will not tire." Each syllable is uttered with a step in the following: "Re-lax, effort-less." Come up with your own phrase.
- ***Competitors breathing*.** When you pass a runner, listen to his or her breathing. In this way, you can learn a lot about their condition, according to the famous ultra marathoner Arthur Newton[3]. If your rival is breathing exceptionally hard after a hill compared to yourself, this indicates poorer condition. However, there are normally heavy breathers and there are heavy breathers due to extra fatigue. Normally, you can tell the difference. When the latter passes you or vice versa, it is safe to discount this individual; he is no doubt suffering from poor conditioning and/or too fast pace, previous workouts that were too intense, or too close to the race, etc. Not his or her day. Therefore, it is safe to pull ahead of the tired heavy breather. I

have used this technique successfully in an 800 meter race against a faster and much younger rival.

- ***Encouragement.*** If you or your coach can arrange it, have your club or teammates cheering you on near the end of the race. This can give you a definite boost and may be a demoralizing blow to your opposition. (I know this helps you to dig deep and to tap those hidden energies.)

REFERENCES

1. Schmidt, P., Tactics in Middle Distance Running, *Track Technique*, Winter 1993-122.
2. Watts, D., Wilson, H., and Horwill, F., *The Complete Middle Distance Runner,* Stanley Paul and Co./Century Hutchinson Ltd., London, England, 1986.
3. Noakes, T., *Lore of Running,* Human Kinetics Publishers, Inc, Champaign, IL, 1991.

CHAPTER

21

There is a great similarity in the physical prowess of the young and old. For example, a 9-year-old world champion runner and a 63-year-old world champion runner are equally fast.

YOUNGER AND OLDER COMPETITORS

Firstly, a champion is not always the winner. A champion is one who defeats his inner fears, runs a personal best, who takes defeat gracefully, who has the respect of his fellow athletes, who has given his utmost, and who comes back from a serious injury or illness. The following will assist to achieve these goals and perhaps a gold medal or more.

Most of the preceding chapters are applicable for all ages, since 9-year-olds and 90-year-olds are bound by the same physical and mental principles. However, the following are some of the finer points and precautions for younger and older athletes. In both cases, gradualness and under-training need to be stressed.

YOUNG COMPETITORS

General

The habit of regular physical activity should be encouraged at an early age to provide a good foundation of health for their adult years. Ideally, there would be participation in a variety of sports to give good muscle balance. Running, in particular, develops the cardiovascular system and provides a good base of conditioning for most other sports.

Sport is a mini-life experience, teaching cooperation, self-control, dealing with success and failure, persistence, hardship, taking orders, compassion, etc. In short, the character-building opportunities are immense.

Although the basic training principles are the same for young and old, young children need to be treated differently than adults because of:

- Slower adaptation to anaerobic work
- Longer recovery required
- Less strength
- Less mental drive
- Less tolerance to heat
- Possible effect on growth

It is important that the parent not put extra stress on the athlete. Having fun needs to be emphasized. Do not encourage the "killer" instinct but encourage achieving a personal best. Then the child will perform at his or her best.

In addition to the following see also Reference 1, *The Competitive Runner's Handbook*, by Glover and Glover which describes for preschool to late teens the practices and recommendations developed by the famous New York Road Runners Club.

Precautions

Precautions are necessary in growing children to prevent growth problems from possible injury, especially in contact sports. The American Academy of Pediatrics Sports Medicine committee "discourages intense activities such as long distance running and weight training until the rapid growth of early adolescence has been completed"(Kidsports[4]).

Also Pat McInally[3], an expert on kids in sports, states: "Too much stress at an early age on bones, muscles and particularly the knee and ankle joint could hamper or stop their running and limit their participation in other sports in the future."

Children are not able to cope with extreme temperatures as well as adults and take more days to acclimate to heat. Ensure that water intake is adequate in hot weather before, during and after exercise. Also, dehydration is more likely in the unfit.

Preschoolers

From 2 to 6, low-key competition, such as short sprints, are safe. Keep it fun. Do not force them into it just because Daddy or Mommy loved to run. At this age, they love games and playing with their friends.

Ages 6 to 12

Between 6 and 12, a good sport to develop running fitness is soccer. My son, Tyler, when age 8 played only soccer and without running training, ran exceptionally well in cross-country.

Six year olds could take part in 400m to 800m aerobic type fun runs. Typical upper limit for cross country races is 2K for seven, eight and nine year olds; and 2.5 to 3K for 10, 11, and 12 year olds, and 4K for 13 and 14 year olds. In cross country training 8 to 12 year olds a volume of about 3000 metres of race pace intervals is reasonable near the end of the season. Before competing in track races at least one season of cross country training is recommended.

I believe that for any of the above distances, a good aerobic base should first be established followed by more aerobic with some fartlek and speed play and hills. Interval training can be done by those in good condition but with limited volume (avoid high mileage), and with intensity always low and increased gradually over many weeks. No race should be attempted without adequate preparation. After all, the basic principles apply for all ages.

Emphasize participating, having fun. A friend of mine, John Faulkner coaches many children of this age in running. He stresses the fun, running games, and relays with their friends and thus is able to tap a lot of their energies. His own children are exceptional runners–a boy 7, and a girl, 9 (in 1999). They are not allowed to run longer than 5K races, although they are eager to. At this age, only one or perhaps two 5K races per year should be allowed, even for exceptionally fit youngsters. A 5K fun run is generally the upper limit for the more experienced older runners in this age group.

Dr. Larry Greene and Dr. Russ Pate in *Training for Young Distance Runners* recommend: "Youths should wait until they are at least 12 to 14 before formal training on a regular basis, i.e., three to seven days [seven is too frequent in my opinion] a week for several months at a time. However, to avoid mental and physical burnout it is important not to subject children of this age to an adult training schedule." I would recommend a maximum of five days per week in training for the 12- to 14-year-olds.

Dr. Richard Mangi, et al[5]., state, "The principles of aerobic training for children are the same as for adults, i.e., three or four sessions per week lasting at least 30 minutes. Young hearts are able to undergo aerobic training; ,e.g., nine year olds have the highest aerobic power per pound of any age group." Girls grow quicker than boys and at about age 12 and 13, have been known to have exceptional stamina.

Arthur Lydiard[6], the famous New Zealand coach, in *Running With Lydiard* states: "Seven seems to be the age from which boys and girls can absorb large amounts of long distance running without any undesirable effects." "It is sustained speed (anaerobic running), not sustained running (aerobic), that does the damage."

See, also the popular Web site www.kidsrunning.com (organized by *Runner's World/* Rodale Press). It offers training advice, running programs, running news and other info, all for kids who love to run. You can even write to the many coaches for advice.

Ages 13 to 16

After puberty, the body can stand more serious training with the guidance of a knowledgeable coach.

Weight training. Light weight training (no maximum lifts) if supervised by qualified people can begin at puberty (12-14 for girls and 14-16 years for boys). Dr. Lyle Micheli[2] (and others) warns that weights *before* adolescence, i.e., *before* puberty, poses the threat of injury, especially to their growth plates (weaker areas at the ends of bones where growth takes place). However, injuries that do occur are due to poor technique and lifting too much weight (i.e., unsupervised lifting). Weight exercises involving the use of medicine balls, or body weight are safer, such as push-ups, chin-ups, pull-ups and sit-ups. However, Ken Sprague[12], owner and operator of the original Gold's Gym for a decade, states: "Properly conducted supervised weight training will not damage bones, inhibit growth, or injure joints in pre-adolescent children. Scientific studies overwhelmingly conclude *supervised* weight training is safe for children, and this conclusion is supported by the American Academy of Pediatrics." Sprague mentions that there is more stress from a young basketball player landing from a height of 18 inches than from the 500-pound leg press.

An excellent reference for parents wishing to involve their children in strength training is the book *Strength Training for Young Athletes* by Kraemer and Fleck[14].

Running training. Smith, Smith and Smoll[4] state: After age 14 or 15 for the average male and 13 to 14 for the average female, there is a striking increase in the body's ability to use oxygen and there is the greatest increase in muscle mass. Therefore, after these ages, the body is ready to respond to intense endurance or (aerobic) training. However, it is at this time also that the growth plates are most vulnerable to injury. Fortunately, they point out that this type of injury is rare in sports. The following quote by Coe and Coe[13] in 1983 suggests that over 14 is a safe age to start interval training: "There is evidence from French sources that *interval training* can have an enlarging but *thinning* effect upon the artery walls if performed by young athletes. It is presumably for this reason that in East Germany it is restricted to those over 14 years of age."

Many track and field clubs in Canada have 13- and 14-year olds training reasonably strenuously but well supervised. For example, the Saugeen Track and Field club is a very successful club in Port Elgin, Ontario with a great deal of spirit and camaraderie. Picture a small resort town with huge maple trees by a great lake, often windy, and you have the location. I can still see myself running along the frozen windy shoreline in daylight and dark. Many dedicated male and female athletes from Port Elgin and the surrounding farm district have gone on to the USA on athletic running scholarships after years of training here. The disciplined cross-country training in the fall on soft hilly trails, often steep, has contributed greatly to their distance training success. The lack of an indoor track facility is compensated for somewhat by indoor strength and circuit training in the winter. Also, the consistent outdoor aerobic training at night under very cold, windy conditions in the winter has no doubt contributed to mental and physical toughness.

Earl and Geordie Farrell have provided disciplined and scientific coaching in this highly respected club for over 24 years. They stress the importance of coaching the individual not the age, as each athlete matures at a different rate and with their own strengths and weaknesses. 13- and 14-year-olds are not allowed to run more than 40 minutes at a time. At this age the program is seasonal, 2-3 phases per year for 10-15 sessions in each phase, with focus on play, running form and modified events. Serious training begins after physical maturity. At 15-16, there is emphasis on speed and strength endurance (anaerobic), as well as aerobic endurance, plus lots of lactic threshold runs. Mileage is about 30-40 miles per week.

A 10K race is generally the upper limit for the more experienced older runners in this age group.

Late Teens

For distance runners (older high school and university athletes), training consists of five phases in the Saugeen Track and Field Club described above: fall (focus on cross-country), winter (aerobic endurance, strength and circuit training), spring (strength endurance, hill and trail running), early summer (speed endurance and early competition), late summer (peaking/competition). At 17 and up, the mileage at the Saugeen club is about 50 miles per week for most athletes at end of high school years (sometimes involving some early morning aerobic runs).

For runners with less experience, talent or enthusiasm for the sport the mileage could be as low as 25 miles per week. Generally the marathon is not recommended until 18 years or older so that growing bones are not affected. Since the basic training principles apply to young and old–the training advice in this book is applicable to teenagers but allowance needs to be made for less strength and experience compared to adults. Also recognize that growing takes away energy from training and racing.

Although racing times are impressive for juniors (16 to 19 year olds), their training volume and intensity is still considerably less (about 15% to 20%) than for similarly talented seniors (over 20).

Relative Intensity of Running Training vs. Age and Gender

Depending on age and gender, the intensity of running training from hardest to easiest is closely as follows: senior male, junior male and senior female, junior female. Note senior is taken as 20 to 30 years and junior as 16 to 19 years inclusive.

THE IN-BETWEEN YEARS

Endurance levels and muscle strength peak at between 20 and 30 years of age, then slowly decline as we get older. Muscle fibers normally decrease a few percent each decade after age 30. After age 35, the *average* person loses half a pound of muscle and gains a pound of fat every year (Dr. Ken Sparks[7]). This doesn't have to be. With consistent exercise (particularly intense exercise), one can reduce muscle loss considerably as one ages. For example, I have maintained my same weight and body fat over the past 10 years. Research has shown that VO_2max declines by about 10% per decade in most individuals but with intense exercise only about half as much. This is largely due to the decrease in maximum heart rate with age.

OLDER COMPETITORS

This section applies to all masters who desire to keep young and stay injury free, but particularly to those over 65.

General

For an athlete to succeed as one gets older, the biggest secret I can suggest is to age more slowly than your rivals. Second in importance is to avoid injury through preventative maintenance. Third, is attention to retention of intensity in the training. Fourth, is more recovery and more rest. Fifth, is proper rest, and proper diet with fewer calories consumed. These and more are discussed below.

It's Never Too Late

There are many examples of master runners who started at a late age and became world champions or showed rapid improvement. I started at age 56 and broke an indoor 400 meters record a year later after a 33-year layoff from running. Scott Tinley and Ken McAlpine[9] reported good examples of improvement in older athletes: e.g., a research study showed a 16% increase in VO_2max (aerobic capacity) among a group of 70 to 79 year olds after only a 13-week training program. Another study reported by Kohrt et al[15], indicated an improvement between 12% to 36% in VO_2max for 53 men and 57 women, previously sedentary for 2 years, and age 60-71. This was achieved by endurance exercise training over a 9- to 12-month period with no significant difference between men or women. Similarly, Coe and Coe[13] reported a 20% improvement in maximum oxygen uptake in 55- to 70-

year-old men, previously inactive, after only an eight-week period of training. An often reported study at Tufts University in Boston indicated a 174% improvement in leg strength for a group of 90-96 year olds volunteers after eight weeks of high intensity strength training; gait speed improved by 48% and thigh muscle increased by 15% (Fiatarone et al[8]). Amazing! All of this indicates it is never too late in life to start and make big gains in fitness, by *gradual progression*, and even to become a champion.

Aging Slower Than Your Rivals

Longevity–this is one of my favorite subjects. Who wouldn't be interested in living longer and at the same time enjoying higher quality living as well. I have given some speeches on this subject, and I sometimes say, "I am going to show you how you can easily earn a million dollars or more and it's practically guaranteed." This really keeps them awake. The secret I let out eventually is that by leading a healthy active life as described below, you will live decades longer. Therefore, you will collect your pension for an extra 20 or 30 years; for example, 25 years at $40,000 per year is one million dollars. Of course, having the right parents helps tremendously but the following will take many years off your biological age and thus add decades to your life.

Your real (biological) age depends on your everyday habits of eating, sleeping, drinking, physical and mental exercising, stress level, or smoking, etc. You can determine your present "real age" from the Internet Web site realage.com; this is based on thousands of individual studies, so it has some validity.

With proper diet and exercise, you can prevent chronic disease, increase your life span by decades and at the same time add more life and speed to your years. The following is a short course in longevity, covering all the essentials:

- ***Avoid atrophy.*** Slowing down is more due to rusting out (atrophy) than aging. Get rid of that "I'm slow because I'm old" thinking.
- ***Supplements.*** To fight the free radicals that damage body cells, take anti-oxidants, vitamin E, C, A, selenium, and grape seed extract daily. Older women may benefit from estrogen replacement. I highly recommend grape seed extract. It is a very powerful antioxidant enhancing the activity of vitamins C and E, helping you to live longer, fight heart disease, stroke, high blood pressure, and with other advantages for athletes; see "Magic Supplements" in Chapter 15.
- ***Improve immune system.*** Take supplements daily (e.g., echinacea, beta carotene, zinc, vitamin C with bioflavonoids) and plenty of fruits and vegetables to improve the immune system. Strengthening the immune system is the preventative maintenance way to prevent disease. Wash the hands frequently. Take aspirin (up to

300mg) each day (or every other day) to thin the blood and reduce possibility of stroke and heart attack.

- ***Get adequate sleep*** and keep a regular sleep routine. Also, if possible, take a 15-30-minute nap every day; a nap too long or too late in the day will interfere with sleep at night. Eat dinner about five hours before bedtime. A late dinner or alcohol or coffee late at night robs you of deep sleep and contributes to aging. Also poor sleep results in less release of growth hormone with consequent lowering of the immune system.
- ***Memory*** deteriorates with age in the normal individual at an increasing rate along with other bodily functions. Memory is a skill requiring constant practice. Your mind needs exercise similar to the body. To reduce memory loss, keep the mind active, for example, with chess, reading, taking courses, writing, memory games, memorizing poetry and intelligent conversation. Physical exercising makes for a more alert mind due to more oxygen to the brain. Also a person with active mind habits survives longer.
- ***Balance*** deteriorates with age and causes falls, but can be improved by exercise. Exercise makes for stronger bones, so that a fall can be more easily survived. One good balance exercise is: stand on one foot for 30 to 60 seconds in bare feet, then the other foot.
- ***VO_2max*** declines by about 1% per year in healthy untrained men but endurance exercise can reduce this decline considerably or even increase oxygen capacity. See "It's Never Too Late" above.
- ***Proper diet.*** Eat plenty of fruits and vegetables for the vitamins and minerals and fiber that they contain. Have a high carbohydrate, low protein, high fiber, low fat diet with minimum sugar and salt. Drink lots of water. Eat fish at least twice a week for the Omega 3 fatty acid to minimize stroke, heart disease and heart arrhythmias (irregular heartbeat).
- A ***high-alkaline, low-acid diet*** (See Chapter 15) will assist to combat heart disease, cancer and other maladies. It also combats lactic acid which accumulates more rapidly in older athletes for any given speed during anaerobic exercise.
- ***Minimize coffee and alcohol*** (it prevents glucose production in the liver and robs energy). Definitely rule out smoking.
- Research indicates that ***under-eating*** improves longevity. Smaller meals result in less energy expended in digestion. Allow enough time between meals for digestion; the digestive system should not be constantly at work.
- Take good care of your ***dental health***, e.g., dental checkups and daily flossing to prevent plaque formation that leads to periodontal disease. With gum disease, bacteria travels through the body causing or worsening health problems; and it has been linked to heart disease, stroke, diabetes, pneumonia and other respiratory diseases.

- ***Activity creates energy.*** It is strange but true that *"activity begets energy"; the more you exercise the more energy you will have.*
- ***Continue regular exercise,*** preferably with some intensity. Exercise is probably the most important of all anti-aging habits. Studies have shown that longevity is affected more by exercise than by your genes. *"Use it or lose it."* It is the intensity, more so than the volume, that keeps you young.

  However, master runners and especially master competitors above 60 need to be cleared for exercise activity by a physician. Then, after the body adapts to the activity, "A trained 60 year old can outperform 95% of untrained 20 year olds" (Dr. Richard Mangi[5]). I have a better quote of my very own: " A very fit 70-year-old can have a better sex life than a not-so-fit 50-year-old."
- ***Stretch*** (t'ai chi, yoga, Pilates exercises, etc.) regularly and ***weight train*** every other day to compensate for the loss of flexibility and strength with age. As we age we lose fast twitch fibers and motor neurons, and hence muscle power (see "Principle of Neural Training" in Chapter 5. Therefore, it is very important to compensate by doing reasonably intense weight training, and rapid intensive movements on a regular basis.
- ***Massage*** on a regular basis will increase joint mobility and flexibility, and strengthen and maintain normal elasticity in muscles.
- ***Hanging from a bar*** for a minute or less, or chin-ups on a regular basis will help to compensate for the compression of the spongy discs in your spine, which occurs with age. This exercise will maintain your posture and prevent shrinkage in height. I call this the "Poor Man's Stretcher." For the more affluent, there is the inversion or tilt table, where you can hang upside down.
- ***Avoid stress*** as much as possible. This has to do with proper attitude and controlled emotions in daily life situations (such as in driving a car, etc.). Practice transcendental meditation. Avoid the hectic, driving, uptight (Type A) behavior. Pace yourself, keep calm. Don't over-react or over-dramatize a situation.
- ***Maintain a positive outlook, and a sense of humor. Laughter has many health benefits.***
- ***Be optimistic.*** We control the quality of our days within us. Positive thinking makes good things happen.
- ***Active positive associates.*** Associate and train with young people and other active, positive people as much as possible.
- ***Have a yearly check-up*** with your doctor.
- ***Have goals and challenges*** in your life. A champion should have goals. Age should be no barrier to new knowledge and experience.
- ***Work on your emotional and spiritual health*** just as you work on your physical health. This involves keeping the mind active, for example, with chess and other games, bridge, reading, studying, and relaxing with music or painting. A healthy, contented mind contributes to a healthy body.

Avoid Injury

As we age, we lose suppleness and strength in the muscles. The joints, ligaments and tendons are less lubricated and more rigid. Also, there is wear and tear due to repetitive training. A chronic injury, particularly the knees, can finish your running career. Aim for the long term. Therefore, preventative maintenance is recommended to compensate for the above.

Injuries are more prevalent as we get older and recovery could take 25% to 50% longer. During my running days at high school and university, I was never injured but at age 70: four times. Injuries can slow you down drastically. For example, at age 71 (year 2000) my injuries (to plantar tendon, hip and broken toe) resulted in training mileage reduced to about 60%, indoor track workouts reduced to about 40% and only three outdoor track workouts. This caused a 4% slower time (+2.5s) in the 400 meters, and 7% (+10s) slower time in the 800 meters compared to the previous year. At this age a fit world class middle distance runner should experience only about 1.5% decline/year.

Therefore, the older athlete has to be extra cautious. The following will assist in preventing injuries:

- ***Stretch*** at least once a day and do weight training two to three times a week. Be careful how you stretch. The wrong stretch or position, or too intense can cause injury.
- ***Plyometrics*** are recommended to strengthen tendons and ligaments. Start easy with skipping and progress from two-legged to one-legged exercises. (In 1999, I had four injuries requiring physiotherapy. These were all for ligaments and tendons and could have been prevented with prior plyometric training.)
- ***Massage.*** Get into the habit of regular massage particularly after a hard training session. Regular massage will also prevent loss of elasticity from intense training over several months. Self massage is beneficial, too.
- ***Practice preventative maintenance.*** For example, massage the plantar tendon daily and do toe raises on a flat surface every other day to prevent plantar fasciitis. If you are a hurdler, do the trail leg exercise daily (as I often do) to strengthen the groin/adductor. Do exercises with surgical tubing to strengthen the quadriceps, hamstring, adductor and abductor muscles.
- If a muscle has been previously injured, make sure to do ***strength training*** for this muscle to keep it strong to prevent reoccurrence of the injury.
- ***Visit the chiropractor*** once a month to ensure your body is in alignment. This will assist to prevent future injuries. ***"Rolfing" massage*** will realign the fascia. The fascia (covering muscles, tendons, ligaments and practically all body parts) is as important as the bones for body support.

- ***Cross-training.*** Pay immediate attention to a small injury. Back off, do cross-training, and get massage or physiotherapy.
- ***Training shoes.*** Wear proper training shoes and replace frequently when worn. Rotate your running shoes frequently.
- ***Run on soft surfaces.*** (trails and grass) as much as possible; avoid running on the roads and sidewalks. The trails are also more relaxing and with more oxygen and less smog.
- ***Increase the cross-training*** and reduce the running training. Cross-training will assist in keeping keep your body in balance by working different muscles.
- ***Adapt gradually.*** Be wary of anything new and different in your training. Your muscles take time to fully adapt—usually six weeks.
- ***Prevent dehydration.*** In exercising during hot weather, ensure adequate fluid intake as this could be more of a problem in the older athlete, especially the unfit older athlete. See the "Water" section in Chapter 15.
- ***Take longer to recover.*** This means more time between repetitions in interval training and more rest days.
- Slow down with any sign of ***abnormal fatigue*** or breathlessness.
- Above all: ***avoid "too much, too soon, too fast."*** Think of this before each training session. Be gradual in all training.
- ***Study Chapter 16 on "Injury Prevention and Causes."***

Effect of Age on Race Results

It is of interest to examine the decline in performance with age from the Age-Graded Tables[10] as this information gives some idea of what to expect as you age.

The results in the table below are based on an examination and plotting of approximate world record race times for 100 meters, 800 meters, mile, and marathon vs. age from these Age-Graded Tables. These race times, if achieved, would produce 100% age grading.

Table 21 • Average Decline in Performance, Percent Per Year, vs. Age

Event	Between 35 to 65	Between 65 to 80	Between 85 to 90
100m	0.73	1.1	1.7
800m	0.88	1.5	2.8
Mile	0.94	1.5	2.7
Marathon	1.1	1.5	2.7

The following is seen from the table:

- There is more drop-off in speed with age as the race distance becomes longer, i.e., sprinters decline least with age and marathoners decline the most.
- From plots of race times vs age it is seen that the there is a more rapid decline after about age 65 +/- 2 years and then an even greater decline after about age 85 +/- 2 years. The more rapid decline with age is to be expected. However, it appears there is something biological happening after about age 65, and then again after about age 85.

Some highly fit world-class individuals decline at a much slower rate up to age 65 and even delay the more rapid decline until several years past 65. For example, my 800 meters indoor time stayed nearly constant from 2:16 at age 60 to 2:17.05 at age 69; the latter indoor race in Boston 1998 was age-rated at 102%. For most less fit, less motivated, individuals, the decline in performance up to about age 65, would be much greater (perhaps 1.5 or 2% per year) rather than 0.7 to 1% per year since these latter numbers are based on world record performers.

Why do sprinters decline in speed or performance at a significantly slower rate than middle distance or marathon runners? The reason for this is strength, flexibility and intensity of exercise. Strength is speed. As we age we lose strength and flexibility. Sprinters are working more on maintaining their strength and flexibility than middle and long distance runners so they decline in speed at a slower rate. In addition, it is well known that to stay young, intensity of exercise is more important than volume. Sprinters have it all since they also have a higher percentage of quality training, i.e., higher intensity than middle distance and marathoner runners, with regular weight training, plyometrics and lots of drills for flexibility.

It is important to age more slowly than your rivals. All this indicates the importance to stay younger and to live longer by regular weight training, frequent stretching and maintenance of intensity and fast movements in training.

Also, don't focus on race times from past years but focus on your particular age graded percentage from the Age-Graded Tables[10]. If you improve in age-graded percentage as you age, you know you are getting better–like an old wine.

Training Older Competitors

Quantity and intensity of training is usually reduced as one ages. For older runners ***less*** (intensity and quantity) is often ***more*** (meaning improved times or improved age-graded percentage). However, it is important to maintain the intensity (quality) although it is reduced. This is what keeps you young and maintains race times as you age. "To stay fast you have to train fast" (Sparkes[7]). To slow down the fast twitch muscle deterioration: speed training intervals, hill training, weight training, fast arms drill, fast feet drill, fast step-ups and fast strides are required on a regular basis. See "Principle of Neural Training" in Chapter 5.

Dr. Jack Daniels[11] recommends "a program for older distance runners that minimizes 'intervals' [VO_2max in his book] and 'repetitions' [anaerobic/speed in his book] and focuses more on threshold training [lactate threshold] as the main quality emphasis. There is no doubt that "tempo" training is less strenuous than VO_2max or speed training but a middle distance runner and a sprinter in particular need the anaerobic/speed type of training even though reduced with age.

As a rough idea of how much to reduce the quantity and intensity during each year–assume the percentage is the same as the percentage reduction in performance from Table 21. So, a 60 year old compared to a 40-year-old of the same caliber (same age-graded percentage) would do about 20 x 1% less intervals. This fits in roughly with my experience in training with younger runners. Also, an 80-year-old compared to a 60-year-old of the same caliber would do about 20 x 2% fewer intervals if they were national class (above about 80% age graded) but about 20 x 3% fewer intervals if they were average club runners. These are only a rough guide. Your body, and particularly the recovery of the heart, will normally dictate how many repetitions are practical. See also the "Recovery" section below. When form drops or speed deteriorates, it's quitting time. Your workout should be such that the cool down is not a big chore and you are not overly tired the next day. Also, as you get older, it becomes even more important always to under-train rather than over-train. Payton Jordan, with many world records in master's sprints and ex-head coach at Stanford University recommends under-training also for sprinters of any age.

Adapt Gradually

Adapt slowly over a longer period of time than when you were younger. Remember it takes about six weeks for a training effect to set into the body. For instance, leaving most of your speed training to the last two or three weeks is a big mistake. All training – stretching, running, and weight training – has to progress gradually over the sharpening period leading up to your main race. Sudden changes lead to possible injury.

There is the "Principle of Diminishing Returns" (see "Principle of Training" in Chapter 5) that you should be aware of. Initially, progress is rapid and as the weeks go by progress is slower and slower. I estimate the last six weeks in the 12 week sharpening schedule will be required to improve by only two or three percent.

Warm-ups and cool downs need to be gradual, too. Start your warm-up with a walk. In doing fast strides or accelerations and speed intervals, the first and last repetition should preferably be slower. Finish your cool down with a walk. It is very important not to stop suddenly after some hard intervals or a race. Keep moving as the heart is working harder for about a minute without the benefit of quick body movement to assist blood flow; also some movement prevents blood pooling in the legs.

See the Principle of "Anti-Shock" in Chapter 5. This deals with avoiding sudden changes in body temperature and sudden changes in heartbeat during and after intense exercise for safety sake. Also, it is wise in doing intense intervals always to train with one or two others, especially during extreme weather conditions; this is particularly pertinent to older runners.

Recovery

As you age, recovery becomes more important. More rest is required to prevent injury and burnout.

- Start the next interval when you *feel ready* to restart. If recovery between intervals is too long, the speed is too fast, or the run is too long.
- Older athletes should take longer to cool down gradually.
- Instead of one rest day per week, you may have to take two or three. Your body will normally tell you how much.
- Instead of the old routine of hard (one day)/easy (the next day), you may have to go to hard/easy/easy days as you get older.
- Taking one easy week per month (periodization) becomes more important as one gets older.
- After the summer track season rest two or three weeks before cross-country or base-training. Another one or two weeks rest is required after the indoor season and the start of the outdoor season. During these rest periods, do cross-training mainly but retain speed with fast strides. Note complete inactive rest of a month could take three months or more to come back to where you left off; so this is not recommended. Also, a year off could require two years or more to come back to near the previous fitness (or to your previous age graded percentage).
- See also Chapter 13 on "Recovery," which lists many essential recovery tips.

INTERVIEW WITH MULTI WORLD RECORD DISTANCE RUNNER ED WHITLOCK

I had the pleasure to interview Ed Whitlock in the fall of 2004. Ed Whitlock's somewhat unorthodox training regime has resulted in several world records and many Canadian records from 1500m to marathon including Canadian marathon records in age group 60-64, 65-69 and a world marathon record in age group 70-74. At age 73 his great age group 70-74 world record of 2:54:48 (age graded 99.98%) in the Toronto Waterfront marathon in 2004 being the most recent. His training apart from frequent distance races involves running long and slow each day exclusively in a 300 meter paved circuit in his [scenic] local cemetery.

Preparation for 2004 world record marathon. For his preparation for the latter 2004 marathon he had 50 training sessions of 3 hour duration in an 11 week period; at one point running 13 days in succession for 3 hours; this is staggering even to contemplate. This indicates the energy of a much younger man. He was adapting his body to his marathon time, and running these sessions without liquid intake. It was a case of running for time not distance or pace. But his pace did improve from about 9 minutes per mile early in the year to just over 8 minutes per mile about 6 weeks before the marathon. On the other days in the 11 weeks he ran shorter long runs or was racing or took a day off. He is convinced this training regime at age 73 was responsible for his good performance. [I have to agree.] He states, "Doing the odd long run would not do it for me." What dedication and perseverance! Also I believe one of Ed's great assets apart from his genes is his tolerant and understanding wife.

Injury prevention. To prevent injuries in spite of a long run every day on hard graveyard pavement he consciously tries to run in a manner that minimizes impact, by running relatively slow with short strides, minimizing bouncing. [I feel his light weight of 112 pounds would also greatly assist to reduce the stress of pounding during running compared to much heavier runners.] But he also looks after his feet, having usually about 10 pairs of running shoes on the go. He states it is OK to feel tired or stiff during the training period. But not OK to have specific pain while running; then it is necessary to stop, rest and get therapy until better.

Physical characteristics. My American friends are always interested in physiological aspects like size and weight, etc. Ed is 5 foot 7 inches tall [looking much taller], weighing an efficient 112 pounds with a resting heart rate in the low 50s, and by treadmill test at age 70 a maximum heart rate of 168 and a VO_2max of 52.8 ml per minute per kg. I thought his VO_2max would be higher. But there is no doubt his running economy is superb as evidenced by his smooth racing style. When racing, his long strides seem to devour the track.

Lifestyle. To provide energy for the frequent long runs Ed sleeps 7. 5 hours and is " heavy on carbohydrates and vegetables, more "bad" fats than recommended, and relatively light on meat." There was some tiredness after the 3 hour long runs for a short time but this did not interfere with normal activities.

YOUNGER AND OLDER COMPETITORS

Marathon strategy. Briefly his marathon strategy is as follows: Plan well ahead. Firstly develop a good base of running. Gradually increase the weekly mileage and get as many long runs as possible. About a week before the marathon decide on a realistic (not optimistic) finishing time objective based on the training and any recent race times. Calculate the pace per mile depending on how the course is marked in miles or kilometers. Adjust the pace on the day depending on climatic conditions. [Keeping track of the pace for 42 kilometres while tired is a mental feat in itself. Also his race pace judgment must be uncanny as he finished more than one minute faster than his targeted finishing time. Amazing!] Ed states, "Don't go faster than this target pace until at least 20 miles." [This is the hard part for most marathoners where they start to slow down drastically, but Ed is able to increase his speed based on his many long runs.] I have observed in many local distance races it is usual for Ed to increase the pace gradually a long way from the finish.] Also he recommends drinking as much as you lose in perspiration and take in some calories by sport drink or other means.

Training philosophy. Ed believes more is better: the more training you do, the longer you train, and the higher intensity the better you will race. To compensate for Father Time he runs more mileage each year and it is obvious that this is working for him. Basically he trains the same all year round to be always ready to race. But certain races have more importance and training tails off after such an event.

Apart from the long runs there are many normal athlete activities missing in his training. For instance there is no stretching, no weight training, no massage, no supplements, no mental training, no cross training and no hill or interval training (to save his Achilles). He feels "better to spend the time running," and states in good humour, "I'm already wasting enough time on my hobby." He uses frequent races to develop speed and toughness and on occasion a fartlek session a day or two before a race. Ed has some natural speed as evidenced by some gold medal performances in the 1500m at the World Masters Championships in Hanover Germany in age group 45-49 (4:09.6), and in Gateshead England in age group 65-69 (4:54.0).

All in all he would recommend his training regime to other distance runners but believes as I do every one must find what works best for them. One must find their own best way. Ed Whitlock, a true inspiration to young and old, has certainly found his best way.

The Final Word

Here's hoping your healthy/active lifestyle and the Ultimate Race Director allows you to collect your million dollars (in pension) but more importantly allows you to run on and on and on with a smile on your face. Also, if you slow down a lot, look on the bright side. You are still able to run and besides, you get to train with (or coach) your grandchildren.

REFERENCES

1. Glover and Glover, *The Competitive Runner's Handbook*, Penguin Books, New York, NY, 1999.
2. Micheli, L., *Sportswise*, Houghton Mifflin Co., Boston, MA, 1990.
3. McInally, P., *Moms and Dads, Kids and Sports*, Charles Scribner's Sons, New York, NY, 1988.
4. Smith, N. J., Smith, R., and Smoll, F. L., *Kidsports*, Addison-Wesley, Reading, MA, 1983.
5. Mangi, R., Jokl, P., and Dayton, W., *Sports Fitness and Training*, Pantheon Books, New York, NY, 1987.
6. Lydiard, A., *Running with Lydiard*, Hodder and Stoughton, Aukland, New Zealand, 1983.
7. Sparks, K., and Kuehls, D., *The Runner's Book of Training Secrets*, Rodale Press, Emmaus, PA, 1996.
8. Fiatarone, M., Marks, E., Ryan, N., et al, "High intensity strength training in nonagenarians. Effects on skeletal muscle." *JAMA* 263: 3029-3034, 1990.
9. Tinley, S., and McAlpine, K., *Sports Endurance*, Rodale Press, Emmaus, PA, 1994.
10. Compiled and edited by World Assoc. of Veteran Athletes (WAVA), "Age Graded Tables", *National Masters News*, Van Nuys, CA, 1994.
11. Daniels, J., *Daniels' Running Formula*, Champaign, IL, 1998.
12. Sprague, K., and Sprague, C., *Weight and Strength Training for Kids and Teenagers*, Jeremy Tarcher Inc., Los Angeles, CA, 1991.
13. Coe, S., and Coe, P., *Running For Fitness*, Pavilion Books, London, England, 1983.
14. Kraemer, W., and Fleck, S. J., *Strength Training for Young Athletes*, Human Kinetics, Champaign, IL, 1993.
15. Kohrt, W. M. et al, "Effects of gender, age, and fitness level on response of VO_2max to training in 60-71 yr olds", *J. Appl. Physiol. 71*(5): 2004-2011, 1991.
16. Bortz, W.,M., *We Live Too Short And Die Too Long*, Bantom Books, New York, NY, 1991.

CHAPTER 22

A chapter for athletes, musicians, dancers,
and all who aspire to greatness:
inspirational quotes from great men and women,
and some by my humble self.

Inspirational Sayings

DREAMS and GOALS

If you've set a goal for yourself and are able to achieve it you have won your race. Your goal may be to come in first, to improve your performance or just to finish the race – it's up to you.

Dave Scott

Motivation is about goal setting. No goal—no motivation.

Earl Fee

The future belongs to those who believe in the beauty of the dream.

Eleanor Roosevelt

Dream of things that never were and ask why not.

George Bernard Shaw

Man is so made, that whenever anything fires his soul, impossibilities vanish.

La Fontaine

I hope I may always desire more than I can accomplish.

Michelangelo Buonarroti (1475-1564)

Discipline is the bridge between goals and accomplishment.

Anon

What you get by achieving your goals is not as important as what you become by achieving your goals.

Zig Zigler

You have to want to be the best before you can even begin to reach for that goal, and you have got to be prepared to sacrifice a lot to get there.

Billie Jean King

HABITS

Motivation gets you started. Habit keeps you going.

Jim Ryun

A winner knows where he is going and how he is going to get there with good consistent habits. A loser dreams of getting there, hopes to get there, knows not the how, and has developed bad habits.

Earl Fee

Order is half of life.

German Proverb

Successful people are successful because they form the habits of things that failures don't like to do.

Albert Gray

First we form habits and then they form us. Conquer your bad habits or they will conquer you.

Rob Gilbert

Power includes the capacity to overcome deeply embedded habits to cultivate higher, more effective ones.

Stephen R. Covey

The greatest people will be those who possess the best capacities, cultivated with the best habits.

James Harris

It's not what you do once in a while, it's what you do day in and day out that makes the difference.

Jenny Craig

We are what we repeatedly do. Excellence then is not an act but a habit.

Aristotle

Working hard becomes a habit, a serious kind of fun. You get self-satisfaction from pushing yourself to the limit, knowing that all the effort is going to pay off.

Mary Lou Retton

First declare and say what you would become, then study and evaluate what actions and habits you need to do to get there, then establish the associated consistent habits, and eliminate the detrimental habits. If you follow through you become a champion.

Earl Fee

EXCELLENCE

The quality of a person's life is in direct proportion to their commitment to excellence.

Vince Lombardi

Excellence is in the defeats. Give attention to the defeats and excellence will follow.

Perry Paxton

The secret of living a life of excellence is merely a matter of thinking thoughts of excellence. [I have tried this principle in living a life of luxury. No matter how hard I think thoughts of luxury it just doesn't work for me.]

Charles Swindall

The excellence is in the details.

Gregory L. Sullivan

We are each like a sleeping giant tied down with many shackles and not knowing or exerting the hidden powers within us. But these powers if awakened and aroused can break these bindings and compel us to gigantic feats not dreamt possible.

Earl Fee

PERSEVERANCE AND ADVERSITY

He who stops being better, stops being good.

Oliver Cromwell

When a person trains once, nothing happens. When a person forces himself to do a thing a hundred, or a thousand times, then he certainly has developed in more ways than physical.

Emil Zatopek

Winning is not everything but the effort to win is.

Zig Zigler

The harder the conflict, the more glorious the triumph.

Thomas Paine

I am willing to put myself through anything; temporary pain or discomfort means nothing to me as long as I can see that the experience will take me to a new [higher] level.

Diana Nyad

There are always two choices—two paths to take. One is easy. And it's only reward is that it's easy.

Anon

Welcome the task that makes you go beyond yourself.

Frank Mcgee

Undertake something that is difficult; it will do you good. Unless you try to do something beyond what you have already mastered, you will never grow.

Ronald E. Osborn

All things are difficult before they become easy.

John Norley

A gem cannot be perfected without friction, nor a man perfected without trials.

Chinese Proverb

No pressure, no diamonds.

Mary Case

Each experience makes us bigger. The setbacks and grieves we endure help us in our marching forward.

Henry Ford

Search for the seed of good in every adversity.

Og Mardino

A certain amount of opposition is a great help in a man. Kites rise against the wind.

John Neal

If the dance of the run isn't fun, then discover another dance, because without fun the good of the run is undone, and a suffering runner quits sooner or later.

Redohe

The whole of what we know is a system of compensations. Each suffering is rewarded; each sacrifice is made up; every debt is paid.

Ralph Waldo Emerson

If it's easy it's probably been done before.

Howard Schatz

It's never too late to be what you might have been.

George Eliot

There's no easy way.

Allan Wells (1980 100m Olympics champion)

If I have made any valuable discoveries, it has been owing more to patient attention, than any other talent. [In other words not patient waiting, but patient hustling.]

Isaac Newton

Expect problems and eat them for breakfast.

Alfred A. Montapert

Genius is nothing more than a great aptitude for patience.

Georges L. Lederc

In the struggle between the stone and water, in time, the water wins.

Japanese Proverb

Ever tried. Ever failed. No matter. Try again. Fail again. Fail better.

Samuel Beckett

I think and think for months and years. Ninety-nine times, the conclusion is false. The hundredth time I am right.

Albert Einstein

It's not that I am so smart, it's just that I stay with the problems longer.

Albert Einstein

Give me six hours to chop down a tree and I will spend four hours sharpening the ax.

Abraham Lincoln

It is the old lesson—a worthy purpose, patient energy for its accomplishment, a resoluteness undaunted by difficulties, and then success.

W.M. Punshon

Run like hell and get the agony over with.

Clarence DeMar

Your decision to be, have or do something out of the ordinary entails facing difficulties that are out of the ordinary as well. Sometimes your greatest asset is simply your ability to stay with it longer than anyone else.

Brian Tracy

Readiness is all.

William Shakespeare

Patiently wave and wear the habit of a champion every day and you will one day be covered in success and wear the crown of glory.

Earl Fee

CONFIDENCE AND CHARACTER

Confidence and courage come through preparation and practice.

Anon

Character cannot be developed in ease and quite. Only through experience, of trial and suffering, can the soul be strengthened, ambition inspired, and success achieved.

Helen Keller

Don't try to be better than your contemporaries or predecessors. Try to be better than yourself.

William Faulkner

Confidence comes from hours, days, weeks, years of constant work and dedication.

Roger Staubach

Getting ahead in a difficult profession requires avid faith in yourself. That is why some with mediocre talent, but with great inner drive, go much further than people with vastly superior talent.

Sophia Loren

The principle is competing against yourself. It's about improvement, about being better than you were the day [or year] before.

Steve Young

I run to see who has the most guts.

Steve Prefontaine

Have confidence that if you have done a little thing well, you can do a bigger thing well too.

Ralph Waldo Emerson

Character is the foundation of all worthwhile success.

John Hayes Hammond

Strive not for winning, but to become the best we can be, not to destroy others....

Lorraine Moller

Practise the power of habitual anticipation and deep positive expectation for realization.

Norman Vincent Peale

Specialize to realize. Believe to achieve.

Earl Fee

The quality of our expectations determines the quality of our actions.

Andre Godin

Manifest plainness,
Embrace simplicity,
Reduce Selfishness,
Have few desires.

Lao-tzu (604BC -531BC)

When you win say nothing. When you lose say less.

Paul Brown

BODY, MIND, SPIRIT

Finishing a marathon forces everyone to bring mind and body together and to reach for extra resources from the power of the human spirit.

Jeff Galloway

As a rule, the mind, residing in a body that has been weakened by pampering, is also weak, and where there is no strength of mind there can be no strength of soul.

Mohandas Gandhi

Difficulties strengthen the mind, as labour does the body.

Seneca

They used to say have a killer instinct but this just adds extra stress. The real enemy is yourself. You are competing against yourself.

Earl Fee

When I finish a training session or a race knowing I have pushed to near the limit and not getting injured—I have a smiling body, mind and spirit.

Earl Fee

To be what we are, and to become what we are capable of becoming, is the only end in life.

Robert Louis Stevenson

RISK

To dare is risk losing your foothold for a moment. Not to dare is to risk losing yourself.

Søren Kierkegaard

You miss 100% of the shots you never take.

Wayne Gretzky

To win without risk is to triumph without glory.

Pierre Corneille

There is a mighty thin line between being a hero and being an idiot [in training].
[I have added the comments in brackets].

Kelly Smith

One can walk proud and tall, even in defeat, after giving your all.

Earl Fee

I risked. I went through the first 5K just a second off my best time.

Billy Mills (Winner of 10K at Tokyo Olympics)

FEAR

The bravest thing you can do when you are not brave is to profess courage and act accordingly.

Corra Harris

Courage is doing what you are afraid to do. There can be no courage unless you're scared.

Eddie Richenbacher

Fear is a darkroom where negatives develop.

Asmon Asif

To use fear as the friend it is, we must retrain and reprogram ourselves. We must persistently tell ourselves that the fear is here–with its gift of energy and heightened awareness–so we can do our best , and learn the most in the new situation.

Peter Mc Williams

Whenever we're afraid, it's because we don't know enough. If we knew and understood enough, we would never be afraid.

Earl Nightingale

You never conquer a mountain. Mountains can't be conquered:
you conquer yourself–your hopes, your fears.

Jim Whitaker

Confront your fears, list them, get to know them, and only then will you be able to put them aside and move ahead.

Jerry Gillie

Feel the fear and do it anyway.

Susan Jeffers

Get your mind off negative thoughts and the thought that this is going to hurt. It's only discomfort anyway. You are not going to war. Think of your strategy and the rewards when you're finished. Think of the good races you have run in the past and some under bad conditions. Remember the nerves and adrenaline are your friends to make you perform beyond yourself. You are your main competitor.

Earl Fee

SUCCESS

Judge your success by what you had to give up to get it.

HH The Dalai Lama

On the road to your big goal there will be blind alleys, and setbacks even with good planning. You have to accept these without discouragement since it's all part of the necessary journey. Consider these drawbacks as a kind of progress. Before success comes you have to pay your dues.

Earl Fee

MISCELLANEOUS

For when The Great Scorer comes to mark against your name,
He writes—not that you won or lost –but how you played the Game.

Grantland Rice

IRONMAN
1008

CREDITS AND COPYRIGHT ACKNOWLEDGEMENTS

Selected material in Chapter 2 reprinted, by permission of
Jerry Lynch, from *Running Within* by Jerry Lynch, Ph.D., and Warren A. Scott, M.D. Human Kinetics, Champaign, IL, Copyright (c) 1999 Jerry Lynch and Warren A. Scott.

Selected material in Chapter 1 and 7 reprinted, by permission of
David Costill, Ph.D., from *Inside Running: Basics of Sports Physiology* by David Costill, Ph.D. Copyright (c) 1986 by Benchmark Press Inc.

Selected material in Chapter 12 reprinted, by permission of
Tom Drum President of "Fraid Nots", from Fraid Nots, Tom Drum Inc. Pompano Beach, FL.

Selected material in Chapter 15 reprinted, by permission of
George Ohsawa Macriobiotic Foundation, Oriville, CA, from Acid and Alkaline by Herman Aihara. Copyright (c) 1986 George Ohsawa Macriobiotic Foundation.

Selected material in Chapter 8 and 9 reprinted, by permission of
Tafnews Press, Mountain View, CA, from *Train Hard, Win Easy* by Toby Tanser. Copyright (c) 1997 by Tafnews Press.

Selected material in Chapter 12 reprinted, by permission of
Dr. Stephen D. Stark, from *The Stark Reality of Stretching* by Dr. Stephen Stark. Copyright (c) 1997 by Dr. Stephen Stark. See www.drstevenstark.com

Selected material in Chapter 6, by permission of
Of Charlie Francis, 1999.

Selected material in Chapter 6 reprinted, by permission of
Payton Jordan, 2000.

Selected material in Chapter 2 reprinted, by permission of
New World Library, Navato, CA, from *Creative Visualization* by Shakti Gawain. Copyright (c) 1995 by Shakti Gawain.

Selected material in Chapter 15 reprinted, by permission of
Bull Publishing Co., Boulder, CO, from *The Ultimate Sports Nutrition Handbook* by Ellen Coleman RD, and Suzanne Nelson Steen, DSc. Copyright (c) 1996 Bull Publishing Co.

Selected material in Chapter 4 reprinted, by permission of
Meyer and Meyer, Aachen, Germany, from *Running to the Top* by Arthur Lydiard. Copyright (c) 1997 by Meyer and Meyer.

See also the reference credits at the end of each chapter.

HUGER
CYCLES
IRONMAN
440

INDEX

W

Y

Z